KNOWLEDGE
MANAGEMENT
IN THEORY
AND
PRACTICE

KNOWLEDGE MANAGEMENT IN THEORY AND PRACTICE

Kimiz Dalkir
McGill University

AMSTERDAM • BOSTON • HEIDELBERG • LONDON
NEW YORK • OXFORD • PARIS • SAN DIEGO
SAN FRANCISCO • SINGAPORE • SYDNEY • TOKYO

ELSEVIER
BUTTERWORTH
HEINEMANN

Elsevier Butterworth–Heinemann
30 Corporate Drive, Suite 400, Burlington, MA 01803, USA
Linacre House, Jordan Hill, Oxford OX2 8DP, UK

♾ Recognizing the importance of preserving what has been written, Elsevier prints its books on
acid-free paper whenever possible.

Library of Congress Cataloging-in-Publication Data
Application submitted

British Library Cataloguing-in-Publication Data
A catalogue record for this book is available from the British Library.
ISBN-13: 978-0-7506-7864-3
ISBN-10: 0-7506-7864-X

For information on all Elsevier Butterworth–Heinemann publications
visit our Web site at www.books.elsevier.com

Printed in the United States of America
06 07 08 09 10   10 9 8 7 6 5 4 3 2

This book is dedicated to my sons, Kemal and Kazmir, who are beginning their journey of discovery.

CONTENTS

FOREWORD

Knowledge management as an organizational innovation has been with us for more than a decade. As a discipline, it has reached a state of maturity where we can now discern the principles, practices, and tools that make it unique. As a discourse, it has engendered new concepts and categories for us to make sense of the many important ways that organizations use knowledge to create value. Given the richness of ideas and innovations that have emerged under the rubric of knowledge management, and given the tremendous interest in schools and organizations to learn about the subject, it is something of a mystery that there are so few textbooks available. Perhaps it is because the field draws upon a wide range of subject areas, or perhaps it is because many different perspectives complicate the discussion of issues that engage knowledge management. Despite these difficulties, or perhaps because of them, there is a pressing need for a textbook that presents a thoughtful, systematic view of knowledge management as a coherent body of management theory and practice. The book in our hands answers this call.

What then is knowledge management? The first chapter of the book gives a well-argued answer, but for our purposes here, we may define knowledge management as a framework for designing an organization's goals, structures, and processes so that the organization can use what it knows to learn and to create value for its customers and community. Thus, there is no single, universal recipe for managing knowledge—each organization has to think through and design its own approach. This design process will have to encompass four sets of organizational enablers posed by these questions: What is the organizational *vision or strategy* driving the need to manage knowledge? What *roles and structures* ought to be in place? How to develop *processes and practices* that promote knowledge sharing and use? Which *tools and platforms* can support these efforts? For each of these enablers, research and practice in knowledge management has identified principles, exemplars, and lessons that can help to plan and execute an effective strategy. Considering these enablers also highlights the special strengths of this textbook.

First and foremost there is the question of vision and strategy—why try to manage knowledge? The book makes clear in its early pages how the creation and application of knowledge can be the engine of organizational performance and growth. In their attempts to pursue this vision, many organizations quickly discover that their most daunting task is to cultivate the norms of trust, cooperation, and mutual respect that nourish the creation and sharing of knowledge. The book recognizes this challenge, and devotes an entire chapter to examining in detail the impact of organizational culture.

Consider next the issue of roles and structures. Departments in organizations are naturally territorial and guarded about losing control of where their information goes to, and how it might be used. The book highlights the importance of leaders such as the Chief Knowledge Officer or the Chief Information Officer who champion the collective benefit of sharing information, and who remove the barriers that prevent cooperation between departments. At the same time, knowledge sharing cannot simply be mandated through formal authority. Some of the most valuable knowledge sharing occurs in communities of practice that are self-organized around informal roles and relationships. A fine chapter in the book discusses communities of practice in the context of knowledge sharing.

The process and practice of knowledge management is a central focus of the book. After a survey of major theoretical approaches in the literature, the book develops a new synthesis that views knowledge management as a continuous cycle of three processes: (1) knowledge creation and capture, (2) knowledge sharing and dissemination, (3) knowledge acquisition and application. This "KM Cycle" model forms the organizational principle of much of the book, and is carefully considered in the first six chapters. The balance between process and practice is a delicate one. A process that is regulated strictly by rules and policies can stifle creativity and experimentation. On the other hand, relying only on informal practices may mean that new learning is dispersed and unavailable to others in the organization.

An alluring aspect of knowledge management is the range of tools and platforms that hold out the promise of transforming the ways we work with information and knowledge. Thus, there are tools that capture and represent content so that it can be accessed efficiently; tools that discover and extract knowledge; tools that facilitate social networking and community building; and tools that support communication and collaboration in groups. While the discussion of tools and techniques takes place throughout the book, a systematic analysis is presented in a well-structured chapter that covers many recent technological developments.

A textbook is a pedagogical apparatus, and this book has incorporated a number of features that will enhance student learning and student-teacher interaction. Each chapter contains learning objectives, side-boxes of short cases, summaries of main messages, and questions for discussion. Beyond these features, the most engaging quality of the book is the combination of experience and enthusiasm that the author brings to the subject: the insights, the resonant examples, the lively language, and the occasional touch of humor. The book is an invitation to students to embark on an exciting and rewarding learning adventure.

Chun Wei Choo
Faculty of Information Studies
University of Toronto

ACKNOWLEDGEMENTS

I would like to thank Karen Maloney of Elsevier/Butterworth-Heinemann for her valuable support and encouragement during the writing of this book. Dr. Chun Wei Choo devoted many hours to a rigorous review of the content, which greatly improved the depth and coverage of the topics addressed. I would also like to extend thanks to the second, anonymous reviewer of the early drafts who thought up wonderful challenges and insisted on conceptual clarity throughout.

Kimiz Dalkir

INTRODUCTION TO KNOWLEDGE MANAGEMENT IN THEORY AND PRACTICE

A light bulb in the socket is worth two in the pocket.

Bill Wolf (1950–2001)

This chapter provides an introduction to the study of knowledge management (KM). A brief history of knowledge management concepts is outlined, noting that much of KM existed before the actual term came into popular use. The lack of consensus over what constitutes a good definition of KM is addressed, and the concept analysis technique is described as a means of clarifying the conceptual confusion that persists over precisely what KM is. The multidisciplinary roots of KM are enumerated, together with their contributions to the discipline. The two major forms of knowledge, tacit and explicit, are compared and contrasted. The importance of KM today for individuals, for communities of practice, and for organizations are described, together with the emerging KM roles and responsibilities needed to ensure successful KM implementations.

LEARNING OBJECTIVES

1. Use a framework and a clear language for knowledge management concepts.
2. Define key knowledge management concepts such as intellectual capital, organizational learning and memory, knowledge taxonomy, and communities of practice using concept analysis.
3. Provide an overview of the history of knowledge management and identify key milestones.
4. Describe the key roles and responsibilities required for knowledge management applications.

INTRODUCTION

The ability to manage knowledge is becoming increasingly more crucial in today's knowledge economy. The creation and diffusion of knowledge have become ever more important factors in competitiveness. More and more, knowledge is being regarded as a valuable commodity that is embedded in products (especially high-technology products) and in the tacit knowledge of highly mobile employees. Although knowledge is increasingly being viewed as a commodity or an intellectual asset, it possesses some paradoxical characteristics that are radically different from those of other valuable commodities. These knowledge characteristics include the following:

- Use of knowledge does not consume it.
- Transferral of knowledge does not result in losing it.
- Knowledge is abundant, but the ability to use it is scarce.
- Much of an organization's valuable knowledge walks out the door at the end of the day.

The advent of the Internet and the World Wide Web have made unlimited sources of knowledge available to us all. Pundits are heralding the dawn of the Knowledge Age supplanting the Industrial Era. Forty years ago, nearly half of all workers in industrialized countries were making or helping to make *things*; today that proportion is down to 20% (Drucker, 1994; Bart, 2000). Labor-intensive manufacturing with a large pool of relatively cheap, relatively homogeneous labor and hierarchical management has given way to knowledge-based organizations. There are fewer people doing more work. Organizational hierarchies are being put aside as knowledge work calls for more collaboration. The only sustainable advance a firm has comes from what it collectively knows, how efficiently it uses what it knows, and how quickly it acquires and uses new knowledge (Davenport and Prusak, 1998). An organization in the Knowledge Age is one that learns, remembers, and acts based on the best available information, knowledge, and know-how.

All of these developments have created a strong need for a deliberate and systematic approach to cultivating and sharing a company's knowledge base—one populated with valid and valuable lessons learned and best practices. In other words, in order to be successful in today's challenging organizational environment, companies need to learn from their past errors and not reinvent the wheel again and again. Organizational knowledge is not intended to replace individual knowledge but to complement it by making it stronger, more coherent, and more broadly applicative. Knowledge management represents a deliberate and systematic approach to ensure the full utilization of the organization's knowledge base, coupled with the potential of individual skills, competencies, thoughts, innovations, and ideas to create a more efficient and effective organization. The Iaccoca Institute found that "CEOs, when asked how much of the knowledge that is available to the organization is actually used, responded 'only about 20%.' Yet if this figure represented average utilization of production capacity, it would only be acceptable to the most foolhardy CEOs"

(Agile People Enterprise Development Group Newsletter, Iacocca Institute, Pennsylvania, November 1996).

Knowledge management (KM) was initially defined as the process of applying a systematic approach to the capture, structure, management, and dissemination of knowledge throughout an organization in order to work faster, reuse best practices, and reduce costly rework from project to project (Nonaka and Takeuchi, 1995; Pasternack and Viscio, 1998; Pfeiffer and Sutton, 1999; Ruggles and Holtshouse, 1999). KM is often characterized by a "pack rat" approach to content: "save it, it may prove useful sometime in the future." Many documents tend to be warehoused, sophisticated search engines are then used to try to retrieve some of this content, and fairly large-scale and costly KM systems are built. Knowledge management solutions have proven to be most successful in the capture, storage, and subsequent dissemination of knowledge that has been rendered explicit—particularly lessons learned and best practices.

The focus of intellectual capital management (ICM), on the other hand, is on those pieces of knowledge that are of *business value* to the organization—referred to as intellectual capital or assets (Bontis and Nikitopoulos, 2001). Although some of these are more visible (e.g., patents, intellectual property), the majority consist of know-how, know-why, experience, and expertise that tend to reside within the head of one or a few employees (Klein, 1998; Stewart, 1997). ICM is characterized by less content—because content is filtered and judged, and only the best are inventoried (the "top ten," for example). ICM content tends to be more representative of a person's real thinking (contextual information, opinions, stories) owing to its emphasis on actionable knowledge and know-how. As a result, endeavors are less costly and the focus shifts to learning (at the individual, community, and organizational level) rather than to the building of systems.

A good definition of knowledge management incorporates both the capturing and storing of the knowledge perspective, together with the valuing of intellectual assets. For example:

> Knowledge management is the deliberate and systematic coordination of an organization's people, technology, processes, and organizational structure in order to add value through reuse and innovation. This coordination is achieved through creating, sharing, and applying knowledge as well as through feeding the valuable lessons learned and best practices into corporate memory in order to foster continued organizational learning.

When asked, most executives often state that their greatest asset is the knowledge held by their employees. They also invariably add that they have no idea how to manage this knowledge! It is essential to identify that knowledge that is of value and is also at risk of being lost to the organization, through retirement, turnover, and competition using the intellectual capital or asset approach. In addition, the selective or value-based knowledge management approach should be a three-tiered one. That is, it should also be applied to three organizational levels: the individual, the group or community, and the organization itself. The best way to retain valuable knowledge is to identify intellectual assets and then to ensure that legacy materials are produced and subsequently stored in such a way as to make their future retrieval and reuse as easy as possible (Stewart, 2000). These tangible by-products need to flow from individual to individual, between members of a community of practice, and, of course, back to the organization itself, in the form of lessons learned, best practices, and corporate memory.

Many knowledge management (KM) efforts have been largely concerned with capturing, codifying, and sharing the knowledge held by people in organizations. Although there is still a lack of consensus over what constitutes a good definition of KM (see the next section), there is widespread agreement as to the goals of an organization that undertakes KM. Nickols (2000) summarizes these goals as follows: "the basic aim of knowledge management is to leverage knowledge to the organization's advantage." Some of management's motives are obvious: the loss of skilled people through turnover, pressures to avoid reinventing the wheel, pressures for organization-wide innovations in processes as well as products, management of risk, and the accelerating rate at which new knowledge is being created. Some typical knowledge management objectives are to:

- Facilitate a smooth transition from those retiring to their successors who are recruited to fill their positions.
- Minimize loss of corporate memory due to attrition and retirement.
- Identify critical resources and critical areas of knowledge so that the corporation "knows what it knows and does it well—and why."
- Build up a toolkit of methods that can be used with individuals, with groups, and with the organization to stem the potential loss of intellectual capital.

WHAT IS KNOWLEDGE MANAGEMENT?

An informal survey conducted by the author identified over 100 published definitions of knowledge management, and of these, at least 72 could be considered very good! Clearly, KM is a multidisciplinary field of study that covers a lot of ground. This finding should not be surprising, for applying knowledge to work is integral to most business activities. However, the field of KM does suffer from the "Three Blind Men and an Elephant" syndrome. In fact, there are likely more than three distinct perspectives on KM, and each leads to a different extrapolation and a different definition.

From the *business perspective*:

Knowledge management is a business activity with two primary aspects:

[T]reating the knowledge component of business activities as an explicit concern of business reflected in strategy, policy, and practice at all levels of the organization; and, making a direct connection between an organization's intellectual assets—both explicit (recorded) and tacit (personal know-how)—and positive business results. (Barclay and Murray, 1997)

Knowledge management is a collaborative and integrated approach to the creation, capture, organization, access and use of an enterprise's intellectual assets. (Grey, 1996)

From the *cognitive science* or *knowledge science perspective*:

Knowledge—the insights, understandings, and practical know-how that we all possess—is the fundamental resource that allows us to function intelligently. Over time, considerable knowledge is also transformed to other manifestations—such as books, technology, practices, and traditions—within organizations of all kinds and in society in general. These transformations result in cumulated [*sic*] expertise and, when used appropriately, increased effectiveness. Knowledge is one, if not THE, principal factor that makes personal, organizational, and societal intelligent behavior possible. (Wiig, 1993, pp. 38–39)

And, from the *process/technology perspective*:

Knowledge management is the concept under which information is turned into actionable knowledge and made available effortlessly in a usable form to the people who can apply it. (*Information Week*, Sept. 1, 2003)

Leveraging collective wisdom to increase responsiveness and innovation. (Carl Frappaolo, Delphi Group, Boston, posted at http://www.destinationkm.com/articles/default.asp?ArticleID=949)

A systematic approach to manage the use of information in order to provide a continuous flow of Knowledge to the right people at the right time enabling efficient and effective decision making in their everyday business. (Steve Ward, Northrop Grumman, posted at http://www.destinationkm.com/articles/default. asp?ArticleID=949)

A knowledge management system is a virtual repository for relevant information which is critical to tasks performed daily by organizational knowledge workers. (What Is KM?, posted at http://www.knowledgeshop.com)

Wiig (1993) also emphasizes that given the importance of knowledge in virtually all areas of daily and commercial life, two knowledge-related aspects are crucial for viability and success at any level. These are knowledge *assets* that must be applied, nurtured, preserved, and used to the largest extent possible by both individuals and organizations; and knowledge-related *processes* to create, build, compile, organize, transform, transfer, pool, apply, and safeguard knowledge that must be carefully and explicitly managed in all affected areas.

Historically, knowledge has always been managed, at least implicitly. However, effective and active knowledge management requires new perspectives and techniques and touches on almost all facets of an organization. We need to develop a new discipline and prepare a cadre of knowledge professionals with a blend of expertise that we have not previously seen. This is our challenge! (Wiig, in Grey, 1996)

Knowledge management is a surprising mix of strategies, tools, and techniques—some of which are nothing new under the sun. Storytelling, peer-to-peer mentoring, and learning from mistakes, for example, all have precedents in education, training, and artificial intelligence practices. Knowledge management makes use of a mixture of techniques from knowledge-based system design, such as structured knowledge acquisition strategies from subject matter experts (McGraw and Harrison-Briggs, 1989) and educational technology (e.g., task and job analysis to design and develop task support systems; see Gery, 1991).

This makes it both easy and difficult to define what KM is. At one extreme, KM encompasses everything to do with knowledge. At the other extreme, it is narrowly defined as an information technology system that dispenses organizational know-how. KM is in fact both of these and many more. One of the few areas of consensus in the field is that KM is a highly multidisciplinary field.

Multidisciplinary Nature of KM

Knowledge management draws upon a vast number of diverse fields such as:

- Organizational science.
- Cognitive science.
- Linguistics and computational linguistics.
- Information technologies such as knowledge-based systems, document and information management, electronic performance support systems, and database technologies.
- Information and library science.
- Technical writing and journalism.
- Anthropology and sociology.
- Education and training.
- Storytelling and communication studies.
- Collaborative technologies such as Computer Supported Collaborative Work and groupware, as well as intranets, extranets, portals, and other web technologies.

This list is by no means exhaustive, but it serves to show the extremely varied roots that gave life to KM and continues to be its basis today. Figure 1-1 illustrates some of the diverse disciplines that have contributed to KM.

The multidisciplinary nature of KM represents a double-edged sword. On the one hand, it is an advantage because almost anyone can find a familiar foundation on which to base their understanding and even practice of KM. Someone with a background in journalism, for example, can quickly adapt his or her skill set to the capture of knowledge from experts and reformulate them as organizational stories to be stored in corporate memory. Someone coming from a more technical database background can easily extrapolate his or her skill set to design and implement knowledge repositories that will serve as the

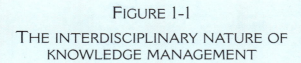

FIGURE 1-1

THE INTERDISCIPLINARY NATURE OF
KNOWLEDGE MANAGEMENT

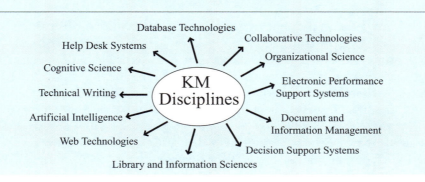

corporate memory for that organization. However, the diversity of KM also presents some challenges with respect to boundaries. Skeptics argue that KM is not and cannot be said to be a separate discipline with a *unique* body of knowledge. This attitude is typically represented by phrases such as "KM is just IM (Information Management)" or "KM is nonsensical—it is just good business practices." It becomes very important to be able to list and describe what set of attributes are necessary and are in themselves sufficient to constitute knowledge management both as a discipline and as a field of practice that can be distinguished from others.

One of the major attributes of KM relates to the fact that it deals with knowledge as well as information. Knowledge is a more subjective way of knowing and is typically based on experiential or individual values, perceptions, and experience. Popular examples to distinguish data from information and from knowledge include the following:

Data: Content that is directly observable or verifiable; a fact—for example, listings of the times and locations of all movies being shown today— I download the listings.

Information: Content that represents analyzed data—for example, "I can't leave before 5 so I will go to the 7:00 P.M. show at the cinema near my office."

Knowledge: At that time of day, it will be impossible to find parking. I remember the last time I took the car I was so frustrated and stressed because I thought I would miss the opening credits. I'll therefore take the commuter train. But first I'll check with Al. I usually love all the movies he hates so I want to make sure it's worth seeing!

Another distinguishing characteristic of KM as opposed to other information management fields is the ability of KM to address knowledge in all of its forms, notably, tacit knowledge and explicit knowledge.

The Two Major Types of Knowledge

"We know more than we can tell"
Polanyi, 1966

Tacit knowledge is difficult to articulate and also difficult to put into words, text, or drawings. In contrast, explicit knowledge represents content that has been captured in some tangible form such as words, audio recordings, or images. Moreover, tacit knowledge tends to reside "within the heads of knowers," whereas explicit knowledge is usually contained within tangible or concrete media. However, it should be noted that this is a rather simplistic dichotomy. In fact, "tacitness" is a property of the knower: what is easily articulated by one person may be very difficult to externalize by another. That is, the same content may be explicit for one person and tacit for another. Somewhat of a paradox is at play here. On the one hand, highly skilled, experienced, and expert individuals may find it harder to articulate their know-how. Novices, on the other hand, are more apt to easily verbalize what they are attempting to do because they are typically following a manual or how-to process. Table 1-1 summarizes some of the major properties of tacit and explicit knowledge.

Typically, the more tacit knowledge is, the more valuable it tends to be. The paradox lies in the fact that the more difficult it is to articulate a concept such as "story," the more valuable that knowledge may be. This is often evidenced when people make reference to knowledge versus know-how, or to knowledge of something versus knowledge of how to do something. Valuable tacit knowledge often results in some observable action when individuals understand and subsequently make use of knowledge. Another perspective is that explicit knowledge tends to represent the final end product, whereas tacit knowledge is the know-how or all of the processes that were required in order to produce that final product.

TABLE 1-1

COMPARISON OF PROPERTIES OF TACIT VS. EXPLICIT KNOWLEDGE

Properties of Tacit Knowledge	Properties of Explicit Knowledge
Ability to adapt, to deal with new and exceptional situations	Ability to disseminate, to reproduce, to access, and to reapply throughout the organization
Expertise, know-how, know-why, and care-why	Ability to teach, to train
Ability to collaborate, to share a vision, to transmit a culture	Ability to organize, to systematize; to translate a vision into a mission statement, into operational guidelines
Coaching and mentoring to transfer experiential knowledge on a one-to-one, face-to-face basis	Transfer of knowledge via products, services, and documented processes

We have a habit of writing articles published in scientific journals to make the work as finished as possible, to cover up all the tracks, to not worry about the blind alleys or how you had the wrong idea at first, and so on. So there isn't any place to publish, in a dignified manner, what you actually did in order to do the work (Richard Feynman, Nobel Lecture, 1966).

A popular misconception is that KM focuses on rendering whatever is tacit into more explicit or tangible forms, and then storing or archiving these forms somewhere, usually in some form of intranet or knowledge portal. This approach is typified by the "build it and they will come" expectation where organizations take an exhaustive inventory of tangible knowledge (i.e., documents, digital records) and make them accessible to all employees. Senior management is then mystified as to why employees are not using this wonderful new resource. In fact, knowledge management is broader and includes leveraging the value of the organizational knowledge and know-how that accumulates over time. This approach is much more holistic and user-centered and begins not with an audit of existing documents but with a needs analysis to better understand how improved knowledge sharing may benefit specific individuals, groups, and the organization as a whole. Successful knowledge-sharing examples are gathered and documented in the form of lessons learned and best practices, and these then form the kernel of organizational stories.

A number of other attributes combine to make up a set of what KM should be all about. Using the concept analysis technique is a good way to identify these attributes.

The Concept Analysis Technique

Concept analysis is an established technique used in the social sciences, such as philosophy and education, in order to derive a "formula" that in turn can be used to generate definitions and descriptive phrases for highly complex terms. We still lack a consensus on knowledge management–related terms, even though these terms do appear to be complex enough to merit the concept analysis approach. Much of the reason of this lack of consensus lies in the fact that a word such as "knowledge" is necessarily subjective, not to mention value-laden in interpretation.

The concept analysis approach rests on obtaining consensus on three major dimensions of a given concept (as shown in Figure 1-2):

1. A list of key attributes that must be present in the definition, vision, or mission statement.
2. A list of illustrative examples.
3. A list of illustrative nonexamples.

This approach is particularly useful in tackling multidisciplinary domains such as intellectual capital, for clear criteria can be developed to enable sorting into categories such as knowledge versus information, document management versus knowledge management, and tangible versus intangible assets. In

FIGURE 1-2

ILLUSTRATION OF THE CONCEPT ANALYSIS TECHNIQUE

Concept Name		
Key Attributes	Examples	Nonexamples
1._____	1._____	1._____
2._____	2._____	2._____
3._____	3._____	3._____
4._____	4._____	4._____
5._____	5._____	5._____
6._____	6._____	6._____
7._____	7._____	7._____

addition, valuable contributions to the organization's intellectual capital are derived through production of ontologies (semantic maps of key concepts), identification of core competencies, and identification of knowledge, know-how, and know-why at risk of being lost through human capital attrition.

Concept analysis can be used to visually map out conceptual information in the process of defining a word (Novak, 1990, 1991). This technique is derived from the fields of philosophy and science education (Bareholz and Tamir, 1992; Lawson, 1994) and is typically used in clearly defining complex, value-laden terms such as democracy or religion. It is a graphical approach to help develop a rich, in-depth understanding of a concept. Figure 1-2 outlines the major components of this approach.

Davenport and Prusak (1998, p. 5) decry the inability to provide a definitive account of knowledge management since "epistemologists have spent their lives trying to understand what it means to know something." Owing to this ongoing lack of clarity and lack of consensus on a definition, knowledge management presents itself as a good candidate for this approach. In visioning workshops, this is the first activity that participants are asked to undertake. The objective is to agree upon a list of key attributes that are both necessary and sufficient in order for a definition of knowledge management to be acceptable. This task is completed by a list of examples and nonexamples, with justifications as to why a particular item was included on the example or nonexample list. Semantic mapping (Jonassen, Beissner, and Yacci, 1993; Fisher, 1990) is the visual technique used to extend the definition by displaying words related to it. Popular terms to distinguish clearly from knowledge management include document management, content management, portal, and knowledge repository. Together, the concept and semantic maps visually depict a model-based definition of knowledge management and its closely related terms.

In some cases, participants are given lists of definitions of knowledge management from a variety of sources so that they can "try out" their concept map of knowledge management by analyzing these existing definitions. Definitions are typically drawn both from the knowledge management literature and, internally, from their own organization. The use of concept definition through concept and semantic mapping techniques can help participants rapidly reach a consensus on a "formulaic" definition of knowledge management—that is, one that focuses less on the actual text or words used and more on which key concepts need to be present, what comprises a necessary and sufficient (complete) set of concepts, and rules of thumb to use in discerning what constitutes an illustrative example of knowledge management.

Ruggles and Holtshouse (1999) identified the following key attributes of knowledge management:

- Generating new knowledge.
- Accessing valuable knowledge from outside sources.
- Using accessible knowledge in decision making.
- Embedding knowledge in processes, products, and/or services.
- Representing knowledge in documents, databases, and software.
- Facilitating knowledge growth through culture and incentives.
- Transferring existing knowledge into other parts of the organization.
- Measuring the value of knowledge assets and/or impact of knowledge management.

Some key knowledge management attributes that continue to recur include the following.

- Both tacit and explicit knowledge forms are addressed; tacit knowledge (Polanyi, 1966) is knowledge that often resides only within individuals; and knowledge that is difficult to articulate such as expertise, know-how, and tricks of the trade.
- There is a notion of added value (the "so what?" of KM).
- There is the notion of application or use of the knowledge that has been captured, codified, and disseminated (the impact of KM).

A "good enough" or satisficing definition of knowledge has been shown to be effective (i.e., settling for "good enough" as opposed to optimizing; when 80% is done because the incremental cost of completing the remaining 20% is disproportionately expensive and/or time-consuming in relation to the expected additional benefits). Norman (1988, pp. 50–74) noted that knowledge may reside in two places: in the heads of people and in the world. It is easy to show the faulty nature of human knowledge and memory. For example, when typists were given caps for typewriter keys, they could not arrange them in proper configuration yet they all could type rapidly and accurately. Why the apparent discrepancy between the precision of behavior and the imprecision of knowledge? The answer is that not all of the knowledge required for precise behavior has to be in the head. It can be distributed partly in the head, partly in the world, and partly in the constraints of the world. Precise behavior can emerge from imprecise knowledge (Ambur, 1999). For this reason once a satisfactory working or operational definition of knowledge management has been formulated, then knowledge management strategy can be confidently tackled.

It is highly recommended that each organization undertake the concept analysis exercise to clarify its understanding of what KM means in its own organization's context. The best way to do so would be to work as a group, enabling them to achieve a shared understanding at the same time that they develop a clearer conceptualization of the KM concept. Each participant can take a turn contributing one good example of what KM is and another example of what KM is not. The entire group can then discuss this example–nonexample pair in order to identify one (or several) key KM attributes. Once the group members feel they have covered as much ground as they are likely to, the key attributes can be summarized in the form of a KM concept "formula" such as: "In our organization, knowledge management must include the following: both tacit and explicit knowledge; a framework to measure the value of knowledge assets; a process for managing knowledge assets. . . ."

HISTORY OF KNOWLEDGE MANAGEMENT

Although the phrase "knowledge management" entered popular usage in the late 1980s (e.g., conferences in KM began appearing, books on KM were published, and the term began to be seen in business-oriented journals), KM has been around for many decades. Librarians, philosophers, teachers, and writers have long been making use of many of the same techniques. However, it could also be argued that knowledge management has been around far longer than the actual term has been in use. Denning (2000) relates how from "time immemorial, the elder, the traditional healer and the midwife in the village have been the living repositories of distilled experience in the life of the community" (available from his website at: http://www.stevedenning.com/history_knowledge_management.html). Some form of narrative repository has been in existence for a long time, and people have found a variety of ways of sharing knowledge in order to build on earlier experience, eliminate costly redundancies, and avoid making at least the same mistakes again. For example, knowledge sharing often took the form of town meetings, workshops, seminars, and mentoring sessions. The primary "technology" used to transfer knowledge consisted of the people themselves. Indeed, much of our cultural legacy stems from the migration of different peoples across continents.

H.G. Wells (1938), though never using the actual term *knowledge management*, described his vision of the "World Brain," which would allow the intellectual organization of the sum total of our collective knowledge. The World Brain would represent "a universal organization and clarification of knowledge and ideas" (p. xvi). Wells anticipated the World Wide Web, albeit in a utopic idealized manner, when he spoke of "this wide gap between . . . at present unassembled and unexploited best thought and knowledge in the world. . . . We live in a world of unused and misapplied knowledge and skill"

(p. 10). The World Brain encapsulates many of the desirable features of the intellectual capital approach to KM: selected, well-organized, and widely vetted content that is maintained, kept up to date, and, above all, put to use to generate value to users, the users' community, and their organization.

What Wells envisaged for the entire world can easily be applied within an organization in the form of an intranet. What is new and is termed *knowledge management* is that we are now able to simulate rich, interactive, face-to-face knowledge encounters virtually through the use of new communication technologies. Information technologies such as an intranet and the Internet enable us to knit together the intellectual assets of an organization and organize and manage this content through the lenses of common interest, common language, and conscious cooperation. We are able to extend the depth and breadth or reach of knowledge capture, sharing, and dissemination activities, as we had not been able to do before, and we find ourselves one step closer to Wells' (1939) "perpetual digest . . . and a system of publication and distribution" (pp. 70–71) "to an intellectual unification . . . of human memory" (pp. 86–87).

In the early 1960s, Drucker was the first to coin the term *knowledge worker* (Drucker, 1964). Senge (1990) focused on the "learning organization" as one that can learn from past experiences stored in corporate memory systems. Barton-Leonard (1995) documented the case of Chapparal Steel as a knowledge management success story. Nonaka and Takeuchi (1995) studied how knowledge is produced, used, and diffused within organizations and how such knowledge contributed to the diffusion of innovation.

A number of people, perceiving the value of measuring intellectual assets, recognized the growing importance of organizational knowledge as a competitive asset (Sveiby, 1996; Norton and Kaplan, 1996; APQC, 1996; and Edvinsson and Malone, 1997). A cross-industry benchmarking study was led by APQC's president Carla O'Dell and completed in 1996. It focused on the following KM needs:

1. Knowledge management as a business strategy.
2. Transfer of knowledge and best practices.
3. Customer-focused knowledge.
4. Personal responsibility for knowledge.
5. Intellectual asset management.
6. Innovation and knowledge creation. (APQC, 1996)

The Entovation timeline (available at http://www.entovation.com/timeline/timeline.htm) identifies the variety of disciplines and domains that have blended together to emerge as knowledge management. Management theorists who have contributed significantly to the evolution of KM include Peter Drucker, Peter Senge, Ikujiro Nonaka, Hirotaka Takeuchi, and Thomas Stewart. An extract of this timeline is given in Figure 1-3.

Milestones in the development of modern technology offer another perspective on the history of KM: industralization beginning in 1800, transportation technologies in 1850, communications in 1900, computerization in the 1950s, virtualization in the early 1980s, and the early efforts at personal-

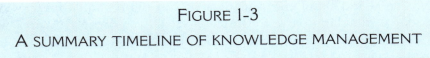

FIGURE 1-3
A SUMMARY TIMELINE OF KNOWLEDGE MANAGEMENT

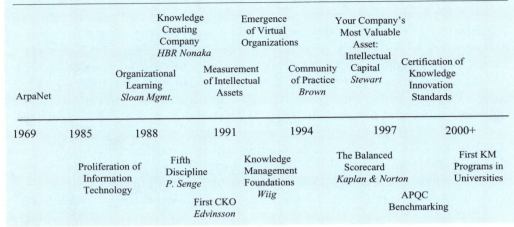

			Knowledge Creating Company *HBR Nonaka*		Emergence of Virtual Organizations		Your Company's Most Valuable Asset: Intellectual	
		Organizational Learning *Sloan Mgmt.*		Measurement of Intellectual Assets		Community of Practice *Brown*	Capital *Stewart*	Certification of Knowledge Innovation Standards
ArpaNet								
1969	**1985**	**1988**		**1991**		**1994**	**1997**	**2000+**
	Proliferation of Information Technology	Fifth Discipline *P. Senge*		Knowledge Management Foundations *Wiig*		The Balanced Scorecard *Kaplan & Norton*		First KM Programs in Universities
			First CKO *Edvinsson*				APQC Benchmarking	

FIGURE 1-4
DEVELOPMENTAL PHASES IN KM HISTORY

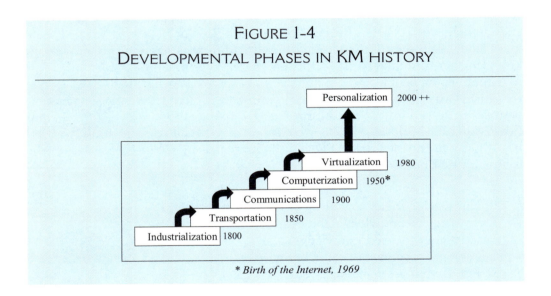

* Birth of the Internet, 1969

ization and profiling technologies in 2000 (Deloitte, Touche, and Tohmatsu, 1999). Figure 1-4 summarizes these developmental phases.

With the advent of the information or computer age, KM has come to mean the systematic, deliberate leveraging of knowledge assets. Technologies enable valuable knowledge to be "remembered" via organizational learning and corporate memory, and they also enable valuable knowledge to be "published"— that is, to be widely disseminated to all stakeholders. The evolution of knowledge management has occurred in parallel with a shift from a retail model based on a catalog (here one should recall Ford's famous quote that you can have a car in any color you like—as long as it is black) to an auction model (as exemplified by eBay) to a personalization model where real-time matching of user needs and services occurs in a win–win exchange model.

In 1969, the launch of ARPANET allowed scientists and researchers to communicate more easily with one another in addition to being able to exchange their large data sets. They came up with a network protocol or language that would allow disparate computers and operating systems to network together across communication lines. Next, a messaging system was added to this data file transfer network. In 1991, the nodes were transferred to the Internet and World Wide Web. At the end of 1969, only four computers and about a dozen workers were connected!!

Simultaneously, many key developments were occurring in information technologies devoted to knowledge-based systems: expert systems that sought to capture "experts on a diskette," intelligent tutoring systems aimed at capturing "teachers on a diskette," and artificial intelligence approaches that gave rise to knowledge engineering in which someone was tasked with acquiring knowledge from subject matter experts, conceptually modeling this content, and then translating it into machine-executable code (McGraw and Harrison-Briggs, 1989). McGraw and Harrison-Briggs describe knowledge engineering as "involving information gathering, domain familiarization, analysis and design efforts. In addition, accumulated knowledge must be translated into code, tested and refined" (p. 5). A knowledge engineer is "the individual responsible for structuring and/or constructing an expert system" (p. 5). The design and development of such knowledge-based systems have much to offer knowledge management, which also aims at the capture, validation, and subsequent technology-mediated dissemination of valuable knowledge from experts.

Books on knowledge management began to appear by the early 1990s, and the field picked up momentum in the mid-1990s with the development of a number of large, international KM conferences and consortia. In 1999, Boisot summarized some of these milestones (see Table 1-2 for an updated summary).

At the 24th World Congress on Intellectual Capital Management in January 2003, a number of KM gurus united in sending out a request to academia to

TABLE 1-2
KNOWLEDGE MANAGEMENT MILESTONES

Year	Entity	Event
1980	DEC, CMU	XCON Expert System
1986	Dr. K. Wiig	Coined KM concept at UN
1989	Consulting firms	Start internal KM projects
1991	HBR article	Nonaka & Takeuchi
1993	Dr. K. Wiig	First KM book published
1994	KM Network	First KM conference
Mid-1990s	Consulting firms	Start offering KM services
Late 1990s	Key vertical industries	Implement KM and start seeing benefits
2000–2003	Academia	KM courses/programs in universities with KM texts

"pick up the KM torch." Among those attending the conference were Karl Sveiby, Leif Edvinsson, Debra Amidon, Hubert Saint-Onge, and Verna Allee. They made a strong case that KM had up until now been led by practitioners "problem-solving by the seat of their pants" and that it was now time to focus on transforming KM into an academic discipline, promoting doctoral research in the discipline, and providing a more formalized training for our future practitioners. Today, over 100 universities around the world offer courses in KM, and many business and library schools offer degree programs in KM (Petrides and Nodine, 2003).

From Physical Assets to Knowledge Assets

Knowledge has become increasingly more valuable than the more traditional physical or tangible assets. For example, traditionally, an airline organization's assets included the physical inventory of airplanes. Today, the airlines' greatest asset is the SABRE reservation system, software that enables the airline not only to manage the logistics of its passenger reservations but also to implement a seat "yield management system." The yield management system refers to an optimization program that is used to ensure that maximum revenue is generated from each seat sold—even if each and every seat carries a distinct price. Similarly, in the manufacturing sector, the value of nonphysical assets such as just-in-time (JIT) inventory systems is rapidly providing more value. These are examples of *intellectual assets*, which generally refer to an organization's recorded information, and human talent where such information is typically either inefficiently warehoused or simply lost, especially in large, physically dispersed organizations (Stewart, 1991).

This has led to a change in focus to the useful lifespan of a valuable piece of knowledge. When is some knowledge of no use? What about knowledge that never loses its value? The notion of knowledge obsolescence and archiving needs to be approached with a fresh eye. It is no longer advisable to simply discard items that are "past their due date." Instead, content analysis and a cost-benefit analysis are needed to manage each piece of valuable knowledge in the best possible way.

Intellectual capital is often made visible by the difference between the book value and the market value of an organization (often referred to as *goodwill*). Intellectual assets are represented by the sum total of what employees of the organization know and what they know how to do. The value of these knowledge assets is at least equal to the cost of re-creating this knowledge. The accounting profession still has considerable difficulty in accommodating itself to these new forms of assets. Some progress has been made (e.g., Skandia was the first organization to report intellectual capital as part of its yearly financial report), but much more work remains to be done in this area. As shown in Figure 1-5, intellectual assets may be found at the strategic, tactical, and operational levels of an organization.

Some examples of intellectual capital include:

1. Competence—the skills necessary to achieve a certain (high) level of performance.

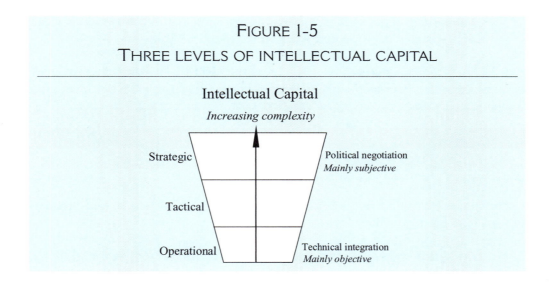

FIGURE 1-5

THREE LEVELS OF INTELLECTUAL CAPITAL

Intellectual Capital

Increasing complexity

Strategic

Political negotiation
Mainly subjective

Tactical

Operational

Technical integration
Mainly objective

2. Capability—strategic skills necessary to integrate and apply competencies.
3. Technologies—tools and methods required to produce certain physical results.

Core competencies, found at a tactical level, are the things that an organization knows how to do well and that provide a competitive advantage. Some examples would be a process, a specialized type of knowledge, or a particular kind of expertise that is rare or unique to the organization. Capabilities, found at a more strategic level, are those things that an individual knows how to do well, which, under appropriate conditions, may be aggregated to organizational competencies. Capabilities are potential core competencies, and sound KM practices are required in order for that potential to be realized. A number of business management texts discuss these concepts in greater detail (e.g., Hamel and Prahalad, 1990). It should be noted that the more valuable a capability is and the less it is shared among many employees, then the more vulnerable the organization becomes should those employees leave.

Organizational Perspectives on Knowledge Management

Wiig (1993) considers knowledge management in organizations from three perspectives, each with different horizons and purposes:

1. *Business Perspective*—focusing on why, where, and to what extent the organization must invest in or exploit knowledge. Strategies, products and services, alliances, acquisitions, or divestments should be considered from knowledge-related points of view.
2. *Management Perspective*—focusing on determining, organizing, directing, facilitating, and monitoring knowledge-related practices and activities required to achieve the desired business strategies and objectives.

3. *Hands-on Perspective*—focusing on applying the expertise to conduct explicit knowledge-related work and tasks.

The business perspective easily maps onto the strategic nature of knowledge management, the management perspective is parallel to the tactical layer, and the hands-on perspective may be equated with the operational level.

WHY IS KM IMPORTANT TODAY?

The major business drivers behind today's increased interest in and application of KM lie in four key areas:

1. *Globalization of business.* Organizations today are more global—multisite, multilingual, and multicultural in nature.
2. *Leaner organizations.* We are doing more and we are doing it faster, but we also need to work smarter as knowledge workers, adopting an increased pace and workload.
3. *"Corporate amnesia."* We are more mobile as a workforce, which creates problems of knowledge continuity for the organization and places continuous learning demands on the knowledge worker. We no longer expect to spend our entire work life with the same organization.
4. *Technological advances.* We are more connected. Advances in information technology not only have made connectivity ubiquitous but have radically changed expectations. We are expected to be "on" at all times, and the turnaround time in responding is now measured in minutes, not weeks.

Today's work environment is more complex because we now need to attend daily to the increase in the number of subjective knowledge items. Filtering over 200 e-mails, faxes, and voicemail messages on a daily basis should be done according to good time management practices and filtering rules, but more often than not, workers tend to exhibit a "Pavlovian reflex" when they note the beeps announcing the arrival of new mail or the ringing of the phone that demands immediate attention. Knowledge workers are increasingly being asked to "think on their feet," with little time to digest and analyze incoming data and information, let alone retrieve, access, and apply relevant experiential knowledge. This is due both to the sheer volume of tasks to address and to the greatly diminished turnaround time. Today's expectation is that everyone is "on" all the time—as evidenced by the various messages expressing annoyance when voicemails are not responded to promptly or e-mails are not acknowledged.

Knowledge management represents one response to the challenge of trying to manage this complex, information-overloaded work environment. As such, KM is perhaps best categorized as a science of complexity. One of the largest contributors to the complexity is that information overload represents only the tip of the iceberg—only that information that has been rendered explicit. KM also must deal with the yet to be articulated or tacit knowledge. To further complicate matters, we may not even be aware of all the tacit knowledge that exists; we may not "know that we don't know." Maynard Keynes (in Wells, 1938, p. 6) hit upon a truism when he stated that "these . . . directive people who are in authority over us, know scarcely anything about the business they have in hand. Nobody knows very much, but the important thing to realize is that they do not even know what is to be known." While Keynes was addressing politics and the economic consequences of peace, today's organizational leaders have echoed his words countless times.

In fact, we are now, according to Snowden (2002), entering the third generation of knowledge management, one devoted to context, narrative, and content management. In the first generation, the emphasis was placed on containers of knowledge or information technologies in order to help us with the dilemma exemplified by the much quoted phrase "if only we knew what we know" (O'Dell and Grayson, 1998). The early adopters of KM, large consulting companies that realized that their primary product was knowledge and that they needed to inventory their knowledge stock more effectively, exemplified this phase. A great many intranets and internal knowledge management systems were implemented during the first KM generation. This was the generation devoted to finding all the information that had up until then been buried in the organization with commonly produced by-products encapsulated as reusable *best practices* and *lessons learned*.

Reeling from information overload, the second generation swung to the opposite end of the spectrum to focus on people, which could be phrased as "if only we knew who knows about." There was growing awareness of the importance of human and cultural dimensions of knowledge management as organizations pondered why the new digital libraries were entirely devoid of content ("information junkyards") and why the usage rate was so low. In fact, the information technology approach of the first KM generation leaned heavily toward a top-down, organization-wide monolithic KM system. In the second generation, it became quite apparent that a bottom-up or grassroots adoption of KM led to much greater success and that there were many grassroots movements—which later became dubbed *communities of practice*. Communities of practice are good vehicles to study knowledge sharing or the movement of knowledge throughout the organization to spark not only reuse for greater efficiency but also knowledge creation for greater innovation.

The third stage of KM brought about an awareness of the importance of shared context: how to describe and organize content so that intended end users are aware it exists and can easily access and apply this content. Shared context creates shared meaning. Content needs to be abstracted from context. This phase is characterized by the advent of metadata to describe the content in addition to the format of content, content management, and knowledge taxonomies. After all, if knowledge is not put to use to benefit the individual, the community of practice, and/or the organization, then knowledge management has failed. Bright ideas in the form of light bulbs in the pocket are not enough; they must be "plugged in," and this can only be possible if people know what there is to be known, can find it when they need to, can understand it, and—perhaps most important—are convinced that this knowledge should be put to work. A slogan for this phase might be something like: "taxonomy before technology" (Koenig, 2002, p. 3).

KM for Individuals, Communities, and Organizations

Knowledge management provides benefits to individual employees, to communities of practice, and to the organization itself. This three-tiered view of KM helps emphasize why KM is important today (see Figure 1-6).

For the individual, KM:

- Helps people do their jobs and save time through better decision making and problem solving.
- Builds a sense of community bonds within the organization.
- Helps people to keep up to date.
- Provides challenges and opportunities to contribute.

For the community of practice, KM:

- Develops professional skills.
- Promotes peer-to-peer mentoring.
- Facilitates more effective networking and collaboration.
- Develops a professional code of ethics that members can follow.
- Develops a common language.

For the organization, KM:

- Helps drive strategy.
- Solves problems quickly.
- Diffuses best practices.
- Improves knowledge embedded in products and services.
- Cross-fertilizes ideas and increases opportunities for innovation.
- Enables organizations to stay ahead of the competition better.
- Builds organizational memory.

Some critical KM challenges are to manage content effectively, facilitate collaboration, help knowledge workers connect and find experts, and help the

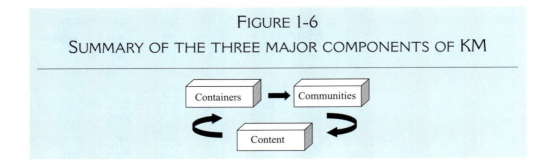

FIGURE 1-6
SUMMARY OF THE THREE MAJOR COMPONENTS OF KM

organization to learn and make decisions based on complete, valid, and well-interpreted data, information, and knowledge.

In order for knowledge management to succeed, it has to tap into what is important to knowledge workers—what is of value to them and to their professional practice as well as what the organization stands to gain. It is important to get the balance right. If the KM initiative is too big, it risks being too general, too abstract, too top-down, and far too remote to catalyze the requisite level of buy-in from individuals. If the KM initiative is too small, however, then it may not be enough to provide sufficient interaction between knowledge workers to generate synergy. The KM technology must be supportive, and management must commit itself to putting into place the appropriate rewards and incentives for knowledge management activities. Last but not least, participants need to develop KM skills in order to participate effectively. These KM skills and competencies are quite diverse and varied, given the multidisciplinary nature of the field, but one particular link is often neglected, and that is the link between KM skills and information professionals' skills. KM has resulted in the emergence of new roles and responsibilities, and a great many of these can benefit from a healthy foundation based not only in information technology (IT) but also in information science. KM professionals have a crucial role to play in all processes of the KM cycle, which is described in more detail in Chapter 2.

KEY POINTS

- KM is not necessarily "completely new" but has been practiced in a wide variety of settings for some time now—albeit under different monikers.
- Knowledge is more complex than data or information; it is subjective, often based on experience, and highly contextual.
- There is no generally accepted definition of KM, but most practitioners and professionals concur that KM treats both tacit and explicit knowledge with the objective of adding value to the organization.
- Each organization should define KM in terms of its own business objectives; concept analysis is one way of accomplishing this.
- KM is all about applying knowledge in new, previously unencumbered or novel situations.
- KM has its roots in a variety of different disciplines.
- The KM generations to date have focused first on containers, next on communities, and finally on the content itself.

DISCUSSION POINTS

1. Use concept analysis to clarify the following terms:
   a. Intellectual capital versus physical assets.
   b. Tacit knowledge versus explicit knowledge.
   c. Community of practice versus community of interest.

2. "Knowledge management is not anything new." Would you argue that this statement is largely true or false? Why or why not? Use historical antecedents to justify your arguments.
3. What are the three generations of knowledge management to date? What was the primary focus of each?
4. What are the different types of roles required for each of the above three generations?

REFERENCES

Ambur, O. (1999). Sixth generation knowledge management: realizing the vision in working knowledge. Retrieved May 18, 2004, from http://mysite.verizon.net/ambur/.

APQC. (1996). *The American Productivity and Quality Centre*. Retrieved May 17, 2004, from http://www.apqc.org.

Barclay, R., and Murray, P. (1997). What is knowledge management? *Knowledge Praxis*. Retrieved May 17, 2004, from http://www.media-access.com/whatis.html.

Bareholz, H., and Tamir, P. (1992), A comprehensive use of concept mapping in design instruction and assessment. *Research in Science and Technology Education, 10*(1): 37–52.

Bart, S. (2000, May). Heeding the sage of the knowledge age. *CRM Magazine*. Retrieved May 18, 2004, from http://www.destinationcrm.com/articles/default.asp?ArticleID=832.

Barton-Leonard, D. (1995). *Wellsprings of knowledge—building and sustaining sources of innovation*. Boston: Harvard Business School Press.

Boisot, M. (1999). *Knowledge assets*. New York: Oxford University Press.

Bontis, N., and Nikitopoulos, D. (2001). Thought leadership on intellectual capital. *Journal of Intellectual Capital, 12*(3): 183–191.

Davenport, T., and Prusak, L. (1998). *Working knowledge*. Boston: Harvard Business School Press.

Deloitte Touche Tohmatsu. (1999, November 4). Riding the e-business tidal wave. Available at http://www.istart.co.nz/index/HM20/PC0/PVC197/EX245/DOCC65/F11843.

Denning, S. (2000). History of knowledge management. Retrieved May 17, 2004, from http://www.stevedenning.com/history_knowledge_management.html.

Drucker, P. (1994, November). The social age of transformation. *Atlantic Monthly*. Retrieved May 18, 2004, from http://www.theatlantic.com/politics/ecbig/soctrans.htm.

Drucker, P. (1964, November 11). Knowledge worker: new target for management. *Christian Science Monitor*. Retrieved May 17, 2004, from http://drucker.cgu.edu/DruckerArchives/data/search/ArticlesBkReviews.asp?clrsess=y.

Edvinsson, L., and Malone, M. (1997). *Intellectual capital: realizing your company's true value by finding its hidden brain power*. New York: HarperCollins.

Feynman, R. (1966). Quotation from Nobel Lecture. Retrieved from http://www.philosphers.co.uk/quotations.

Fisher, K. M. (1990). Semantic networking: the new kid on the block. *Journal of Research in Science Teaching, 27*(10): V1001–1018.

Gery, G. (1991). *Electronic performance support systems*. Cambridge, MA: Ziff Institute.

Grey, D. (1996, March). What is knowledge management? *The Knowledge Management Forum*. Available at http://www.km.forum.org/what_is.htm.

Hamel, G., and Prahalad, C. (1990, May–June). The core competence of the corporation. *Harvard Business Review*.

Information Week (Sept. 1, 2003). Ten Principles for Knowledge Management Success. Available at http://whitepapers.informationweek.com.

Jonassen, D. H., Beissner, K., and Yacci, M. A. (1993). *Structural knowledge: techniques for conveying, assessing and acquiring structural knowledge*. Hillsdale, NJ: Lawrence Erlbaum Associates.

Klein, D. (1998). *The strategic management of intellectual capital*, pp. 1–3. Oxford, UK: Butterworth-Heinemann, Oxford.

Koenig, M. (2002). The third stage of KM emerges. *KM World*, 11(3). Retrieved May 19, 2004, from http://www.kmworld.com/publications/magazine/index.cfm?action=readarticle&Article_ID=1223&Publication_ID=67.

Lawson, M. J. (1994). Concept mapping. In T. Husen and T. N. Postlewaite (Eds.), *The international encyclopedia of education*, 2nd ed., Vol. 2, pp. 1026–1031, Oxford: Elsevier Science.

McGraw, K., and Harrison-Briggs, K. (1989). *Knowledge acquisition: Principles and guidelines*. Englewood Cliffs, N.J.: Prentice Hall.

Nickols, F. (2000). KM overview. Retrieved May 18, 2004, from http://home.att.net/~discon/KM/KM_Overview_Context.htm.

Nonaka, I., and Takeuchi, H. (1995). *The knowledge-creating company: how Japanese companies create the dynamics of innovation*. New York: Oxford University Press.

Norman, D. A. (1988). *The design of everyday things*. New York: Doubleday.

Norton, N., and Kaplan, D. (1996). *The balanced scorecard: translating strategy into action*. Boston: Harvard Business School Press.

Novak, J. (1991). Clarify with concept maps: a tool for students and teachers alike. *The Science Teacher*, 58(7): 45–49.

Novak, J. (1990). Concept mapping: a useful tool for science education. *Journal of Research in Science Teaching*, 60(3): 937–940.

O'Dell, C., and Grayson, C. (1998). *If only we knew what we know: the transfer of internal knowledge and best practice*. New York: Simon & Schuster.

Pasternack, B., and Viscio, A. (1998). *The centerless corporation*. New York: Simon & Schuster.

Petrides, L., and Nodine, T. (2003, March). Knowledge management in education: defining the landscape. *The Institute for the Study of Knowledge Management in Education*.

Pfeiffer, J., and Sutton, R. (1999). *The knowing-doing gap: How smart companies turn knowledge into action*. Boston: Harvard Business School Press.

Polanyi, M. (1966). *The tacit dimension*. Gloucester, MA: Peter Smith.

Ruggles, R., and Holtshouse, D. (1999). *The knowledge advantage*. Dover, N.H.: Capstone Publishers.

Senge, P. (1990). *The fifth discipline: the art and practice of the learning organization*. New York: Doubleday.

Snowden, D. (2002). Complex acts of knowing: paradox and descriptive self-awareness. *Journal of Knowledge Management*, 6(2): 100–111.

Stewart, T. (2000, September 4). Software preserves knowledge, people pass it on. *Fortune*.

Stewart, T. (1997). *Intellectual capital*. New York: Doubleday.

Stewart, T. (1991, June). Intellectual capital: your company's most valuable asset. *Fortune Magazine*, 44–60.

Sveiby, K. (1996). What is knowledge management? Retrieved May 17, 2004, from http://www.sveiby.com/articles/KnowledgeManagement.html.

Wells, H. G. (1938). *World brain*. Garden City, NY: Doubleday, Doran & Co.

Wiig, K. (1993). *Knowledge management foundations*. Arlington, TX: Schema Press.

THE KNOWLEDGE MANAGEMENT CYCLE

A little knowledge that acts is worth infinitely more than much knowledge that is idle.

Kahlil Gibran (1883–1931)

This chapter describes the major phases involved in the knowledge management cycle, encompassing the capture, creation, codification, sharing, accessing, application, and reuse of knowledge within and between organizations. Four major approaches to KM cycles are presented from Meyer and Zack (1996), Bukowitz and Williams (2000), McElroy (2003), and Wiig (1993). A synthesis of these approaches is then developed as a framework for following the path information takes to become a valuable knowledge asset for a given organization. This chapter concludes with a discussion of the strategic and practical implications of managing knowledge throughout the KM cycle.

LEARNING OBJECTIVES

1. Describe how valuable individual, group, and organizational knowledge is captured, created, codified, shared, accessed, applied, and reused throughout the knowledge management cycle.
2. Compare and contrast major KM life-cycle models, including the Zack, Bukowitz and Williams, McElroy, and Wiig life-cycle models.
3. Define the key steps in each process of the KM cycle and provide concrete examples of each.
4. Identify the major challenges and benefits of each phase of the KM cycle.
5. Describe how the integrated KM cycle combines the advantages of other KM life-cycle models.

Effective knowledge management requires an organization to identify, generate, acquire, diffuse, and capture the benefits of knowledge that provide a strategic advantage to that organization. A clear distinction must be made between information—which is digitizable—and true knowledge assets—which can only exist within the context of an intelligent system. As we are still far from the creation of artificial intelligence systems, this means that knowledge assets reside within the human knowers, and not the organization per se. A knowledge information cycle can be envisaged as the route information follows in order to become transformed into a valuable strategic asset for the organization via a knowledge management cycle.

One of the major KM processes aims at identifying and locating knowledge and knowledge sources within the organization. Valuable knowledge is then translated into explicit form, often referred to as *codification of knowledge*, in order to facilitate more widespread dissemination. Networks, practices, and incentives are instituted to facilitate person-to-person knowledge transfer as well as person–knowledge content connections in order to solve problems, make decisions, or otherwise act based on the best possible knowledge foundation. Once this valuable, field-tested knowledge and know-how is transferred to an organizational knowledge repository, it is said to become part of "corporate memory." This is sometimes also referred to as "ground truth."

As was the case with a generally accepted definition of KM, a similar lack of consensus exists with respect to the terms used to describe the major steps in the KM cycle. Table 2-1 summarizes the major terms found in the KM literature.

Upon closer inspection, however, the differences are not really that great. The terms used differ, but there does appear to be some overlap in the different types of steps involved in a KM cycle. To this end, four models were selected based on their ability to meet the following criteria:

- They are implemented and validated in real-world settings.
- They are comprehensive with respect to the different types of steps found in the KM literature.
- They include detailed descriptions of the KM processes involved in each step.

These four models are the Zack, from Meyer and Zack (1996), the Bukowitz and Williams (2000), the McElroy (2003), and the Wiig (1993) KM cycles.

MAJOR APPROACHES TO THE KM CYCLE

The Zack KM Cycle

The Zack KM cycle is derived from work on the design and development of information products (Meyer and Zack, 1996). A number of lessons learned from the cycle that physical products follow within an organization can be

TABLE 2-1
A COMPARISON OF KEY KM CYCLE PROCESSES

Nickols (1999)	Wiig (1993)	McElroy (1999)	Rollet (2003)	Bukowitz & Williams (2003)	Zack (1996)
Acquisition	Creation	Individual and group learning	Planning	Get	Acquisition
Organization	Sourcing	Knowledge claim validation	Creating	Use	Refinement
Specialization	Compilation	Information acquisition	Integrating	Learn	Store/retrieve
Store/access	Transformation	Knowledge validation	Organizing	Contribute	Distribution
Retrieve	Dissemination	Knowledge integration	Transferring	Assess	Presentation
Distribution	Application		Maintaining	Build/sustain	
Conservation	Value realization		Assessing	Divest	
Disposal					

applied to the management of knowledge assets. Information products are broadly defined as information "sold" to internal or external customers such as databases, news synopses, and customer profiles. Meyer and Zack (1996) propose that research and knowledge about the design of physical products can be extended into the intellectual realm to serve as the basis for a KM cycle.

This approach provides a number of useful analogies, such as the notion of a product platform (the knowledge repository) and the information process platform (the knowledge refinery) to emphasize the notion of value-added processing required in order to leverage the knowledge of an organization. The KM cycle consists primarily of creating a higher value-added "knowledge product" at each stage of knowledge processing. For example, a basic database may represent an example of knowledge that has been created. Value can then be added by extracting trends from this data. The original information has been repackaged to provide trend analyses that can serve as the basis for decision making within the organization. Similarly, competitive intelligence can be gathered and synthesized in order to repackage "raw" data into meaningful, interpreted, and validated knowledge that is of immediate value to users. That is to say, it can be put into action directly. Yet another example is a newsgathering service that summarizes or repackages information to meet the needs of distinct, different individuals through profiling and personalization of value-added activities.

Meyer and Zack echoed other authors in stressing "the importance of managing the evolution and renewal of product architecture for sustained competitive success. . . . different architectures result in different product functionality, cost, quality and performance. Architectures are . . . a basis for product innovation" (p. 44). Research and knowledge about the design of physical information products can inform the design of a KM cycle. In Meyer and Zack's approach, the interfaces between each stage are designed to be seamless and standardized. Experience suggests the critical importance of specifying internal and external user interfaces in order to do so.

The Meyer and Zack KM cycle processes are composed of the technologies, facilities, and processes for manufacturing products and services. The authors suggest that information products are best viewed as a repository comprising information content and structure. Information content is the data held in the repository that provides the building blocks for the resulting information products. The content is unique for each type of business or organization. For example, banks have content relating to personal and commercial accounts; insurance companies hold information on policies and claims; and pharmaceutical companies accumulate a large body of scientific and marketing knowledge around each product under design or currently sold.

In addition to the actual content, the other important elements to consider are the overall structure and approach to how the content is stored, manipulated, and retrieved. The information unit is singled out as the formally defined atom of information to be stored, retrieved, and manipulated. This notion of a unit of information is a critical concept that should be applied to knowledge items as well. A focus at the level of a knowledge object distinguishes KM from document management. Although a document management system (DMS) stores, manipulates, and retrieves documents as integral wholes, KM can easily identify, extract, and manage a number of different knowledge items (sometimes referred to as *knowledge objects*) within the same document. The unit under study is thus quite different, both in nature and in scale. This again links us back to the notion that KM is not about the exhaustive collection of voluminous content but rather about more selective sifting and modification of existing captured content. The term often used today is *content management systems*.

Different businesses once again make use of unique meaningful information units. For example, a repository of financial statements is held in Mead's Data System Nexis, and the footnotes can be defined as information units. A user is able to select a particular financial statement for analysis based on key attributes of the footnotes. An expertise location system may have, as knowledge objects, the different categories of expertise that exist within that organization (e.g., financial analysis). These attributes are used to search for, select, and retrieve specific knowledgeable individuals within the company.

The structure for the repository further includes schemes for labeling, indexing, linking, and cross-referencing the information units that together comprise the content of KM. Although the Meyer and Zack key cycle addresses information products, the approach can easily be extended to knowledge products. Knowledge does indeed possess unique attributes, but this does not mean we should adopt a *tabula rasa* approach and reinvent a decade's worth of tried, tested, and true methods and approaches to content management. This is particularly true of explicit, formal, and codified knowledge where this type of knowledge follows mostly similar processes as information products do in general. In the case of tacit knowledge, content management approaches need to be further adapted, but once again, solid content management should serve as a point of departure.

The repository becomes the foundation upon which a firm creates its family of information and knowledge products. This means that the greater the scope, depth, and complexity, the greater the flexibility for deriving products and thus the greater the potential variety within the product family. Such repositories often form the first kernel of an organizational memory or corporate memory for the company. A sample repository for a railway administration organization is shown in Figure 2-1.

Meyer and Zack analyzed the major developmental stages of a knowledge repository and mapped these stages onto a KM cycle. The stages are acquisition, refinement, storage/retrieval, distribution, and presentation/use. They refer to this cycle as the "refinery." Figures 2-2 and 2-3 summarize the major stages in the Meyer and Zack cycle.

Acquisition of data or information addresses the issues regarding sources of "raw" materials such as scope, breadth, depth, credibility, accuracy, timeliness, relevance, cost, control, and exclusivity. The guiding principle is the well-known adage of "garbage in, garbage out." That is, source data must be of the highest quality; otherwise the intellectual products produced downstream will be inferior.

Refinement is the primary source of value added; it may be physical (e.g., migrating from one medium to another) or logical (restructuring, relabeling,

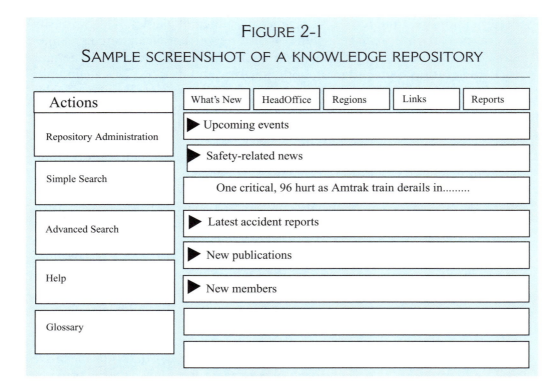

FIGURE 2-1

SAMPLE SCREENSHOT OF A KNOWLEDGE REPOSITORY

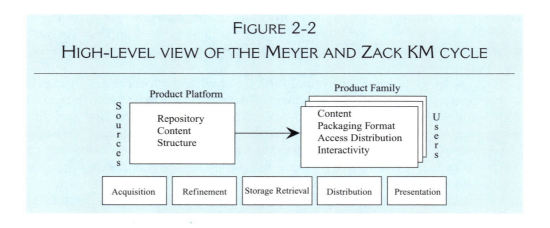

FIGURE 2-2

HIGH-LEVEL VIEW OF THE MEYER AND ZACK KM CYCLE

indexing, and integrating.) Refining also refers to cleaning up (e.g., "sanitizing" content so as to ensure complete anonymity of sources and key players involved) or standardizing (e.g., conforming to templates of a best practice or lessons learned as used within that particular organization). Statistical analyses can be performed on content at this stage to conduct a meta-analysis (high-level summary of key themes and patterns found in a collection of knowledge objects). This stage of the Meyer and Zack cycle adds value by creating more readily usable knowledge objects and by storing the content more flexibly for future use.

FIGURE 2-3

HIGH-LEVEL VIEW OF THE MEYER AND ZACK KM CYCLE
(CONTINUED)

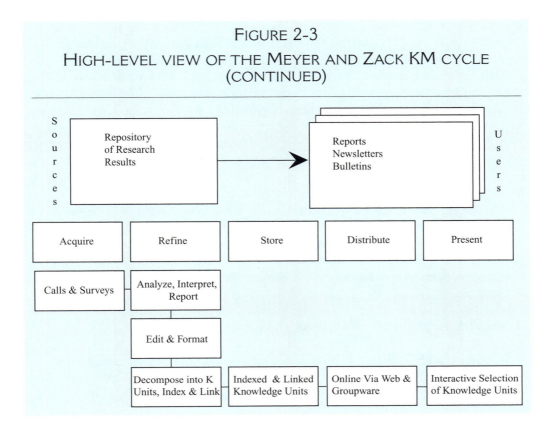

Storage/retrieval forms a bridge between the upstream acquisition and refinement stages that feed the repository and downstream stages of product generation. Storage may be physical (file folders, printed information) or digital (database, knowledge management software).

Distribution describes how the product is delivered to the end user (e.g., fax, print, e-mail) and encompasses not only the medium of delivery but also its timing, frequency, form, language, and so on.

The final step is *presentation* or *use*. It is at this stage that context plays an important role. The effectiveness of each of the preceding value-added steps is evaluated here: does the user have enough context to be able to make use of this content? If not, the KM cycle has failed to deliver value to the individual and ultimately to the organization.

In order for the cycle to work as intended, front-end knowledge needs to be provided. This is typically in the form of rules in how to identify source information, acquire it, refine it, and subsequently add it to the firm's information repository. There may also be a similar need at the final stage—rules on how content may be distributed and used such as copyright, attribution, confidentiality, and other restrictions that may apply.

The repository and the "refinery" together enable the management of valuable knowledge of a firm. They in turn need to be supported by the firm's core capabilities in information technology, internal knowledge about its business, external knowledge about current and emerging environments, as well as how it organizes and manages itself. The flexibility with which the firm can create content-based products forms the basis of the firm's ability to realize market leverage from its information assets.

Although not explicitly described in the Meyer and Zack cycle, there is also a notion of having to continually renew the repository and the refinery in order to avoid obsolescence. Renewal should be added to the cycle diagram in the form of a feedback loop that involves rethinking the basic content and structure of the repository to decide whether different, newer products or repackaging is required. This may mean increasing the depth of an analysis, updating a report, providing greater integration, allowing more sophisticated cross-linking, or achieving greater standardization of content.

The Meyer and Zack model is one of the most complete descriptions of the key elements involved in the knowledge management model. Its strength derives primarily from its comprehensive information processing paradigm, which is almost completely adaptable to knowledge-based content. In particular, the notion of refinement is a crucial stage in the KM cycle and one that is often neglected.

The Bukowitz and Williams KM Cycle

Bukowitz and Williams (2000) describe a knowledge management process framework (p. 9) that outlines "how organizations generate, maintain and deploy a strategically correct stock of knowledge to create value" (p. 8). This framework is shown in Figure 2-4.

In this framework, knowledge consists of knowledge repositories, relationships, information technologies, communications infrastructure, functional skill sets, process know-how, environmental responsiveness, organizational intelligence, and external sources. The get, learn, and contribute phases are tactical in nature. They are triggered by market-driven opportunities or demands, and they typically result in day-to-day use of knowledge to respond to these demands. The assess, build/sustain, or divest stages are more strategic, triggered by shifts in the macroenvironment. These stages focus on more long-range processes of matching intellectual capital to strategic requirements.

The first stage, *get*, consists of seeking out information needed in order to make decisions, solve problems, or innovate. The challenge today is not so

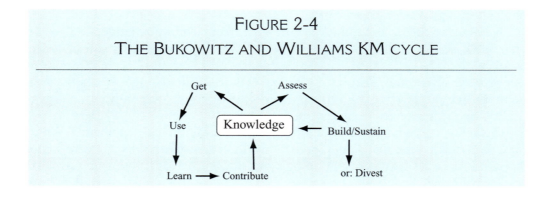

FIGURE 2-4
THE BUKOWITZ AND WILLIAMS KM CYCLE

much in finding information but in dealing effectively with the enormous volume of information that can be obtained. Technology has made great strides in providing access to an ever-increasing pool of information. The resultant "information overload" has created a critical need to sift through the vast volume of content, identify the knowledge of value, and then to manage this knowledge effectively and efficiently. Information professionals have traditionally fulfilled this role, and they are certainly needed, now more than ever. User needs must be well understood in order to match information seekers with the best possible content. This involves knowing where knowledge resources exist and can be accessed.

Where knowledge management diverges from information management is that "getting" of content encompasses not only traditional explicit content (e.g., a physical or electronic document) but also tacit knowledge. This means information users need be connected not only to content but also to content experts—people—where most of the valuable tacit knowledge resides. The term *cybrarian* is sometimes used to describe the new knowledge professional role. The key tasks are to organize knowledge content, maintain timeliness, completeness, and accuracy, profile users' information needs, access/navigate/filter voluminous content in order to respond to users' needs, and help train users with new knowledge repository technologies (*information literacy*).

The next stage, *use*, deals with how to combine information in new and interesting ways in order to foster organizational innovation. The focus is primarily on individuals and then on groups. The narrow focus on innovation as the reason for making use of intellectual assets is somewhat limiting in this KM cycle. The authors discuss a number of techniques to promote serendipity and out-of-the-box thinking or creativity-enhancing techniques. Although promoting the greatest, most fluid flow of knowledge is a worthwhile pursuit, the uses of knowledge are much wider in scope than innovation.

The *learn* stage refers to the formal process of learning from experiences as a means of creating competitive advantage. An organizational memory is created so that organizational learning becomes possible from both successes (best practices) and failures (lessons learned). The links between learning and creating value are harder to establish than those of getting and using information. Learning in organizations is important because it represents the transition step between the application of ideas and the generation of new ones. Time must be taken to reflect on experience and consider its possible value elsewhere. There should be a strong link between organizational strategy and organizational learning activities. Learning is absolutely essential after the "getting" and "using" of content; otherwise, the content is simply warehoused somewhere and does not make a difference in how things are done within the organization.

The *contribute* stage of the KM cycle deals with getting employees to post what they have learned to the communal knowledge base (e.g., a repository). Only in this way can individual knowledge be made visible and available across the entire organization, where appropriate. The last caveat is added, for the tendency is to warehouse all knowledge, which should not be the focus of KM. These sequences of steps are used by many authors, and they have the unfortunate effect of creating the misconception that KM is all about making public all that resides within the heads of individuals. Needless to say, the impact on the motivation of employees plummets considerably! The point of the exercise is not to post everything on the company intranet but to cull those experiences from which others in the organization may also benefit. This implies that the experience has potential to be generalized. In fact, a great deal of content to be shared organization-wide must first be repackaged in a "generic" format in order to be of use to a wider audience.

Examples of content that employees should be encouraged to contribute include the sharing of best practices and lessons learned so that others do not repeat the same mistakes. The authors describe a number of carrots and sticks that can be used to promote knowledge sharing. In effect, practice has proven that knowledge sharing occurs quite well without any heavy direct pay-per-contribution schemes, or with equally onerous punish-the-withholders mentality. In order for successful knowledge sharing to occur, it must "make sense." That is, the benefits to both the organization and the individuals must exist and must be clearly perceived as such. The other critical success factor appears to involve the successful deployment of knowledge brokers—professionals who assume the responsibility of gathering, repackaging, and promoting knowledge nuggets throughout the organization. A good system should be in place to maintain the results of organizational learning—a good organizational memory management system, often in the form of an intranet of some sort. Part of good organizational memory management practice should be to always maintain attribution, require authorization for dissemination, provide feedback mechanisms, and keep track of knowledge reuse. One of the best rewards of contributing is to be notified of how "popular" your contributions were (which is analogous to a citation index for scholarly publications).

Next, the *assess* stage deals more with the group and organizational level. Assessment refers to the evaluation of intellectual capital and requires that the organization define mission-critical knowledge and map current intellectual capital against future knowledge needs. The organization must also develop metrics to demonstrate that it is growing its knowledge base and profiting from its investments in intellectual capital. The theory of the organization needs to be expanded to include capturing the impact of knowledge on organizational performance. This includes identifying new forms of capital such as human capital (competencies), customer capital (the customer relationship), organizational capital (knowledge bases, business processes, technology infrastructure, values, norms, and culture), and intellectual capital (the relationship between human, customer, and organizational capital). Assessment must take these new types of assets into account and focus on how easily and flexibly the organization can convert its knowledge into products and services of value to the customer. A new set of frameworks, processes, and metrics that evaluate the knowledge base must be incorporated into the overall management process.

The *build and sustain* step in the KM cycle ensures that the organization's future intellectual capital will keep the organization viable and competitive. Resources must be allocated to the growth and maintenance of knowledge, and they should be channeled in such a way as to create new knowledge and reinforce existing knowledge. At the tactical level, the inability to locate and apply knowledge to meet an existing need results in a lost opportunity. At the strategic level, coming up short on the "right" knowledge delivers a much more serious blow—loss of competitiveness and ultimately of organizational viability as well.

The final step in the Bukowitz and Williams KM cycle is the *divest* step. The organization should not hold on to assets—physical or intellectual—if they are no longer creating value. In fact, some knowledge may be more valuable if it is transferred outside the organization. In this step of the KM cycle, organizations need to examine their intellectual capital in terms of the resources required to maintain it and whether these resources would be better spent elsewhere. This involves understanding the why, when, where, and how of formally divesting parts of the knowledge base. An opportunity cost analysis of retaining knowledge should be incorporated into standard management practice. It is necessary to be able to understand which parts of the knowledge base will be unnecessary for sustaining competitive advantage and industry viability.

Traditional divestiture decisions regarding knowledge include obtaining patents, spinning off companies, outsourcing work, terminating a training program and/or employees, replacing/upgrading technologies, and ending partnerships, alliances, or contracts. However, KM requires a planned purposeful form of divesting, which means that the decision to be made is a strategic one, not an operational task. Ideally, unnecessary knowledge should not have been acquired in the first place; the organization should put into place processes to clearly discriminate between forms of knowledge that can be leveraged and those that are of limited use. Knowledge that is a drain on resources should be converted into value. This often involves converting rather than getting rid of knowledge—for example, by redeploying the knowledge elsewhere within or outside of the organization.

The Bukowitz and Williams KM cycle introduces two new critical phases: the learning of knowledge content and the decision as to whether to maintain this knowledge or divest the organization of this knowledge content. This KM cycle is more comprehensive than the Meyer and Zack cycle because the notion of tacit as well as explicit knowledge management has been incorporated.

The McElroy KM Cycle

McElroy (1999) describes a knowledge life cycle that consists of the processes of knowledge production and knowledge integration, with a series of feedback loops to organizational memory, beliefs, and claims and the business-processing environment. The high-level processes are shown in Figure 2-5.

McElroy emphasizes that organizational knowledge is held both subjectively in the minds of individuals and groups and objectively in explicit forms. Together, they comprise the distributed organizational knowledge base of the company. Knowledge use in the business-processing environment results in outcomes that either match expectations or fail to do so. Matches reinforce existing knowledge, leading to its reuse, whereas mismatches lead to adjustments in business-processing behavior via single-loop learning (Argyris and Schon,

FIGURE 2-5

HIGH-LEVEL PROCESSES IN THE McELROY KM CYCLE

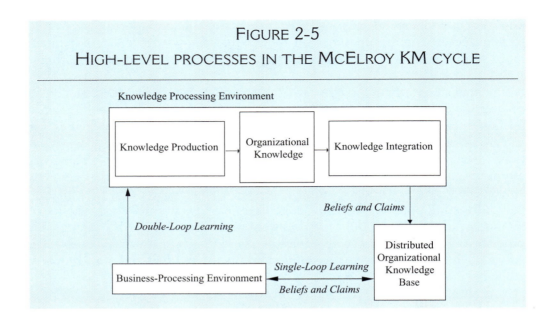

1978). Successive failures from mismatches will lead to doubt and ultimately rejection of existing knowledge, which will in turn trigger knowledge processing to produce and integrate new knowledge, this time via double-loop learning (Argyris and Schon, 1978).

Problem claim formulation represents an attempt to learn and state the specific nature of the detected knowledge gap. Knowledge claim formulation follows as a response to validated problem claims via information acquisition and individual and group learning. New knowledge claims are tested and evaluated via knowledge claim evaluation processes. Evaluation of knowledge claims leads to surviving knowledge claims that will be integrated as new organizational knowledge or falsified/undecided knowledge claims. The record of all such outcomes becomes part of the distributed organizational knowledge base via knowledge integration. Once integrated, they are used in business processing. Experience gained from the use of knowledge in the organizational knowledge base gives rise to new claims and resulting beliefs, triggering the cycle to begin all over again.

In knowledge production, the key processes are individual and group learning; knowledge claim formulation; information acquisition; codified knowledge claim; and knowledge claim evaluation. Figure 2-6 illustrates these knowledge production processes.

Individual and group learning represents the first step in organizational learning. Knowledge is information until it is validated. Knowledge claim validation involves codification at an organizational level. A formalized procedure is required for the receipt and codification of individual and group innovations. Information acquisition is the process by which an organization deliberately or serendipitously acquires knowledge claims or information produced by others, usually external to the organization. This stage plays a fundamental role in formulating new knowledge claims at the organizational level. Exam-

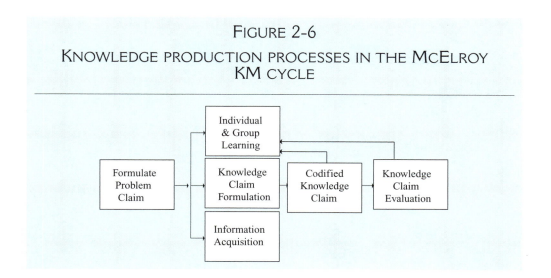

FIGURE 2-6

KNOWLEDGE PRODUCTION PROCESSES IN THE MCELROY
KM CYCLE

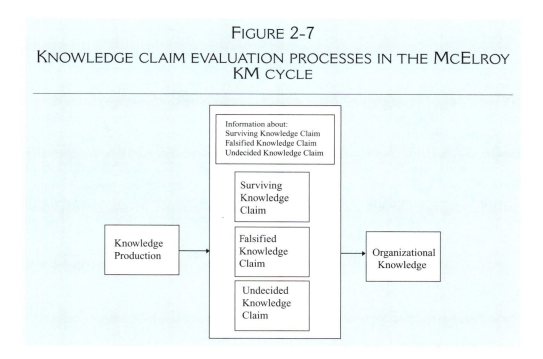

FIGURE 2-7

KNOWLEDGE CLAIM EVALUATION PROCESSES IN THE MCELROY
KM CYCLE

ples include competitive intelligence, subscription services, library services, research initiatives, think tanks, consortia, and personalized information services. Knowledge claim evaluation is the process by which knowledge claims are evaluated to determine their veracity and value. This implies that they are of greater value than existing knowledge in the organizational knowledge base. Figure 2-7 shows some of the components of this stage of the knowledge cycle.

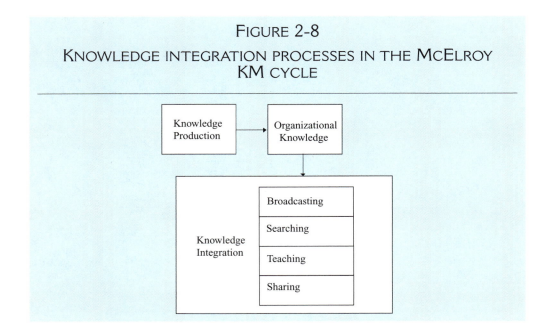

FIGURE 2-8

KNOWLEDGE INTEGRATION PROCESSES IN THE MCELROY
KM CYCLE

Knowledge integration is the process by which an organization introduces new knowledge claims to its operating environment and retires old ones. This includes all knowledge transmission such as teaching, knowledge sharing, and other social activities that either communicate an understanding of previously produced organizational knowledge to knowledge workers or integrate newly minted knowledge. Figure 2-8 describes this stage of the KM cycle.

One of the great strengths of the McElroy cycle is the clear description of how knowledge is evaluated and a conscious decision is made as to whether or not it will be integrated into the organizational memory. The validation of knowledge is a step that clearly distinguishes knowledge management from document management. The KM cycle does more than address the storage and subsequent management of documents or knowledge that has been warehoused "as is." The KM cycle focuses on processes to identify knowledge content that is of value to the organization and its employees.

The Wiig KM Cycle

Wiig (1993) focuses on the three conditions that need to be present for an organization to conduct its business successfully: it must have a business (products/services) and customers; it must have resources (people, capital, and facilities); and it must have the ability to act. The third point is emphasized in the Wiig KM cycle.

Knowledge is the principal force that determines and drives the ability to act intelligently. With improved knowledge we know better what to do and how to do it. Wiig identifies the major purpose of KM as an effort "to make the enterprise intelligent-acting by facilitating the creation, cumulation [sic], deployment and use of quality knowledge" (p. 39). Working smarter means that we must approach our tasks with greater expertise—that we must acquire as much relevant and high-quality knowledge as possible and apply it better in a number of different ways. Working smarter "involves making use of all the best knowledge we have available" (p. 51).

Wiig's KM cycle addresses how knowledge is built and used as individuals or as organizations. There are four major steps in this cycle, as shown in Figure 2-9:

1. Building knowledge.
2. Holding knowledge.
3. Pooling knowledge.
4. Applying knowledge.

Although the steps are shown to be independent and sequential, this is a simplification since we may perform some of the functions and activities in parallel. It is also possible to cycle back to repeat functions and activities performed earlier but with a different emphasis and/or level of detail. The cycle addresses a broad range of learning from all types of sources: personal experience, formal education or training, peers, and intelligence from all sources. We can then hold knowledge either within our heads or in tangible forms such as books or databases. Knowledge can be pooled and used in a variety of different ways depending on the context and the purpose.

The cycle focuses on identifying and relating the functions and activities that we engage in to make products and services as knowledge workers.

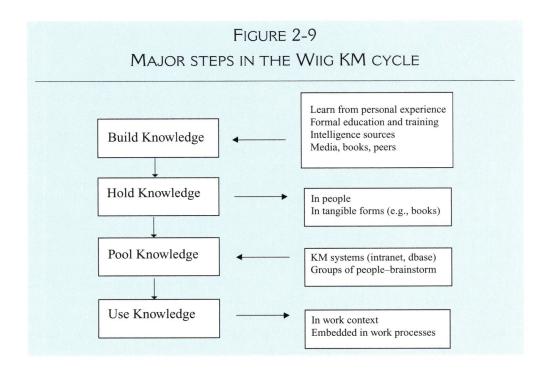

FIGURE 2-9

MAJOR STEPS IN THE WIIG KM CYCLE

Building knowledge refers to activities ranging from market research to focus groups, surveys, competitive intelligence, and data mining applications. Building knowledge consists of five major activities:

1. Obtain knowledge.
2. Analyze knowledge.
3. Reconstruct/synthesize knowledge.
4. Codify and model knowledge.
5. Organize knowledge.

Knowledge creation may occur through R&D projects, innovations by individuals to improve the way they perform their tasks, experimentation, reasoning with existing knowledge, and hiring of new people. Knowledge may also be created through knowledge importing (e.g., elicit knowledge from experts and from procedure manuals, engage in joint ventures to obtain technology, or transfer people between departments). Finally, knowledge may be created through observing the real world (e.g., making site visits, observing processes after the introduction of a change).

Knowledge analysis consists of:

- Extracting what appears to be knowledge from obtained material (e.g., analyze transcripts and identify themes, listen to an explanation, and select concepts for further consideration).
- Abstracting extracted materials (e.g., form a model or a theory).
- Identifying patterns extracted (e.g., trend analysis).
- Explaining relations between knowledge fragments (e.g., compare and contrast, causal relations).
- Verifying that extracted materials correspond to the meaning of original sources (e.g., meaning has not been corrupted through summarizing, collating, and so on).

Knowledge synthesis or reconstruction consists of generalizing analyzed material to obtain broader principles, generating hypotheses to explain observations, establishing conformance between new and existing knowledge (e.g., corroborating validity in light of what is already known), and updating the total knowledge pool by incorporating the new knowledge.

Codifying and modeling knowledge involves how we represent knowledge in our minds (mental models, for example), how we then assemble the knowledge into a coherent model, how we document the knowledge in books and manuals, and how we encode it in order to post it to a knowledge repository.

Finally, knowledge is organized for specific uses and according to an established organizational framework (such as standards and categories). Examples include a help desk service or a list of frequently asked questions (FAQs) on the company intranet. This organization is usually done using some form of knowledge ontology (conceptual model) and taxonomy (classification rules). Examples include an official list of key words or categories, knowledge object attribute specifications, and guidelines for translation.

Holding knowledge consists of remembering, accumulating knowledge in repositories, embedding knowledge in repositories, and archiving knowledge. *Remembering knowledge* means that the individual has retained or remembered that item of knowledge (i.e., knowledge has been internalized or understood by a given individual). *Accumulating knowledge* in a repository means that a computer-resident knowledge base has been created and that knowledge has been encoded, permitting it to be stored in organizational memory. *Embedding knowledge* consists of ensuring that it is part of business procedures (e.g., added to a procedures manual or training course). Finally, *archiving knowledge* involves creating a scientific library and systematically retiring out-of-date, false, or no longer relevant knowledge from the active repository. Archiving typically involves storing the content in another, less costly, or less bulky medium for less frequent future retrieval.

Examples of knowledge held by companies include intellectual property, patents, knowledge documented in the form of research reports, technical papers, or tacit knowledge, which remains in the minds of individuals but which may be elicited and embedded in the knowledge base or repository (e.g., tips, tricks of the trade, case studies, videotapes of demonstrations by experts, and task support systems). In this way, the organization's holdings of valuable knowledge are documented in repositories or in people and are therefore available for future reference and use.

Knowledge pooling consists of coordinating, assembling, and accessing and retrieving knowledge. *Coordination of knowledge* typically requires the formation of collaborative teams to work with particular content in order to create a "who knows what" network. Once knowledge sources are identified, they are then *assembled* into background references for a library or repository in order to facilitate subsequent access and retrieval. Focus groups are often used in order to arrive at a consensus as to how this can best be achieved. *Access and retrieval* then addresses being able to consult with knowledgeable people about difficult problems, obtaining a second opinion from an expert, or discussing a difficult case with a peer. Knowledge can be accessed and retrieved directly from the repository as well (e.g., using a knowledge base system to obtain advice on how to do something or reading a knowledge document in order to arrive at a decision).

Organizations may pool knowledge in a variety of ways. The employee who does not have the necessary knowledge and know-how to solve a particular problem can contact others in the organization who have solved similar problems either by obtaining the information from the organizational knowledge repository or by finding an expert through the expertise locator network and contacting that person directly. The individual can then organize all this information and request that more experienced knowledge workers validate the content.

Finally, there are innumerable ways to apply the knowledge, including the following:

- Use established knowledge to perform a routine task—for example, make standard products, provide a standard service, or use the expert network to find out who is knowledgeable about a particular area.

- Use general knowledge to survey exceptional situations at hand—for example, determine what the problem is and estimate potential consequences.
- Use knowledge to describe the situation and scope of the problem—for example, identify the problem and show generally how to handle it.
- Select relevant special knowledge to handle the situation—for example, identify who you need to consult with or want to address the problem.
- Observe and characterize the situation with special knowledge—for example, make a comparison with known patterns, take a history, and collect and organize required information to act.
- Analyze the situation with knowledge—for example, judge whether it can be handled internally or whether outside help will be required.
- Synthesize alternative solutions with knowledge—for example, identify options and outline possible approaches.
- Evaluate potential alternatives using special knowledge—for example, determine the risks and benefits of each possible approach.
- Use knowledge to decide what to do—for example, rank alternatives, select one, and do a reality check.
- Implement the selected alternative—for example, execute the task and authorize the team to proceed.

When knowledge is applied to work objects, routine and standard tasks are approached in a different way than difficult or unusual tasks. Routine or standard tasks are typically carried out using "compiled" knowledge that we can readily access and use almost unconsciously or automatically. Difficult tasks are usually performed in a more deliberate and conscious manner, for knowledge workers cannot use automated knowledge in unanticipated situations.

Figure 2-10 summarizes the key activities in the Wiig KM cycle. A major advantage of the Wiig approach to the KM cycle is the clear and detailed description of how organizational memory is put into use in order to generate value for individuals, groups, and the organization itself. The myriad of ways in which knowledge can be applied and used are linked to decision-making sequences and individual characteristics. Wiig also emphasizes the role of

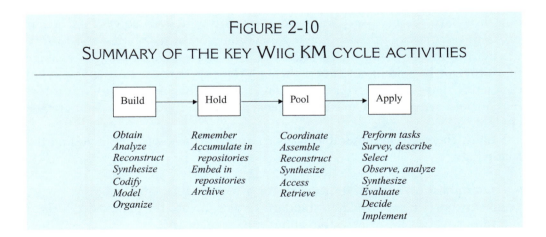

FIGURE 2-10

SUMMARY OF THE KEY WIIG KM CYCLE ACTIVITIES

Build	Hold	Pool	Apply
Obtain	Remember	Coordinate	Perform tasks
Analyze	Accumulate in	Assemble	Survey, describe
Reconstruct	repositories	Reconstruct	Select
Synthesize	Embed in	Synthesize	Observe, analyze
Codify	repositories	Access	Synthesize
Model	Archive	Retrieve	Evaluate
Organize			Decide
			Implement

knowledge and skill, the business use of that knowledge, constraints that may prevent that knowledge from being fully used, opportunities and alternatives to managing that knowledge, and the expected value added to the organization.

AN INTEGRATED KM CYCLE

On the basis of our preceding study of some major approaches to KM cycles, we can distill an integrated KM cycle. The three major stages are:

1. Knowledge capture and/or creation.
2. Knowledge sharing and dissemination.
3. Knowledge acquisition and application.

In the transition from knowledge capture/creation to knowledge sharing and dissemination, knowledge content is assessed. Knowledge is then contextualized in order to be understood ("acquisition") and used ("application"). This stage then feeds back into the first one in order to update the knowledge content. The integrated KM cycle is outlined in Figure 2-11.

Knowledge capture refers to the identification and subsequent codification of existing (usually previously unnoticed) internal knowledge and know-how within the organization and/or external knowledge from the environment. Knowledge creation is the development of new knowledge and know-how—innovations that did not have a previous existence within the company. When knowledge is inventoried in this manner, the next critical step is to present an assessment against selection criteria that will follow closely the organizational goals. Is this content valid? Is it new or better? That is, is it of sufficient value to the organization such that it should be added to the store of intellectual capital?

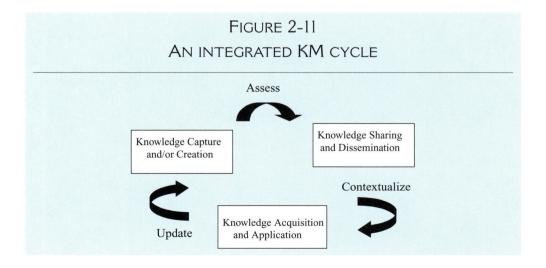

FIGURE 2-11
AN INTEGRATED KM CYCLE

Once it has been decided that the new or newly identified content is of sufficient value, the next step is to contextualize this content. This involves maintaining a link between the knowledge and those knowledgeable about that content: the author or originator of the idea and subject matter experts, as well as those who have garnered significant experience in making use of this content. Contextualization also implies identifying the key attributes of the content in order to better match to a variety of users—for example, personalization to translate the content into one preferred by the end user or creation of a short executive summary to better accommodate the time constraints of a senior manager. Finally, contextualization will often succeed when the new content is firmly, yet seamlessly, embedded in the business processes of the organization. The integrated cycle subsumes most of the steps involved in the KM cycles discussed in this chapter. Table 2-2 shows this mapping in more detail.

The knowledge management cycle is then reiterated as users understand and decide to make use of content. The users will validate usefulness, and they will signal when it becomes out of date or when this knowledge is not applicable. Users will help validate the scope of the content or how generalizable the best practices and lessons learned can be. They will also, quite often, come up with new content, which they can then contribute to the next cycle iteration.

TABLE 2-2
INTEGRATED KM CYCLE STEPS

Meyer & Zack (1996)	Bukowitz & Williams (2003)	McElroy (1999)	Wiig (1993)	Integrated KM Cycle
Acquisition	Get	Individual & group learning	Creation	Create/capture
Refinement	Use	Knowledge claim validation	Sourcing	Create/capture
Store/retrieve	Learn	Information acquisition	Compilation	Create/capture
Distribution	Contribute	Knowledge validation	Transformation	Create/capture and contextualize
Presentation	Assess	Knowledge integration	Dissemination	Share, disseminate, and assess
	Build/sustain		Application	Acquisition and application
	Divest		Value realization	Update

A major international consulting organization wanted to capture lessons learned from its major projects. This represented a first step toward becoming a learning organization. From a scan of what similar companies were doing, their competitive intelligence led them to select the implementation of an after-action review (AAR) in the form of a project postmortem. The AAR was a new procedure, and it was initially piloted with a group of experienced consultants. Project managers who became experienced with the postmortem were subsequently asked to become resource people for those willing to learn and try it out. A new role of knowledge journalist was created; the idea was to appoint a neutral, objective person who had not been a member of the original project team to facilitate the postmortem process and capture the key learnings from the project. Finally, the postmortem was added as a final step for all project managers before they could officially and formally deem a project to be completed.

STRATEGIC IMPLICATIONS OF THE KM CYCLE

Knowledge represents the decisive basis for intelligent, competent behavior at the individual, group, and organization level. Only a conscious and organized reflection of lessons learned and best practices discovered will allow companies to leverage their hard-won knowledge assets. A knowledge architecture needs to be designed and implemented in order to enable the staged processing and transformation of knowledge, much like information products are processed, and to ensure that the knowledge objects reach intended end users and are put to good use. The objective is to retain and share knowledge with a wider audience. Information and communication technologies such as groupware, intranets, and knowledge bases or repositories provide the necessary infrastructure to do so. Business processes and cultural enablers offer the necessary incentives and opportunities for all knowledge workers to become active participants throughout the knowledge management cycle.

PRACTICAL CONSIDERATIONS FOR MANAGING KNOWLEDGE

Understanding the different stages of managing knowledge throughout the KM cycle is important, though not enough. From a practical perspective, managing knowledge requires an organizing principle—a framework—that will help us classify the different types of activities and functions needed to deal with all knowledge-related work within and between organizations. This framework is often encapsulated in the form of a KM theory or model. Several major KM models are presented in the next chapter.

KEY POINTS

- There are a number of different approaches to the knowledge management cycle such as those by McElroy, Wiig, Bukowitz and Willams, and Meyer and Zack.
- By comparing and contrasting these approaches and by validating them through experience gained to date with KM practice, the major stages are identified as knowledge capture and creation, knowledge sharing and dissemination, and knowledge acquisition and application.
- The critical processes throughout the KM cycle assess the worth of content based on organizational goals, contextualize content in order to better match with a variety of users, and continuously update with a focus on updating, archiving as required, and modifying the scope of each knowledge object.

DISCUSSION POINTS

1. Discuss the different KM cycle approaches and how to integrate them into a comprehensive, integrated approach to the effective management of knowledge within an organization.
2. Provide an example of how each major KM cycle stage listed below can add value to knowledge and increase the strategic worth of the knowledge asset:
   a. Capture
   b. Codify
   c. Create
   d. Share
   e. Acquire
   f. Apply
3. Where are the key decision points in the KM cycle? What types of information would you require in order to decide whether the knowledge content would continue to the next step of the cycle?

REFERENCES

Argyris, C., and Schon, D. (1978). *Organizational learning: a theory of action perspective*. New York: McGraw-Hill.

Bukowitz, W., and Williams, R. (2000). *The knowledge management fieldbook*. London: Prentice Hall.

McElroy, M. (2003). *The new knowledge management: complexity, learning and sustainable innovation*. Boston, MA: Butterworth-Heinemann.

McElroy, M. (1999, April). The knowledge life cycle. Presented at the ICM Conference on KM. Miami, FL.

Meyer, M., and Zack, M. (1996). The design and implementation of information products. *Sloan Management Review*, 37(3): 43–59.

Nickols, F. (1996). Cooperative development of a classification of knowledge management functions. In P. Murray, *Knowledge Praxis*. Retrieved May 25, 2004, from http://www.media-access.com/classification.html.

Wiig, K. (1993). *Knowledge management foundations*. Arlington, TX: Schema Press.

KNOWLEDGE MANAGEMENT MODELS

Furious activity is no substitute for understanding.

H. H. Williams (1858–1940)

To succeed, a knowledge management initiative must have a robust theoretical foundation. The major KM activities described in the KM cycle in the previous chapter require a conceptual framework to operate within; otherwise the activities will not be coordinated and will not produce the expected KM benefits. Knowledge management models are presented from Choo (1998), Weick (2001), Nonaka and Takeuchi (1995), Wiig (1993), von Krogh and Roos (1995), Boisot (1998), Beer (1984), and Bennet and Bennet (2004). All the models present different perspectives on the key conceptual elements that form the infrastructure of knowledge management. This chapter describes, compares, and contrasts each model in order to provide a sound understanding of the discipline of KM.

LEARNING OBJECTIVES

1. Understand the key tenets of the major knowledge management theoretical models in use today.
2. Link the KM frameworks to key KM concepts and the major phases of the KM cycle.
3. Explain the complex adaptive system model of KM and how it addresses the subjective and dynamic nature of content to be managed.

INTRODUCTION

In an economy where the only certainty is uncertainty,
the one sure source of lasting competitive advantage is knowledge.
I. Nonaka (1995)

Although few would argue that knowledge is not important, the overriding problem is that few managers and information professionals understand how to manage knowledge in knowledge-creating organizations. The tendency is to focus on "hard" or quantifiable knowledge, and KM is often seen as some sort of information processing machine. The advent of knowledge management was initially met with a fair degree of criticism, with many people feeling this was yet another buzzword that would quickly pass into history. Instead, KM established itself credibly as both an academic discipline of study and a professional field of practice, and one reason it was so successful was the work done on theoretical or conceptual models of knowledge management. Early in the development of KM, more pragmatic considerations about its processes were soon complemented by the need to understand what was happening in organizational knowing, reasoning, and learning.

A more holistic approach to KM has become necessary as the complex subjective and dynamic nature of knowledge has become a more pressing issue. Cultural and contextual influences further increased the complexity involved in KM, and these factors also had to be taken into account in a model or framework that could situate and explain the key KM concepts and processes. Finally, measurements were needed in order to be able to monitor progress toward and attainment of expected KM benefits.

This holistic approach encompasses all the different types of content to be managed, ranging from data to information to knowledge, but also from tacit to explicit and back to tacit-knowledge-type conversions. All the KM models presented in this chapter attempt to address knowledge management from a holistic and comprehensive perspective.

Davenport and Prusak (1998, p. 2) provide the following distinctions between data, information, and knowledge, which also serve to recap the examples presented in Chapter 1:

Data: A set of discrete, objective facts about events.
Information: A message, usually in the form of a document or an audible or visible communication.
Knowledge: A fluid mix of framed experiences, values, contextual information, and expert insight that provides a framework for evaluating and incorporating new experiences and information. It originates and is applied in the minds of knowers. In organizations, it often becomes embedded not only in documents or repositories but also in organizational routines, processes, practices, and norms.

Davenport and Prusak (1998) refer to this distinction between data, information, and knowledge as an operational one, and they argue that we can transform information into knowledge by means of comparison, consequences, connections, and conversation. They stress that knowledge-creating activities take place between and within humans and that we have to consider knowledge among the most important corporate assets.

Yet there is no need to choose one over the other or to create mutually exclusive categories. A great deal of overlap and a great deal of value are evident in the many different types of content. In this respect, *content management* is perhaps a better, more general term than knowledge management.

Nonaka and Takeuchi (1995) provide a more philosophical distinction, starting from the traditional definition of knowledge as "justified true belief." They define knowledge as "a dynamic human process of justifying personal belief toward the "truth" (p. 58). They contend that in order to produce innovation, it is necessary to create knowledge. For them, organizational knowledge creation is "the capability of a company as a whole to create new knowledge, disseminate it throughout the organization and embody it in products, services, and systems" (p. 58).

The concept of tacit knowledge, as we saw in Chapter 1, has been clarified by Polanyi (1966), who stresses the importance of the "personal" way of knowledge construction, affected by emotions and acquired at the end of the process involving every individual's active creation and organization of the experiences. When a person tacitly knows, he or she acts, decides, uses the body, and experiences great difficulty in explaining this process in words, rules, and algorithms. The act of tacitly knowing is without distance from things and performances, and the knowing interaction between persons is one of an unaware observation and social, "communitarian" closeness.

Polanyi posits that all knowledge is either tacit or rooted in tacit knowledge. On one hand, tacit knowledge is not easily expressed in formalized ways, and is context-specific, personal, and difficult to communicate. On the other hand, explicit knowledge is the codified one, expressed in formal and linguistic ways, easily transmittable and storable, and expressible in words and algorithms, but it represents only the tip of the iceberg of the entire body of knowledge. This definition of the tacit/explicit concepts emphasizes the importance of considering adequately the tacit dimension.

The 80/20 rule appears to apply here; that is, roughly 80% of our knowledge is in tacit form as individuals, as groups, and as an organization. Only 15 to 20% of valuable knowledge has typically been captured, codified, or rendered tangible and concrete in some fashion. This is usually in the form of books, databases, audio or video recordings, graphs or other images, and so forth. The tacit/explicit mobilization (in the epistemological dimension) and the individual/group/organizational sharing and diffusion (in the ontological dimension) have to take place in order to create knowledge and produce innovation. Each of the KM models presented in the next section addresses this point in different but complementary ways.

MAJOR THEORETICAL KM MODELS

The following models were selected because they possess the following critical characteristics:

1. They represent a holistic approach to knowledge management (i.e., they are comprehensive and take into consideration people, process, organization, and technology dimensions).
2. They have been reviewed, critiqued, and discussed extensively in the KM literature, by practitioners, academics, and researchers alike.
3. The models have been implemented and field tested with respect to reliability and validity.

This list is not meant either to be exhaustive or a definitive short list, but the models have been selected with a view to providing the widest possible perspective on KM as a whole, combined with a deeper, more robust theoretical foundation for explaining, describing, and better predicting the best way to manage knowledge.

The von Krogh and Roos Model of Organizational Epistemology

The von Krogh and Roos KM model (1995) distinguishes between individual knowledge and social knowledge, and they take an epistemological approach to managing organizational knowledge: the organizational epistemology KM model. Whereas the definition of *organization* has been problematic and the term is often used interchangeably with information, a number of issues must be addressed:

- How and why individuals within an organization come to know.
- How and why organizations, as social entities, come to know.
- What counts for knowledge of the individual and the organization.
- What are the impediments in organizational KM.

The cognitivist perspective (e.g., Varela, 1992) proposes that a cognitive system, whether it is a human brain or a computer, creates representations (i.e., models) of reality and that learning occurs when these representations are manipulated. A cognitive organizational epistemology views organizational knowledge as a self-organizing system in which humans are transparent to the information from the outside (i.e., we take in information through our senses, and we use this information to build our mental models). The brain is a machine based on logic and deduction that does not allow any contradictory propositions. The organization thus picks up information from its environment and processes it in a logical way. Alternative courses of action are generated through information search, and the cognitive competence of an organization depends on the mobilization of individual cognitive resources—a "linear" summation of individuals to form the organizational whole.

The connectionist approach, on the other hand, is more holistic than reductionist. The brain is not assumed to sequentially process symbols but to perceive "wholeness," global properties, patterns, synergies, and gestalts. Learning rules govern how the various components of these whole networks are connected. Information is not only taken in from the environment but also generated internally. Familiarity and practice lead to learning. Individuals form nodes in a loosely connected organizational system, and knowledge is an emergent phenomenon that stems from the social interactions of these individuals. In this perspective, knowledge resides not only in the minds of individuals but also in the connections among these individuals. A collective mind is formed as the representation of this network, and it is this that lies at the core of organizational knowledge management.

Von Krogh and Roos adopt the connectionist approach. In their organizational epistemology KM model, knowledge resides both in the individuals of an organization and, at the social level, in the relations between the individuals. Knowledge is said to be "embodied"; that is, "everything known is known by somebody" (von Krogh and Roos, 1995, p. 50). Unlike cognitivism, which views knowledge as an abstract entity, connectionism maintains that there can be no knowledge without a knower. This notion fits nicely with the concept of tacit knowledge, which is very difficult to abstract out of someone and is made more concrete. It also reinforces the strong need to maintain links between knowledge objects and those who are knowledgeable about them—authors, subject matter experts, and experienced users who have applied the knowledge both successfully and unsuccessfully.

In 1998, von Krogh, Roos, and Kleine examined the fragile nature of KM in organizations in terms of the mind-set of the individuals, communication in the organization, the organizational structure, the relationship between the members, and the management of human resources. These five factors could impede the successful management of organizational knowledge for innovation, competitive advantage, and other organizational goals. For example, if the individuals do not perceive knowledge to be a crucial competence of the firm, then the organization will have trouble developing knowledge-based competencies. If there is no legitimate language to express new knowledge in the individual, contributions will fail. If the organizational structure does not facilitate innovation, KM will fail. If individual members are not eager to share their experiences with their colleagues on the basis of mutual trust and respect, there will be no generation of social, collective knowledge within that organization. Finally, if those contributing knowledge are not highly evaluated and acknowledged by top management, they will lose their motivation to innovate and develop new knowledge for the firm.

Organizations need to put knowledge enablers in place that will stimulate the development of individual knowledge, group sharing of knowledge, and organizational retention of valuable knowledge-based content. This approach was further refined (von Krogh, Ichijo, and Nonaka, 2000) to propose a model of knowledge enabling rather than knowledge management. Knowledge enabling refers to the "overall set of organizational activities that positively affect knowledge creation" (p. 4). This typically involves facilitating relationships and conversations as well as sharing local knowledge across an organization and across geographical and cultural borders.

The connectionist approach appears to be the more appropriate one for underpinning a theoretical model of knowledge management, especially owing to the fact that the linkage between knowledge and those who "absorb" and make use of the knowledge is viewed as an unbreakable bond. The connectionist approach provides a solid theoretical cornerstone for a model of knowledge management and is a component of the models discussed in this chapter.

The Nonaka and Takeuchi Knowledge Spiral Model

Nonaka and Takeuchi (1995) studied the success of Japanese companies in achieving creativity and innovation. They quickly found that it was far from a mechanistic processing of objective knowledge. Instead, they discovered that organizational innovation often stemmed from highly subjective insights that can best be described in the form of metaphors, slogans, or symbols. The Nonaka and Takeuchi model of KM has its roots in a holistic model of knowledge creation and the management of "serendipity." The tacit/explicit spectrum of knowledge forms (the epistemological dimension) and the individual/group/organizational or three-tier model of knowledge sharing and diffusion (the ontological dimension) are both needed in order to create knowledge and produce innovation.

Nonaka and Takeuchi argue that a key factor behind the Japanese enterprises' successful track record in innovation stems from the more tacit-driven approach to knowledge management. They maintain that Western culture considers knower and known as separate entities (harkening back to the cognitivist approach, which places greater importance on communicating and storing explicit knowledge). In contrast, the Japanese, through the structural characteristics of their language and through influences such as Zen Buddhism, believe in the oneness of humanity and nature, body and mind, self and other (Nonaka and Takeuchi, 1995). Accordingly, it may be easier for Japanese managers to engage in the process of "indwelling," a term used by Polanyi (1966) to define the individual's involvement with objects through self-involvement and commitment, in order to create knowledge. In such a cultural environment, knowledge is principally "group knowledge," easily converted and mobilized (from tacit to explicit, along the epistemological dimension) and easily transferred and shared (along the individual to the group to the organization, in the ontological dimension).

Nonaka and Takeuchi underline the necessity of integrating the two approaches, from the cultural, epistemological, and organizational points of view, in order to acquire new cultural and operational tools for better knowledge-creating organizations. Their construct of the *hypertext organization* formalizes the need for integrating the traditionally opposed concepts of Western and Japanese schools of thought.

The Knowledge Creation Process

Knowledge creation always begins with the individual. A brilliant researcher, for example, has an insight that ultimately leads to a patent. Or a middle manager has an intuition about market trends that becomes the catalyst for an important new product concept. Similarly, a shop floor worker draws upon years of experience to come up with a process innovation that saves the company millions of dollars. In each of these scenarios, an individual's personal, private knowledge (predominately tacit in nature) is translated into valuable, public organizational knowledge. Making personal knowledge available to others in the company is at the core of this KM model. This type of knowledge creation process takes place continuously and occurs at all levels of the organization. In many cases, the creation of knowledge happens in an unexpected or unplanned way.

According to Nonaka and Takeuchi, there are four modes of knowledge conversion that

> constitute the "engine" of the entire knowledge-creation process. These modes are what the individual experiences. They are also the mechanisms by which individual knowledge gets articulated and "amplified" into and throughout the organization (p. 57). Organizational knowledge creation, therefore, should be understood as a process that organizationally amplifies the knowledge created by individuals and crystallizes it as a part of the knowledge network of the organization. (p. 59)

> Knowledge creation consists of a social process between individuals in which knowledge transformation is not simply a unidirectional process but it is interactive and spiral. (pp. 62–63)

Knowledge Conversion

There are four modes of knowledge conversion, as illustrated in Figure 3-1:

1. From tacit knowledge to tacit knowledge: the process of *socialization*.
2. From tacit knowledge to explicit knowledge: the process of *externalization*.
3. From explicit knowledge to explicit knowledge: the process of *combination*.
4. From explicit knowledge to tacit knowledge: the process of *internalization*.

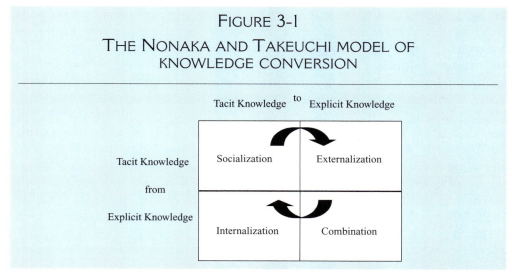

FIGURE 3-1

THE NONAKA AND TAKEUCHI MODEL OF
KNOWLEDGE CONVERSION

Source: Nonaka and Takeuchi, 1995, p. 62.

Socialization (tacit-to-tacit) consists of sharing knowledge in face-to-face, natural, and typically social interactions. It involves arriving at a mutual understanding through the sharing of mental models, brainstorming to come up with new ideas, apprenticeship or mentoring interactions, and so on. Socialization is among the easiest forms of exchanging knowledge because it is what we do instinctively when we gather at the coffee machine or engage in impromptu corridor meetings. The greatest advantage of socialization is also its greatest drawback: because knowledge remains tacit, it is rarely captured, noted, or written down anywhere. It remains in the minds of the original participants. Although socialization is a very effective means of knowledge creation and sharing, it is one of the more limited means. It is also very difficult and time-consuming to disseminate all knowledge using only this mode.

Davenport and Prusak (1998) point out that:

> Tacit, complex knowledge, developed and internalized by the knower over a long period of time, is almost impossible to reproduce in a document or a database. Such knowledge incorporates so much accrued and embedded learning that its rules may be impossible to separate from how an individual acts. (p. 70)

This means that the process of acquiring tacit knowledge is not strictly tied to the use of language but rather to experience and to the ability to transmit and to share it. This idea must not be confused with that of a simple transfer of information because knowledge creation does not take place if we abstract the transfer of information and of experiences from associated emotions and specific contexts in which they are embedded. Socialization consists of sharing experiences through observation, imitation, and practice.

For example, Honda organizes "brainstorming camps" during which detailed discussions take place to solve difficult problems in development projects. These informal meetings are usually held outside the workplace, off-site, where everybody is encouraged to contribute to the discussion and nobody is allowed to refer to the status and qualification of employees involved. The only behavior not admitted during these discussions is simple criticism that is not followed by constructive suggestions. Honda uses brainstorming meetings not only to develop new products but also to improve its managerial systems and its commercial strategies. Brainstorming represents not only occasions for creative dialogue but also a moment when people share experience and, then, tacit knowledge. In this way, they create harmony among themselves, they feel they are a part of the organization, and they feel linked to one another by sharing the same goals. Many other organizations hold similar "Knowledge Days" or "Knowledge Cafés" to encourage this type of tacit-to-tacit knowledge sharing.

The process of *externalization* (tacit-to-explicit) gives a visible form to tacit knowledge and converts it to explicit knowledge. It can be defined as "a quintessential knowledge creation process in that tacit knowledge becomes explicit, taking the shapes of metaphors, analogies, concepts, hypotheses, or models" (Nonaka and Takeuchi, 1995, p. 4). In this mode, individuals are able to articulate the knowledge and know-how and, in some cases, the know-why and the care-why. Previously tacit knowledge can be written down, taped, drawn, or made tangible or concrete in some manner. An intermediary is often needed at this stage; it is always more difficult when we transform one type of knowledge into another. A knowledge journalist is someone who can interview knowledgeable individuals in order to extract, model, and synthesize in a different way (format, length, level of detail, etc.) and thereby increase its scope (a wider audience can understand and apply this content now).

Once externalized, knowledge is tangible and permanent. It can be shared more easily with others and leveraged throughout the organization. Good principles of content management will need to be brought into play in order to make future decisions about archiving, updating, and retiring externalized knowledge content. It is particularly important not to lose attribution and authorship information when tacit knowledge is made explicit. This involves codifying metadata or information about the content along with the actual content.

For example, Canon decided to design and produce a mini-copier that can be used occasionally for personal use. This new product was very different from expensive industrial copiers, which also engendered high maintenance costs. Canon had to design something that was relatively inexpensive with reasonable maintenance costs. The Canon mini-copier project members, aware that the drum was the most frequent problem, designed a type of drum that would last through a fair amount of usage. They then had to be creative and design a drum that did not cost more than the mini-copier! How did they come up with this innovation? After long discussions, one day the leader of the unit that had to solve this problem brought along some cans of beer, and as the team was brainstorming, someone noted that beer cans had low costs and used the same type of aluminum as copier drums did. The rest, as they say, is history.

The next stage of knowledge conversion in the Nonaka and Takeuchi model is *combination* (explicit-to-explicit), the process of recombining discrete pieces of explicit knowledge into a new form. Some examples would be a synthesis in the form of a review report, a trend analysis, a brief executive summary, or a new database to organize content. No new knowledge is created per se; it is a new combination or representation of existing or already explicit knowledge. In other words, combination occurs when concepts are sorted and systematized in a knowledge system. Some examples would be populating a database when we teach, when we categorize and combine concepts, or when we convert explicit knowledge into a new medium such as a computer-based tutorial. For example, in developing a training course or curriculum for a university course, existing, explicit knowledge would be recombined into a form that better lends itself to teaching and to transferring this content.

Another example is that of Kraft General Foods when it planned and developed a new point-of-sale (POS) system, one that would track not only items sold but also information about the buyers. Its intent was to use this information to plan new models to sell, new combinations of products, of products and services, of services, and so on. The POS system collects and analyzes information and then helps marketing people to plan information-intensive marketing programs called micro-merchandising.

The last conversion process, *internalization* (explicit-to-tacit), occurs through diffusing and embedding newly acquired behavior and newly understood or revised mental models. Internalization is strongly linked to "learning by doing."

Internalization converts or integrates shared and/or individual experiences and knowledge into individual mental models. Once internalized, new knowledge is then used by employees who broaden it, extend it, and reframe it within their own existing tacit knowledge bases. They understand, learn, and buy into the new knowledge, and this is manifested as an observable change; that is, they now do their jobs and tasks differently.

For example, General Electric has developed a system of documenting all customer complaints and inquiries in a database that can be accessed by all its employees. This system allows the employees to find answers to new customers' questions much more quickly because it facilitates the sharing of employees' experiences in problem solving. This system also helps the workers to internalize others' experiences in answering questions and solving problems.

Knowledge, experiences, best practices, lessons learned, and so on go through the conversion processes of socialization, externalization, and combination, but they cannot halt at any one of these stages. Only when knowledge is internalized into individuals' tacit knowledge bases in the form of shared mental models or technical know-how does this knowledge become a valuable asset to the individual, to their community of practice, and to the organization. In order for organizational knowledge creation to take place, however, the entire conversion process has to begin all over again: the tacit knowledge accumulated at the individual level needs to be socialized with other organizational members, thereby starting a new spiral of knowledge creation (Nonaka and Takeuchi, 1995, p. 69). When experiences and information are transferred through observation, imitation, and practice, then we are back in the socialization quadrant. This knowledge is then formalized and converted into explicit knowledge, through use of analogy, metaphor, and model, in the externalization quadrant. This explicit knowledge is then systematized and recombined in the combination quadrant, whereupon it once again becomes part of individuals' experiences. In the internalization quadrant, knowledge has once again become tacit knowledge.

Knowledge Spiral

Knowledge creation is not a sequential process. Rather, it depends on a continuous and dynamic interaction between tacit and explicit knowledge throughout the four quadrants. The knowledge spiral (see Figure 3-2) shows how organizatins articulate, organize and systematize individual tacit knowledge. Organizations produce and develop tools, structures, and models to accumulate and share knowledge. The knowledge spiral is a continuous activity of knowledge flow, sharing, and conversion by individuals, communities, and the organization itself.

The two steps in the knowledge spiral that are the most difficult are those involving a change in the type of knowledge, namely, *externalization*, which converts tacit into explicit knowledge, and *internalization*, which converts

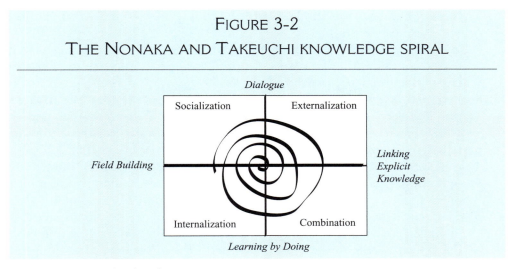

FIGURE 3-2

THE NONAKA AND TAKEUCHI KNOWLEDGE SPIRAL

Source: Nonaka and Takeuchi, 1995, p. 71.

explicit into tacit knowledge. These two steps require a high degree of personal commitment, and they will typically involve mental models, personal beliefs and values, and a process of reinventing yourself, your group, and the organization as a whole. A metaphor is a good way of expressing this "inexpressible" content. For example, a slogan, a story, an analogy, or a symbol of some type can encapsulate complex contextual meanings. A metaphor is often used to convey two ideas in a single phrase and may be defined as "accomplishes in a word or phrase what could otherwise be expressed only in many words, if at all" (Sommer and Weiss, 1995, p. vii). All of these vehicles are good models for representing a consistent, systematic, and logical understanding of content without any contradictions. The better and the more coherent the model, and the better the model fits with existing mental models, the higher the likelihood of successful implementation of a knowledge spiral.

It is possible to structure metaphors, models, and analogies in an organizational KM design. The first principle is to have built-in redundancy to make sure information overlaps. Redundancy will make it easier to articulate content, to share content, and to make use of it. An example is to set up several competing groups, to build in a rotational strategy so that workers do a variety of jobs, and to provide easy access to company information via a single integrated knowledge base.

Knowledge sharing and use occurs through the "knowledge spiral," which, "starting at the individual level and moving up through expanding communities of interaction, . . . crosses sectional, departmental, divisional and organizational boundaries" (Nonaka and Takeuchi, 1995, p. 72). Nonaka and Takeuchi argue that an organization has to promote a facilitating context in which the organizational knowledge-creation process and the individual one can easily take place, acting as a spiral. They describe the following "Enabling Conditions for Organizational Knowledge Creation":

1. *Intention*: an organization's aspiration to its goals (strategy formulation in a business setting).
2. *Autonomy*: condition whereby individuals act autonomously, according to the "minimum critical specification" principle, and are involved in cross-functional self-organized teams.
3. *Fluctuation and Creative Chaos*: condition that stimulates the interaction between the organization and the external environment and/or creates fluctuations and breakdowns by means of creative chaos or strategic equivocality.
4. *Redundancy*: existence of information that goes beyond the immediate operational requirements of organizational members; competing multiple teams on the same issue; and strategic rotation of personnel.
5. *Requisite Variety*: internal diversity to match the variety and complexity of the environment, and to provide everyone in the organization with the fastest access to the broadest variety of necessary information; flat and flexible organizational structure interlinked with effective information networks.

The Nonaka and Takeuchi model has proven to be one of the more robust ones in the field of KM, and it continues to be applied in a variety of settings. One of its greatest strengths is its simplicity—both in terms of understanding the basic tenets of the model and in terms of being able to quickly internalize and apply the KM model. One of its major shortcomings is that, though valid, it does not appear to be sufficient to explain all of the stages involved in managing knowledge. The Nonaka and Takeuchi model focuses on the knowledge transformations between tacit and explicit knowledge, but the model does not address larger issues of how decision making takes place by leveraging both forms of knowledge.

The Choo Sense-making KM Model

Choo (1998) has described a model of knowledge management that stresses sense making (largely based on Weick, 2001), knowledge creation (based on Nonaka and Takeuchi, 1995) and decision making (based on, among other concepts, bounded rationality; see Simon, 1957). The Choo KM model focuses on how information elements are selected and subsequently fed into organizational actions. Organizational action results from the concentration and absorption of information from the external environment into each successive cycle, as illustrated in Figure 3-3. Each phase, sense making, knowledge creation, and decision making, has an outside stimulus or trigger.

In the sense-making stage, one attempts to make sense of the information streaming in from the external environment. Priorities are identified and used to filter the information. Individuals construct common interpretations from the exchange and negotiate information fragments combined with their previous experiences. Weick (2001) proposed a theory of sense making to describe how chaos is transformed into sensible and orderly processes in an organization through the shared interpretation of individuals. *Loosely coupled system* is a term used to describe systems that can be taken apart or revised without

FIGURE 3-3
OVERVIEW OF CHOO'S (1998) KNOWLEDGE
MANAGEMENT MODEL

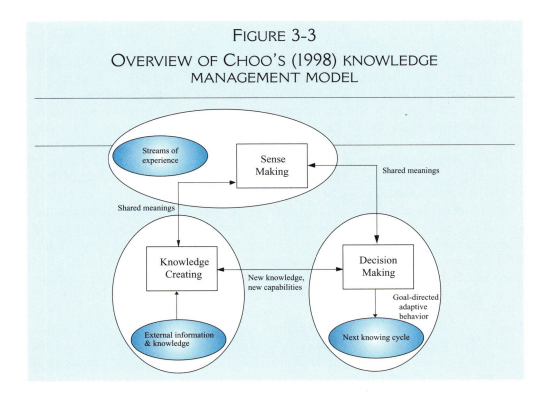

damaging the entire system. A human being is "tightly coupled," whereas the human genome is "loosely coupled." Loose coupling permits adaptation, evolution, and extension. Sense making can be thought of as a loosely coupled system whereby individuals construct their own representation of reality by comparing current with past events.

Weick (2001) proposes that sense making in organizations consists of four integrated processes: (1) ecological change, (2) enactment, (3) selection, and (4) retention.

Ecological change is a change in the environment that is external to the organization—one that disturbs the flow of information to participants—and triggers an ecological change in the organization. Organizational actors enact their environment by attempting to closely examine elements of the environment.

In the *enactment* phase, people try to construct, rearrange, single out, or demolish specific elements of content. Many of the objective features of their environment are made less random and more orderly through the creation of their own constraints or rules. Enactment clarifies the content and issues to be used for the subsequent selection process.

Selection and *retention* are the phases in which individuals attempt to interpret the rationale for the observed and enacted changes by making selections. The retention process in turn furnishes the organization with an organizational memory of successful sense-making experiences. This memory can be reused in the future to interpret new changes and to stabilize individual interpretations into a coherent organizational view of events and actions. These phases also serve to reduce any uncertainty and ambiguity associated with unclear, poorly defined information.

Knowledge creating may be viewed as the transformation of personal knowledge between individuals through dialogue, discourse, sharing, and storytelling. This phase is directed by a knowledge vision of "as is" (current situation) and "to be" (future, desired state). Knowledge creation widens the spectrum of potential choices in decision making by providing new knowledge and new competencies. The result feeds the decision-making process with innovative strategies that extend the organization's capability to make informed, rational decisions. Choo (1998) draws upon the Nonaka and Takeuchi (1995) model for a theoretical basis of knowledge creation.

Decision making is situated in rational decision-making models that are used to identify and evaluate alternatives by processing the information and knowledge collected to date. There are a wide range of decision-making theories such as the theory of games and economic behavior (e.g., Dixit and Nalebuff, 1991; Bierman and Fernandez, 1993), chaos theory, emergent theory, and complexity theory (e.g., Gleick, 1987; Fisher, 1984; Simon, 1969; Stewart, 1989; Stacey, 1992). There is even a garbage can theory of decision making (e.g., Daft, 1982; Daft and Weick, 1984; Padgett, 1980).

The Garbage Can model (GCM) of organizational decision making was developed in reference to "ambiguous behaviors," that is, explanations or interpretations of behaviors that at least appear to contradict classical theory. The GCM was greatly influenced by the realization that extreme cases of aggregate uncertainty in decision environments would trigger behavioral responses, which, at least from a distance, appear to be "irrational" or at least not in compliance with the total/global rationality of "economic man" (e.g., "act first, think later"). The GCM was originally formulated in the context of the operation of universities and their many interdepartmental communications problems.

The Garbage Can model attempted to expand organizational decision theory into the then uncharted field of organizational anarchy, which is characterized by "problematic preferences," "unclear technology," and "fluid participation." "The theoretical breakthrough of the garbage can model is that it disconnects problems, solutions, and decision makers from each other, unlike traditional decision theory. Specific decisions do not follow an orderly process from problem to solution, but are outcomes of several relatively independent streams of events within the organization" (Daft, 1982, p. 139).

Simon (1957) identified the principle of bounded rationality as a constraint for organizational decision making: "The capacity of the human mind for formulating and for solving complex problems is very small compared with the size of the problems whose solution is required for objectively rational behavior in the real world—or even for a reasonable approximation to such objective rationality" (p. 198).

Simon suggested that persons faced with ambiguous goals and unclear means of linking actions to those goals seek to fulfill short-term subgoals. Subgoals are objectives that the individual believes can be achieved by allocating resources under his or her control. These subgoals are generally not derived from broad policy goals, but rather from experiences, education, the community, and personal needs. Simon (1976) first proposed bounded rationality theory as a limited or constrained rationality to explain human decision-making behavior. When confronted with a highly complex world, the mind constructs a simple mental model of reality and tries to work within that model. The model may have weaknesses, but the individual will try to behave rationally within the constraints or boundaries of that model.

Individuals can be bound in a decisional process by a number of factors such as:

- Limits in knowledge, skills, habits, and responsiveness.
- Availability of personal information and knowledge.
- Values and norms held by the individual, which may differ from those of the organization.

This theory has long been accepted in organizational and management sciences. Bounded rationality is characterized by individual use of limited information analysis, evaluation and processing, shortcuts and rules of thumb (sometimes called *heuristics*), and "satisficing" behavior, which means it may not be fully optimized but it is good enough. The 80/20 rule (e.g., Clemson, 1984) is a good example of the application of satisficing behavior—for example, in a brainstorming session, when you feel that you may not have fully exhausted all the possibilities but have managed to capture roughly 80% of them. Continuing would result in the law of diminishing returns, so much more effort would be required to incorporate the remaining 20% that generally participants would agree that what they have so far is "good enough" for them to proceed.

One strength of the Choo KM model is the holistic treatment of key KM cycle processes extending to organizational decision making, which is often lacking in other theoretical KM approaches. This makes the Choo model one of the more "realistic" or feasible models of KM, for the model represents organizational actions with "high fidelity." The Choo KM model is particularly well suited to simulations and hypothesis- or scenario-testing applications.

The Wiig Model for Building and Using Knowledge

Wiig (1993) approached his KM model with the following principle: in order for knowledge to be useful and valuable, it must be organized. Knowledge should be organized differently depending on what use will be made of the knowledge. For example, in our own mental models, we tend to store our knowledge and know-how in the form of semantic networks. We can then choose the appropriate perspective based on the cognitive task at hand.

Knowledge organized within a semantic network can be accessed and retrieved using multiple-entry paths that map onto different knowledge tasks to be completed. Some useful dimensions to consider in Wiig's KM model include: (1) completeness, (2) connectedness, (3) congruency, and (4) perspective and purpose.

Completeness addresses the question of how much relevant knowledge is available from a given source. Sources may be human minds or knowledge bases (i.e., tacit or explicit knowledge). We first need to know that the knowledge is out there. The knowledge may be complete in the sense that all that is available about the subject is there, but if no one knows of its existence and/or availability, they cannot make use of this knowledge.

Connectedness refers to the well-understood and defined relations between the different knowledge objects. Very few knowledge objects are totally disconnected from the others. The more connected a knowledge base is (i.e., the greater the number of interconnections in the semantic network), then the more coherent the content and the greater its value.

A knowledge base is said to possess *congruence* when all the facts, concepts, perspectives, values, judgments, and associative and relational links between the knowledge objects are consistent. There should be no logical inconsistencies, no internal conflicts, and no misunderstandings. Most knowledge content will not meet such ideals where congruency is concerned. However, concept definitions should be consistent, and the knowledge base as a whole needs to be constantly "fine-tuned" to maintain congruency.

Perspective and purpose refer to the phenomenon through which we "know something" but often from a particular point of view or for a specific purpose. We organize much of our knowledge using the dual dimensions of perspective and purpose (e.g., just-in-time knowledge retrieval or just enough—"on-demand" knowledge).

Semantic networks are useful ways of representing different perspectives on the same knowledge content. Figures 3-4 through 3-8 present examples of different perspectives on the same knowledge object ("car") using semantic networks.

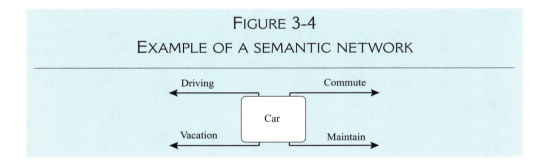

FIGURE 3-4

EXAMPLE OF A SEMANTIC NETWORK

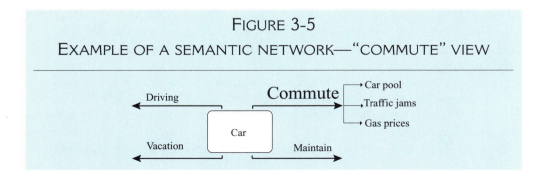

FIGURE 3-5

EXAMPLE OF A SEMANTIC NETWORK—"COMMUTE" VIEW

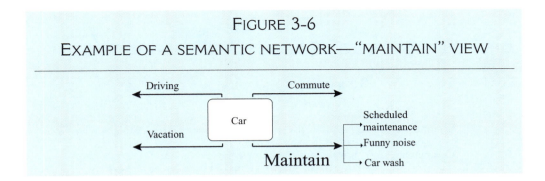

FIGURE 3-6

EXAMPLE OF A SEMANTIC NETWORK—"MAINTAIN" VIEW

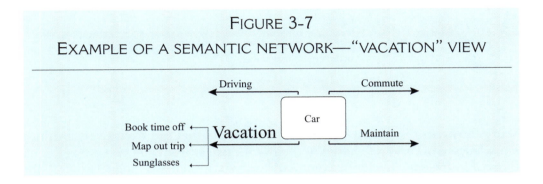

FIGURE 3-7

EXAMPLE OF A SEMANTIC NETWORK—"VACATION" VIEW

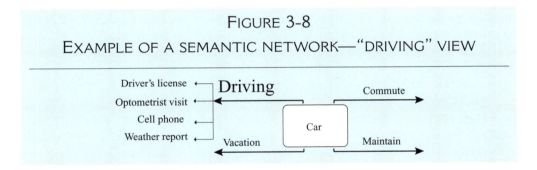

FIGURE 3-8

EXAMPLE OF A SEMANTIC NETWORK—"DRIVING" VIEW

Wiig's KM model goes on to define different levels of internalization of knowledge. Wiig's approach can be seen as a further refinement of Nonaka and Takeuchi's fourth quadrant, internalization. Table 3-1 briefly defines each of these levels. In general, there is a continuum of internalization, starting with the lowest level, the novice, who "does not know he does not know"—who does not have even an awareness that the knowledge exists—and extending to the mastery level where there is a deep understanding not just of the know-what, but the know-how, the know-why, and the care-why (i.e., values, judgments, and motivations for using the knowledge).

Wiig (1993) also defines three forms of knowledge: public knowledge, shared expertise, and personal knowledge. *Public knowledge* is explicit, taught, and routinely shared knowledge that is generally available in the public domain. An example would be a published book or information on a public website.

TABLE 3-1
WIIG KM MODEL—DEGREES OF INTERNALIZATION

Level	Type	Description
1	Novice	Barely aware or not aware of the knowledge and how it can be used.
2	Beginner	Knows that the knowledge exists and where to get it but cannot reason with it.
3	Competent	Knows about the knowledge, can use and reason with the knowledge given external knowledge bases such as documents and people to help.
4	Expert	Knows the knowledge, holds the knowledge in memory, understands where it applies, reasons with it without any outside help.
5	Master	Internalizes the knowledge fully, has a deep understanding with full integration into values, judgments, and consequences of using that knowledge.

Shared expertise is proprietary knowledge assets that are exclusively held by knowledge workers and shared in their work or embedded in technology. This form of knowledge is usually communicated via specialized languages and representations. Although he does not use the term, this knowledge form would be common in communities of practice and among informal networks of like-minded professionals who typically interact and share knowledge in order to improve the practice of their profession. Finally, *personal knowledge* is the least accessible but most complete form of knowledge. It is typically more tacit than explicit and is used nonconsciously in work, play, and daily life.

In addition to the three major *forms* of knowledge (personal, public, and shared), Wiig (1993) defines four *types* of knowledge: factual, conceptual, expectational, and methodological. *Factual knowledge* deals with data and causal chains, measurements, and readings—typically, directly observable and verifiable content. *Conceptual knowledge* involves systems, concepts, and perspectives (e.g., concept of a track record, a bullish market). *Expectational knowledge* concerns judgments, hypotheses, and expectations held by knowers. Examples are intuition, hunches, preferences, and heuristics that we make use of in our decision making. Finally, *methodological knowledge* deals with reasoning, strategies, decision-making methods, and other techniques. Examples would be learning from past mistakes or forecasting based on analyses of trends.

Together, the three forms of knowledge and the four types of knowledge combine to yield a KM matrix that forms the basis of the Wiig KM model. Table 3-2 outlines the Wiig KM model.

To summarize, Wiig (1993) proposes a hierarchy of knowledge that consists of public, shared, and personal knowledge forms. His hierarchy of knowledge forms is shown in Figure 3-9.

The major strength of the Wiig model is that, despite having been formulated in 1993, the organized approach to categorizing the type of knowledge

TABLE 3-2
THE WIIG KM MATRIX

Form of Knowledge	Type of Knowledge			
	Factual	Conceptual	Expectational	Methodological
Public	Measurement, reading	Stability, balance	When supply exceeds demand, price drops	Look for temperatures outside the norm
Shared	Forecast analysis	"Market is hot"	A little water in the mix is okay	Check for past failures
Personal	The "right" color, texture	Company has a good track record	Hunch that the analyst has it wrong	What is the recent trend?

FIGURE 3-9
WIIG HIERARCHY OF KNOWLEDGE FORMS

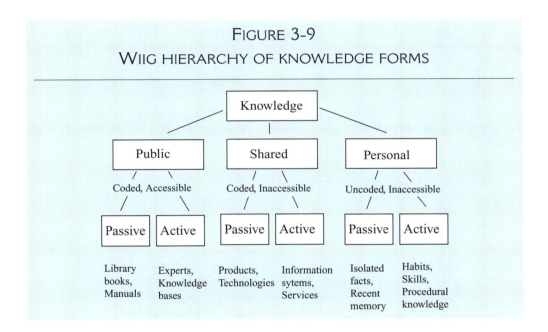

to be managed remains a powerful theoretical model of KM. The Wiig KM model is perhaps the most pragmatic of the models in existence today and can easily be integrated into any of the other approaches. This model enables practitioners to adopt a more detailed or refined approach to managing knowledge based on the type of knowledge but goes beyond the simple tacit/explicit dichotomy. Its major shortcoming is the paucity of research and/or practical experience involving the implementation of this model.

The Boisot I-Space KM Model

The Boisot KM model is based on the key concept of an "information good" that differs from a physical asset. Boisot distinguishes information from data by emphasizing that information is what an observer will extract from data as a function of his or her expectations or *prior knowledge*. The effective movement of information goods is largely dependent on senders and receivers sharing the same coding scheme or language. A knowledge good is one that also possesses a context within which it can be interpreted. Effective knowledge sharing requires that senders and receivers share the context as well as the coding scheme.

Boisot (1998) proposes the following two key points:

1. The more easily data can be structured and converted into information, the more diffusible it becomes.
2. The less data that has been so structured requires a shared context for its diffusion, the more diffusible it becomes.

Together, they underpin a simple conceptual framework, the Information Space or I-Space KM model. Data is structured and understood through the processes of codification and abstraction. Codification refers to the creation of content categories—the fewer the number of categories, the more abstract the codification scheme. It is assumed that the well-codified abstract content is much easier to understand and apply than the highly contextual content. Boisot's KM model addresses the tacit form of knowledge by noting that in many situations, the loss of context due to codification may result in the loss of valuable content. This content needs a shared context for its interpretation and implies face-to-face interaction and spatial proximity—which is analogous to socialization in the Nonaka and Takeuchi model (1995).

The I-Space model can be visualized as a three-dimensional cube with the following dimensions (see Figure 3-10): (1) codified—uncodified; (2) abstract—concrete; and (3) diffused—undiffused.

The activities of codification, abstraction, diffusion, absorption, impacting, and scanning all contribute to learning. Where they take place in sequence—and to some extent they must—together they make up the six phases of a social learning cycle (SLC). These activities are described in Table 3-3.

The Boisot model incorporates a theoretical foundation of social learning and serves to link together content, information, and knowledge management in a very effective way. In an approximate sense, the codification dimension is linked to categorization and classification; the abstraction dimension is linked to knowledge creation through analysis and understanding; and the third diffusion dimension is linked to information access and transfer. There is a strong potential to make use of the Boisot I-Space KM model as to map and manage an organization's knowledge assets as the social learning cycle—something that the other KM models do not directly address. However, the Boisot model appears to be somewhat less well known and less accessible, and as a result has not had widespread implementation. More extensive field-testing of this

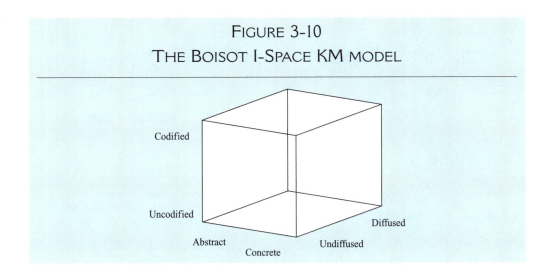

FIGURE 3-10
THE BOISOT I-SPACE KM MODEL

Codified

Uncodified

Abstract   Diffused

Concrete   Undiffused

model would provide feedback regarding its applicability as well as more guidelines on the best way to implement the I-Space approach.

Complex Adaptive System Models of KM

The Intelligent Complex Adaptive Systems (ICAS) KM theory views the organization as an intelligent complex adaptive system—the ICAS model of KM (e.g., Beer, 1981; Bennet and Bennet, 2004). Beer (1981) was a pioneer in the treatment of the organization as a living entity. In his Viable System model (VSM), a set of functions is distinguished, which ensures the viability of any living system and organizations in particular. The VSM is based on the principles of cybernetics or systems science, which make use of communication and control mechanisms to understand, describe, and predict what an autonomous or viable organization will do.

Complex adaptive systems consist of many independent agents that interact with one another locally. Together, their combined behavior gives rise to complex adaptive phenomena. Complex adaptive systems are said to "self-organize" through this form of emergent phenomena. There is no overall authority that is directing how each one of these independent agents should be acting. An overall pattern of complex behavior emerges as a result of all their interactions.

The Viable System model has been applied to a wide range of complex situations, including the modeling of an entire nation (implemented by President Salvador Allende in Chile in 1972). The model enables managers and their consultants to elaborate policies and to develop organizational structures in the clear understanding of the recursions in which they are supposed to operate, and to design regulatory systems within those recursions that obey certain fundamental laws of cybernetics (e.g., Ashby's Law of Requisite Variety). As such, the usefulness of the VSM as a theoretical grounding for KM becomes quite clear.

TABLE 3-3

THE SOCIAL LEARNING CYCLE IN BOISOT'S I-SPACE KM MODEL

Phase	Name	Description
1	Scanning	▪ Identifying threats and opportunities in generally available but often fuzzy content. ▪ Scanning patterns such as unique or idiosyncratic insights that then become the possession of individuals or small groups. ▪ Scanning may be very rapid when the data is well codified and abstract and very slow and random when the data is uncodified and context-specific.
2	Problem solving	▪ The process of giving structure and coherence to such insights—that is, codifying them. ▪ In this phase they are given a definite shape, and much of the uncertainty initially associated with them is eliminated. ▪ Problem solving initiated in the uncodified region of the I-space is often both risky and conflict-laden.
3	Abstraction	▪ Generalizing the application of newly codified insights to a wider range of situations. ▪ Involves reducing them to their most essential features—that is, conceptualizing them. ▪ Problem solving and abstraction often work in tandem.
4	Diffusion	▪ Sharing the newly created insights with a target population. ▪ The diffusion of well-codified and abstract content to a large population will be technically less problematic than that of content that is uncodified and context-specific. ▪ Only a sharing of context by sender and receiver can speed up the diffusion of uncodified data. ▪ The probability of a shared context is inversely proportional to population size.
5	Absorption	▪ Applying the new codified insights to different situations in a "learning by doing" or a "learning by using" fashion. ▪ Over time, such codified insights come to acquire a penumbra of uncodified knowledge that helps to guide their application in particular circumstances.
6	Impacting	▪ The embedding of abstract knowledge in concrete practices. ▪ The embedding can take place in artifacts, technical or organizational rules, or behavioral practices. ▪ Absorption and impact often work in tandem.

Source: Adapted from Boisot, 1998.

A number of researchers have made use of complex adaptive system theories in deriving a theoretical basis for KM. David Snowden (2000), the director of Cynefin, a research group at IBM, describes his approach as follows: "Complex adaptive systems theory is used to create a sense-making model that utilizes self-organizing capabilities of the informal communities and identifies a natural flow model of knowledge creation, disruption and utilization" (p. 1).

Cynefin is a Welsh word with no direct equivalent in English but as a noun can be translated as *habitat* or, as an adjective, as *acquainted* or *familiar*. The Cynefin research center focuses on action research in organizational complexity and is open to individuals and to organizations. One of Snowden's (2000) major points is that the focus on tacit–explicit knowledge conversion (e.g., the Nonaka and Takeuchi model, 1995) that has dominated knowledge management practice since 1995 provides a limited, but useful, set of models and tools. The Cynefin model instead proposes the following key types of knowledge: known, knowable, complex, and chaotic. Snowden's Cynefin model is less concerned about tacit–explicit conversions because of its focus on descriptive self-awareness than on prescriptive organization models.

Bennet and Bennet (2004) also describe a complex adaptive system approach to KM, but the conceptual roots are somewhat different from the Beer VSM. Bennet and Bennet believe strongly that the traditional bureaucracies or popular matrix and flat organizations are not sufficient to provide the cohesiveness, complexity, and selective pressures that ensure the survival of an organization. A different model is proposed, one in which the organization is viewed as a system that is in symbiotic relationship with its environment, that is, "turning the living system metaphor into reality" (p. 25). The Intelligent Complex Adaptive System (ICAS) model is composed of living subsystems that combine, interact, and coevolve to provide the capabilities of an advanced, intelligent technological and sociological adaptive enterprise. Complex adaptive systems are organizations that are composed of a large number of self-organizing components, each of which seeks to maximize its own specific goals but which also operates according to the rules and context of relationships with the other components and the external world.

In an ICAS, the intelligent components consist of people who are empowered to self-organize but who remain part of the overall corporate hierarchy. The challenge is to take advantage of the strengths of people while getting them to cooperate and collaborate to leverage knowledge and to maintain a sense of unity of purpose. Organizations take from the environment, transform those inputs into higher-value outputs, and provide them to customers and stakeholders. Organizational intelligence becomes a form of competitive intelligence that helps facilitate innovation, learning, adaptation, and quick responses to new unanticipated situations. Organizations solve problems by creating options, and they use internal and external resources to add value above and beyond the value of the initial inputs. They must also do this in an effective and efficient manner. Knowledge becomes the most valuable of these resources because it is critical in taking effective action in a variety of uncertain situations. This is often used to distinguish information management (predictable reactions to known and anticipated situations) and knowledge management (use of existing or new reactions to unanticipated situations). Knowledge will typically consist of experience, judgment, insight, context, and the "right" information. Understanding and meaning become prerequisites to taking effective action, and they create value by ensuring the survival and growth of the organization.

The key processes in the ICAS KM model can be summarized as:

1. Understanding.
2. Creating new ideas.
3. Solving problems.
4. Making decisions.
5. Taking actions to achieve desired results.

Since only people can make decisions and take actions, this model emphasizes the individual knowledge worker and his or her competency, capacity, learning, and so on. These knowledge assets are leveraged through multiple networks (communities of practice, for example) to make available the knowledge, experience, and insights of others. This type of tacit knowledge is leveraged through dynamic networks and makes a broader "highway" available to connect data, information, and people through virtual communities and knowledge repositories.

To survive and successfully compete, an organization also requires eight emergent characteristics, according to this model: (1) organizational intelligence, (2) shared purpose, (3) selectivity, (4) optimum complexity, (5) permeable boundaries, (6) knowledge centricity, (7) flow, and (8) multidimensionality.

An emergent characteristic is the result of nonlinear interactions, synergistic interactions, and self-organizing systems. The ICAS KM model follows along the lines of the other approaches in that it is connectionist and holistic in nature. The emergent ICAS characteristics are outlined in Figure 3-11. These emergent properties serve to endow the organization with the internal capability to deal with the future unanticipated environments yet to be encountered.

Organizational intelligence refers to the capacity of the firm to innovate, acquire knowledge, and apply that knowledge to relevant situations. In the ICAS model, this property refers to the organization's ability to perceive, interpret, and respond to its environment in such a way as to meet its goals and satisfy its stakeholders. This is very similar to the approach taken in the Choo sense-making model. Unity and a shared purpose represent the organization's ability to integrate and mobilize its resources through a continuous, two-way communication with its large number of relatively independent subsystems, much like the VSM. Optimum complexity represents the right balance between internal complexity (i.e., number of different relevant organizational states) to deal with the external environment without losing sight of the overall goal and the notion of a firm that despite its size does not lose its common identity. The major difference here with VSM is the notion of relevant states—not all possible states. This selectivity is in keeping with the notion of evaluating content in KM as opposed to a more exhaustive warehousing approach.

FIGURE 3-11
OVERVIEW OF THE ICAS MODEL

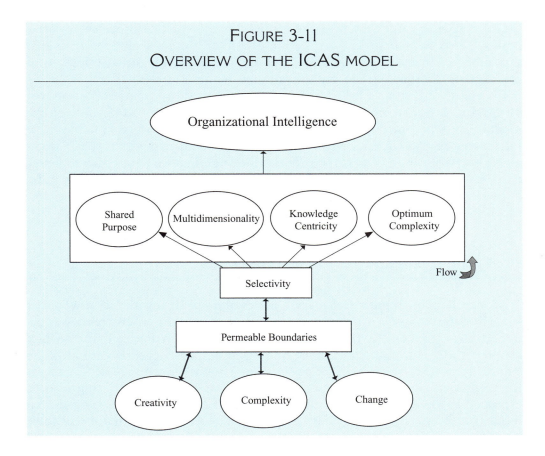

The process of selectivity consists of filtering incoming information from the outside world. Good filtering requires broad knowledge of the organization, specific knowledge of the customer, and a strong understanding of the firm's strategic goals. Knowledge centricity refers to the aggregation of relevant information from self-organization, collaboration, and strategic alignment. Flow enables knowledge centricity and facilitates the connections and continuity needed to maintain unity and give coherence to organizational intelligence. Permeable boundaries are essential if ideas are to be exchanged and built upon. Finally, multidimensionality represents organizational flexibility that ensures that knowledge workers have the competencies, perspectives, and cognitive ability to address issues and solve problems. This is sometimes seen as being analogous to developing human instinct.

Each of these characteristics must emerge from the nature of the organization. They cannot be designed by managerial decree; they can only be nurtured, guided, and helped along. In summary, there are four major ways in which the ICAS model describes organizational knowledge management: (1) creativity, (2) problem solving, (3) decision making, and (4) implementation.

Creativity is the generation of new ideas, perspectives, understanding, concepts, and methods to help solve problems, build products, offer services, and so on. Individuals, teams, networks, or virtual communities are useful in *problem solving*, and they take the outputs of the creative processes as their inputs. *Decision making* is the selection of one or more alternatives generated during the problem-solving process, and *implementation* is the carrying out of the selected alternative(s) in order to obtain the desired results.

Complex KM models based on adaptive system theory show both an evolution and a return to systems thinking roots in the KM world. All of the models presented in this chapter are relevant, and each offers valuable theoretical foundations in understanding knowledge management in today's organizations. What they all share is a connectionist and holistic approach to better understand the nature of knowledge as a complex adaptive system that includes knowers, the organizational environment, and the "bloodstream" of organizations—the knowledge-sharing networks.

STRATEGIC IMPLICATIONS OF KM MODELS

Models help us to put the disparate pieces of a puzzle together in a way that leads to a deeper understanding of both the pieces and the ensemble they make up. Models supplement the concept analysis approach outlined in the first chapter in order to take our understanding to a deeper level. KM models are still fairly new to the practice or business of knowledge management, and yet they represent the way ahead. A coherent model of knowledge-driven processes is crucial to the KM initiatives' ability to address strategic business goals, even if only partially. This is not to say that KM is a silver bullet or that it will solve all organizational problems. Those areas of knowledge-intensive work and intellectual capital development that are amenable to KM processes, on the other hand, require a solid foundation of understanding of what KM is, what the key KM cycle processes are, and how these fit in to a model that enables us to interpret, to establish cause and effect, and to successfully implement knowledge management solutions.

PRACTICAL IMPLICATIONS OF KM MODELS

For many years now, KM practitioners have been practicing "KM on the fly." Many valuable empirical lessons and best practices have been garnered through experience with many diverse organizations. However, KM needs to be grounded in more robust, sound theoretical foundations—something more than "it worked well last time so . . . ." The KM models' key role is to ensure a certain level of completeness or depth in the practice of KM: a means of ensuring that all critical factors have been addressed. The second practical benefit of a model-driven KM approach is that models not only enable a better description of what is happening but also help provide a better prescription for meeting organizational goals. KM models help to explain what is happening now, and they provide us with a valid blueprint or road map for getting organizations where they want to be with their knowledge management efforts.

KEY POINTS

- Knowledge management encompasses data, information, and knowledge (sometimes referred to collectively as *content*) and addresses both tacit and explicit forms of knowledge.
- The von Krogh and Roos KM model takes an organizational epistemology approach and emphasizes that knowledge resides both in the minds of individuals and in the relations they form with other individuals.
- The Nonaka and Takeuchi KM model focuses on knowledge spirals that explain the transformation of tacit knowledge into explicit knowledge and then back again as the basis for individual, group, and organizational innovation and learning.
- Choo and Weick adopt a sense-making approach to model knowledge management that focuses on how information elements are fed into organizational actions through sense making, knowledge creating, and decision making.
- The Wiig KM model is based on the principle that in order for knowledge to be useful and valuable, it must be organized through a form of semantic network that is connected, congruent, and complete, and that has perspective and purpose.
- Complex adaptive systems are particularly well suited to model KM as they view the organization much like a living entity concerned with independent existence and survival. Beer, as well as Bennet and Bennet, have applied this approach to describe the cohesiveness, complexity, and selective pressures that operate on intelligent complex adaptive systems (ICAS).

DISCUSSION POINTS

1. Compare and contrast the cognitivist and connectionist approaches to knowledge management. Why is the connectionist approach more suited to the von Krogh KM model? What are the strengths of this approach? What are its weaknesses? Use examples to make your points.
2. Describe how the major types of knowledge (e.g., tacit and explicit) are transformed in the Nonaka and Takeuchi knowledge spiral model of KM. Use a concrete example to make your point (e.g., a "bright" idea that occurs to an individual in the organization).
   a. Which transformation would prove to be the most difficult? Why?
   b. Which transformation would prove to be fairly easy? Why?
   c. What other key factors would influence how well the knowledge spiral model worked within a given organization?
3. In what ways is the Choo and Weick KM model similar to the Nonaka and Takeuchi KM model? In what ways do the two models differ?
   a. How does the integration of a bounded rationality approach to decision making strengthen this model? Give some examples.
   b. List some of the key triggers that are required in order for the sense-making KM model approach to be successful.

4. How is the Wiig KM model related to the Nonaka and Takeuchi model? In what important ways do they differ?
   a. List some examples of internalization to illustrate how each of the five levels differs.
   b. How do public, private, and shared knowledge differ? What are the implications of managing these different types of knowledge according to the Wiig KM model?
5. Outline the general strategy you would use in order to implement the Boisot I-Space KM model. Where would you expect to encounter difficulties? What would be some of the expected benefits to the organization of applying this approach?
6. What is the major advantage of a complex adaptive system approach to a KM model? What are some of the drawbacks?
   a. Provide an everyday example of requisite variety. Next, apply this to the management of knowledge in an organization. What are the key elements needed in order to successfully regulate a complex adaptive system? Why?

REFERENCES

Beer, S. (1981). *Brain of the firm*. 2nd ed. New York: John Wiley & Sons.

Bennet, A., and Bennet, D. (2004). *Organizational survival in the new world: the intelligent complex adaptive system. A new theory of the firm*. Burlington, MA: Elsevier Science.

Bierman, H., and Fernandez, L. (1993). *Game theory with economic applications*. Reading, MA: Addison-Wesley.

Boisot, M. (1998). *Knowledge assets*. Oxford: Oxford University Press.

Choo, C. (1998). *The knowing organization*. New York: Oxford University Press.

Clemson, B. (1984). *Cybernetics—a new management tool*. Turnbridge Wells, Kent, UK: Abacus Press.

Daft, R. L. (1982). Bureaucratic versus nonbureaucratic structure and the process of innovation and change. *Research in the Sociology of Organizations, 1*: 129–166.

Daft, R. L., and Weick, K. E. (1984). Toward a model of organizations as interpretation systems. *Academy of Management Review, 9*: 284–295.

Davenport, T., and Prusak, L. (1998). *Working knowledge*. Boston: Harvard Business School Press.

Dixit, A., and Nalebuff, B. (1991). *Thinking strategically*. New York: W. W. Norton.

Fisher, B. A. (1984). Decision emergence: the social process of decision-making. In R. S. Cathcart and L. A. Samovar (Eds.), *Small group communication: a reader*, 4th ed. (pp. 149–156). Dubuque, IA: Wm. C. Brown.

Gleick, J. (1987). *Chaos—making a new science*. Harmondsworth, Middlesex, UK: Penguin Books.

Nonaka, I., and Takeuchi, H. (1995). *The knowledge-creating company: how Japanese companies create the dynamics of innovation*. New York: Oxford University Press.

Padgett, J. F. (1980). Managing garbage can hierarchies. *Administrative Science Quarterly, 25*: 538–604.

Polanyi, M. (1966). *The tacit dimension*. London: Routledge and Kegan.

Simon, H. (1976). *Administrative behavior: a study of decision-making processes in administrative organization. 3rd ed.* New York: Free Press.

Simon, H. (1969). *The sciences of the artificial.* Cambridge, MA: MIT Press.

Simon, H. (1957). *Models of man: social and rational.* New York: John Wiley & Sons.

Snowden, D. (2000). Complex acts of knowing: paradox and descriptive self-awareness. *Journal of Knowledge Management*, 6(2): 1–33.

Sommer, E., and Weiss, D. (1995). *Metaphors dictionary. 1st ed.* Florence, KY: Thomson Publishing Company.

Stacey, R. D. (1992). *Managing the unknowable: strategic boundaries between order and chaos in organizations.* San Francisco, CA: Jossey-Bass.

Stewart, I. (1989). *Does God play dice? The mathematics of chaos.* Oxford, UK: Basil Blackwell.

Varela, F. (1992). Whence perceptual meaning? A cartography of current ideas. In F. Varela and J. P. Dupuy (Eds.). *Understanding Origin: Scientific Ideas on the Origin of Life, Mind, and Society* (A Stanford University Interational Symposium) Boston Studies Phil.Sci, Kluwer Assoc., Dordrecht, 1992.

Varela, F., and Dupuy, J. P. (Eds.). *Understanding Origin: Scientific Ideas on the Origin of Life, Mind, and Society* (A Stanford University Interational Symposium) Boston Studies Phil.Sci, Kluwer Assoc., Dordrecht, 1992.

Von Krogh, G., Ichijo, K., and Nonaka, I. (2000). *Enabling knowledge creation: how to unlock the mystery of tacit knowledge and release the power of innovation.* Oxford: Oxford University Press.

Von Krogh, G., and Roos, J. (1995). *Organizational epistemology.* New York: St. Martin's Press.

Von Krogh, G., Roos, J., and Kleine, D. (1998). *Knowing in firms: understanding, managing and measuring knowledge.* London: Sage Publications.

Weick, K. (2001). *Making sense of the organization.* Malden, MA: Basil Blackwell.

Wiig, K. (1993). *Knowledge management foundations: thinking about thinking. How people and organizations create, represent and use knowledge.* Arlington, TX: Schema Press.

KNOWLEDGE CAPTURE AND CODIFICATION

If written directions alone would suffice,
libraries wouldn't need to have the rest of the universities attached.
Judith Martin (1938–) *Washington Post* columnist and author

This chapter addresses the first phase of the knowledge management cycle, knowledge capture and/or creation. The major approaches, techniques, and tools used to elicit tacit knowledge, to trigger the creation of new knowledge, and to subsequently organize this content in a systematic manner (codification) are presented. These approaches represent a multidisciplinary methodology that integrates what we have found to be successful in a variety of other fields such as knowledge acquisition for the development of expert systems, instructional design techniques for course content creation and organization, task analysis techniques used in the development of performance support systems, and taxonomic approaches that originate from library and information studies.

LEARNING OBJECTIVES

1. Become familiar with the basic terminology and concepts related to knowledge capture and codification.
2. Describe the major techniques used to elicit tacit knowledge from subject matter experts.
3. Define the major roles and responsibilities that come into play during the knowledge capture and codification phase.
4. Outline the general taxonomic approaches used in classifying knowledge that has been captured.

5. Analyze the type of knowledge to be captured and codified, select the best approach to use, and discuss its advantages and shortcomings for a given knowledge elicitation application.

INTRODUCTION

The first high-level phase of the knowledge management cycle, as seen in Figure 4-1, begins with knowledge capture and codification. More specifically, tacit knowledge is captured or elicited, and explicit knowledge is organized or coded.

In knowledge capture, a distinction needs to be made between the capture or identification of existing knowledge and the creation of new knowledge. In most organizations, explicit or already identified and coded knowledge typically represents only the tip of the iceberg. Traditional information systems departments deal primarily with highly structured (records or forms-oriented) data that makes up much less than 5% of a company's information. In knowledge management, we need to also consider knowledge that we know is present in the organization, which we can then set out to capture. There remains, however, that interesting area of knowledge that we do not know about. This as-yet-unidentified knowledge will require additional steps in its capture and codification. Finally, there is knowledge that we know we do not have. We will need to facilitate the creation of this new, innovative content (see Figure 4-2).

Capturing the knowledge in an organization is not purely about technology. Indeed, many firms find that IT plays only a small part in ensuring that information is available to those who need it. The approach needed depends on the kind of business, its culture, and the ways in which people solve problems. Some organizations generally deliver standard products and services, while others are constantly looking for new ways of doing things. Knowledge capture can therefore span a whole host of activities, from organizing customer information details into a single database to setting up a mentoring program. We

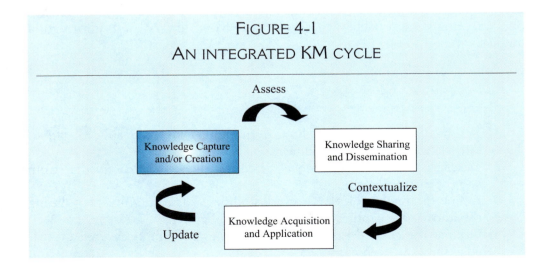

FIGURE 4-1
AN INTEGRATED KM CYCLE

FIGURE 4-2
THE KNOWN-UNKNOWN MATRIX

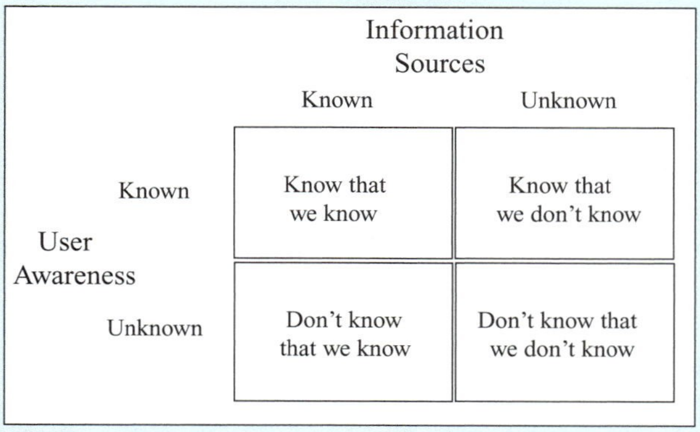

	Information Sources	
	Known	**Unknown**
User Awareness — **Known**	Know that we know	Know that we don't know
User Awareness — **Unknown**	Don't know that we know	Don't know that we don't know

Source: Frappaolo, 2004.

need to capture both types of knowledge—explicit and tacit. Knowledge about standardized work, for example, can be described explicitly and is easily captured in writing. On the other hand, where there is innovation and creativity, people also need some direct contact (Moorman and Miner, 1997).

Knowledge capture cannot therefore be a purely mechanistic "add-on" because it has to do with the discovery, organization, and integration of knowledge into the "fabric" of the organization. Knowledge has to be captured and codified in such a way that it can become a part of the existing knowledge base of the organization. Every organization has a history, which provides a backdrop to the growth and evolution of the organization.

Every organization also has a memory. The embodiment of the organizational memory is the experience of its employees, combined with the tangible data and knowledge stores in the organization (Walsh and Ungson, 1991). Bush (1945) envisioned instruments that, if properly developed, give one access to and command over the inherited knowledge of the ages. Knowledge that is not captured in this way becomes devalued and is eventually ignored. Knowledge is more than statements, declarations, and observations: it represents an intellectual currency that produces the most value when circulated. It may have unrealized potential and value, but unless it is spent, its value is not tested.

In today's fast-paced economy, an organization's knowledge base is quickly becoming its only sustainable competitive advantage. As such, this resource must be protected, cultivated, and shared among organizational members. Until recently, companies could succeed based on individual knowledge of a handful of strategically positioned workers. Increasingly, however, competitive advantage is to be gained by making individual knowledge available within the organization, transforming it into organizational knowledge. Organizational knowledge complements individual knowledge, making it stronger and broader. The full utilization of an organization's knowledge base, coupled with the potential of individual skills, competencies, thoughts, innovations, and ideas, will enable a company to compete more effectively in the future. Competitiveness is becoming increasingly dependent on an organization's agility or ability to respond to changes in a very timely manner. The major component of agility lies in the skills and learning abilities of the knowledge workers within that organization.

Without doubt knowledge capture may be difficult, particularly in the case of tacit knowledge. Tacit knowledge management is the process of capturing the experience and expertise of the individual in an organization and making it available to anyone who needs it. The capture of explicit knowledge is the systematic approach of capturing, organizing, and refining information in a way that makes information easy to find, and facilitates learning and problem solving. Knowledge often remains tacit until someone asks a direct question. At that point, tacit can become explicit, but unless that information is captured for someone else to use again at a later date, learning, productivity, and innovation are stifled.

Once knowledge is explicit, it should be organized in a structured document that will enable multipurpose use. The best KM tools create knowledge and then leverage it across multiple channels, including phone, e-mail, discussion forums, Internet telephony, and any new channels that come online. A wide variety of techniques may be used to capture and codify knowledge, and many of these techniques have their origins in fields other than knowledge management (e.g., artificial intelligence, sociology, and instructional design), which are described here.

TACIT KNOWLEDGE CAPTURE

Traditionally, knowledge capture has emphasized the individual's role in gathering information and creating new knowledge. The literature does not reflect any consensus on the role of the individual in knowledge acquisition. Some authors (e.g., Nelson and Winter, 1982) believe that the firm is a learning entity unto itself; that is, it has some cognitive capabilities that are quite apart from the individuals who comprise it. In contrast, other authors (e.g., Dodgson, 1993) do not believe that organizations per se can acquire knowledge and learn; rather, they say, only individuals can learn. A middle ground is needed where individuals in the firm play a critical role in acquiring organizational knowledge.

Learning at the individual level, however, is widely accepted to be a fundamentally social process—something that cannot occur without some form of group interaction. Individuals thus learn from the collective, and at the same time the collective learns from individuals (e.g., Crossan, Lane, and White, 1999). According to Crossan's 4I model (see Figure 4-3), organizational learning involves a tension between assimilating new learning (exploration) and using what has been learned (exploitation). Individual, group, and organizational levels of learning are linked by the social and psychological processes of intuiting, interpreting, integrating, and institutionalizing (the four I's). Zietsma et al. (2002) modified this slightly by including the process of attend-

FIGURE 4-3

THE 4I MODEL OF ORGANIZATIONAL LEARNING

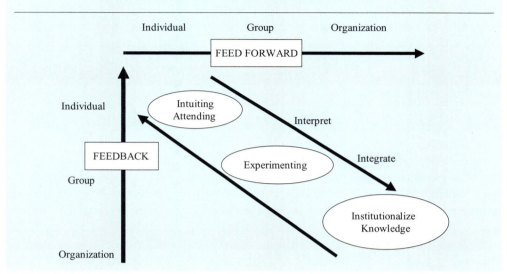

Source: Crossan, Lane, and White, 1999.

ing at the stage of intuiting and the process of experimenting at the stage of interpreting.

In KM, this knowledge creation or capture may be done by individuals who work for the organization or a group within that organization, by all members of a community of practice (CoP), or by a dedicated CoP individual. It is really done on a personal level as well, for almost everyone performs some knowledge creation, capture, and codification activities in carrying out their job. Cope (2000) refers to this as PKM (personalized KM). Within the firm, individuals share perceptions and jointly interpret information, events, and experiences (Cohen and Levinthal, 1990), and at some point, knowledge acquisition extends beyond the individuals and is coded into corporate memory (Inkpen, 1995; Spender, 1996; Nonaka and Takeuchi, 1995). Unless knowledge is embedded into corporate memory, the firm cannot leverage the knowledge held by individual members of the organization. Organizational knowledge acquisition is the "amplification and articulation of individual knowledge at the firm level so that it is internalized into the firm's knowledge base" (Malhotra, 2000, p. 334). The value of tacit knowledge sharing was discovered in a surprising way at Xerox (Roberts-Witt, 2002), as illustrated later in this chapter.

Many of the tacit knowledge capture techniques described in this chapter derive from techniques that were originally used in artificial intelligence—more specifically, in the development of expert systems. An expert system incorporates know-how gathered from experts and is designed to perform as experts do. The term *knowledge acquisition* was coined by the developers of such systems to refer to various techniques such as structured interviewing, protocol or talk aloud analysis, questionnaires, surveys, observation, and simulation. Some authors (e.g., Keritsis, 2001) even use the term *digital cloning*.

Knowledge management in business settings is similarly concerned with knowledge capture, finding ways to make tacit knowledge explicit (e.g., documenting best practices) or creating expert directories to foster knowledge sharing through human–human collaboration (Smith, 2000). In 1989, for example, Feigenbaum contrasted traditional libraries as "warehouses of passive objects where books and journals wait for us to use our intelligence to find them, to interpret them and cause them finally to divulge their stored knowledge" (p. 122) with a library of the future where "books" would interact and collaborate with users.

Tacit Knowledge Capture at Individual and Group Levels

Knowledge acquisition from individuals or groups can be characterized as the transfer and transformation of valuable expertise from a knowledge source (e.g., human expert, documents) to a knowledge repository (e.g., corporate memory, intranet). This process involves reducing a vast volume of content from diverse domains into a precise, easily usable set of facts and rules. "The idea of acquiring knowledge from an expert in a given field for the purpose of designing a specific presentation of the acquired information is not new. Reporters, journalists, writers, announcers and instructional designers have been practicing knowledge acquisition for years . . . system analysts have functioned in a very similar role in the design and development of conventional software systems" (McGraw and Harrison-Briggs, 1989, pp. 8–9).

The approach used to capture, describe, and subsequently code knowledge depends on the type of knowledge: explicit knowledge is already well described, but we may need to abstract or summarize this content. Tacit knowledge, on the other hand, may require much more significant up-front analysis and organization before it can be suitably described and represented. The ways in which we can tackle tacit knowledge range from simple graphical representations to sophisticated mathematical formulations.

In the design and development of knowledge-based systems, or expert systems, knowledge engineers interviewed subject matter experts, produced a conceptual model of their critical knowledge, and then "translated" this model into a computer-executable model such that an "expert on a diskette" resulted (e.g., Hayes-Roth, Waterman and Lenat, 1983). The global aim of such systems was to extract and render explicit the primarily procedural knowledge that comprised specialized know-how—typically in a very narrow field. *Procedural knowledge* is knowledge of how to do things, how to make decisions, how to diagnose, and how to prescribe. The other type of knowledge, *declarative knowledge*, denotes descriptive knowledge or knowing "what" as opposed to knowing "how." It soon became apparent that certain types of content were easily extracted and modeled in this manner—anything that was similar to an interactive online manual or help function in such fields as engineering, manufacturing, decision support, and medicine.

A wonderful by-product of the work in artificial intelligence was the array of innovative knowledge acquisition techniques that were created. The interactions with subject matter experts that were needed to render tacit knowledge explicit made up the knowledge engineer's toolkit. Quite a few of these techniques are imminently relevant and applicable to the process of tacit knowledge capture in knowledge management applications. The major tasks carried out by knowledge engineers included:

- Analyzing information and knowledge flow.
- Working with experts to obtain information.
- Designing and implementing an expert system.

Only the last point would differ, and it could be replaced by "designing and implementing a knowledge management system or knowledge repository." On the other side were the subject matter experts, and they had to be able to:

- Explain important knowledge and know-how.
- Be introspective and patient.
- Have effective communication skills.

Subject or domain experts were usually "sole sources of information whose expertise companies wish to preserve" (McGraw and Harrison-Briggs, 1989, p. 7). Today, many organizations face knowledge continuity concerns due to a wave of retiring baby boomers who represent knowledge "walking out the door." The concerns are quite similar, and the techniques used show a great deal of overlap. For example, multiple experts were often participants in knowledge engineering sessions in order to cover the range of expertise they represented, to validate the content, to provide different perspective, and so on. A number of group knowledge acquisition techniques were developed and used successfully with such groups. These approaches would be a perfect fit for knowledge acquisition at the community of practice level.

Another artificial intelligence researcher, Parsaye (1988), outlined the following three major approaches to knowledge acquisition from individuals and groups:

1. Interviewing experts.
2. Learning by being told.
3. Learning by observation.

All three approaches are applicable to tacit knowledge capture, but no one approach should be used to the total exclusion of the others. In many cases, a combination of these approaches will be required to capture tacit knowledge. The following section presents a toolkit and guidelines on the strengths and drawbacks of each as a means of helping select the best combination of techniques for different knowledge capture situations.

Interviewing Experts

Two of the more popular techniques for optimizing the interviewing of experts are structured interviewing and stories.

Structured Interviewing

Structured interviewing of subject matter experts is the most often used technique to render key tacit knowledge of an individual into more explicit forms. In many organizations, structured interviewing is performed through exit interviews that are held when knowledgeable staff near retirement age. Content management systems are well suited to publishing their lessons learned and best practices accumulated over their years of experience at the organization. Structured interviewing techniques require strong communication and conceptualization skills. In addition, interviewers need to have a good grasp of the subject matter at hand. These sessions yield specific data that is often declarative in response to focused questions. Structured interviews may also be used to clarify or refine knowledge originally elicited during unstructured interactions. The interviewer should outline specific goals and questions for the knowledge acquisition session. The interviewee should be provided with session goals and sample lines of questioning but usually not the specific questions to be asked.

Two major types of questions are used in interviewing: open and closed questions. Open questions tend to be broad and place few constraints on the expert. They are not followed by choices because they are designed to encourage free response (Oppenheim, 1966). These types of questions allow interviewers to observe the expert's use of key vocabulary, concepts, and frames of reference. The expert can also offer information that was not specifically asked for. Some examples would be:

- "How does that work?"
- "What do you need to know before you decide?"
- "Why did you choose this one rather than that one?"
- "What do you know about . . ."
- "How could . . . be improved?"
- "What is your general reaction to . . . ?"

Closed questions set limits on the type, level, and amount of information an expert will provide. A choice of alternatives is always given. A moderately closed question would be something like: "which symptom led you to conclude that . . . ?" A very strong closed question is one that can only be answered by yes or no.

The structured interviewing process is primarily a people-focused one, and as such, techniques that serve to facilitate the interactions can greatly contribute to the successful outcome of such sessions. Reflective listening helps in cases where words may have multiple meanings. The interview participants may hold very different mental models, and personal characteristics such as background, attitude, training, and level of comfort with current position in the organization, may influence how an expert communicates his or her knowledge. The four major techniques used in reflective listening include paraphrasing, clarifying, summarizing, and reflecting feelings.

Paraphrasing is the restating of the perceived meaning of the speaker's message but using your own words. The goal is to check the accuracy with which the message was conveyed and understood. Examples include:

- "What I believe you said was . . ."
- "If I am wrong, please correct me but I understood you to say . . ."
- "In other words, . . ."
- "As I think I understand it . . ."

Clarifying lets the expert know that the message was not immediately understandable. These responses encourage the expert to elaborate or clarify the original message so that the interviewer gets a better idea of the intended message. One should always focus on the message and not on the expert's ability to communicate, and the expert should be encouraged to elaborate or explain by using open questions wherever possible. Examples include:

- "I don't understand . . ."
- "Could you please explain . . ."
- "Please repeat that last part again . . ."
- "Could you give me an example of that . . ."

Summarizing helps the interviewer compile discrete pieces of information and form a knowledge acquisition session into a meaningful whole. It also helps confirm that the expert's message was heard and understood correctly. The summary should be expressed in the words of the interviewer. Examples would be:

- "To sum up what you have been saying . . ."
- "What I have heard you say so far . . ."
- "I believe that we are in agreement that . . ."

Finally, *reflecting feelings* mirrors back to the speaker the feelings that seem to have been communicated. The main focus is on emotions, attitudes, and reactions, and not on the content itself. The purpose is to clear the air of some emotional reaction or negative impact of the message. Some examples are:

- "You seem frustrated about . . ."
- "You seem to feel that you were put on the spot . . ."
- "I sense that you are uncomfortable with . . ."

Transcripts of interviews are then analyzed in order to identify key concepts, common themes, and major methods or techniques that were mentioned. If multiple experts were interviewed for the same procedure or subject, then conflict resolution might be needed. Usually, each individual will be interviewed more than once so that interviewers can validate their understanding of the knowledge that has been elicited, fill in any missing gaps, and better conceptualize the content in an organized manner. Each interview will raise additional questions, whether these are aimed at clarifying, correcting, or expanding upon critical elements. After a number of interviews and follow-up sessions, the interviewer will be able to start identifying key themes and have a preliminary framework for organizing these themes. Unlike the initial interview sessions, where new content is generated and captured, subsequent interviews are more focused and target a more detailed level.

The best test of whether enough content has been captured is to switch roles: the interviewer can assume the role of novice practitioner and verbally or physically go through the key tasks discussed to date. The interviewee can then validate until both are satisfied that the knowledge has been understood and captured in as complete and valid a manner as possible.

Stories

Stories are another excellent vehicle for both capturing and coding tacit knowledge. An organizational story is a detailed narrative of management actions, employee interactions, and other intraorganizational events that are communicated informally within the organization. A story can be defined as the telling of a happening or a connected series of happenings, whether true or fictitious (Denning, 2001). Snowden (2001) defines a narrative as: "not just about telling, constructing or even eliciting stories, it is about allowing the patterns of culture, behaviour, and understanding that are revealed by stories to emerge" (p. 1). An organizational story can be defined as a detailed narrative of past management actions, employee interactions, or other key events that have occurred and that have been communicated informally (Swap et al., 2001). Conveying information in a story provides a rich context, causing the story to remain in the conscious memory longer and creating more memory traces than is possible with information not in context. Stories can greatly increase organizational learning, communicate common values and rule sets, and serve as an excellent vehicle for capturing, coding, and transmitting valuable tacit knowledge.

A number of conditions must be in place, however, in order to ensure that storytelling in its various enacted forms creates value in a particular organization. Sole and Wilson (2002) argue that although all stories are narratives, not all narratives are good knowledge-sharing stories. As an example, they cite movies, which tell stories designed primarily to entertain and therefore need not necessarily be authentic—or even believable. In contrast, in organizational storytelling, stories are often used to promote knowledge sharing, inform, and/or prompt a change in behavior, as well as communicate the organizational culture and create a sense of belonging. In order to achieve these organizational objectives, knowledge-sharing stories need to be authentic, believable, and compelling. Stories need to evoke some type of response, and, above all, they need to be concise (Denning, 2001), so that the moral of the story or the organizational lesson to be learned can be easily understood, remembered, and acted upon. In other words, organizational stories should have an impact: they should prevent similar mistakes from being repeated, or they should promote organizational learning and adoption of best practices stemming from the collective organizational memory.

Denning (2001) describes the power of a springboard story, knowledge that has been captured in the form of a brief story that has the ability to create a strong impact on its audience. He outlines a number of key elements required to use stories to encapsulate valuable knowledge, such as:

- The explicit story should be relatively brief and detailed just enough that the audience can understand it.
- The story must be intelligible to the specific audience so that they are "hooked."
- The story should be inherently interesting.
- The story should spring the listener to a new level of understanding.
- The story should have a happy ending.
- The story should embody the change message.
- The change message should be implicit.
- The listeners should be encouraged to identify with the protagonist.
- The story should deal with a specific individual or organization.
- The protagonist should be prototypical of the organization's main business.
- Other things being equal, true is better than invented.
- One should test, test, and test again.

The use of fables such as those found in Aesop (1968) is often quite helpful in capturing tacit knowledge. A simple approach is to invite participants to a workshop where they are given several classic fables to read; they are asked to recollect some of what they have heard and to identify the lesson to be learned in each. Fables are particularly useful with multicultural groups since fables are ubiquitous in all cultures, but they definitely differ one from the other. Participants are given a fable minus the "punch line," and they are asked to fill in the moral of the story. Asking for a punch line is a highly effective way of acquainting participants with the objectives of stories or the purpose of organizational storytelling—that is, what the reader should learn from it. Participants also become sensitized to the fact that stories, like fables, need to be concise. A fable can consolidate multiple viewpoints and recollections of different individuals because it is not dependent on a single story to deliver its message (Snowden, 2001). Finally, the best way to end a fable—the punch line—is to have an ironic end in which the reader realizes how a happy ending could have come about without the narrative actually stating this in any form.

The following vignettes on IBM and Xerox illustrate the value of storytelling in the capture of tacit knowledge.

IBM

Knowledge disclosure is a key way of identifying the organizational culture. Knowledge disclosure techniques such as storytelling allow us to uncover knowledge in the context of its use. IBM views stories as a powerful means of knowledge discovery and knowledge transfer. They are very good for conveying complex messages simply. Storytelling is a unifying and defining component of all communities. Stories exist in all organizations; managed and purposeful storytelling provides a powerful mechanism for the disclosure of intellectual or knowledge assets in companies. It can also

Continued

provide a nonintrusive, organic means of producing sustainable cultural change. Storytelling is an excellent means of conveying values and other complex tacit knowledge.

Stories are endemic within each and every organization. They should be fostered, leveraged, and managed. We all tell stories in our daily work to share our experience and knowledge. Tacit knowledge is the most powerful means of sharing knowledge, and this knowledge is usually shared through informal networks. Organizations need to accept the fact that stories exist in their organization, identify the stories that persist, leverage these stories to effect cultural change, and foster an environment conducive to sharing knowledge and learning through stories. The best teachers, presenters, and knowledge sharers tell stories naturally in order to convey learning points and share their experiences. Stories put the knowledge in context and then make the learning memorable and the learning experience more compelling. Failure stories, or lessons learned, help a community to learn from its mistakes.

IBM has a four-stage storytelling approach: (1) anecdotal elicitation through interviews, observation, and story circles; (2) anecdotal deconstruction to analyze cultural issues, ways of working, values, rules, and beliefs to yield the story's key messages; (3) intervention/communication design with a story constructed or enhanced; and (4) story deployment. Storytelling workshops can be run to elicit the knowledge and cultural values of an organization as well as both its best and worst practices. Capturing anecdotal or tacit knowledge builds an accurate picture of the existing culture, discloses enablers and inhibitors to sharing, and identifies business issues. Values—moral principles or standards—are identified. Rules—the code of discipline that drives or conforms behavior—are also identified. And finally, beliefs—the collection of ideas that a community regards as true or shares faith in—are elicited.

Storytelling is a cathartic process through which employees can share experiences and build social capital and networks. Perhaps most importantly of all, it achieves agreement among the participants.

Once anecdotes are captured, they can be stored in a repository and aligned with communities, processes, and subject areas. They can then be used to trigger and support discussion forums (e.g., lunch and learn), databases, intellectual capital management systems (e.g., training), document management systems, bulletin boards, online chats, portals (e.g., community kickoff days), and intranets (e.g., competency/skill profiling).

Ultimately, it is the people who make communities, and effective communities have valuable stories. In order to help support effective communities, you need to understand what their issues are, what they need, and what facilities and solutions would best suit them.

Source: IBM Knowledge Socialization Project, IBM Research. http://www.research.ibm.com

It is, of course, not enough to create rich environments where people can share. Xerox provides lots of these environments: online Knowledge Universe with a catalog of best practices, chat rooms for CoPs, a company Yellow Pages, and a section of the public website, Knowledge Street, which is devoted to promoting knowledge sharing. Also required are good ideas, leadership, and motivated people. A few years ago, Jack Whalen, a sociologist, spent some time in a Xerox customer service call center outside Dallas studying how people used Eureka. The trouble was that the employees were not using it. Management therefore decided workers needed an incentive to change. To this end, they held a contest in which workers could win points (convertible into cash) each time they solved a customer problem, by whatever means. The winner was an eight-year veteran named Carlos, who had more than 900 points. Carlos really knew his stuff and everyone else knew this too. Carlos never used the software.

The runner-up, however, was a shock to everyone. Trish had been with the company only a few months, had no previous experience with copiers, and did not even have the software on her machine. Yet her 600 points doubled the score of the third-place winner. Her secret: she sat right across from Carlos. She overheard him as he talked, and she persuaded him to show her the inner workings of copiers during lunch breaks. She asked other colleagues for tips too. This story illustrates how knowledge gets shared. The point is not the software but how many people can sit next to Carlos! There is no single best practice for sharing knowledge—both technology and subject matter experts are needed. And sometimes storytelling is the best way to transfer knowledge. Most managers see this as a waste of time, but instead of breaking up the coffee machine cliques, companies should make opportunities for storytelling at informal get-togethers that are loosely organized as offsite meetings, and also through videotapes and bragging sessions.

Source: Eureka Project at Xerox. APQC Case Study. http://www.apqc.org

Learning by Being Told

In learning by being told, the interviewee expresses and refines his or her knowledge, and at the same time, the knowledge manager clarifies and validates the knowledge artifact that renders this knowledge in explicit form. This form of knowledge acquisition typically involves domain and task analysis, process tracing, and protocol analysis and simulations. Task analysis is an approach that looks at each key task an expert performs and characterizes the tasks in terms of prerequisite knowledge/skills required, criticality, consequences of error, frequency, difficulty, and interrelationships with other tasks and individuals, as well as how the task is perceived by the person (routine, dreaded, or eagerly anticipated).

Process tracing and protocol analysis are adapted from psychological techniques. They involve asking the subject matter expert to "think aloud" as he or she solves a problem or undertakes a task. The information used, questions asked, actions taken, alternatives considered, and decisions taken are the types of knowledge acquired in such sessions (e.g., Svenson, 1979; McGraw and Seale, 1987; Gammack and Young, 1985). Simulations are especially effective for later stages of knowledge acquisition, validating, refining, and completing the knowledge capture process. Tools may include software programs and "props" such as models, schematics, and maps.

Learning by Observation

There are at least two types of discernible expertise: skill or motor based (e.g., operating a piece of machinery, riding a bike) and cognitive expertise (e.g., making a medical diagnosis). Expertise is a demonstration of the application of knowledge. The learning-by-observation approach involves presenting the expert with a sample problem, scenario, or case study that the expert then solves. Although we cannot observe someone's knowledge, we can observe and identify expertise. The key is to use audio or video to record what the expert knows. People think of video mainly as a presentation device. However, experience has shown again and again that video recordings of informal and unrehearsed expert demonstrations form a permanent record of task knowledge—one that can be mined repeatedly. However, one should always accommodate the particular expert or interviewee at all times; many individuals end up feeling much less comfortable if they know they are being recorded. The happy medium is to bring along recording equipment but allow the subject the choice and hand over the controls to them—so they can mute whenever they wish to "speak off the record." For physical demonstrations, inexpensive digital camcorders are recommended. For software demonstrations, screen capture movie software that records the action directly from the desktop is recommended. Together, simple equipment and simple techniques can capture an amazing range of information and demonstrations.

Other Methods of Tacit Knowledge Capture

A number of other techniques may be used to capture tacit knowledge from individuals and from groups, including:

- Ad hoc sessions.
- Road maps.
- Learning histories.
- Action learning.
- E-learning.
- Learning from others through business guest speakers and benchmarking against best practices.

Ad hoc sessions are a means of rapidly mobilizing a community of practice or informal professional network to a member's call for help. These are usually brainstorming sessions of no more than 30 minutes and can take place as face-to-face meetings or make use of technologies such as instant messaging, e-mail, teleconferencing, and chat rooms.

Road maps are more formal in nature. They tend to be facilitated problem-solving meetings that are scheduled, convened, and follow an agenda. The objective is to solve day-to-day problems in a public forum, which often leads to the development of guidelines and even standards for continuous process improvement within the company. These sessions may also be "registered" so that they can also be used for internal benchmarking initiatives. Internal benchmarking consists of monitoring progress against goals over time (comparing snapshots to an initial baseline) and/or comparing the performance of one unit to that of another within the same company.

"Those who cannot remember the past are condemned to repeat it" is an oft-repeated quote from George Santayana. Learning histories (Roth and Kleiner, 2000) are a very useful means of capturing tacit knowledge, especially in group settings. They represent a retrospective history of significant events that occurred in the organization's recent past, as described in the voice of the people who took part in them. Organizational history is often researched through a series of initial individual interviews where participants are asked to remember and reflect upon the event followed by a facilitated workshop with all participants in order to capture that group's memory.

The learning history process consists of (1) planning, (2) reflective interviews, (3) distillation, (4) writing, (5) validation, and (6) dissemination.

Planning establishes the scope of the learning history to be captured; the scope is a function of the business objective targeted by the learning history. Each learning history exercise should be well founded on a problem or challenge that was overcome by the organization. The learning history serves to describe what happened, why it happened, how the organization reacted, and what current organizational members should learn from this experience. The second phase, reflective interviews, consists of asking participants to talk about what happened from their own point of view. By asking them about their analysis, evaluation, and the judgment they used, insights will emerge. The capture and codification of these insights will help increase the organization's reflective capacity.

The third phase, distillation, consists of synthesizing the information that was gathered from the interviews into a summary format that will make it very easy for others to access, read, and understand. The interview transcripts, along with notes from the facilitated learning history workshop, can then be analyzed to identify key themes and subthemes as well as specific quotes to be used. The key themes are documented at a more abstract level (they need not have specific dates or other details in order to convey the major points to be made), and the quotes are verified and authorization obtained in order to print them with an attribution. The content is then written up, validated, and published in order to disseminate the learning history and to anchor it as part of the organizational memory. The results are often transcribed in a Q/A format as shown in Table 4-1. A learning history is thus a systematic review of successes and failures in order to capture best practices and lessons learned as they

TABLE 4-1

SAMPLE LEARNING HISTORY TEMPLATE

Theme Title	For example, "Repurposing of objectives for the ACME Division in 1995 in response to new environmental regulations"
Part 1: Overview of Theme	Brief overview of the event, emphasizing why it was a significant event in the organization's history, why it needs to be well understood in order to better meet today's objectives, who was involved, what triggered the event, and so on.
Part 2: Description	Chronological commentary, conclusions, and the questions that were asked together with the responses; quotes representing key responses to questions should appear as separate right-hand-side column and be aligned with the content the quote refers to.
Part 3: Summary	Brief summary of quotes, additional questions to provide more clarity to the theme; a stand-alone section that can be made available and be understood by those who were not participants in the original event.
Part 4: Best Practices	Describe any best practices that group consensus identified. Include the following information: ■ Date prepared ■ Point of contact (name, contact information) ■ Members who contributed to the development of the best practice ■ Problem statement (what does best practice address) ■ Background (enough context to understand the problem and the proposed solution) ■ Best practice description (model, business rules—use graphics where appropriate)
Part 5: Lessons Learned	Describe any lessons learned identified by the group. Include the following information: ■ Date prepared ■ Point of contact (name, contact information) ■ Members who contributed to the development of the best practice ■ Problem statement (what does best practice address) ■ Background (enough context to what happened, what went wrong, and how to prevent a recurrence) ■ Lesson learned description (model, business rules—use graphics where appropriate)

pertain to a significant organizational event or project. Some typical questions posed in learning history knowledge capture include:

- What was your role in the project/initiative?
- How would you judge its success or failure?
- What would you do differently if you could?
- What recommendations do you have for other people who may face a similar situation?
- What innovative things were done along the way?

Learning histories are typically presented in two side-by-side columns with a narrative in one column and evaluative comments in the other. This allows readers to arrive at their own conclusions. The learning history must always be validated by the original participants before it is finally disseminated throughout the organization. Dissemination works best when it is an organized activity. Action learning is based on the fact that people tend to learn by doing. Small groups can be formed with participants who share common issues, goals, or learning needs. They can meet regularly, report on progress, brainstorm alternatives, try out new things, and evaluate the results. This is a form of task-oriented group work and learning that is well suited for narrow, specialized domains and specific issues. One good theme for such small groups would be to analyze a learning history and discuss what they would have done differently and why in order to promote a better understanding of the event in question.

E-learning solutions typically involve capturing valuable procedural knowledge and documenting a history of all procedural changes, together with an explanation or justification for the change made (George and Kolbasuk, 2003). In this way, a historical thread is maintained, and the context within which changes were deemed to be necessary is not lost. In addition to a repository for such knowledge, a process needs to be established whereby employees who are planning to leave have the time and the necessary support to organize and store their reference materials, procedural experience accumulated throughout the years, and valuable knowledge to benefit others in the future. For example, it be very useful to capture how they solve problems. Next, online courses could be created based on the information from threaded discussion archives. In this way, traditional and computer-based training systems can be combined to capture and make available previously uncodified, typically tacit knowledge and know-how. The knowledge capture approach is similar to the subject matter expert's work with an instructional designer to design course content and accompanying hands-on activities.

An example is NASA, where 60% of aerospace workers were slated to reach retirement age all within a few years of each other. These impending retirements threatened the loss of valuable knowledge of the Apollo-era missions unless they could be transferred to remaining and future workers. NASA began a mentoring program that makes use of e-learning and virtual collaboration to capture valuable knowledge and know-how and to keep this content online. The solution included a mix of e-mail, threaded discussions, and live collaborative sessions. Almost all major organizations around the world face a similar situation. The demographic pressure created by the baby boomers, who have always led by their sheer numbers, has created a growing need for knowledge continuity applications to make sure that valuable knowledge does not "walk out the door."

Learning from others can involve activities such as external benchmarking, which involves learning about what the leaders are doing in terms of their best practices, either through publications or site visits, and then adapting and adopting their best practices. Benchmarking helps identify better ways of doing business. Other learning sources include attending conferences and expositions and commissioning specific studies. Inviting guest speakers to an organization presents yet another opportunity to bring a fresh perspective or point of view. Speakers may be selected on the basis of targeted interests, and they may be

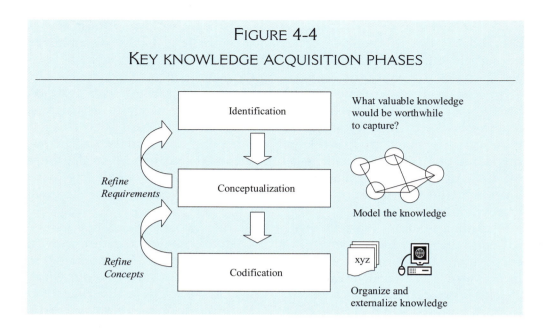

FIGURE 4-4

KEY KNOWLEDGE ACQUISITION PHASES

internal or external to the organization. Typically, they give a seminar or workshop and leave behind a set of reference materials.

Figure 4-4 summarizes the key steps involved in knowledge acquisition at the individual and group level. Identification refers to the process of characterizing key problem aspects such as participants, resources, goals, and existing reference materials. Conceptualization involves specifying the key concepts and the key relationships among them in the form of a concept or knowledge map. Codification renders this validated content into an explicit form that can then be more readily disseminated throughout the organization.

The importance of recordkeeping during knowledge capture, especially tacit knowledge capture, cannot be emphasized enough. Original transcripts, recordings, and reference materials need to be carefully organized in a knowledge acquisition database. The source of each piece of key knowledge must be carefully recorded for future reference, and key findings should also be systematically captured. Templates are often used to structure and standardize knowledge acquisition processes. A sample knowledge acquisition session template is shown in Figure 4-5. Sending back transcripts and summary forms to the people interviewed serves to validate and complete the content; it also gives the interviewee the chance to edit comments so that they are not taken out of context.

Tacit Knowledge Capture at the Organizational Level

Organizational knowledge acquisition is a qualitatively different process from that which occurs at individual and group levels. Whereas at the group level we are primarily concerned with identifying and coding valuable knowledge, which is mostly tacit in nature, organizational knowledge capture takes place on a more macro level. A good approach is proposed by Malhotra

FIGURE 4-5

Knowledge Acquisition Session Notes

Project Name _____

Date _____

Person interviewed _____

Interviewer _____

Technique _____

Objective _____

Duration _____

Reference materials collected _____

Recorded session? Y/N _____

Next scheduled interview _____

Next topics to be addressed _____

Summary of key findings _____

Points to be clarified/followed up _____

Others to interview to complete knowledge acquisition _____

Special considerations _____

What worked well with this expert _____

What should be different next time _____

Key areas of expertise of interviewee _____

Number of years with the organization _____

(2000), who outlines four major organizational knowledge acquisition processes: (1) grafting, (2) vicarious learning, (3) experiential learning, and (4) inferential processes.

Grafting involves the migration of knowledge between firms. It is a learning process whereby the firm gains access to task- or process-specific knowledge that was not previously available within the firm. This is typically achieved through mergers, acquisitions, or alliances in that there is a direct passing of knowledge between firms (Huber, 1991). An example would be technology transfer or other forms of explicit knowledge. *Vicarious learning* processes occur through one firm observing other firms' demonstrations of techniques or procedures. Examples are benchmarking studies where companies can adopt the best practices of other industry leaders. This knowledge is more tacit than that obtained through grafting (Inkpen and Beamish, 1997), for it involves learning how to do something or know-how.

Experiential knowledge acquisition involves knowledge acquisition within a given firm—that is, knowledge created by doing and practicing. Repetition-based experience relies on the learning curve to establish routines and procedures. This type of knowledge is initially tacit but can be easily codified and transferred (Pennings, Barkema, and Douma, 1994; Starbuck, 1992). Argyris and Schon (1978) refer to the processes of single- and double-loop learning. Single-loop learning involves the refinement and improvement of existing procedures and technologies as opposed to developing new ones (adaptivity for efficiency). In *inferential processes* (e.g., Mintzberg, 1990), learning is within the firm and occurs by doing. However, knowledge acquisition occurs primarily through interpretation of events, states, changes, and outcomes relative to the activities undertaken and decisions made. Learning is experimental, deductive learning that seeks to make sense of occurrences and to establish causal links between actions and outcomes. This type of learning is sometimes called double-loop learning because it involves changing underlying assumptions and frameworks (adaptivity for effectiveness).

The results of all four types of organizational knowledge capture will ultimately reside in some type of knowledge repository. This is the recipient of organizational memory, and containers are usually some form of database on an intranet or extranet. The capture of such knowledge has, in large part, already occurred, which means we can proceed more directly to the codification of this content.

EXPLICIT KNOWLEDGE CODIFICATION

Knowledge can be shared through personal communication and interaction, as we saw in the first quadrant, socialization, of the Nonaka and Takeuchi KM model. This occurs naturally all the time and is very effective, though rarely is it cost-effective. Knowledge codification is the next stage of leveraging knowledge. By converting knowledge into a tangible, explicit form such as a document, that knowledge can be communicated much more widely and with less cost. Interaction is limited in scope to those within hearing or able to have face-to-face contact. Documents can be disseminated widely over a corporate intranet, and they persist over time, which makes them available for reference as and when they are needed, both by existing and by future staff. They constitute the only "real" corporate memory of the organization.

There are, of course, costs and difficulties associated with knowledge codification. The first issue is that of quality, which encompasses (1) accuracy, (2) readability/understandability, (3) accessibility, (4) currency, and (5) authority/credibility.

Knowledge codification serves the pivotal role of allowing what is collectively known to be shared and used. Knowledge held by a particular person enables that person to be more effective. If people interact to share their knowledge within a community of practice, then that practice becomes more effective. If knowledge is codified in a material way (i.e., it is rendered explicit), then it can be shared more widely in terms of both audience and time duration. Knowledge must be codified in order to be understood, maintained, and improved upon as part of corporate memory. The codification of explicit knowledge can be achieved through a variety of techniques such as cognitive mapping, decision trees, knowledge taxonomies, and task analysis.

Cognitive Maps

Once expertise, experience, and know-how have been rendered explicit, typically through some form of interviewing, the resulting content can be represented as a cognitive map. A cognitive or knowledge map is a representation of the "mental model" of a person's knowledge and provides a good form of codified knowledge. A mental model is a symbolic or qualitative representation of something in the real world. It is how human minds process and make sense of their complex environments. A cognitive map is a powerful way of coding this captured knowledge because it also captures the context and the complex interrelationships between the different key concepts. It is in fact also very important to include individual views, perceptions, judgments, hypotheses, and beliefs as they form part of the interviewee's subjective worldview. The nodes in a map are the key concepts, and the links represent the interrelationships between the concepts. These may be drawn manually by taping small note pages on a wall, a whiteboard, or visualization software, ranging from simple brainstorming mapping tools to 3-D depictions. Figure 4-6 shows an example of a cognitive map in response to the question: "describe the major differences between tacit and explicit knowledge objects."

Cognitive mapping is based on concept mapping (Leake et al., 2003), which allows experts to directly construct knowledge models. Concept maps represent concepts and relations in a two-dimensional graphical form, with nodes representing key concepts connected by links representing propositions. These are quite similar to semantic networks used by such diverse disciplines as linguistics, education, and knowledge-based systems. The goal of such systems is

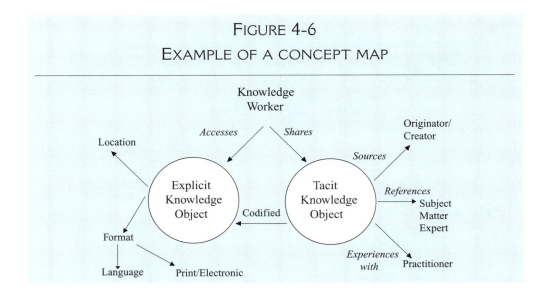

FIGURE 4-6

EXAMPLE OF A CONCEPT MAP

to better organize explicit knowledge and to store it in corporate memory for long-term retention.

Another widely used tool for explicit knowledge coding is the Common-KADS methodology (Schreiber et al., 2000; Shadbolt, O'Hara, and Crow, 1999), which is a knowledge engineering methodology centered on six models of an organization:

1. Task model of the organization's business processes.
2. Agent model of the executors' use of knowledge, both human and artificial, to carry out the various tasks in the organization.
3. Knowledge model that explains in detail the knowledge structures and types required for performing tasks.
4. Communication model that models the communicative transactions between agents.
5. Design model that specifies the architectures and technical requirements needed to implement a system that embodies the functions detailed by the knowledge and communication models.

In order to implement KADS, the organization is analyzed to identify knowledge-oriented problems, describe the organizational aspects that may affect knowledge solutions (e.g., culture, resources), and describe the business processes in terms of agents required, location, knowledge assets deployed, and measures of knowledge intensiveness and significance (e.g., mission criticality). Next the knowledge used in the organization is described in terms of possessors and processes used, whether or not it is in the right form and location, of the right quality, and available at the right times. The feasibility of suggested solutions is then checked against the knowledge problems identified in the first step. This approach allows a systematic cost-benefit analysis to be carried out for the processes of knowledge capture.

Decision Trees

Decision trees are another widely used method to codify explicit knowledge. This representation is both compact and efficient. The decision tree is typically in the form of a flowchart, with alternate paths indicating the impact of different decisions being made at that juncture point. A decision tree can represent many "rules," and when you execute the logic by following a path down it, you are effectively bypassing rules that are not relevant to the case in hand. You do not have to look at every rule to see if it "fires," and you also take the shortest route to the correct outcome. Their graphical nature makes them very easy to understand, and they are obviously very well suited for the coding of process knowledge. An example would be a preventive maintenance process for factory equipment. The captured knowledge from maintenance workers could be coded in a decision tree to help future maintenance workers carry out parts replacement and other work on a schedule-based decision rather than reacting to parts becoming worn out. Another example, shown in Figure 4-7, helps guide the decision to consolidate or to develop a new product as a risk management decision tree.

FIGURE 4-7

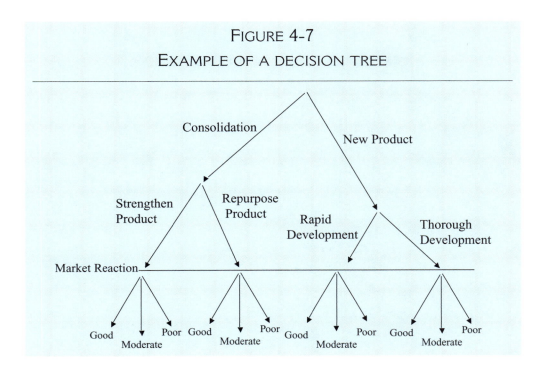

FIGURE 4-7
EXAMPLE OF A DECISION TREE

Knowledge Taxonomies

Concepts can be viewed as the building blocks of knowledge and expertise. We each use our own internal definitions of concepts to make sense of the world around us. Once key concepts have been identified and captured, they can be arranged in a hierarchy that is often referred to as a structural knowledge taxonomy. Knowledge taxonomies allow knowledge to be graphically represented in such a way that it reflects the organization of concepts within a particular field of expertise or for the organization at large. A knowledge dictionary is a good way to keep track of key concepts and terms that are used. This may be compiled as you acquire and code knowledge. It should clearly define and clarify the professional "jargon" of the subject matter domain.

Taxonomies are basic classification systems that enable us to describe concepts and their dependencies—typically in a hierarchical fashion. The higher up the concept is placed, the more general or generic the concept is. The lower the concept is placed, the more specific an instance it is of higher-level categories. An example is shown in Figure 4-8.

An important concept that underlies taxonomies is the notion of inheritance. Each node is a subgroup of the node above it, which means that all of the properties of the higher-level node are automatically transferred from "parent" to "child." As shown in Figure 4-8, if the higher-level node is a houseplant and the lower-level nodes are foliage and flowering plants, both of these two subgroups possess all the characteristics of houseplants. In fact, taxonomies originated as biological classification schemes.

FIGURE 4-8

EXAMPLE OF A KNOWLEDGE TAXONOMY

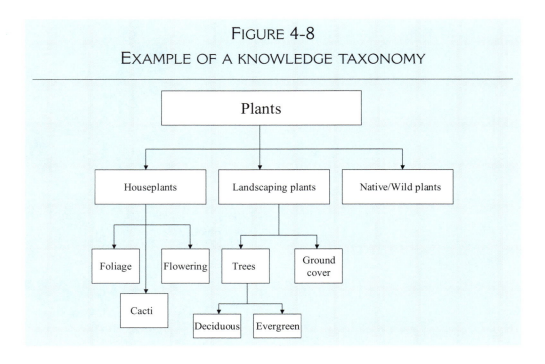

Taxonomies are most useful in the organization of declarative knowledge such as that embodied by diagnostic systems. The construction of a taxonomy involves identifying, defining, comparing, and grouping elements. Organizational knowledge taxonomies, however, are driven not by basic first principles or "real" attributes but by consensus. All the organizational stakeholders need to agree on the classification scheme to be used to derive the taxonomy—it cannot be theoretical but empirical. This is how we code this type of knowledge in our work.

A number of concept sorting techniques may be used in coding organizational knowledge, ranging from manual to completely automated processes. An example of a manual process would be to have participants sort cards into groupings. An automated example would be something like the RepGrid technique developed by Shaw (1981) based on Kelly's (1955) personal construct theory. Most automated systems use a form of cluster analysis to identify groupings in a set of data (e.g., hierarchical cluster analysis; see Johnson, 1967), multidimensional scaling (e.g., Kruskal, 1977), or network scaling (e.g., Schvaneveldt, Durso, and Dearholt, 1985). Cluster analysis is a method of producing classifications from data that is initially unclassified. In hierarchical cluster analysis, the groupings are arranged in the form of a hierarchical tree. Repertory grid analysis is a technique based on a theory that states each person functions as a scientist who classifies or organizes his or her world. Based on these classifications, the individual is able to construct theories and act based on these theories. A repertory grid depicts this theoretical framework for a

TABLE 4-2

MAJOR TAXONOMIC APPROACHES TO
KNOWLEDGE CODIFICATION

Taxonomic Approach	Key Features
Cognitive or concept map	▪ Key content represented as a node in a graph, and the relationships between these key concepts are explicitly defined. ▪ Can show multiple perspectives or views on the same content. ▪ Fairly easy to produce and intuitively simple to understand but difficult to use for knowledge related to procedures.
Decision tree	▪ Hierarchical or flowchart type of representation of a decision process. ▪ Very well suited to procedural knowledge—less able to capture conceptual interrelationships. ▪ Easy to produce and easy to understand.
Manual knowledge taxonomy	▪ Object-oriented approach that allows lower or more specific knowledge to automatically incorporate all attributes of higher-level or parent content they are related to. ▪ Very flexible—can be viewed as a concept map or as a hieararchy. ▪ More complex; will therefore require more time to develop as it must reflect user consensus.
Automated knowledge taxonomy	▪ A number of tools are now commercially available for taxonomy construction. ▪ Most are based on statistical techniques such as cluster analysis to determine which types of content are more similar to each other and can constitute subgroups or thematic sets. ▪ Good solution if there is a large amount of legacy content to sort through. ▪ More expensive and still not completely accurate—will need to validate and refine for maximum usefulness.

given individual. The different taxonomic approaches to the codification of explicit knowledge are summarized in Table 4-2.

When creating a knowledge taxonomy of the organization, it is vitally important to identify content owners. This helps ensure that content will always be kept up to date. The organization will also have a clear idea of which staff members are holders of specialized knowledge. This knowledge taxonomy (sometimes called a *knowledge map*) should also make use of metadata, tagging on "information about information"—for example, tagging content with content owners, "best before" dates, classification information such as key words, business-specific information such as intended audience, and vertical industry addressed. An illustration follows.

The Siemens AG ShareNet system[1] is essentially an intranet covering both codified and personalized knowledge. The ShareNet organization consists of a global editor, contributors, a decision committee for the evolution of ShareNet, and about 100 ShareNet managers, one in each country, who support contributors in capturing project experiences and marketing know-how. These managers drive the development of reusable knowledge. They spend 50% of their time on this function and are supported by an 18-strong central team. Siemens rates the taxonomy as being very important. They came up with a shared taxonomy for business processes. The incentive system is also quite interesting: ShareNet shares are given for urgent responses, discussion group responses, objects published, reuse feedback, and so on. A total of 3500 shares means that an individual receives an invitation to attend a conference. Siemens continues to have a KM department whose main responsibilities are to set up communities and provide a central support service to these communities. For example, there are corporate-funded CoP kickoff workshops. Their initial budget was $600,000 and is now $10 million, mainly in the form of ShareNet Managers' time.

Source: BEEP Knowledge System Case Study. http://www.beepknowledgesystem.org.

Information professionals, as well as journalists and professional writers, are the ideal candidates to capture knowledge and develop knowledge taxonomies, as it is within the realm of library and information science skill sets. Capturing organizational knowledge is almost always a process of adding value to the original content. Restructuring and rewriting, for example, are ways of directly increasing the value of organizational knowledge assets. By using professional writers, key information can be distilled into a more effective form. This process will also identify knowledge gaps and provide a mechanism for filling them. The act of analyzing and reworking the information will help clarify what the organization knows and what it needs to know. It is neither necessarily cheap nor easy, but it will capture key knowledge, improve consistency, and enhance generalizability throughout the organization. Writing good content is the best way of creating knowledge assets within an organization.

STRATEGIC IMPLICATIONS OF KNOWLEDGE CAPTURE AND CODIFICATION

Knowledge capture and codification are particularly critical when an issue of knowledge continuity arises (e.g., Field, 2003; Beazley, Boenisch, and Harden, 2003). Whereas knowledge management is concerned with capturing and sharing know-how valuable to colleagues performing similar jobs throughout a company, knowledge continuity management focuses on passing critical knowledge from exiting employees to their replacements. Whereas most of the literature focuses on transfer of this departing individual knowledge to successors of the departing individual, the problem is not so localized. Knowledge continuity should not only focus on the specific knowledge to be transferred between individuals but should also address strategic concerns at group and organizational levels. The organization needs to be aware of its critical knowledge assets; these are captured and codified in the form of a knowledge map or taxonomy. Organizations also need to take into account the impact of a departure on the communities to which they belong, whether the departure is due to a baby boomer retiring or other reasons. Their leaving may literally leave a serious gap in the fabric of the community network.

At its core, knowledge continuity management is about communication (Field, 2003)—employees need to understand just what it is that they know, that others need to know, and why this content needs to be shared with their peers. The more critical a job is to the company, the more important it is that it is part of a continuity management system. The more sophisticated, complex, and tacit the worker's knowledge, the more difficult it will be to pass on—and even more important that it be passed on. These raise important questions concerning security and access, in addition to a code of ethics that ensures that all concerned are treated in a professional manner.

Field (2003) makes a number of recommendations, including:

- Set up a knowledge profile for all critical workers.
- Foster mentoring relationships.
- Encourage communities of practice.
- Ensure that knowledge sharing is rewarded.
- Protect people's privacy.
- Create a bridge to organizational memory for long-term retention of the valuable content.

PRACTICAL IMPLICATIONS OF KNOWLEDGE CAPTURE AND CODIFICATION

Although the benefits of capturing tacit knowledge and codifying explicit knowledge are obvious to organizations, they are often fairly vague at the level of the individual knowledge worker. The continuing prevalence of the "knowledge is power" paradigm makes it difficult to "sell" employees on the importance of having their knowledge retained by the organization as a future hedge for when they are no longer working there. Knowledge is a curious asset—one that cannot be owned but is merely borrowed or rented. Some knowledge remains within the organization when employees leave, but this needs to be the "right" kind of knowledge and workers will need to be able to access and make use of it.

Recommendations for promoting knowledge capture and codification follow.

1. *Acknowledge knowledge contributors.* Turning tacit knowledge into explicit knowledge is difficult for many users and often meets with resistance, despite the obvious benefits. Acknowledge workers who not only create original content, but also help improve the content over time by adding context from customer interactions. KM software should offer reports to identify those who are contributing, or help to tap the tacit knowledge by building profiles of experts based on their contributions.

2. *Remember to forget.* The role of unlearning or reframing cannot be emphasized enough (e.g., Fiol and Lyles, 1985). The organizational knowledge base should not be viewed as unlimited storage space to be filled. Although there may not be any technological constraints, certainly some conceptual constraints need to be taken into consideration. Unlearning involves disposing of old frameworks and breaking away from the status quo—a form of double-loop learning. Van de Ven and Polley (1992) suggest that unlearning involves responses to mistakes, and failures can play an important role in knowledge acquisition and deployment—if they are viewed as learning opportunities. As Thomas Edison (1847–1931) put it: "I have not failed. I've just found 10,000 ways that won't work."

3. *Don't spill any knowledge during transfer.* Conversion of tacit to explicit knowledge must be accomplished without significant loss of knowledge (e.g., Brown and Duguid, 2000). The advantages of communicability do not always outweigh the disadvantages of "knowledge leakage." It is just as valuable to maintain a link to knowers—individuals within the organization who are adept at making use of complex knowledge. The goal is to carry out the "right" amount of knowledge acquisition and codification.

4. *Remember the paradox of knowledge value.* The more tacit knowledge is, the more value it holds. Tacit knowledge is generally of greater value and of greater competitive advantage to a firm. It may be in the firm's interest to maintain that content at a certain minimal level of tacitness so that it is not easily acquired or imitated by others.

KEY POINTS

- Firms need to adapt and adjust to some degree if they are to survive.
- Firms need to learn—the question is whether they do so in an ad hoc informal manner or whether there is deliberate intention to learn.
- Emergent knowledge acquisition (Malhotra, 2000) is spontaneous and unplanned. Because it is haphazard, there is no guarantee that anything will be retained in the organization's corporate memory.
- Methodical, systematic, intentional knowledge acquisition is of great strategic value to a firm.
- Knowledge bases must be populated and contents deployed in order to maximize efficiency and effectiveness throughout the organization.

DISCUSSION POINTS

1. Why is it difficult to directly codify tacit knowledge?
2. What are some of the pitfalls that may be encountered in capturing tacit knowledge? How would you address these pitfalls?
3. What is the purpose of a learning history? What are its key components?
4. What are the major taxonomic approaches to codifying knowledge that has been captured? What sorts of criteria would help you decide which one(s) to use in a given organization? How would you maintain such a taxonomy?
5. Define knowledge continuity management and discuss its strategic implications for knowledge capture and codification.

NOTE

[1] CoPs 2000 Conference, UK.

REFERENCES

Aesop's Fables (1968). G. F. Townsend, Trans. NJ: Doubleday and Co. (Original work published 1544).

Argyris, C., and Schon, D. (1978). *Organizational learning: a theory of action perspective.* New York: McGraw-Hill.

Beazley, H., Boenisch, J., and Harden, D. (2003). *Continuity management: preserving corporate knowledge and productivity when employees leave.* New York: John Wiley & Sons.

Brown, J., and Duguid, P. (2000, May–June). Balancing act: how to capture knowledge without killing it. *Harvard Business Review*, 3–7.

Bush, V. (1945). As we may think. *Atlantic Monthly, 176*(1): 101–108.

Cohen, W., and Levinthal, D. (1990). Absorptive capacity: a new perspective on learning and innovation. *Administrative Science Quarterly, 35*: 128–152.

Cope, M. (2000). *Know your value? Value what you know.* New York: Financial Times Prentice Hall.

Crossan, M., Lane, W., and White, R. (1999). An organizational learning framework: from intuition to institution. *Academy of Management. The Academy of Management Review 24*(3): 522–537.

Denning, S. (2001). *The springboard: how storytelling ignites action in knowledge-era organizations.* Boston: Butterworth-Heinemann.

Dodgson, M. (1993). Organizational learning: a review of some literatures. *Organization Studies, 14*(3): 375–394.

Feigenbaum, E. (1989). Toward the library of the future. *Long Range Planning, 22*(1): 122.

Field, A. (2003, April). When employees leave the company, how can you make sure their expertise doesn't? *Harvard Management Communication Letter.*

Fiol, C., and Lyles, M. (1985). Organizational learning. *Academy of Management Review, 10*: 803–813.

Frappaolo, C. (2004). What is your knowledge IQ? Intelligent Portals. Available online at http://www.intelligentkm.com/feature/08/feat1.jhtml?_requestid=4287.

Gammack, J., and Young, R. (1985). Psychological techniques for eliciting expert knowledge. In M. Bramer (Ed.), *Research and development in expert systems* (pp. 105–112). London: Cambridge University Press.

George, T., and Kolbasuk, M. (2003, March 10). E-learning helps companies capture the knowledge of retiring employees and gain competitive edge. *Educational Advantage*. Retrieved from www.informationweek.com.

Hayes-Roth, F., Waterman, D., and Lenat, D. (1983). *Building expert systems*. Reading, MA: Addison-Wesley.

Huber, G. (1991). Organizational learning: the contributing processes and a review of the literatures. *Organizational Science, 2*: 88–117.

Inkpen, A. (1995). *The management of international joint ventures*. New York: Routledge.

Inkpen, A., and Beamish, P. (1997). Knowledge, bargaining power, and the instability of international joint ventures. *Academy of Management Review, 22*: 177–202.

Kelly, G. (1955). *The psychology of personal constructs*. New York: W. W. Norton.

Keritsis, G. (2001). Knowledge management—digital cloning (KES). *IT Toolbox Knowledge Management*. Retrieved from http://knowledgemanagement.ittoolbox.com/documents/document.asp?i=1156.

Kruskal, J. (1977). Multidimensional scaling and other methods for discovering structure. In K. Enslein, A. Ralson, and H. S. Wilf (Eds.), *Statistical methods for digital computers*. No. 07-011. London: Sage Publishers.

Leake, D., Maguitman, A., Reichherzer, T., Canas, A., Carvalho, M., Arguedas, M., Brenes, S., and Eskridge, T. (2003). Aiding knowledge capture by searching for extensions of knowledge models. In *Proceedings, K-Cap '03*, October 23–25, 2003. Sanibel Island, FL: ACM.

Malhotra, Y. (2000). *Knowledge management and virtual organizations*. London: Idea Group Publishing.

McGraw, K., and Harrison-Briggs, K. (1989). *Knowledge acquisition: principles and guidelines*. Englewood Cliffs, NJ: Prentice Hall.

McGraw, K., and Seale, M. (1987). Structured knowledge acquisition techniques for combat aviation. In *Proceedings, NAECON'87, 4*: 1340–1348, Dayton, Ohio.

Mintzberg, H. (1990). Strategy formation: schools of thought. In J. Frederickson (Ed.), *Perspectives of strategic management*. New York: Harper Business.

Moorman, C., and Miner, A. (1997). The impact of organizational memory on new product performance and creativity. *Journal of Marketing Research, 34*: 91–106.

Nelson, R., and Winter, S. (1982). *An evolutionary theory of economic change*. Cambridge, MA: Belknap Press.

Nonaka, I., and Takeuchi, H. (1995). *The knowledge creating company*. New York: Oxford University Press.

Oppenheim, A. (1966). *Questionnaire design and attitude measurement*. New York: Basic Books.

Parsaye, K. (1988). Acquiring and verifying knowledge automatically. *AI Expert, 3*(5): 48–63.

Pennings, J., Barkema, H., and Douma, S. (1994). Organizational learning and diversification. *Academy of Management Journal, 37*: 608–640.

Roberts-Witt, S. (2002, March 26). A "Eureka" moment at Xerox. *PC Magazine*. Available at http://www.pcmag.com/article2/0,4149,28792,00.asp.

Roth, G., and Kleiner, A. (2000). Developing organizational memory through learning histories. In James W. Cortada and John A. Woods (Eds.), *The knowledge management yearbook 2000–2001* (pp. 123–144). Burlington, MA: Butterworth-Heinemann.

Schreiber, G., Akkermans, H., Anjewierden, A., de Hoog, R., Shadbolt, N., Van de Velde, W., and Wielinga, B. (2000). *Knowledge engineering and management: the commonKADS methodology.* Cambridge, MA: MIT Press.

Schvaneveldt, R., Durso, F., and Dearholt, T. (1985). Pathfinder scaling with network structures. Memorandum in Computer and Cognitive Science, MCCS-85-9, Computing Research Laboratory, New Mexico State University.

Shadbolt, N., O'Hara, K., and Crow, L. (1999). The experimental evaluation of knowledge acquisition techniques and methods: history, problems and new directions. *International Journal of Human-Computer Studies,* 51(4): 729–755.

Shaw, M. (1981). *Recent advances in personal construct theory.* New York: Academic Press.

Smith, L. (2000, December–January). Knowledge discovery, capture and creation. *Bulletin of the American Society for Information Science,* 26(2).

Snowden, D. (2001). Narrative patterns: the perils and possibilities of using story in organizations. Available at http://www.kwork.org/Resources/narrative.pdf.

Sole, D., and Wilson, D. (2002). Storytelling in organizations: the power and traps of using stories to share knowledge in organizations. *The Knowledge Management Advantage.* Retrieved February 23, 2004, from http://www.kmadvantage.com/docs/km_articles/Storytelling_in_Organizations.pdf.

Spender, J-C. (1996). Making knowledge the basis of a dynamic theory of the firm. *Strategic Management Journal,* 17: 45–62.

Starbuck, W. (1992). Learning by knowledge intensive firms. *Journal of Management Studies,* 29: 713–740.

Svenson, O. (1979). Process descriptions of decision making. *Organizational Behavior and Human Performance,* 23: 86–112.

Swap, W., Leonard, D., Shields, M., and Abrams, L. (2001). Using mentoring and storytelling to transfer knowledge in the workplace. *Journal of Management Information Systems* 18(1): 95–114.

Van de Ven, A., and Polley, D. (1992). Learning while innovating. *Organization Science,* 3: 92–116.

Walsh, J., and Ungson, G. (1991). Organizational memory. *Academy of Management Review,* 16: 57–91.

Zietsma, C., Winn, M., Branzei, O., and Vertinsky, I. (2002). The war of the woods: facilitators and impediments of organizational learning processes. *British Journal of Management,* 13: S61–S74.

KNOWLEDGE SHARING AND COMMUNITIES OF PRACTICE

Knowledge exists to be imparted.

Ralph Waldo Emerson (1803–1882)

This chapter addresses the social nature of knowledge, knowledge sharing, and communities of practice. A number of important conceptual frameworks are presented to examine the social construction of meaning. Knowledge-sharing groups such as communities of practice are placed in historical context, and their evolution in organizations is described with particular emphasis on the development of social capital. Techniques and technologies such as social networks are presented as a means of visualizing and analyzing knowledge flows during knowledge-sharing activities, and some common barriers to knowledge sharing are described.

LEARNING OBJECTIVES

1. Describe the key components of a community of practice.
2. Outline the major phases in the life cycle of a community and the corresponding information and knowledge management needs for each.
3. Define the major roles and responsibilities in a community of practice, with particular emphasis on the integration of library and information professionals' skills.
4. Analyze the flow of knowledge in a community of practice using appropriate tools and techniques to identify enablers and obstacles to knowledge sharing.
5. Discuss how communities can be linked to organizational memory in order to foster organizational learning and innovation.

Once knowledge has been captured and codified, it needs to be shared and disseminated throughout the organization (see Figure 5-1).

With the advent of personal computers and the World Wide Web, it seems to be implicitly assumed that all web users are good researchers or searchers. Unfortunately, this has not been accompanied by any type of training or what is sometimes referred to as "information literacy," which is defined as "a set of abilities requiring individuals to recognize when information is needed and have the ability to locate, evaluate and use effectively the needed information" (ALA, 1989). "Information seeking" rarely appears as a requirement in job descriptions, and yet, International Data Corporation (IDC) (Feldman, 2004) estimates that knowledge workers spend from 15 to 35% of their time searching for information. These workers typically succeed in finding what they seek less than 50% of the time. At the same time, economists have raised the alarm about the "productivity paradox," which refers to a surprising decline in productivity (as measured by standard indices), despite massive investment in computers (Harris, 1994).

This means that although 80 to 85% of a company's information is hard-to-access tacit knowledge, it does not appear that explicit knowledge is any easier to find and use. One IDC estimate (Feldman, 2004) found that 90% of a company's accessible information is used only once. The amount of time spent reworking or re-creating information because it has not been found or, worse, going ahead and making decisions based on incomplete information is increasing at an alarming rate. The IDC study estimates that an organization with 1000 knowledge workers loses a minimum of $6 million per year in time spent just searching for information. The cost of reworking information because it has not been found costs that organization a further $12 million a year. We can only imagine but not yet calculate the increase in creativity and original thinking that might be unleashed if knowledge workers had more time to think instead of futilely trying to find existing information.

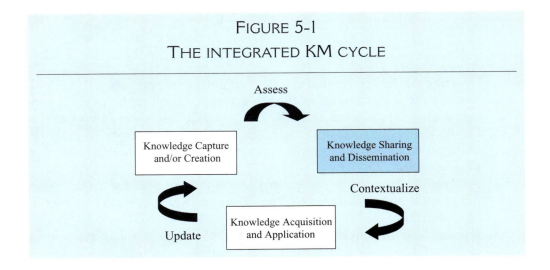

FIGURE 5-1
THE INTEGRATED KM CYCLE

THE COST OF NOT FINDING INFORMATION

The annual cost of a poorly designed knowledge base interface such as an intranet can be easily calculated using the Excellent Intranet Cost Analyzer (available from http://www.dack.com/web/cost_analyzer.html). There is a cost to not finding information. Although it is impossible to measure the exact cost of employees not finding information on a company's intranet, the tool below gives a ballpark figure.

Instructions:

1. Enter the number of company employees.
2. Enter the average number of intranet pages each employee visits per day.
3. Enter the average number of seconds of confusion per page a company's intranet users will experience. That is, the number of seconds a user says, "This isn't what I'm looking for," or "Dammit! I'm lost." A typical range is between 5 and 20 seconds.
4. Enter the average employee's annual salary.
5. Push the Calculate button.

In 2000, the IBM Institute conducted a survey of 40 managers at large accounting organizations to identify the sources of information people used in organizations that had a well-developed knowledge management system or infrastructure (Bartlett, 2000). The results showed that people still first turned to people in order to find information, solve problems, and make decisions. In fact, the company knowledge base was ranked only fourth among the five choices for preferred sources of information, as shown in Table 5-1.

Cross and Parker (2004) found that people are the most critical conduits of information and knowledge. Knowledge workers typically spend a third of their time looking for information and helping their colleagues do the same. A knowledge worker is five times more likely to turn to another person rather than an impersonal source such as a database or knowledge management systems. Only one in five knowledge workers consistently finds the

TABLE 5-1
RESULTS OF THE IBM INSTITUTE SURVEY

Information Source	Number of respondents who chose this source	% of respondents who chose this source
People	34	85%
Prior material	16	40%
Web	10	25%
Knowledge base	4	12%
Other	4	12%

information needed to do their jobs, and Cross and Parker (2004) have found that knowledge workers spend more time re-creating existing information they were unaware of than creating original material.

A similar type of study was undertaken with a large aviation company in the United States. This longitudinal study, which took place over seven years, studied the ways individuals in this large organization sought out and found information. The research team actually sat down with and observed highly skilled professionals as they went about their daily work. Not only did these workers prefer to contact other people in order to find, retrieve, and make use of information, but this also turned out to be a more successful strategy to use.

Other people are the preferred source of information for a number of reasons. One is of course that it is often faster, but this is not the only reason. When we turn to another person, we not only end up with the information we were looking for but we also learn where it is to be found, how to reformulate our question or query, whether we were on the right track, and where we strayed. Last but not least, the information is coming to us from a known and usually trusted, credible source. In other words, people are the best means of getting not only a direct answer but "metaknowledge" about our search target and our search capabilities. Talking to other people provides a highly valuable learning activity that is primarily a tacit–tacit knowledge transfer, for this type of knowledge is seldom rendered explicit, nor is it captured in any form of document.

All these studies point to one key dimension, and that is that learning is a predominantly social event (Cohen and Prusak, 2001). Present-day organizations have difficulty providing opportunities for such social one-to-one knowledge exchanges to continue to exist in their traditional form—that is, as informal hallway, water cooler, coffee machine, or even designated smoking area chats due to the large number of employees and/or the fact that they may not all be in close proximity to one another. Technology offers a new medium through which employees who share similar professional interests, problems, and responsibilities can share knowledge. This is typically through e-mail groups, discussion groups, and other interactions in some sort of virtual shared workspace that is typically hosted by the organization's intranet. These groups are often referred to as communities of practice (CoPs).

A community of practice refers to "a group of people having common identity, professional interests and that undertake to share, participate and establish a fellowship" (American Heritage Dictionary, Pickett, 2000). A community of practice can also be defined as a group of people, along with their shared resources and dynamic relationships, who assemble to make use of shared knowledge, in order to enhance learning and create a shared value for the group (Seufert, von Krogh, and Bach, 1999; Adams and Freeman, 2000). The term *community* suggests that these groups are not constrained by typical geographic, business unit, or functional boundaries but rather by common tasks, contexts, and interests. The word "practice" implies knowledge in action— how individuals *actually* perform their jobs on a day-to-day basis as opposed to more formal policies and procedures that reflect how work *should* be performed. The concept of a community of practice as a knowledge-sharing community within organizational settings originated with Lave and Wenger (1991). Many organizations have implemented communities of practice, as illustrated in the following vignettes on Ericsson and ICL.

ERICSSON

Jumping straight into deploying knowledge management technology was a temptation for telecommunications supplier Ericsson Canada Inc. "We have a tendency to grab technology first," says Anders Hemre, director of enterprise performance at the company's Montreal research unit. But before doing so, Ericsson officials wisely took a step back to look at the company's culture, values, and people.

Through surveys, Hemre found that the research group's growth-doubling to 1700 workers in four years by 1999 had undercut the sense of community. So Ericsson identified informal groups that had formed around work-related topics, such as Java programming or the mobile Internet, and worked to help those cliques expand and form new groups to further disseminate ideas and information. People gather informally to discuss work outside their cubicles every day, but to capture that and put a little bit of structure to it to help it along, without over-engineering or over-managing it, is the trick.

Once the groups were identified by talking to employees in the various research divisions, Ericsson appointed a community leader for each group and gave workers time to meet on a regular basis. There was no agenda for these meetings, which still take place. A community is formed for learning, but it is not necessarily organized or managed heavy-handedly.

Organik requires employees to create profiles by filling out a form that Ericsson stores in an Oracle database. When a person searching for an expert finds a match in the database, Organik will send an e-mail notifying that person that his help is being requested.

Source: Hemre, A. (2005).

ICL

ICL Ltd. has changed its entire organization into communities that fall into two types: professional and interest. All employees belong to a professional community dependent on their function (Sales, Project Management, Consultancy, etc.), and any employee can belong to one or more communities of interest (KM, Quality Improvement, etc.). For example, a consultant will belong to the professional community of consultants and work and develop within this framework. The consultant can

Continued

also specialize in KM and therefore belong to the KM community of interest where members share, discuss, and develop in the KM field. The KM community meets at regular intervals, guest speakers are invited to meetings, and lots of tacit knowledge exchange takes place. It develops into a true community spirit. The interest community will typically regulate itself and have an administrator to facilitate the web space and other coordination activities.

Source: Lank (1997).

Desmarest (1997) distinguished two basic orientations to KM: information-based (codifying and storing content) and people or interaction-based (connecting knowers). As we saw in Chapter 4, information-based approaches focus primarily on knowledge capture and codification. The information-based approach tends to emphasize explicit knowledge rather than tacit and favors the externalization objective. The learner is viewed as a *tabula rasa*, or blank slate, into which content is simply poured in. Rodin's "The Thinker" is an image that captures this notion well—an individual, alone, deep in thought. This narrow focus, or "tunnel vision," neglects context, background, history, common knowledge, and social resources. As Seely Brown puts it: "information and individual are inevitably and always part of rich social networks" (Seely Brown and Duguid, 2002, p. xxv). Critics maintain that this oversimplifies knowledge and, in particular, ignores the social context of knowledge (e.g., Seely Brown and Duguid, 2002; Conrad and Poole, 2002).

People or interaction-based approaches, on the other hand, place a great deal of emphasis on knowledge-sharing interactions, which in today's organizations tend to be associated with communities of practice (Thomas, Kellogg, and Erickson, 2001). This social constructivist approach to learning and knowledge transfer seems to be much better suited to the discipline of knowledge management.

THE SOCIAL NATURE OF KNOWLEDGE

Knowledge management needs to view knowledge as something that is actively constructed in a social setting (McDermott, 2000). Group members produce knowledge by their interactions, and a group memory is created. Social constructivism views knowledge not as an objective entity but as a subjective, social artifact (Berger and Luckmann, 1966). Social constructivists argue that knowledge is produced through the shared understandings that emerge through social interactions. As individuals and groups of people communicate, they mutually influence each other's views and create or change shared constructions of reality (Klimecki and Lassleben, 1999). The social constructivist perspective views knowledge as context dependent and thus as something that cannot be completely separated from "knowers" (Lave and Wenger, 1991). Context helps distinguish between knowledge management and document management: whereas document management can be carried out in a more or less automated manner, knowledge management cannot be accomplished without involving people as well as tangible content.

Huysman and deWit (2002) describe a collective acceptance of shared knowledge as being the key method of generating value to the organization. Until knowledge is collectively accepted and institutionalized across the organization, organizational-level learning cannot occur and organizational memory cannot be developed. Ortenblad (2002) explained that, unlike the functionalist paradigm in which learning starts in the individual, the interpretive paradigm suggests that learning begins in the relationships between individuals. As the community grows and its knowledge base is more broadly shared across the organization, the community's practices become regularly, widely, and sufficiently adopted so as to be described as institutionalized knowledge (Huysman and DeWit, 2002).

Since individual memory is limited, we need to embed this knowledge in useful, more permanent forms such as documents and e-mails. This institutionalized knowledge then becomes an organizational legacy that remains in the corporate memory for subsequent generations. It is critical to remember that the context of each item of knowledge must also be captured: when it occurred, who is knowledgeable about it, who submitted it, and so on. Without this context, the knowledge product is not complete and cannot be successfully used, applied, or even understood. An illustration is provided in the vignette Thomas & Betts.

THOMAS & BETTS

Networks, by definition, connect everyone to everyone.[1] Hierarchies, by definition, do not; rather, they create formal channels of communication and authority. When a network becomes the main means by which information is conveyed and work gets done in an organization, our hierarchical crutches are knocked down. Rank is unclear. Networks operate informally with few rules; they depend on trust. The first dimension of trust is competence: I can trust you if you are good at what you do. Second, trust needs a community. Networks naturally spawn internal groups of like-minded individuals. When these emerge around a common discipline, they are communities of practice. Communities of practice create and validate competence. The boss may not know who the best worker is, but the community will always know.

At Thomas & Betts Corporation, a $2.2 billion electrical parts maker in Memphis, Tennessee, motivation is decidedly nontechnical. Board games in which teams compete in solving business problems teach managers the importance of sharing ideas and information. "It gives employees a good sense of the roles and functions other people play in the company," says

Continued

Gary Bodam, director of training and development. Once they realize that their willingness to share knowledge affects the bottom line in games, they are more open to making changes in how they operate in the real world, he says. But Thomas & Betts is also using technology to foster knowledge sharing. The company runs an E-learning-management system from ThoughtWare Technologies Inc. that tracks employees' continuing education, such as public speaking or engineering. The data is logged in a Systems-Applications-Products human resources system that can be used by managers looking for the best candidates for jobs. As Bodam states, "It's all become part of the overall knowledge base by which we'll try to move the organization forward."

SOCIOGRAMS AND SOCIAL NETWORK ANALYSIS

Social network analysis (SNA) is the mapping and measuring of relationships and flows between people, groups, organizations, computers, or other information/knowledge processing entities (Krebs, 2000). The nodes in the network are the people and groups, while the links show relationships or flows between the nodes (see Figure 5-2). SNA provides both a visual and a mathematical analysis of complex human systems to identify patterns of interaction such as average number of links between people in an organization or community, number of subgroups, information bottlenecks, knowledge brokers, and knowledge hoarders.

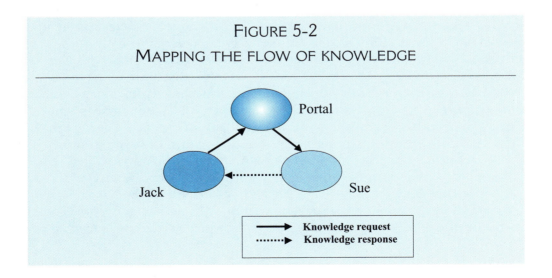

FIGURE 5-2

MAPPING THE FLOW OF KNOWLEDGE

In the context of knowledge management, social network analysis (SNA) enables relationships between people to be mapped in order to identify knowledge flows: from whom do people seek information and knowledge? With whom do they share their information and knowledge? In contrast to an organizational chart that shows formal relationships—who works where and who reports to whom—a social network analysis chart shows informal relationships—who knows who and who shares information and knowledge with whom (see Figure 5-3). It therefore allows managers to visualize and understand the many relationships that can either facilitate or impede knowledge creation and sharing (Anklam, 2003). Because these relationships are normally invisible, SNA is sometimes referred to as an organizational X ray, showing the real networks that operate underneath the surface organizational structure (Donath, 2002; Freeman, 2004).

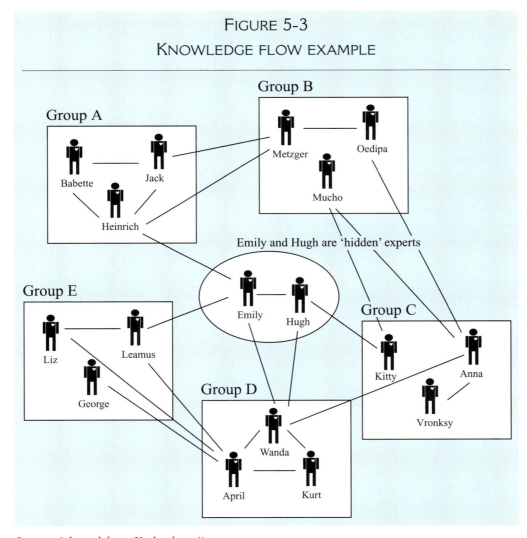

FIGURE 5-3

KNOWLEDGE FLOW EXAMPLE

Source: Adapted from Krebs, http://www.orgnet.com.

Once social relationships and knowledge flows can be seen, they can be evaluated and measured. Network theory is sympathetic with systems theory and complexity theory. Social networks are also characterized by a distinctive methodology encompassing techniques for collecting data, statistical analysis, visual representation, and so on. The results of social network analyses can be used at the level of individuals, departments, or organizations to identify information bottlenecks and to accelerate the flow of knowledge and information across functional and organizational boundaries. A social network should be regarded as a dynamic or moving target and will need to be constructed more than once. For example, the data gathering and analysis process can provide a baseline against which you can then plan and prioritize the appropriate changes and interventions to improve the social connections and knowledge flows within the group or network.

The process of social network analysis typically involves the use of questionnaires and/or interviews to gather information about the relationships between a defined group or network of people. The responses gathered are then mapped using a software tool specifically designed for the purpose. Key stages of the process will typically include:

- Identifying the network of people to be analyzed (e.g., team, workgroup, department).
- Clarifying objectives and formulating hypotheses and questions.
- Developing the survey methodology and designing the questionnaire.
- Surveying the individuals in the network to identify the relationships and knowledge flows between them.
- Using a software mapping tool to visually map out the network.
- Analyzing the map and the problems and opportunities highlighted using interviews and/or workshops.
- Designing and implementing actions to bring about desired changes.
- Mapping the network again after a suitable period of time.

In order for SNA maps to be meaningful, it is important to know what information you need to gather in order to build a relevant picture of your group or network. Good survey design and questionnaire design are therefore key considerations. Questions will be typically based on factors such as:

- Who knows who and how well?
- How well do people know each other's knowledge and skills?
- Who or what gives people information about *xyz*?
- What resources do people use to find information/feedback/ideas/advice about *xyz*?
- What resources do people use to share information about *xyz*?

Although there are quite a number of different SNA tools, there is a need for a user-friendly end-to-end solution that can be applied in a variety of business settings (Dalkir and Jenkins, 2004). Existing tools have little support, are usually proprietary, have little track record, and tend to be heavily weighted toward the statistical analysis of data once it has been gathered, with little support for the initial data collection activities.

Community Yellow Pages

All communities are about connections between people, and these connections are often used to develop corporate yellow pages or an expertise location system. Though initially community based, such expertise locators can eventually be integrated to form a corporatewide yellow pages. Lamont (2003) emphasizes their contribution to organizational learning initiatives such as facilitating mentoring programs, identifying knowledge gaps, and providing both performance support and follow-up to formal training activities. Figures 5-4 and 5-5 illustrate a typical application for a large, distributed European publishing company.

A wide range of software exists for the development of corporate yellow pages (see Table 5–2 for some examples). Most create an initial profile of an individual's expertise based on an analysis of published documents, questionnaires, or interviews, while others focus on e-mails. These are very popular KM applications, and they are often the first KM implementation a company will undertake primarily because they can be developed fairly quickly (on the order of one to two months), and they can provide almost instantaneous benefits to individuals, communities, and the organization itself.

Yellow pages, or expertise location systems, were among the earliest KM applications, and they remain one of the best ways to initiate wider-scale knowledge sharing in organizations. Two examples are from Texaco and British Petroleum.

FIGURE 5-4
EXAMPLE OF A CORPORATE YELLOW PAGES

Directories	Libraries	Discussion Area	Support
Products	Best Practices Library	Discussion Themes	Glossary of Terms
Projects	Lessons Learned	Project Management	Frequently Asked Questions
External Suppliers	Stories	Risk Management	
Publishing Companies	Training Modules		
Network of Experts			

FIGURE 5-5

EXAMPLE OF A CORPORATE YELLOW PAGES (CONTINUED)

Network of Experts

Function	Geographic Area	Business Area	Expertise
Vice President	Northeast	Sales	Content Management
Director	West Coast	Operations	Electronic Production
Line Manager	Midwest	Distribution	Knowledge Management
Operator	South	Finance	Publishing Management

Expertise		
Content Management		
Jane Dennys	Head Office	555 434-4564
Will Jameson	Regional Office 6	555 212-3212
Electronic Production		
Jan Zariski	Regional Office 6	555 212-3233
Sarah Marxman	Regional Office 6	555 212-3232

TABLE 5-2

SOFTWARE TO DEVELOP YELLOW PAGES OR EXPERTISE LOCATION SYSTEMS

Name	Description	Website
Kamoon's Connect	Profiles set up by analyzing unstructured repositories to identify documented expertise	http://www.kamoon.com/
AskMe	Web-based questionnaire used on a voluntary basis; can track Q&A to identify any knowledge gaps	http://www.askmecorp.com/
Sopheon's Organik	Q&A format, provides answers to questions and then stores the answers in a repository for future reference	http://www.sopheon.com/
Tacit's KnowledgeMail	Learns about people automatically through analysis of e-mails as well as document repositories and Lotus Notes databases. Search results include experts and links to content.	http://www.tacit.com/

Texaco's knowledge management arsenal includes PeopleNet (Gonsalves and Zaino, 2001), a custom-built application that lets employees build a personal profile and post it as a web page on the company's intranet. The content of the profile does not have to be purely work-related: pictures and hobby lists coexist alongside users' summaries of their job expertise. The PeopleNet content and the company's e-mail systems are linked through KnowledgeMail from Tacit Knowledge Systems Inc., which monitors an employee's e-mail, moving phrases that seem to reflect a person's expertise on a particular subject into a private profile accessible only to that employee. The person then chooses which phrases to publish in a public directory to help others distinguish him or her as a potential expert in an area. Someone searching for an expert in marketing crude oil, for example, would get a list of people associated with that phrase; clicking on a name in that list would call up a profile of the person in KnowledgeMail, as well as a link to the person's PeopleNet profile.

Three hundred people at Texaco have used KnowledgeMail through a pilot program in its first year and a half. It is considered to be a successful KM application. John Old, the company's director of information, recounts a meeting in which Texaco executives were sharing ideas on knowledge management with a business partner. In demonstrating KnowledgeMail, a colleague typed the word "wireless," and the top name on the retrieved list was a systems architect who was in the room but had never been identified as someone knowledgeable in wireless technology. "In any large company, there are lots of conversations in e-mail that you're not aware of, and there are lots of hidden experts," Old says.

BP's yellow pages[2] are entirely bottom up. About 20,000 (of 80,000) have personal pages. It takes about 10 minutes to produce one using a form-filling approach, which contains a self-appraisal of skills and interest. No one vets the content, but people rarely oversell themselves! People who leave BP may still have a page. Every 3 seconds someone makes a connection. The yellow pages are widely embedded in the BP intranet; they are integrated into the search environment and are now a part of how they do business.

Source: Cohen, 1999.

KNOWLEDGE-SHARING COMMUNITIES

The notion of a community is not necessarily a new concept. As far back as 1887, writers such as the German sociologist Ferdinand Tonnies compared and contrasted the more direct, more total, and more significant interactions to be found in a community as opposed to the more formal, more abstract, and more instrument-driven relationships to be found in a society (Loomis, 1957). Tonnies argued that there are two basic forms of human will: the essential will, which is the underlying, organic, or instinctive driving force; and arbitrary will, which is deliberative, purposive, and future (goal) oriented. Tonnies called groups that form around essential will, in which membership is self-fulfilling, *Gemeinschaft* (often translated as community). Groups in which membership was sustained by an instrumental goal or definite end he termed *Gesellschaft* (often translated as society). Gemeinschaft was exemplified by the family or neighborhood, and Gesellschaft by the city or the state.

More recently, Anselm Strauss (1978), another sociologist, described Internet communities as "social worlds." Even before there was an Internet, there were "invisible colleges," which consisted of academics, who though spread out around the world, nonetheless developed a sense of collective identity with their colleagues, their field, and their professional position within that field via constant communications (Price, 1963). Their shared communications and mental models gave rise to a discipline, a professional group. Sharing and circulating knowledge appears to be an age-old effective social glue. These early communities were made possible by the printing press and are sometimes referred to as "textual" communities because they primarily circulate written documents. An important characteristic that these early communities share with today's virtual communities is that they organized themselves. The biggest divergence is that whereas documents tend to be fixed, information or knowledge to be shared is fluid in nature.

The first virtual communities emerged about a decade after the establishment of the Internet. The Internet itself was an initiative called ARPANET, which was intended as a means of making it easier for researchers to share large data files. In the early 1980s, a network called USENET was set up to link university computing centers that used the UNIX operating system. One function of USENET was to distribute "news" on various topics throughout the network. Initially, all of the newsgroups focused on technical or scholarly subjects, but so-called alt and rec groups that focused on nontechnical topics such as food, drugs, and music began to appear, which constituted the first evidence of people organizing themselves into virtual networks.

Before long, the number of newsgroups started to grow exponentially. USENET, for example, had 158 newsgroups in 1984. The number grew to 1732 in 1991 and to 10,696 in 1994. Today there are more than 25,000 different newsgroups in existence. The Well, based in the San Francisco Bay Area, flourished as a place where online pioneers could gather to meet and talk with one another and is one of the oldest virtual communities around. Rheingold (1993) was one of the first to assert that online networks were emerging as an important social force that could provide rich and authentic community experiences. Hagel and Armstrong (1997) argued that virtual communities have economic as well as social significance. Like Rheingold, they recognize that virtual communities are based on the affinity among their participants that encourages them to participate in ongoing dialog with each other. Knowledge sharing between participants can generate "webs of personal communication" that reinforce a sense of identification with the community.

Although the literature discusses virtual communities in abundant detail, the technology-mediated interactions were supplanted by a substantial amount of old-fashioned telephone exchanges, face-to-face meetings, and general "neighborliness" (Rheingold, 1993). When videoconferencing first began to be widely used as an alternative to face-to-face business meetings, it was quickly found that this medium worked well but only after participants had met in person and established some sort of social presence. If participants met one another for the first time during a videoconference, or a teleconference for that matter, the interactions were much more awkward and slower, and the knowledge that was exchanged tended to be less significant (Hayden, Hanor, and Harrison, 2001). Psychologists have found that in face-to-face talks, only 7% of the meaning is conveyed by words, while 38% is communicated by intonation and 55% through visual cues and up to 87% of messages are interpreted on a nonverbal, visual level (Telstra, 2000).

Seely Brown (2002) points out the neglect of the social aspects of knowledge sharing when he notes that documents do more than merely carry information. They "help structure society, enabling social groups to form, develop and maintain a sense of shared identity" (p. 189). The community-forming character of the Internet is by now quite well known. In fact, a number of technologies that were originally intended to transmit information, such as the Minitel system in France that used to book travel and served as an electronic phone book, quickly became used as messaging systems between users. Similarly, transactional websites such as eBay and Amazon.com hold value not only in terms of their product offerings but also in the ability of visitors to the site to annotate content and thus communicate with other visitors.

Although technology is a feature of some communities, technological means of interacting are not a necessary component of communities. Technology comes into play when members are more dispersed and when they have fewer occasions to meet face to face. The critical components of a community lie in the sharing of common work problems between members, a membership that sees the clear benefits of sharing knowledge among themselves and that has developed norms of trust, reciprocity, and cooperation.

Types of Communities

All communities share some basic characteristics, regardless of the type of community. Wenger (1998) identifies these characteristics as joint enterprise, mutual engagement, and shared repertoire (see Figure 5-6).

Joint enterprise refers to the glue that binds members together—why they want to interact with one another. Reasons for interacting with one another will typically be a personal goal and contribution toward the community's goal. *Mutual engagement* refers to how members become part of the community.

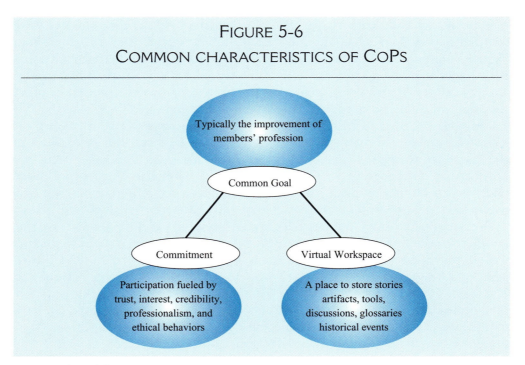

FIGURE 5-6
COMMON CHARACTERISTICS OF CoPs

Typically the improvement of members' profession

Common Goal

Commitment

Virtual Workspace

Participation fueled by trust, interest, credibility, professionalism, and ethical behaviors

A place to store stories artifacts, tools, discussions, glossaries historical events

Source: Adapted from Wenger, 1998.

They do not automatically belong because they say so, because they have a certain job title, or because they know someone. There are membership rules, and each member agrees to carry out certain roles and responsibilities in order to help achieve the goals of the CoP. Finally, a *shared repertoire* refers to the shared workspace in which members can communicate with one another, and store and share knowledge products, their profiles, and so on. The shared repertoire is typically space on a server; it may be an intranet within an organization or on the Internet. What is important is that there is a place for real-time exchanges and asynchronous discussions, and that these interactions leave behind tangible archives—the social capital and intellectual capital created by the community. All communities thus need shared cultural objects, a means of sharing them and a means of storing them.

In other words, networks form because people need one another to reach common goals. Mutual help, assistance, and reciprocity are common to all functioning networks. Another important characteristic is that these networks be not only self-organizing but also self-regulating. For example, no one "decrees" that a community will exist (although many organizations have made this mistake). It is not a top-down formal organization as a task force or project team would be. There is no one person "in charge" of the community, although there may be founding members. Similarly, if someone is in it only for themselves, the other members will quickly realize this, as is illustrated by Hardin's (1968) tragedy of the commons scenario.

TRAGEDY OF THE COMMONS

Picture a pasture open to all. It is to be expected that each herdsman will try to keep as many cattle as possible on the commons. Such an arrangement may work satisfactorily for centuries because tribal wars, poaching, and disease keep the numbers of both man and beast well below the carrying capacity of the land. Finally, however, comes the day of reckoning, that is, the day when the long-desired goal of social stability becomes a reality and logic of the commons remorselessly generates tragedy. As a rational being, each herdsman seeks to maximize his gain. "What is the utility *to me* of adding one more animal to my herd?" Since the herdsman receives all the proceeds from the sale of the additional animal, the positive utility is nearly + 1. The negative impact is the additional overgrazing created by one more animal. However, the effects of overgrazing are shared by all the herdsmen; the negative utility for any particular herdsman is only a fraction of −1. The only sensible course for him to pursue is to add another animal to his herd, and another, and so forth. But this is the conclusion reached by each and every rational herdsman sharing a commons. Therein lies the tragedy.

There are many types of CoPs, and they are typically defined as a function of some common focal points such as:

- A profession such as engineering, law, or medicine.
- A work-related function or process such as production, distribution, marketing, sales, and customer service.
- A recurring, nagging problem situated in a process or function.
- A topic such as technology, knowledge retention, or innovation.
- An industry such as automotive, banking, or healthcare.

A CoP may also be described in terms of its goals, such as the development of best practices or benchmarking. A CoP may be self-organizing or sponsored by the organization. It may also be distinguished on the basis of the type of recognition (or lack thereof) it has from the host organization (Wenger, 1998): unrecognized, bootlegged, legitimized, supported, and institutionalized. These categories often reflect the maturity level of a community, but not all communities will necessarily aspire to become institutionalized (Iverson and McPhee, 2002).

An online community can take many forms, but most such communities will contain:

1. Member-generated content (e.g., profiles, home pages, ratings, reviews).
2. Member-to-member interaction (e.g., discussion forums, member yellow pages).
3. Events (e.g., guest events, expert seminars, virtual meetings, or demos).
4. Outreach (e.g., newsletters, volunteer/leader/mentoring programs, polls/surveys).

It is important to distinguish a community of practice from other groups such as work teams or project groups. Many online communities may be termed communities of interest because they have an open membership that is catalyzed by interest in a common theme such as a hobby. A community of practice is more like a professional organization. CoPs have a business case, a code of ethics, a mission statement, and so forth. They are there for a reason, and they produce results that are of value to the profession. Typically, a CoP goal would have something to do with the improvement of the common profession or professional theme of interest to members. However, the manner in which they are formed is quite unlike a professional organization, as communities self-organize and emerge in a bottom-up manner.

Roles and Responsibilities in CoPs

Communities consist of people, not technology (Cook, 1999). Community members may take an active role by contributing to discussions or providing assistance to other members. This is referred to as "participation." Other members may simply read what others have posted without taking an active role themselves. These types of members used to be referred to as "lurkers," but given the somewhat derogatory connotation of the term, this has been replaced by "legitimate peripheral participation."

In almost every case, the more participation that occurs in the community, the greater the value created for both community members and community creators. However, it is important to keep in mind that in most communities, readers outnumber posters by 10:1 or more. People who visit a community regularly but who do not post anything typically represent 90% or more of the total community participation. Passive members are not really passive in most cases, for they may be actively using and applying the content they have accessed online.

Kim (2000) lists the key roles as (1) visitors, (2) novices, (3) regulars, (4) leaders, and (5) elders.

Visitors may visit once or twice and may or may not join. At this point, they are merely curious and are seeking to find out what the community is all about. *Novices* are new members, who typically keep to themselves at first until they have learned enough about the community and the other members. At this point, they become *regulars*, members who provide regular contributions and who interact with other members on a sustained basis. *Leaders* are members who have the time and energy to take on more official roles such as helping with the operation of the community. *Elders* are akin to subject matter experts: they are familiar with the professional theme and the community, and they have become respected sources of both subject matter knowledge and cultural knowledge. Elders maintain the community history and agree to be consulted from time to time by other community members.

Communities of practice require a number of key roles to be filled. These need not necessarily be a single individual working full-time. More often, they are revolving roles much like everyone taking a turn at being a scribe at business meetings today. However, real work remains to be done in order for the community to succeed, and this translates into real time. Depending on the type of organization, the number of members, and other scope variables, a good rule of thumb is to budget 10 to 20% of a knowledge worker's time as being devoted to CoP work.

Nickols (2000) defines more official community roles. The major CoP roles include a champion, a sponsor, a facilitator, a practice leader, a knowledge service center or office (KSO), and members. The *champion* ensures support at the highest possible level, communicates the purpose, promotes the community, and ensures impact. The *sponsor* serves as the bridge between the CoP and the rest of the formal organization, communicates the company's support for a CoP, and may remove barriers such as time, funding, and other resources. The sponsor is instrumental in establishing the mission and expected outcomes for the community. Community members are recruited for their expertise relevant to the practice or strategic services. They are there to better share knowledge, know-how, and best practices that will benefit the business through active participation. They participate in discussions, raising issues and concerns regarding common needs and requirements, alert other members to any changes in conditions and requirements, are on the lookout for ways to enhance CoP effectiveness (e.g., by recruiting high-value members), and, above all, they learn.

CoP *facilitators* have perhaps the most demanding role. They are responsible for clarifying communications and for making sure that everyone participates and that dissident views are heard and understood. They are the chief organizers of events such as meetings (face-to-face as well as virtual meetings). They administrate all communications by drawing out reticent members, reconciling opposing points of view, posing questions to further discussion, and keeping discussions on topic. The *practice leader* is the acknowledged leader of the CoP "themes." The leader provides thought leadership for the practice or strategic service, validates innovations and best practices, and promotes adherence to them. He or she identifies emerging patterns and trends in CoP activities and knowledge base as well as in other areas that may impact the practice. Leaders resolve conflicts, evaluate CoP performance with respect to expectations, approve memberships, and lead the way in prioritizing issues and improvements to be tackled. CoP practice leaders serve as models to coach other members, or they arrange to provide coaching, and they are always alert to the potential need for CoP changes (e.g., more members, different members, and different member composition).

CoP *knowledge services* are information/knowledge integrators who serve to interface with all CoPs to ensure clarity and lack of duplication of the information disseminated within and from the CoPs. They maintain information-sharing relationships with all CoPs, inform CoP members about relevant activities elsewhere, and inform others about relevant CoP activities. The knowledge center coordinates information from CoP members to avoid duplication, redundancies, and poor quality (e.g., in postings to CoP websites and forums), and they filter knowledge and requests for help (e.g., yellow pages). Finally, all *members* of the CoP share responsibility for marketing and promoting the CoP, generating interest in it, promoting enthusiasm among current members, and demonstrating its value. Everyone must ensure continued support and resources from sponsor(s), recruit high-potential prospective members, and invite them to special CoP events. Members are expected to better leverage the knowledge created and learning generated by the CoP, to write and publish articles or results descriptions in company publications, and to publish articles in external journals or magazines and then distribute them internally.

In addition, some new types of roles arise from CoPs such as membership managers, discussion moderators, knowledge editors, knowledge librarians, archivists, usage analysts, and knowledge brokers. A *CoP membership manager* has to deal with the registration and ongoing membership directory work. A *CoP moderator* is much like a radio/TV show host, serving as a conversation manager who helps keep discussions focused, injects new topics and provocative points of view when discussion lags, and seeds discussion with appropriate content. Moderators must often be critical in order to ensure value generation. A *knowledge editor* collects, sanitizes, and synthesizes content created, and provides a value-added link for the content produced. A *knowledge librarian* or community taxonomist is responsible for organizing and managing the collection of knowledge objects generated by the community. A *knowledge archivist* maintains and organizes content generated by participants over time. A CoP *usage analyst* studies data on participants' behaviors within the community and makes recommendations to the moderator. Finally, a *knowledge broker* is someone who can join up with a number of different communities in order to identify commonalities and redundancies, create synergy, form alliances, and feed in to organizational memory and learning (e.g., map of intellectual assets, yellow pages, or expertise directory, CoP best practices, and lessons learned).

Finally, some new roles and structures will be set up at the organizational level. For example, the World Bank (see: http://www.worldbank.org/ks/) has more than 100 *thematic groups*, which is the term used for communities of practice. A KM Board oversees all CoPs. It is a small central unit (5 members) that has overall coordination and facilitation duties for synergies and redundancies in the CoPs, opportunities for cross-CoP sharing, feeding the organization memory, and assessing the value of each CoP. A governance body (KM Council) is responsible at the corporate level for overall KM policy formulation.

Knowledge management at CIDA (Canadian International Development Agency) was inspired by the World Bank. CIDA has implemented over 400 best practices, lessons learned, and 30 communities of practice (see http://www.acdi-cida.gc.ca/cida_ind.nsf/0/7D4E485700F8511B85256 E910045D3D2?OpenDocument).

Branch-sharing activities are coordinated through the CIDA KM Secretariat. The CIDA KM Secretariat in the Senior VP's office has a staff of four to five, which enables better knowledge sharing within and among branches. This office works closely with two organizations: (1) the Branch KM Leaders group, which has a representative from each of the 13 agency branches, and develops the KM agenda, expected results, communication strategy, and specific KM issues; and (2) the Network (CoP) Leaders group, which consists of the leaders of each pilot CoP network, and helps networks learn from each other, achieve their objectives, share lessons learned, and solve problems.

CANADIAN INTERNATIONAL DEVELOPMENT AGENCY (CIDA)

CIDA[3] focuses on the dissemination of information, results, and lessons learned. CIDA was spending about $100 million on repeating and reinventing knowledge the organization already had. Knowledge is created through bringing together partners and shareholders in the organization around issues and practices to produce new ideas, perspectives, and insights. In the application of knowledge, CIDA has requested that partners and shareholders collaborate online on specific projects. As part of the Canadian government, CIDA needs to make all information and services available to citizens electronically through a project called Government Online. This means making information such as immigration services, goods and trade, and development assistance available outside of Canada as well.

CIDA uses an extranet, which is a culmination of the various intranets and the Internet. Access is controlled to promote free-flowing discussion and information sharing. CIDA uses its extranets to promote knowledge sharing through its Partners Forum, Field Representatives Forum, and Strategic Information Management Forum. Finally, regional forums allow different CIDA branches to share among themselves. The first step is to disseminate information that can be used as formal or explicit knowledge. The second step is to encourage members of each extranet to develop new knowledge through online discussions. The third step entails the implementation of this new knowledge in the design, development, and management of specific projects. The goal is to harvest the results of this implementation effort and to disseminate those results as formal/explicit knowledge through the Agency's intranet. To date, CIDA has documented about 4000 best practices and lessons learned.

CIDA has about 30 CoPs involving about 1200 people. A KM Forum was organized involving about 150 people from various departments and partners. These networks are the primary knowledge-sharing vehicles within CIDA. CIDA management now provides support to the CoPs and has developed expert directories to promote interaction from both within and outside the organization. CIDA is currently involved in using profiling and metadata to map and identify appropriate forms of access to knowledge and expertise within the agency. An example is the Online Project Management, which develops tools to support KM within the organization. CIDA is also extending knowledge skills to its partners and is encouraging interaction between them through its Strategic Information Management Forum initiative.

Knowledge Sharing in Virtual CoPs

The establishment of a community identity depends heavily on knowledge sharing. Even something as simple as an online or paper newsletter will provide the backbone for a community to develop. A sense of community arises from reading the same text, the same article, and the same announcement as discussions can grow around this kernel. Personalization efforts will, to some extent, work against this sense of community as different members receive different content.

Different knowledge-sharing technologies or channels should always be seen as complementary and as mutually exclusive. All types of communications represent some form of conversation, and each communication medium has its strengths and weaknesses. It is important to choose the appropriate mix of channels in order to optimize knowledge sharing. Most communities organize their knowledge-sharing interactions as informal exchanges between peers, and communication genres are chosen primarily on the basis of the developing relationship between community members (Zucchermaglio and Talamo, 2003). The choice of communication medium appears to be a function of specific professional tasks and the stage of maturity of community development. The authors conducted a longitudinal study of an interorganizational community of practice over a three-year period. For example, it took about six months for communications to become predominantly informal and e-mail-based among community members. Concurrent with this was an increasing formality in how community members communicated with those external to the community, which indicates that a sense of community boundary has been established.

One important type of knowledge sharing that occurs in a community involves the evolution of a best practice (an improved way of doing things) or lessons learned (learning from both successful and unsuccessful events). Figure 5-7 shows how a good idea can evolve and be transferred within CoPs in order to be ultimately incorporated into the organizational memory or knowledge repository. The knowledge-sharing processes involved include searching, evaluating, validating, implementing (transferring and enabling), reviewing, and routinizing (Jarrar and Zairi, 2000).

Table 5-3 shows the results of an APQC study that looked at how best practice knowledge was shared and transferred within organizations (APQC,

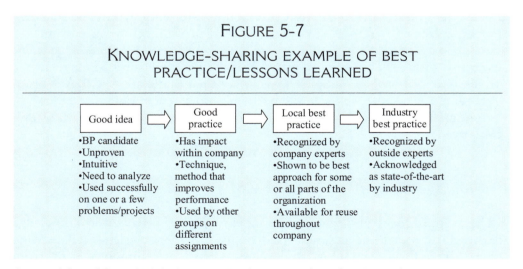

FIGURE 5-7

KNOWLEDGE-SHARING EXAMPLE OF BEST PRACTICE/LESSONS LEARNED

Source: Adapted from APQC, American Productivity and Quality Center, http://www/apqc.org.

Table 5-3

APQC (1999) Study on How Knowledge Is Transferred within a Company

Verbally at team meetings	23%
Departmental meeting	21%
Written instructions	17%
Ad hoc verbally	16%
Intranet	9%
Video	5%

1999). Their findings show that 51% of knowledge sharing occurred as part of a formal process within the organization, 39% was ad hoc, more tacit, and likely within a CoP and, perhaps most striking, 10% of the best practices were never shared. This type of obstacle in knowledge sharing or knowledge flow is very difficult to pick up. Social network analysis (SNA) is one technique that can help identify such knowledge hoarding or knowledge "black holes," where content is received but nothing is ever sent out.

We can also look more closely at the types of exchanges that occur in knowledge sharing. The majority of the knowledge exchanges consist of requests, revisions, modifications, or some form of repackaging, publications, references (e.g., telling people about, who knows about), recommendations, reuse, and reorganization (e.g., adding on of categories, metadata). Reuse is also an excellent measure of the success of the knowledge sharing, and it can be thought of as being analogous to a citation index. Scholars and researchers produce a number of scientific publications, but a metric that is perhaps even more meaningful than the number of papers published is the citation index, which keeps track of how many others have made use of this work. When others do refer to their work, this is evidenced by specific citations and references to the original work or a reuse of the original content. It is possible to track such reuse in a knowledge management system as well; in some organizations, this knowledge is used to evaluate how good a knowledge sharer a given employee is.

Knowledge-sharing communities are not just about providing access to data and documents: they are about interconnecting the social network of people who produced the knowledge. A good knowledge management system should include information not just on the people who produced the knowledge but also on those who will make use of it. There is as much value in talking to people experienced in using knowledge as there is in talking to the original authors (subject matter experts). One way to facilitate knowledge sharing is by making the knowledge visible. Knowledge sharing can be made more visible by making the interactions online visible in some way so that "I know that you know *xyz*" and "I know that you know that I know *abc*." Visible interactions help create a mutual awareness, mutual accountability, and mutual engagement to knit group members more closely together.

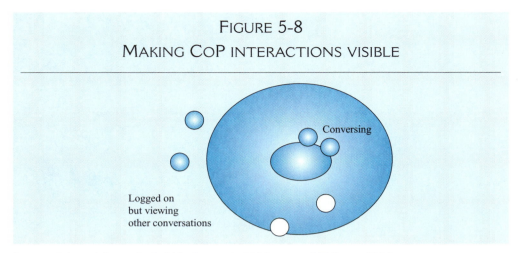

FIGURE 5-8
MAKING CoP INTERACTIONS VISIBLE

Conversing

Logged on
but viewing
other conversations

Source: Adapted from the Babble System in Erickson and Kellogg, 2000.

Figure 5-8 shows a high-level representation of how a CoP can be rendered more visible using social computing systems such as the Babble system (Erickson and Kellogg, 2000). Babble was designed as an online multiuser environment to support the creation, explanation, and sharing of knowledge through text-based conversations.

Social computing refers to digital systems that draw upon social information and context to enhance the activity and performance of people, organizations, and systems. Examples include recommender systems such as those that advise you on which books you would enjoy, which music you would like to hear, and which movies you would like to see. Social presence is an important concept in virtual networks because it refers to how much of a sense members have that other people are present. Since communities are all about social interactions for learning and knowledge exchange, it is very important that a social connection be felt. The use of buddy lists is another example of establishing social presence. This feature lets you know who else is currently online when you log on to a virtual space.

OBSTACLES TO KNOWLEDGE SHARING

A number of obstacles can hinder knowledge sharing within organizations. Chief among these obstacles is the notion that knowledge is property and ownership is very important. One of the best ways to counteract this notion is to reassure individuals that authorship and attribution will be maintained. In other words, they will not lose the credit for a knowledge product they created. Maintaining the connection between knowledge and the people who are knowledgeable about it is paramount in any knowledge management system. There is a prevalent notion of knowledge as power. The more that information is shared between individuals, the more opportunities for knowledge creation occur. There is, however, a risk in sharing what you know because, in most cases, individuals are most commonly rewarded for what they know, not what they share. As a result, hoarding of knowledge often leads to negative consequences such as empire building, reinvention of the wheel, feelings of isolation, and resistance to ideas from outside an organization. The best way to address concerns is to adapt the rewards and censure systems that exist in the organization. In other words, it is important to stop rewarding knowledge hoarding and start providing valued incentives for knowledge sharing.

Another common reason given for not sharing knowledge is that either the provider is unsure that the receiver will understand and correctly use the knowledge and/or the recipient is unsure about the truth or credibility of the knowledge in question. Both issues disappear in the context of a community, as it is a self-regulating system that continually vets and validates both content and membership.

Finally, the organizational culture and climate may either help or hinder knowledge sharing. An organizational culture that encourages discovery and innovation will help, whereas one that nurtures individual genius will hinder. An organization that rewards collective work will help create a climate of trust, whereas a culture that is based on social status will hinder knowledge sharing. Without a receptive knowledge-sharing culture in place, effective knowledge exchanges cannot occur. Significant organizational changes may need to take place before effective knowledge sharing can begin to take place.

Another caveat: while the assessment may show that organizational knowledge sharing is weak due to any or all of the factors above, knowledge sharing may be flourishing quite well—only it has not been detected. This condition is often referred to as the phenomenon of the "undernet."

The Undernet

Organizations often conclude that knowledge sharing does not occur because no one is using the organizational knowledge repository. Knowledge sharing may in fact be occurring. Often employees simply create their own networks instead of going through an official or formal organization-wide network. KM succeeds when it is a grassroots or demand-driven initiative rather than a top-down technology push.

Knowledge flows well when members perceive that there is a climate of trust, that the members with whom they exchange knowledge are credible, and that knowledge exchange is bidirectional. In small organizations, these undernets bring different specialties together, such as engineering, design, and marketing. But in larger organizations these specialties tend to separate into their own groups. When that happens, the communities develop different ways of working and even adopt different vocabularies, and they no longer understand each other. Knowledge still flows easily within specialties but not across them (Seely Brown, 2002).

Social network analysis is a very useful tool, for it provides the means of identifying the "undernets" in an organization (Weinberger, 1999). The undernet is defined as the intranets that escape the official gaze of the organization. They represent how people really share knowledge, and they constitute the skeleton of the communities of practice that have emerged. Weinberger aptly refers to these undernets as the "lifeblood" of the organization. In fact, many corporate top-down knowledge management initiatives are met with lack of interest and lack of activity, and investigation invariably turns up the existence of the "other" network—the one people really use!

The undernet is often referred to as KM's dirty little secret: however much you invest in high-tech knowledge banks, employees in search of an answer tend to make their first port of call the folks they know from the water cooler. An example is the Kraken vs. KnowledgeCurve system at Pricewaterhouse-Coopers (PWC) as discussed in an interview with Julia Collins (CIO Magazine, March 1, 2001, available from http://www.cio.com/archive/030101/passport_colins.html). Although PWC has considerable investment in formal knowledge management databases, called KnowledgeCurve, the Kraken is an informal and unofficial Lotus Notes e-mail list that has been garnering more attention lately. Named after a mythological sea monster in a poem by Alfred Lord Tennyson, the Kraken is a sort of global glue, sharing knowledge across national borders. Kraken is much less sophisticated as a system goes—just e-mail—so what is the secret of its success?

Knowledge sharing in Kraken is a manifestation of a community of practice. In fact, 80% of the messages in Kraken begin with a question: Does anybody know? Has anybody ever done . . . ? Such questions often result in four- to five-page responses. This is knowledge sharing among professionals with concrete decisions to make and problems to solve. In order to do so, they need to connect to their peers, and the undernet is the result of their connections. Ideally, such grassroots or bottom-up knowledge systems should be accommodated by the organization-wide systems. Knowledge brokers are individuals who are able to move among more than one network, and they can play a key role in putting together a company's "big picture." Formal, top-down KM systems tend to encapsulate more formal, explicit knowledge, whereas community networks tend to be less formal and more tacit and to have more "work in progress" content. Ellen Knapp, PWC's Chief Knowledge Officer, puts it this way: "KnowledgeCurve is about teaching. Kraken is about learning. You can't have one without the other" (Stewart, 2000).

ORGANIZATIONAL LEARNING AND SOCIAL CAPITAL

Human capital refers to a person's education, skills, and background necessary to be productive in an organization or profession. However, sociologists such as Coleman (1994) and Granovetter and Swedborg (2001) argue that there is much more to explaining the differences in individual success than individual characteristics alone. The concrete personal relationships and networks of relations generate trust, establish expectations, and create and enforce norms. These webs of social relationships influence individual behavior and ultimately organizational success. The term *social capital* has been coined to refer to the institutions, relationships, and norms that shape the quality and quantity of an organization's social interactions (Lesser and Prusak, 2001). Social capital is not just the sum of the individuals that comprise an organization; it is the glue that holds them together.

Nahapiet and Ghoshal (1998) define social capital as "the sum of the actual and potential resources embedded within, available through, and derived from the network of relationships possessed by an individual or social unit. It thus comprises both the network and the assets that may be mobilized through that network" (p. 243). While the concept is still evolving, there have been increasing calls for expanded "investment" on the part of business, government, and other organizations to promote the development and maintenance of social capital. Social capital facilitates the creation of new intellectual capital. Organizations, as institutional settings, are conducive to the development of high levels of social capital. It is because of their denser social capital that firms, within certain limits, have an advantage over markets in creating and sharing intellectual capital.

Knowledge-sharing communities are the primary producers of social capital, as they provide the opportunity for individuals to develop a network with members who share similar professional interests. The community provides a "Who's who" in the form of yellow pages to help make connections between members. The community provides a reference mechanism to quickly enable members to evaluate content, solve problems, and make decisions based on vetted, validated, and current knowledge. Social networks can increase productivity by reducing the costs of doing business. Social capital facilitates coordination and cooperation. At the same time, social capital has an important "downside" (Portes and Landholt, 1996): communities, groups, or networks that are isolated, parochial, or working at cross-purposes to the organization's collective interests.

A broader understanding of social capital accounts for both the positive and negative aspects by including vertical as well as horizontal associations between people, and includes behavior within and among organizations, such as firms. This view recognizes that horizontal ties are needed to give communities a sense of identity and common purpose. However, without "bridging" ties that transcend various social divides (e.g., religion, ethnicity, socioeconomic status), horizontal ties can become a basis for pursuing narrow interests, and can actively preclude access to information and material resources that would otherwise be of great assistance to the community (e.g., tips about job vacancies, access to credit).

Measuring the Value of Social Capital

Organizations have begun to implement a large number of communities of practice in hopes of achieving such benefits as:

- Building loyalty and commitment among stakeholders.
- Promoting innovation through better sharing of best practices.

- Improving efficiency of processes.
- Generating greater revenue and revenue growth.
- Decreasing employee turnover and attrition.

It remains a challenge to be able to evaluate whether these objectives are in fact achieved by communities—or even to measure whether progress has been made toward such goals. Communities of practice come packaged with a business plan: they are there for a business reason, and as such they must be evaluated just like any other business initiative in order to be able to calculate the return on the company's investment.

One way of measuring value is to calculate the additional value that a community member represents in comparison to the average site visitor. For example, in a transactional website, if a community member purchases twice as much per month as the average user, then the community is generating additional revenue. Similar comparisons may be made with respect to usage for noncommercial sites. It appears that communities that are actively managed have higher participation rates and consequently bring greater value to the organization. Most companies lack experience in community management and will have to find resources that possess the necessary expertise, processes, tools, and infrastructure to get the job done.

Community development costs may be based on hardware and software costs (one-time and ongoing), community strategy development costs (one-time), and ongoing community management costs. Benefits other than usage are much more difficult to assess. For example, the benefits of the closer relationship that develops between the community members often leads to higher employee retention rates. Organizational learning is likely accelerated, and process efficiencies are attained as a result, but it is difficult to quantify these valuable outcomes. Another example would be the power of viral marketing or word of mouth that uses a community as a conduit. Such recommendations would be much more targeted and relevant. When we add to that the fact that they come from trusted peer sources, then the outcomes may be much more favorable in terms of the internalization and application of this shared content.

Another approach is to attempt to measure the value of the social capital that has been produced as a result of the knowledge sharing. Social capital has been measured in a number of innovative ways, though for a number of reasons obtaining a single "true" measure is probably not possible, or perhaps even desirable. Measuring social capital may be difficult, but it is not impossible, using different types and combinations of qualitative, comparative, and quantitative research methodologies (Woolcock and Narayan, 2000; Sveiby and Simons, 2002). Measurement is especially challenging because social capital is comprised of concepts such as trust, community, and networks, which are difficult to quantify. The challenge is increased when one considers that the quest is to measure not just the quantity but also the quality of social capital on a variety of scales. A useful form is that of a story or vignette of success due to the existence of a knowledge-sharing community, such as the community that is working toward a cure for SARS.

A global team of scientists working on a vaccine for the SARS virus (Severe Acute Respiratory Syndrome) have been collaborating online to store common knowledge on a website, to look up experts, and to create communities. They make use of a KM tool from Knexa (http://www.knexa.com) to stay in touch and to receive pertinent, up-to-date information without having to actively search for it. This website has become a virtual home to the collection of international scientists working on the SARS problem. Although much material has been published on how incentives are needed to get people to embark upon KM solutions, this is not the case here. The major incentive is that this knowledge network makes it easier for them to successfully do their job. Several groups can work simultaneously instead of sequentially to move ahead more quickly.

Source: Haimila, 2003.

It may also be possible to adapt methods used in measuring the social capital of countries or societies. For example, in his research comparing northern and southern Italy, Putnam (1995) examines social capital in terms of degree of civic involvement, as measured by voter turnout, newspaper readership, membership in choral societies and football clubs, and confidence in public institutions. Northern Italy, where all these indicators are higher, showed significantly improved rates of governance, institutional performance, and development when other orthodox factors were controlled for. Putnam's recent work on the United States (2000) uses a similar approach, combining data from both academic and commercial sources to show a persistent long-term decline in the United States' stock of social capital. Putnam validates data from various sources against the findings of the General Social Survey, widely recognized as one of the most reliable surveys of American social life. Other examples include the World Values Survey, which measured interpersonal trust in 22 countries by asking questions such as: "Generally speaking, would you say that most people can be trusted or that you can't be too careful in dealing with people?" (Knack and Keefer, 1997). The Social Capital Initiative at the World Bank funds social capital projects that will help define and measure social capital, its evolution, and its impact (e.g., Narayan and Cassidy, 2001).

STRATEGIC IMPLICATIONS OF KNOWLEDGE SHARING

Some of the strategically important benefits of knowledge sharing include:

- Connecting professionals across platforms, across distances.
- Standardizing professional practices.
- Avoiding mistakes.

- Leveraging best practices.
- Reducing time to talent.
- Building reputation.
- Taking on stewardship for strategic capabilities.

Knowledge resides in communities in the form of social capital. The key is often connecting people to solve problems, to develop new capabilities (learn), to improve work practices, and to share what is new in the field. The type of knowledge that is transferred is shared expertise. Unlike formal education and training where public knowledge is transferred, CoPs provide apprenticing situations over long periods of time. These need a shared background (context) and shared language in order to share expertise and will also need to be technology-mediated using e-mail, the telephone, groupware, videoconferencing, and intranets or websites.

Employees today are more often loyal to their profession than to a particular company. In turn, companies are no longer able to afford employment for life; layoffs have occurred even in Japan where "salarymen" could expect to work at a company for life. One of the biggest benefits of communities of practice is that they help retain employees. If a knowledge worker is working at an organization where he or she is able to be an active member of one or more communities of practice, this will be a significant incentive to stay with that organization. Lesser and Storck (2001) examined the relationships that form in these communities and suggested that the obligations, norms, trust, and identification that come with being a community member enhance the members' ability to share knowledge with and learn from community participants. The community also serves as a powerful tool to welcome new members into the organization. New employees can quickly "plug in" to the network, connect, get help, pick up the organizational culture, and develop a sense of identity and belonging.

Another key benefit of communities lies in the now popular notion of "six degrees of separation" where every person can be linked to another by six links (Watts, 1999). This notion goes back to the famous 1967 experiment by Milgram (1967) where he asked each of 160 people in Kansas and Nebraska to direct a letter to a particular person in Massachusetts by sending it to an acquaintance whom they thought might be able to forward it to the target. To Milgram's surprise, 42 letters eventually arrived after an average of only 5.5 hops. Networks are powerful conduits for the sharing of knowledge—powerful in terms of the reach of the network and the speed with which knowledge can be exchanged, but also powerful in that content is not merely conveyed but explicitly or implicitly "vouched for" because it is being sent from a trusted, credible source.

PRACTICAL IMPLICATIONS OF KNOWLEDGE SHARING

Whereas communities of practice do emerge and run on their own, a minimal level of investment and support is crucial (Wenger, McDermott, and Snyder,

2002). First and foremost, senior management should ensure that the organizational climate or culture is one that encourages networking. In addition to financial support, it is important that employees are given the time they need to fulfill their knowledge-sharing roles and responsibilities. They will need a physical place to meet for the face-to-face meetings, which should occur at least once a year. They should receive a travel budget if one is required. Their group membership should be recognized and evaluated as part of the performance review. Additional resources such as community moderators, journalists, librarians, taxonomists, and archivists should be facilitated as well. Experience has shown that one of the most important factors contributing to the success of a community is that of an active and effective facilitator.

A conversation is more than an intellectual endeavor: it is a fundamentally social process, as is learning. People need to connect; they need to speak to an audience and note how they are being received and adjust accordingly. People portray themselves through conversations reflecting their personal agendas, personal style, and ability to take credit and share blame. In a virtual world, it is important to realize that all such connections and conversations are public and that, once digitized, conversations can persist. This means that anyone can access them at some time in the future. It is important that knowledge-sharing interactions be maintained at a professional level at all times and that all members of a virtual network be aware of and agree to adhere to a professional code of ethics, both online and offline.

KEY POINTS

- The cost of not finding information is extremely high for both individuals and the organization as a whole.
- It is not always about knowing what but "knowing who knows what," which can take the form of a corporate yellow pages or expertise location system.
- Learning is primarily a social activity.
- Knowledge sharing occurs quite efficiently and effectively in communities of practice where members share a professional interest and goal.
- In order for effective knowledge sharing to occur in CoPs, a number of key roles need to be in place such as knowledge sponsor, champion, facilitator, practice leader, knowledge support office, membership managers, discussion moderators, knowledge editors, librarians, archivists, usage analysts, and knowledge brokers.
- Virtual communities are the primary sources of social capital produced that are of value to the organization.
- Social network analysis can be used to visualize the people and their connections in virtual communities.
- Some of the key obstacles to knowledge sharing are notions such as knowledge is property, knowledge is power, credibility of the content and the source, organizational culture, and the presence of undernets.

DISCUSSION POINTS

1. What are the major distinguishing characteristics of a community of practice that a community of interest would not possess?
2. Compare and contrast some different types of communities of practice. Describe how they would differ with respect to their goals.
3. What are the key differences between the functionalist and the social constructivist perspectives on knowledge? Why is the social constructivist perspective better suited to knowledge management?
4. Describe the roles and responsibilities of a knowledge broker in a virtual community. Provide examples of how they could help promote knowledge sharing and increase the value of the social capital of the firm.
5. What is the difference between human and social capital?
6. What are some of the key deterrents to knowledge sharing and knowledge flow within an organization? How could you help overcome them?
7. List some of the ways in which social network analysis techniques can be used to better understand how knowledge is circulated within an organization.
8. What lesson can be learned from the tragedy of the commons? Provide some modern-day examples and discuss how you would ensure that effective knowledge sharing will take place.
9. What are some popular technologies used to develop corporate yellow pages? How do they compare?
10. What are some of the key steps you would need to carry out in order to conduct a social network analysis of an organization? What would you need to know before you could start? What sorts of questions could the SNA answer?

NOTES

[1] A. Gonsalves and J. Zaino, Employees Share Pearls of Wisdom, *Information Week*, September 10, 2001.
[2] CoPs 2000 Conference, UK.
[3] http://www.acdi-cida.gc.ca/cida_ind.nsf/AllDocIds/1FDF10C0471C273685256C560056D0DF?OpenDocument

REFERENCES

Adams, E., and Freeman, C. (2000). Communities of practice: bridging technology and knowledge assessment. *Journal of Knowledge Management*, 4(1): 38–44.
ALA. (1989). *Presidential Committee on Information Literacy. Final Report.* Chicago: American Library Association, 1989. Available from http://www.ala.org/ala/acrl/acrlpubs/whitepapers/presidential.htm.

Anklam, P. (2003). KM and the social network. *Knowledge Management Magazine*, 6(8). Available from http://www.kmmagazine.com/xq/asp/sid.2CE3D98A-36A0-4D67-A4E1-7852ABAE6AC1/articleid.F79B4E31-7854-4B6A-9202-164FB18672D3/qx/display.htm.

APQC. (1999). Creating a knowledge-sharing culture. Consortium *Benchmarking Study*. Houston, TX: American Productivity and Quality Center.

Bartlett, J. (2000, December). Knowing people. *Knowledge Management*. Available at http://www.destinationcrm.com/km/dcrm_km_article.asp?id=830.

Berger, P. L., and Luckmann, T. (1966). *The social construction of reality*. New York: Doubleday and Co.

Cohen, D. (1999). Knowing the drill. Virtual teamwork at BP. Available at http://www.providersedge.com.

Cohen, D., and Prusak, L. (2001). *In good company*. Boston: Harvard Business School Press.

Coleman, J. (1994). Social capital in the creation of human capital. *American Journal of Sociology ('94 Supplement)*: 97.

Conrad, C., and Poole, M. (2002). *Strategic organizational communication in a global economy*. 5th ed. Fort Wayne, IN: Harcourt College Publishers.

Cook, P. (1999). I heard it through the grapevine: making knowledge management work by learning to share knowledge, skills and experience. *Industrial and Commercial Training*, 31(3): 101–105.

Cross, R., and Parker, A. (2004). *The hidden power of social networks: understanding how work really gets done in organizations*. Boston: Harvard Business School Press.

Dalkir, K., and Jenkins, M. (2004, December). Social network analysis in context: from a research methodology to a business tool. In *Proceedings, International Conference on Knowledge Management (ICKM2004)*, Singapore.

Desmarest, M. (1997). Understanding knowledge management. *Long Range Planning*, 30: 374–384.

Donath, J. (2002). A semantic approach to visualizing online conversations. *Communications of the ACM*, 45(4): 45–49.

Erickson, T., and Kellogg, W. (2000). Social translucence: an approach to designing systems that support social processes. *ACM Transactions on Human-Computer Interaction*, 7(1): 59–83.

Feldman, S. (2004, March). The high cost of not finding information. *KM World*, 13(3). Available at http://www.keyworld.com.

Freeman, L. C. (2004). Visualizing social networks. *Carnegie Mellon Journal of Social Structure*. Available at http://zeeb.library.cmu.edu:7850/JoSS/article.html.

Gonsalves, A., and Zaino, J. (2001, September 10). Employees share pearls of wisdom. *Information Week*. Available at http://www.informationweek.com.

Granovetter, M., and Swedberg, R. (2001). *The sociology of economic life*. Boulder, CO: Westview Press.

Hagel, J., and Armstrong, A. (1997). *Net gain: Expanding markets through virtual communities*. Boston: Harvard Business School Press.

Haimila, S. (2003). KM rushes to SARS cure. Canadian effort enhanced by "virtual" home web site. *Key World*, 12(7). Available at http://www.keyworld.com.

Hardin, G. (1968). The tragedy of the commons. *Science (162)*: 1243–1248.

Harris, D. (Ed.) (1994). *Organizational linkages: understanding the productivity paradox*. Washington, DC: National Academy Press.

Hayden, K., Hanor, J., and Harrison, R. (2001). Multipoint videoconferencing: using constructivist strategies to engage adult learners. Retrieved on July 12, 2004, from http://www.uwex.edu/disted/conference/Resource_library/proceedings/02_28.pdf.

Hemre, A. (2005). Building and sustaining communities of practice at Ericsson Research Canada. Ch. 9. In M. Rao (Ed.), *KM tools and techniques*. Amsterdam, Netherlands: Elsevier.

Huysman, M., and DeWit, D. (2002). *Knowledge sharing in practice*. Dordrecht, Netherlands: Kluwer Academic Publishers.

Iverson, J., and McPhee, R. (2002). Knowledge management in communities of practice. *Management Communication Quarterly*, 16(2): 259–266.

Jarrar, Y. F., and Zairi, M. (2000). Internal transfer of best practice for performance excellence: a global survey. *Benchmarking: An International Journal*, 7(4): 239–246.

Kim, A. (2000). *Community building on the web*. Berkeley, CA: Peachpit Press.

Klimecki, R., and Lassleben, H. (1999). Modes of organizational learning: indications from an empirical study. *Management Learning*, 29(4): 405.

Knack, S., and Keefer, P. (1997). Does social capital have an economic payoff? A cross-country investigation. *Quarterly Journal of Economics*, 112: 1251–1288.

Krebs, V. (2000). The social life of routers: applying knowledge of human networks to the design of computer networks. *The Internet Protocol Journal*, 3(4): 14–25.

Lamont, J. (2003, January). Expertise location and the learning organization. *KM World Magazine*, 12(1). Available from http://www.kmworld.com/publications/magazine/.

Lank, E. (1997). Valuing key knowledge. A case study. *KM Magazine 1*(1). Available at http://www.kmmagazine.com.

Lave, J., and Wenger, E. (1991). *Situated learning: legitimate peripheral participation*. New York: Cambridge University Press.

Lesser, E., and Prusak, L. (2001). Communities of practice, social capital, and organizational knowledge. In J. W. Cortada and J. A. Woods (Eds.), *The knowledge management yearbook 2000–2001*. Boston: Butterworth-Heinemann.

Lesser, E., and Storck, J. (2001). Communities of practice and organizational performance. *IBM Systems Journal*, 40(4): 831–841.

Loomis, C. (Ed. and Trans.) (1957). *Community and society: gemeinschaft und gesellschaft* by Ferdinand Tonnies (pp. 223–231). Ann Arbor: Michigan State University Press.

McDermot, R. (1999). Why information technology inspired but cannot deliver knowledge management. *California Management Review*, 41(4): 103–117.

Metcalfe, R. (1996, July 15). There oughta be a law. *The New York Times*, 15 July 1996. Late Edition, Final, Section D, Page 7, Column 1.

Milgram, S. (1967). The small world problem. *Psychology Today*, 1: 60–67.

Nahapiet, J., and Ghoshal, S. (1998). Social capital, intellectual capital, and the organizational advantage. *Academy of Management Review*, 23(2): 242–266.

Narayan, D., and Cassidy, M. F. (2001). A dimensional approach to measuring social capital: development and validation of a social capital inventory. *Current Sociology*, 49(2): 59–105.

Nickols, F. (2000). Community of practice start up kit. The distance consulting company. Available at http://home.att.net/~nickols/.

Ortenblad, A. (2002). Organizational learning: a radical perspective. *International Journal of Management Reviews*, 4(1): 87–100.

Pickett, J. P., et al. (2000). *The American heritage dictionary of the English language* 4th ed. Boston: Houghton Mifflin.

Portes, A., and Landholt, P. (1996, May–June). The downside of social capital. *The American Prospect 26*: 18–21, 94. Also available from http://epn.org/prospect/26/26-cnt2.

Price, D. (1963). *Little science, big science*. New York: Columbia University Press.

Putnam, R. (2000). *Bowling alone: the collapse and revival of American community.* New York: Simon and Schuster.

Putnam, R. (1995). Bowling alone: America's declining social capital. *Journal of Democracy,* 6(1): 65–87.

Rheingold, H. (1993). *The virtual community: homesteading on the electronic frontier.* Reading, MA: Addison-Wesley.

Seely Brown, J. (2002). John Seely Brown talks about knowledge flow. Excerpt of an interview from CSC World. Available from http://www.csc.com.

Seely Brown, J., and Duguid, P. (2002). *The social life of information.* Boston: Harvard Business School Press.

Seufert, A., von Krogh, G., and Bach, A. (1999). Towards knowledge networking. *Journal of Knowledge Management,* 3(3): 180–190.

Snowden, D. (2001). Narrative patterns: the perils and pitfalls of using stories in organisations. *Knowledge Management ARK,* July 2001: 1–7. Available at http://www.kwork.org/Resources/narrative.pdf.

Stewart, T. (2000). Why Kraken and conversation work so well. *Fortune Magazine.* Available from http://www.fortune.com/fortune/careers/edge/2000/09/04/index.html.

Strauss, A. (1978). A social world perspective. *Studies in Symbolic Interaction,* 1(1): 119–128.

Sveiby, K., and Simons, R. (2002). Collaborative climate and effectiveness of knowledge work—an empirical study. *Journal of Knowledge Management,* 6(5): 420–433.

Telstra. (2000). Retrieved on July 12, 2004, from http://www.commvis.com.au/effectiveness_of_videoconferenci.htm.

Thomas, J. C., Kellogg, W. A., and Erickson, T. (2001). The knowledge management puzzle: human and social factors in knowledge management. *IBM Systems Journal,* 40(4): 863–885.

Watts, D. (1999). Networks, dynamics and the small world phenomenon. *American Journal of Sociology,* 105(2): 493–527.

Weinberger, D. (1999). The undernet. *Intranet Journal.* Retrieved on July 12, 2004, from http://www.intranetjournal.com/articles/199912/ia_12_17_99a.html.

Wenger, E. (1998). *Learning, meaning and identity.* Cambridge, UK: Cambridge University Press.

Wenger, E., McDermott, R., and Snyder, W. (2002). *Cultivating communities of practice.* Boston: Harvard Business School Press.

Woolcock, M., and Narayan, N. (2000). Social capital: implications for development theory, research and policy. *World Bank Research Observer,* 15(2): 225–250.

Zucchermaglio, C., and Talamo, A. (2003). The development of a virtual community of practice using electronic mail and communicative genres. *Journal of Business and Technical Communications,* 17(3): 259–284.

KNOWLEDGE APPLICATION

All that is gold does not glitter; not all those that wander are lost.

J.R.R. Tolkein (1892–1973)

This chapter brings us to the final step in the knowledge management cycle when the knowledge that has been captured, coded, shared, and otherwise made available is put to actual use. If this step is not accomplished successfully, all of the KM efforts will have been in vain, for KM can succeed only if the knowledge is used. However, it now becomes imperative to understand which knowledge is of use to which set of people and how best to make it available to them so that they not only understand how to use it but believe that using this knowledge will lead to an improvement in their work. The use of learning taxonomies, task support systems, and personalization or profiling techniques can help ensure the best possible match between user and content. Expertise location systems and other collaboration aids can help groups of people find and apply valuable knowledge and know-how. Content management systems can be designed to optimize knowledge application on an organization-wide basis.

LEARNING OBJECTIVES

1. Understand how user and task modeling approaches can help promote effective knowledge use at the individual, group, and organizational level.
2. Describe how an organizational knowledge management architecture is designed.
3. Define organizational learning and describe the links between individual and organizational learning.
4. Compare and contrast learning and understanding with internalization of knowledge.

145

5. List the different knowledge support technologies that can help users put knowledge into action.

INTRODUCTION

Knowledge management typically addresses one of two general objectives: knowledge reuse to promote efficiency and innovation to introduce more effective ways of doing things. Knowledge application refers to the actual use of knowledge that has been captured or created and put into the KM cycle (see Figure 6-1).

Knowledge eventually is made accessible to all the knowledge workers in the organization, with an implicit assumption that they will be used. This assumption turns out to be a rather large and often unfounded one. If we recall the Nonaka and Takeuchi model from Chapter 3, we can see that having captured, coded, reorganized, and made knowledge available, we are still only in the third quadrant. The knowledge spiral needs to be completed by successful internalization of knowledge. This process of internalization, it should be recalled, consists not only in accessing and understanding the content but in consciously deciding that this is indeed a good—ideally better—way of doing things, and hence the knowledge is applied to a real-world decision or problem.

This is *knowledge reuse*, the process whereby useful nuggets of knowledge or knowledge objects are made available in a library of such objects. These knowledge objects can be annotated references, components (programs or text), templates, patterns, or other types of containers. For example, consulting companies often reuse project proposal templates because they convey the company brand, contain useful reusable objects such as testimonials, company description, and so on. The goal is to reduce the time it takes to complete tasks as well as to help maintain higher standards regarding the quality of the work to be done. The benefits to new employees are enormous as they are able to

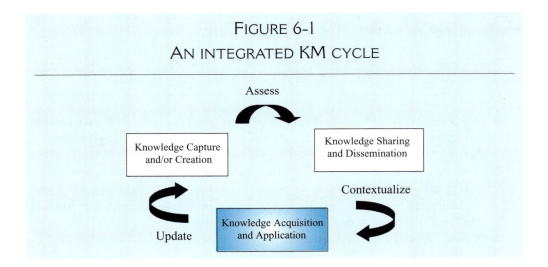

FIGURE 6-1
AN INTEGRATED KM CYCLE

attain "day one" performance with the help of such a reuse library; that is, they are able to perform at a fairly high level on their first day on the job. The other major benefit is the work that is not done—because it was possible to see that someone else had already done it. The savings involved in not "reinventing the wheel" can be considerable.

KM aims to support learning organizations that provide all employees with access to corporate memory so that both the individuals and the organization as a whole improve. Corporate memory is often incomplete because it has captured only explicit knowledge. KM also attempts to make accessible the valuable tacit knowledge, which is added to the corporate memory. While it is possible to reuse tacit knowledge (and this is done all the time during knowledge-sharing interactions), reuse tends to refer to packaged explicit knowledge. Reuse of explicit knowledge affords a longer-term advantage. Whereas tacit knowledge reuse can benefit the individual who sought the advice of a more experienced colleague, knowledge objects that are accessible through the knowledge repository are accessible to all workers and they remain so for as long as they are useful.

That being said, it is imperative to try to include or at least be able to point to where the tacit knowledge associated with a given knowledge object resides. It is never possible or even desirable to try to render all knowledge explicit. If knowledge workers can easily locate and communicate with individuals in the company that are connected to a given knowledge object (e.g., they are familiar with how it is used, they have been trained, etc.), then the ability to apply or to make use of this knowledge is greatly increased. In the example of the proposal writing knowledge object or template, hyperlinks can easily be included not only to good examples of past proposals that were successful (best practices) but also to the individuals involved in their preparation so that they can be contacted for advice, a read-through, or other forms of help.

The essence of problem solving, innovation, creativity, intuitive design, good analysis, and effective project management involves more tacit, rather than explicit, knowledge. By putting tacit knowledge in a principal role and cultivating tacit knowledge environments, KM can play an important role in application development, particularly in reuse. Another aspect of the explicit knowledge problem is the fallacy that documentation (explicit knowledge) equals understanding. We seek understanding in order to successfully reuse a component. However, the larger and more complex the component, the harder it is to gain the required understanding from documentation alone. Understanding, in this context at least, is a combination of documentation and conversation—conversation about the component and the context in which that component operates. No writer of documentation can anticipate all the questions a component user may have. Even if this were possible, the resulting documentation would be so extensive and cumbersome that potential users would simply develop their own component rather than wade through the documentation.

Knowledge management systems that focus on gathering, recording, and accessing reams of "knowledge" at the expense of person-to-person interactions have proven to be expensive and less than satisfactory. Organizations that fail to understand tacit knowledge will repeat many of the mistakes made with methodologies such as Computer Assisted Software Engineering (CASE). A common assumption in the past was that all relevant knowledge could be bundled up in nice, neat, easily accessible packages of "best practices" that practitioners could then "repeat."

When we attack reuse as a knowledge management problem, we begin to ask new questions, or at least look for different avenues for finding solutions to the problem. How do we go about finding the component we need? How do we gain confidence that the component does what we want it to do and does not do strange things that we do not want? What is the distance (organizationally or geographically) between the component developer and users? Are there other people who have used this component whom we could talk to and learn from? Do we have access to the author of this component? Have others found this component to be effective? How should we go about testing this component? How easily will this component integrate into our environment?

Dixon (2000) outlines factors that affect knowledge transfer: characteristics of the receiver (skills, shared language, technical knowledge), the nature of the task (routine, nonroutine), and the type of knowledge being transferred (a continuum from explicit to tacit). The author then identifies five categories of knowledge transfer that she has observed, from Near Transfer ("transferring knowledge from a source team to a receiving team that is doing a similar task in a similar context but in a different location") to Serial Transfer ("the source team and the receiving team are one and the same"). Dixon then describes techniques that work well for each of these five types of transfer.

The objective of this chapter is not to describe the practices for knowledge transfer in detail, but rather to point out that merely coding a component and scratching out a few lines of documentation will rarely be enough to facilitate knowledge transfer. Other researchers such as Hatami, Galliers, and Huang (2003) found that a key to organizational success in the face of global competition is the ability to capture organizational learning, to effectively reuse the knowledge through efficient means, and to synthesize these into more intelligent problem recognition, strategic analysis, and choices in strategic directions. By tapping into their organization's memory, decision makers can make more intelligent business decisions. This is achieved when individuals access data, information, and knowledge residing in repositories. However, retrieval alone is not enough—knowledge application must follow, and the success of knowledge application appears to be a function of the characteristics of the individual, the knowledge content, the purpose of reuse for the particular task at hand, and the organizational context or culture.

KNOWLEDGE APPLICATION AT THE INDIVIDUAL LEVEL

Characteristics of Individual Knowledge Workers

Individual differences play a major role in knowledge-sharing behaviors (Hicks and Tochtermann, 2001). Knowledge workers vary with respect to their familiarity with the subject matter and their personality and cognitive styles. Cohen and Levinthal (1990) found that sharing is more likely to occur when a foundation of prior relevant knowledge exists. A number of studies (e.g., Ford et al., 2002; Kuhlthau, 1993; Spink et al., 2002) found significant correlations between online searching behaviors and the cognitive styles of learners. On the other hand, the business world heavily favors the use of instruments such as the Myer-Briggs Type Indicator (MBTI) personality style assessment (Myers et al., 1998) to assess differences in personality styles. Some research has been done to correlate MBTI type with knowledge-sharing behaviors. Webb (1998), in a study of the consulting firm Price Waterhouse Coopers, showed that a strong outgoing personality was important in knowledge sharing regardless of qualifications and prior experience.

Characteristics of the individual who is seeking to apply or reuse knowledge are likely to play a role in how effective he or she is at finding, understanding, and making use of organizational knowledge. Individual characteristics may include, for example, personality style, their preferences regarding how individuals best learn, how they prefer to receive their information, as well as how they can best be helped to put the knowledge to work. This may range from something as simple as asking for and subsequently accommodating the language the user prefers to work in to more sophisticated modeling of the user in terms of their abilities and their goals. One good framework that is of use here is the Bloom taxonomy of learning objectives (Bloom, Mesia, and Krathwohl, 1964), which was designed to help teachers set learning goals for learning activities. The taxonomy can be easily adapted to knowledge application goals for each knowledge object in a repository.

One way of visualizing personalization is to think of the one-person company or the one-person library. All of the knowledge resources in a given repository can be made to appear as if they were there at the disposal of a given person, reflecting their preferences, their background, and so forth. Figure 6-2 illustrates this concept of "many-to-one" interactions.

Personalization and profiling are currently a popular means of characterizing visitors to a given website. This is particularly true of virtual stores where customer data can then be analyzed in order to improve marketing efforts. However, in knowledge management we are less concerned with database marketing applications of personalization than with ensuring that information retrieval and knowledge application processes are tailor-made for each knowledge worker. The easier it is for a knowledge worker to find, understand, and internalize the knowledge, the greater their success in actually applying this knowledge. An alternative approach to user modeling is proposed in Figure 6-3.

Instead of using profiling technologies to better understand all customers, we can make use of similar techniques to follow or trace a given individual's interactions with a number of corporate memory interfaces. This alternative approach will yield a user model that will help us to better understand the types of human-knowledge interactions that have occurred in order to optimize knowledge application within the organization. For example, push technologies are based on user models that look at historical information requests

FIGURE 6-2

ILLUSTRATION OF THE PERSONALIZATION CONCEPT

Personalization: many-to-one interactions

The one-person:

office
store
school
library
.......?

FIGURE 6-3

ALTERNATIVE APPROACH TO PERSONALIZATION

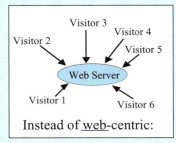

Instead of <u>web</u>-centric:

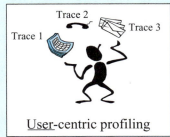

<u>User</u>-centric profiling

in order to push or automatically send out similar new content that becomes available.

We will need to be able to find and use content based on individuals' personal model, and how they perceive the knowledge world around them. This is often influenced by their particular background (e.g., IT vs. sociology), how long they have been in the company, how expert they are in the topic, as well as a whole spectrum of preferences ranging from the linguistic to the format they prefer to receive knowledge (e.g., visuals who prefer diagrams to those who prefer to read text). These are often represented as semantic networks (see Figures 6-4 and 6-5).

There are also systems that monitor users' tasks online and interpret them in context, based on traces they leave behind. These systems work well for tasks that are well identified and where knowledge can be described in a clear ontology (e.g., a postal address template). In general, this approach is based on a user interacting with a computer system to perform a task that leads to changes in the system. An observer agent (a software routine) observes these changes according to an observation model to generate a log or trace of what the user has done. The trace is then analyzed to identify and extract significant

FIGURE 6-4

EXAMPLE OF A SEMANTIC NETWORK

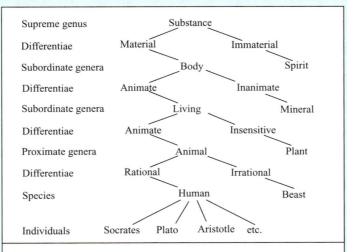

Supreme genus	Substance
Differentiae	Material — Immaterial
Subordinate genera	Body — Spirit
Differentiae	Animate — Inanimate
Subordinate genera	Living — Mineral
Differentiae	Animate — Insensitive
Proximate genera	Animal — Plant
Differentiae	Rational — Irrational
Species	Human — Beast
Individuals	Socrates Plato Aristotle etc.

Tree of Porphyry, as it was drawn by the logician Peter of Spain (1329). It illustrates the categories under substance, which is called the supreme genus or the most general category.

FIGURE 6-5

EXAMPLE OF A SEMANTIC NETWORK (CONTINUED)

Birds
build their nests in — Trees
eat — Worms
fly using their — Wings
made of — Feathers

Figure 6-6
Dynamic Profiling System Design

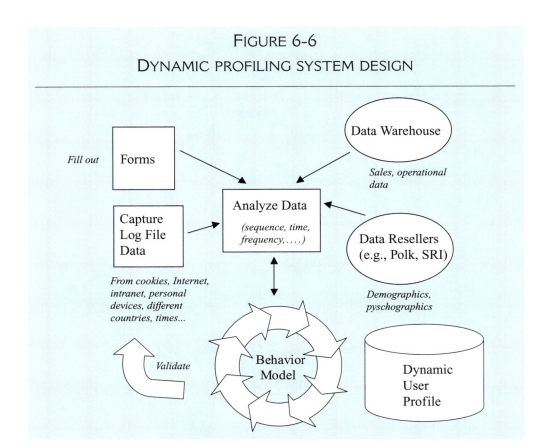

episodes and interpret them according to explained task signatures. Each episode represents a pattern, and each pattern can be mapped onto a task, a subtask, or a more specific step that forms part of the subtask. For example, if the user is trying to locate, open, and print out a particular file, three distinct episodes can be identified: behaviors related to locating, opening, and printing the file. These episodes can then be reused by assistant agents that help the user to do what they are trying to do. The assistance episodes themselves can also be reused in the future (see Figure 6-6). In this way, the system has modeled how users behave when they are undertaking these particular types of tasks.

The important factor to note here is that user modeling is an ongoing process, not a one-shot deal. Dynamic profiling systems need to be developed based on a mix of human and automated trace facilities, in order to be able to continually adapt to changes in the environment, changes in the organization, and changes in the individuals themselves (e.g., different job responsibilities, different preferences, new competencies, and new interests).

Bloom's Taxonomy of Learning Objectives

Bloom (1956) divided knowledge into a hierarchical scheme that distinguishes between psychomotor skills, the affective domain (e.g., attitudes), and the cognitive domain (e.g., knowledge). The cognitive domain is more commonly used, although attitudinal changes are often required in knowledge management too. Bloom emphasizes that learning is hierarchical, with learning (objectives) at the highest level dependent on the achievement of lower-level knowledge and skills first.

The cognitive domain taxonomy is shown in Table 6-1. The levels from low to high are: knowledge, comprehension, application, analysis, synthesis, and evaluation.

TABLE 6-1
BLOOM TAXONOMY OF THE COGNITIVE DOMAIN

	Level	Description	Action verbs that can be used
1	Knowledge	Remembering of previously learned material.	Recall, repeat, define, describe, list, identify, label, match, name, state.
2	Comprehension	Ability to grasp the meaning of material (e.g., translating from one form to another, estimating future trends, explaining or giving examples of).	Classify, convert, discuss, explain, generalize, give an example of, paraphrase, restate in your own words, summarize, review.
3	Application	Ability to use learned material in new and concrete situations by applying rules, methods, concepts, principles, laws, and theories.	Articulate, assess, chart, computer construct, determine, develop, discover, establish, extend, operationalize, participate, predict, provide, show, solve, use, apply, demonstrate, sketch, practice, illustrate.
4	Analysis	Ability to break down material into its component parts so that its organizational structure may be understood. Identification of parts, relationships between parts, recognition of organizational principles.	Break down, correlate, diagram, differentiate, discriminate, distinguish, focus, infer, outline, point out, recognize, separate, subdivide, compare, contrast, inspect, inventory, relate, examine.
5	Synthesis	Ability to put parts together to form a new whole. Creative behaviors stressed in the formulation of something new.	Adapt, categorize, collaborate, combine, communicate, compile, compose, create, design, devise, facilitate, formulate, generate, incorporate, individualize, initiate, integrate, model, plan, propose, assemble, organize.
6	Evaluation	Ability to judge the value of material based on definite criteria.	Appraise, conclude, criticize, decide, defend, judge, justify, support, evaluate, rate, value, score, prioritize, select.

Source: Adapted from Bloom, 1956.

The affective domain includes the manner in which we deal with things emotionally, such as feelings, values, appreciation, enthusiasms, motivations, and attitudes. The five major categories are listed in Table 6-2.

The psychomotor domain includes physical movement, coordination, and use of the motor skills areas. Development of these skills requires practice and is measured in terms of speed, precision, distance, procedures, or techniques in execution. The seven major categories are listed in Table 6-3.

These taxonomic categories can be used "inside out" to help understand what users are trying to do. The level of internalization can be identified for effective performance; for example, one can set a minimum threshold that must be reached in order for the worker to be able to understand and make appropriate use of the knowledge object. This feature can in turn be incorporated into a user model. The Bloom taxonomy serves as a means of determining not only what knowledge workers are expected to do (usually referred to as skills or expertise) but also the level of performance that is expected (also referred to as mastery level). For example, by using the cognitive skill portion of the Bloom taxonomy, it is possible to characterize a particular knowledge object, say, a best practice procedure on how best to present a project team members' resumes when preparing a project proposal. The knowledge worker who prepares the bid is expected to have a level of understanding that allows for the critical judgment needed to execute this task at the required proficiency level. He or she must not only be skilled in the selection of team members to be included in the proposal but also be able to repackage their resumes in the form that has been shown to be the best based on past successes. Another example, using the affective domain Bloom taxonomy, once again can make use of this best practice but this time address the best way to judge whether candidates who meet the technical skill requirements also possess the appropriate "soft skills," such as being a good team player, having a collaborative approach to work, and not hoarding knowledge or claiming individual credit for group work.

The Bloom taxonomy provides a good basis for assessing knowledge application. All too often in KM, simply having accessed content is taken to mean that knowledge workers are using (and reusing) this content. It is far more useful to assess the impact that the knowledge residing in the knowledge base has had on learning, understanding, and "buying in" to a new way of doing things. Only through changes in behavior can knowledge use be inferred; the taxonomy provides a more detailed framework to evaluate the extent to which knowledge has been internalized (using the Nonaka and Takeuchi, 1995, model). For example, at the lower cognitive skill levels, simply being aware that knowledge exists within the organization is easily observed when knowledge workers are able to locate the content within a knowledge repository. Access is typically tracked using log file statistics, which are similar to the number of hits or visitors that a website has attracted. Knowledge application, however, requires that knowledge workers have attained much higher levels of comprehension such as analysis, synthesis, and evaluation. Only at these levels can knowledge be said to truly be applied. In contrast to someone who can point to a template in the knowledge base, knowledge application will be

TABLE 6-2

AFFECTIVE DOMAIN AS CHARACTERIZED IN THE BLOOM TAXONOMY

Receiving phenomena: Awareness, willingness to hear, selected attention.

Examples: Listen to others with respect. Listen for and remember the name of newly introduced people.

Key words: asks, chooses, describes, follows, gives, holds, identifies, locates, names, points to, selects, sits, erects, replies, uses.

Responding to phenomena: Active participation on the part of the learners. Attends and reacts to a particular phenomenon. Learning outcomes may emphasize compliance in responding, willingness to respond, or satisfaction in responding (motivation).

Examples: Participates in class discussions. Gives a presentation. Questions new ideals, concepts, models, and so on in order to fully understand them. Knows the safety rules and practices them.

Key words: answers, assists, aids, complies, conforms, discusses, greets, helps, labels, performs, practices, presents, reads, recites, reports, selects, tells, writes.

Valuing: The worth or value a person attaches to a particular object, phenomenon, or behavior. This ranges from simple acceptance to the more complex state of commitment. Valuing is based on the internalization of a set of specified values, while clues to these values are expressed in the learner's overt behavior and are often identifiable.

Examples: Demonstrates belief in the democratic process. Is sensitive toward individual and cultural differences (value diversity). Shows the ability to solve problems. Proposes a plan to social improvement and follows through with commitment. Informs management on matters that one feels strongly about.

Key words: completes, demonstrates, differentiates, explains, follows, forms, initiates, invites, joins, justifies, proposes, reads, reports, selects, shares, studies, works.

Organization: Organizes values into priorities by contrasting different values, resolving conflicts between them, and creating a unique value system. The emphasis is on comparing, relating, and synthesizing values.

Examples: Recognizes the need for balance between freedom and responsible behavior. Accepts responsibility for one's behavior. Explains the role of systematic planning in solving problems. Accepts professional ethical standards. Creates a life plan in harmony with abilities, interests, and beliefs. Prioritizes time effectively to meet the needs of the organization, family, and self.

Key words: adheres, alters, arranges, combines, compares, completes, defends, explains, formulates, generalizes, identifies, integrates, modifies, orders, organizes, prepares, relates, synthesizes.

Internalizing values (characterization): Has a value system that controls their behavior. The behavior is pervasive, consistent, predictable, and, most importantly, characteristic of the learner. Instructional objectives are concerned with the student's general patterns of adjustment (personal, social, emotional).

Examples: Shows self-reliance when working independently. Cooperates in group activities (displays teamwork). Uses an objective approach in problem solving. Displays a professional commitment to ethical practice on a daily basis. Revises judgments and changes behavior in light of new evidence. Values people for what they are, not how they look.

Key words: acts, discriminates, displays, influences, listens, modifies, performs, practices, proposes, qualifies, questions, revises, serves, solves, verifies.

Source: Adapted from Bloom, 1956.

TABLE 6-3

BLOOM TAXONOMY OF THE PSYCHOMOTOR DOMAIN

Perception: The ability to use sensory cues to guide motor activity. This ranges from sensory stimulation, through cue selection, to translation.

Examples: Detects nonverbal communication cues. Estimates where a ball will land after it is thrown and then moves to the correct location to catch the ball. Adjusts heat of stove to correct temperature by smell and taste of food. Adjusts the height of the forks on a forklift by comparing where the forks are in relation to the pallet.
Key words: chooses, describes, detects, differentiates, distinguishes, identifies, isolates, relates, selects.

Set: Readiness to act. It includes mental, physical, and emotional sets. These three sets are dispositions that predetermine a person's response to different situations (sometimes called mind-sets).

Examples: Knows and acts upon a sequence of steps in a manufacturing process. Recognizes one's abilities and limitations. Shows desire to learn a new process (motivation). *Note*: This subdivision of psychomotor is closely related to the "Responding to phenomena" subdivision of the affective domain.
Key words: begins, displays, explains, moves, proceeds, reacts, shows, states, volunteers.

Guided response: The early stages in learning a complex skill that includes imitation and trial and error. Adequacy of performance is achieved by practicing.

Examples: Performs a mathematical equation as demonstrated. Follows instructions to build a model. Responds to hand signals of instructor while learning to operate a forklift.
Key words: copies, traces, follows, reacts, reproduces, responds.

Mechanism: The intermediate stage in learning a complex skill. Learned responses have become habitual, and the movements can be performed with some confidence and proficiency.

Examples: Uses a personal computer. Repairs a leaking faucet. Drives a car.
Key words: assembles, calibrates, constructs, dismantles, displays, fastens, fixes, grinds, heats, manipulates, measures, mends, mixes, organizes, sketches.

Complex overt response: The skillful performance of motor acts that involve complex movement patterns. Proficiency is indicated by a quick, accurate, and highly coordinated performance, requiring a minimum of energy. This category includes performing without hesitation and automatic performance. For example, players often utter sounds of satisfaction or expletives as soon as they hit a tennis ball or throw a football because they can tell by the feel of the act what the result will produce.

Examples: Maneuvers a car into a tight parallel parking spot. Operates a computer quickly and accurately. Displays competence playing the piano.
Key words: assembles, builds, calibrates, constructs, dismantles, displays, fastens, fixes, grinds, heats, manipulates, measures, mends, mixes, organizes, sketches. *Note*: The key words are the same as Mechanism, but will have adverbs or adjectives that indicate that the performance is quicker, better, more accurate, and so on.

Continued

TABLE 6-3—*Continued*

BLOOM TAXONOMY OF THE PSYCHOMOTOR DOMAIN

Adaptation: Well developed skills, and the individual can modify movement patterns to fit special requirements.	Examples: Responds effectively to unexpected experiences. Modifies instruction to meet the needs of the learners. Performs a task with a machine that it was not originally intended to do. (Machine is not damaged, and there is no danger in performing the new task.) Key words: adapts, alters, changes, rearranges, reorganizes, revises, varies.
Origination: Creating new movement patterns to fit a particular situation or specific problem. Learning outcomes emphasize creativity based upon highly developed skills.	Examples: Constructs a new theory. Develops a new and comprehensive training program. Creates a new gymnastic routine. Key words: arranges, builds, combines, composes, constructs, creates, designs, initiates, makes, originates.

Source: Adapted from Bloom, 1956.

manifested by a change in how a knowledge worker goes about doing his or her job.

It is equally important to take the affective component into consideration when analyzing knowledge application. Often, knowledge fails to be used not because it has not been understood but because the knowledge worker is not convinced that this new best practice or lesson learned represents any significant improvement over the way he or she is already working. An attitudinal change is more often than not a critical prerequisite to internalization. It is not enough that someone be made aware of and understand a given practice. People must also believe that it is indeed a better way of doing things and that they stand to gain by adopting this new way of working.

The psychomotor domain is less widely used in knowledge management and is often more related to physical work and skills. Individualized learning to facilitate knowledge application appears in the vignette on Hughes Space and Communications.

HUGHES SPACE AND COMMUNICATIONS

Hughes Space and Communications (HSC) is a unit of Hughes Electronics Corporation, a subsidiary of General Motors. HSC has 6000 employees who develop, produce, and launch state-of-the-art space and communications systems for military, commercial, and scientific uses. It is the world's largest producer of commercial communication satellites. At HSC, KM is not viewed in terms of traditional departmental boundaries. It is not a process, a function, or an organization. It is a skill that is part of managing

Continued

a business, and it should be one of the tools that every manager possesses in his or her repertoire. Traditional management tends to take a "top-down" approach to implementation. In KM, it is better to lead not by direction but by service, providing people with the necessary assistance to enable them to improve the work they are already doing.

For example, a lessons learned system can be described as a closed-loop learning system. People experience something in their work, either through analysis, discovery, or dialogue. There are both good and bad discoveries, but in either event, something is learned. The key is in extracting what was learned and in providing a connection between what was learned and what is practiced. Lessons need to be documented and disseminated to the masses in a form that is easily accessible to all. Feedback is then collected and incorporated back into the documentation process. The challenge is to continuously insert these lessons into what is happening on the job.

HSC also has a coordinated business intelligence-gathering effort that includes a system that pulls information from over 60 online sources, a process for analyzing it, and ongoing dialoguing and sharing among HC and other Hughes marketing people. This effort began as a joint project of a few marketing people and the corporate library. It received a boost when it was featured at a knowledge fair that showcased existing knowledge management activities to people from throughout HSC.

HSC has an intranet but has not just put Netscape on everyone's desktop and then expected them to start using it effectively to do their jobs. Instead, they implemented the intranet gradually, selectively deploying in pilot areas that focused on supporting a high-value business need such as lessons learned, gated processes, yellow pages, or a common user interface to existing systems. Using one-on-one tutorials, each person was trained in how to use the intranet and Internet to do a specific job. When pilots proved successful, they were then deployed into enterprise-wide business applications.

Source: Foundation Strategic Innovation Report, Computer Science Corporation. Available at http://www.csc.com.

A user model is not enough, however, for the facilitation of knowledge application. We also need to know what the users are doing and what their goals or purposes are in applying this knowledge object. To this end, we will also require a task model. As with the user model, the task model will serve to better characterize why someone would apply a particular knowledge item.

A user and task-adapted approach is highly recommended in order to facilitate internalization processes. This means that we need to know enough about the users and what they are trying to do in order to support them in the best possible way. This is, of course, quite similar to what a good reference librarian or coach would do—that is, try to understand who you are and what you are trying to accomplish before beginning to attempt to help out. Someone who is browsing to pick up general information and background on a subject of interest may be mistakenly taken for someone who is "lost in a sea of information" or someone who has a looming deadline to meet and is looking for a specific template to help him or her complete the task at hand as quickly as possible without too many errors. Such a person would not appreciate being flooded with too much information. They are looking only for the specially selected, vetted, and guided nuggets of knowledge—sometimes referred to as just-in-time (JIT) knowledge and just-enough knowledge. The latter are best exemplified by task support systems or Electronic Performance Support Systems (EPSSs).

Task Analysis and Modeling

Task analysis studies what knowledge workers must do with respect to specific actions to be taken and/or cognitive processes that must be called upon to achieve a particular task (e.g., Preece et al., 1994). The most commonly used method is task decomposition, which breaks down higher-level tasks into their subtasks and operations. The lower levels may make use of task flow diagrams, decision flowcharts, or even screen layouts to better illustrate the step-by-step process that has to be undertaken in order to complete a task successfully. A good task analysis should show the sequencing of activities by ordering them from left to right. In order to break down a task, a question should be asked, "how is this task done?" If a subtask is identified at a lower level, it is possible to build up the structure by asking "why is this done?"

The task decomposition can be carried out using the following stages:

1. Identify the task to be analyzed.
2. Break this down into four to eight subtasks. These subtasks should be specified in terms of objectives and, between them, should cover the whole area of interest.
3. Draw the subtasks as a layered diagram ensuring that it is complete.
4. Decide upon the level of detail into which to decompose. Making a conscious decision at this stage will ensure that all the subtask decompositions are treated consistently. It may be decided that the decomposition should continue until flows are more easily represented as a task flow diagram.
5. Continue the decomposition process, ensuring that the decompositions and numbering are consistent. It is usually helpful to produce a written account as well as the decomposition diagram.
6. Present the analysis to someone else who has not been involved in the decomposition but who knows the tasks well enough to check for consistency.

Task flow analysis can include details of interactions between the user and the current system, or other individuals, and any problems related to them. Copies of screens from the current system may also be taken to provide details of interactive tasks. Task flows will not only show the specific details of current work processes but may also highlight areas where task processes are poorly understood, are carried out differently by different staff, or are inconsistent with the higher-level task structure. An example of a task analysis is shown in Table 6-4.

Such task analyses are an important first step in the design of knowledge application support systems. A popular form of these analyses has been around long before the term *knowledge management* came into common usage. Electronic Performance Support Systems (EPSSs) were and continue to be widely used to provide on-the-job learning and advice. E-learning is also currently enjoying a high level of usage and can be seen as a subset of EPSS, as described in the next sections.

EPSS

In the groundbreaking book, *Electronic Performance Support Systems*, Gery (1991) defined EPSS as an integrated electronic environment that is available to and easily accessible by each employee and is structured to provide immediate, individualized online access to the full range of information, software, guidance, advice and assistance, data, images, tools, and assessment and monitoring systems to permit job performance with minimal support and intervention by others.

TABLE 6-4
EXAMPLE OF A TASK ANALYSIS

Task Analysis for Task: Tying shoelaces

For more experienced individuals	For novices
1. Grab one lace in each hand.	1. Pinch the laces.
2. Pull the shoe laces tight with a vertical pull.	2. Pull the laces.
3. Cross the shoe laces.	3. Hang the ends of the laces from the corresponding sides of the shoe.
4. Pull the front lace around the back of the other.	4. Pick up the laces in the corresponding hands.
5. Put that lace through the hole.	5. Lift the laces above the shoe.
6. Tighten the laces with a horizontal pull.	6. Cross the right lace over the left one to form a tepee.
7. Make a bow.	7. Bring the left lace toward the student.
8. Tighten the bow.	8. Pull the left lace through the tepee.
	9. Pull the laces away from one another.
	10. Bend the left lace to form a loop.
	11. Pinch the loop with the left hand.
	12. Bring the right lace over the fingers and around the loop.
	13. Push the right lace through the hole.
	14. Pull the loops away from one another.

An electronic performance support system can also be described as any computer software program or component that improves employee performance by reducing the complexity or number of steps required to perform a task, providing the performance information an employee needs to perform a task, or introducing a decision support system that enables an employee to identify the action appropriate for a particular set of conditions (see Figure 6-7).

The EPSS point of view has been revolutionary. Its significance was how it reframed our thinking from the training paradigm of "fill 'em up with knowledge and skills and then put 'em to work." EPSS practitioners and business sponsors came to understand that people could be put on task far sooner—almost from day one—if we provided an appropriate suite of integrated supports in the context of performing real-work tasks.

Performance support systems such as EPSS help distill content into useful chunks. The famous experiment by Miller (1956) found that our span of immediate memory is severely limited. In fact, we can only hold seven (plus or minus two) discrete items in our minds at the same time. Psychologists then did quite a bit of research on how chunking, or combining items into more general categories, can help to overcome this human information processing bottleneck. This is also the reason why mnemonics work in helping us to remember. For example, in trying to recall a list of things to do, one mnemonic trick is to visualize each item as being in a different room of your house.

The EPSS capitalizes on such useful methods by reducing, say, a document into discrete knowledge chunks (see Figure 6-8). Each chunk then becomes a knowledge object, and the EPSS can direct you to the specific piece of knowledge you need in order to carry out the task at hand. This is another important distinction in how KM carries out content management as opposed to systems such as document management systems. KM operates at a finer level of granularity—the work has been done a priori, so users need not wade

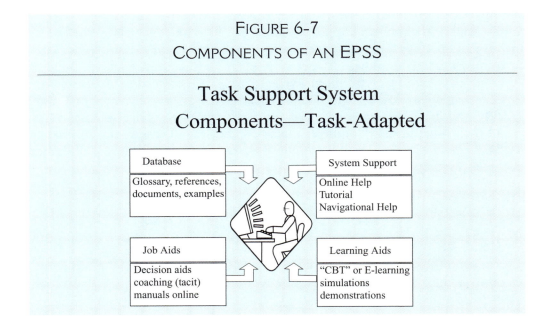

FIGURE 6-7
COMPONENTS OF AN EPSS

FIGURE 6-8

CHUNKING IN CONTENT MANAGEMENT

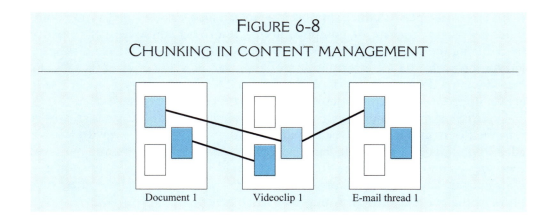

through thick technical documents or other "containers" of knowledge. These have been broken down into the valuable knowledge nuggets that are of greatest use.

Content management in KM thus involves breaking down documents into their conceptual components and mapping them out using concept indexes, semantic networks, or hierarchical knowledge taxonomies. Decomposition is also a prerequisite for the development of EPSS. Understanding the EPSS vision remains far from common. Indeed, *misunderstanding* of the EPSS vision is far more common—a result, in part, of misapplication of the term by people who sought "currency" in being on the bandwagon, despite the fact that they were selling traditional CBT, online reference materials, and the like. Still, after roughly eight years since the coining of the phrase, there are quite a few success stories for "true" performance support systems. What we call EPSS may change: a movement has begun to replace the term with *Performance Centered Systems*, in an attempt to recapture the original intent and to better appeal to the IS community. But the concept is here to stay, justified by the value these systems have provided to the visionary organizations that sponsored them.

Electronic Performance Support Systems can help an organization to reduce the cost of training staff while increasing productivity and performance. They can empower an employee to perform tasks with a minimum amount of external intervention or training. By using this type of system, an employee, especially new employees, will not only be able to complete their work more quickly and accurately, but as a secondary benefit they will also learn more about their job and their employer's business. For an update on this approach, see Dickleman (2003). An EPSS application at Sun Microsystems is described in the accompanying vignette.

SUN MICROSYSTEMS

Sun Microsystems, an $8 billion company, has launched SunWEB,[1] an intranet linking its 20,300 employees worldwide. At last count, the company had more than 1000 internal web servers putting up more than a quarter of

Continued

a million web and electronic pages. The intranet has not only saved $25 million a year but has also helped achieve big savings by enhancing its relationships with customers and suppliers by putting knowledge online. Sun has also begun thinking about how to use this powerful network to enhance the knowledge, skills, and capabilities of its employees and partners. SunTAN is their new intranet-based knowledge and training system, an interactive, network-based curriculum management and sales support system. SUN has tremendous learning and knowledge needs: 90% of its revenues are from products that are less than a year old, and it has consistently experienced widening product lines and shorter life cycles. As a result, the company found it could not train its sales professionals fast or effectively enough. It could no longer rely on traditional classroom-based training, which was too long, overwhelmed people with information, and cost about $2225 a week per individual (not counting lost sales time).

SunTAN consolidates sales training information, sales support resources, product updates and materials, competitive intelligence, and an array of other content on the Sun intranet. This distributed learning architecture ensures that the richest, most bandwidth-intensive, and most actively used media (e.g., a video demonstrating the latest line of new server products) is distributed to and stored on local servers at regional sales offices rather than the company's headquarters. Users can then download them at their convenience. In the new world of distance training, the only knowledge you need to retain is knowledge of the location of where you can get the information you need. It changes so often that it no longer makes sense to retain it. It is a pull rather than a push model. It is critical that funding for it comes from business units and that content also comes from resources other than a centralized training group. In this way, SunTAN serves as a just-in-time knowledge or performance support system enabling sales personnel to rapidly access critical information while they have a customer on the phone. Moreover, they can train in a self-directed way at their desktops without abandoning their customers for a weeklong training course.

SunTAN was originally developed for Sun's direct sales reps and sales engineers, but it is now available to the company's 20,000 resellers who account for more than 60% of worldwide sales. Additional features that will be integrated in this environment include database technology to track and profile individual usage of the system. This will be used to create customized learning paths and alert employees when relevant resources become available. A collaborative product called Kansas will be integrated into this environment to allow users to pull in as many as nine different video feeds onto a single screen for a high-tech meeting or panel discussion. Another add-on technology will be a conceptual indexer that will allow users to search and retrieve video content with key words much in the same way that they now search text. Some SUN customers are requesting that SunTAN's training content be made available within their own intranet firewalls.

Malcolm (1998) discussed the extension of the EPSS concept to apply to groups (CoPs) and to house content that could be dynamically updated within an organization's knowledge repository. Performance support systems today have been designed primarily for use by the individual: they support an individual as he or she works to accomplish some performance goal. In the commercial market, programs that help you prepare your income tax returns, write a will, or create a newsletter template all illustrate this level of support. In corporations, systems that support customer service representatives—whether in a call center for financial transactions or travel reservations, or face to face in the lobby of a hotel—also represent an individual's use of an EPSS. Imagine a group around a table with the means to project a computer display. The group would work through the steps of the process together, brainstorming and receiving group processing advice from a built-in "coach." The work product belonged to the group, and it was the group's performance that had been enhanced by the EPSS.

Another way to look at this challenge is to say that yet another conceptual merger needs to take place—this time assimilating the discipline of knowledge management—that is, capturing and sharing vital business information from a variety of sources, not just top down, in order to enable better decision making in a dynamic business environment. We in the field of performance support have much to learn from it, just as those who study knowledge capture and sharing have much to learn from us about how to integrate various kinds of support into the context of performing work.

Examples are fairly common in the large consulting firms where dynamically updated EPSSs are integrated within the organizational knowledge repository in order to make the complex task of sharing critical business and personal development information much easier.

Barron (2000) summarizes the current state of the art of EPSS and related approaches in the following manner: "take an eLearning course; chunk it into discrete learning bites; surround it with technology that assesses a learner's needs and delivers the appropriate learning nuggets; add collaborative tools that allow learners to share information. What do you get? Something that looks a whole lot like knowledge management."

The best approach, then, requires a user model or trace—a record of the interaction between the user and the system. The user model would capture the objects of interest or focus—that is, what content was accessed, when, how often, in which sequence, and so on. A log of user interactions can be abstracted to produce a user and task signature. Together, these will yield a model of the user and the task the user is attempting to perform. These two sources of information can help provide the best possible support for knowledge application in that particular case. Figure 6-9 illustrates a sample user and task model.

A good example of task and user modeling is a knowledge service center. An R&D organization relies upon a dedicated team of 10 information professionals who are continually updating their user and task models in order to optimize knowledge services. For example, each researcher's profile is updated regularly to reflect changing interests, new skills, and/or new projects. In addition, each information request is also analyzed periodically to assess the level of noise versus the level of "hits"—that is, how often was the information judged to be useful? This analysis is used to further refine or fine-tune the profiles so that the next information request will yield increasingly better results.

It is assumed that episodes related to particular tasks usually share some common features. Once these common features or patterns have been identified for a given task, they can be considered a signature of the task—evidence that the user is performing this task.

FIGURE 6-9
SAMPLE USER AND TASK MODEL

		Task Characteristics					Features	
Users	Tasks	Frequency	Consequence of Errors	Difficulty	Inter-dependencies	Type of Support	Complexity	Desirability
U(1) - Manager	T(1) T(2) T(3)	Weekly Monthly Quarterly	Low Moderate High	Low Moderate High	T(7), T(4)	Template Example	Low Moderate High	Low Moderate High
U(2) - Technical	T(2) T(7) T(8)							
U(3) - Sales	T(1) T(2) T(3) T(5)							
Help Desk	Support Request	Daily	High	Moderate	N/A	Knowledge Repositories	Moderate	High
I.T.	Problem Report	Daily	Moderate	Moderate	N/A	Manuals	Moderate	Moderate
Research	Tech. Watch	Monthly	Low	Low	Strategic Objectives	-	Moderate	Moderate
CKO	Strategic Priorities	Quarterly	High	Moderate	Business Units	-	High	High
U(n)	T(n)							

KNOWLEDGE APPLICATION AT GROUP AND ORGANIZATIONAL LEVELS

Knowledge management systems (KMSs) are tools aimed at supporting knowledge management. They evolved from information management tools that integrated many aspects of computer-supported collaborative work (CSCW) environments with information and document management systems (Ganesan, Edmonds, and Spector, 2001; Greif, 1988; Kling, 1991). Key characteristics of a KMS are support for:

1. Communication among various users.
2. Coordination of users' activities.
3. Collaboration among user groups on the creation, modification, and dissemination of artifacts and products.
4. Control processes to ensure integrity and to track the progress of projects.

Systems that support KM provide specific functions related to communication (e-mail and discussion forums); coordination (shareable calendars and task lists); collaboration (shareable artifacts and workspaces); and control (internal audit trails and automatic version control). A user-centered KMS contributes to an organizational culture of sharing by providing a sense of belonging to a community of users and by supporting reciprocity among users (Marshall and Rossett, 2000). KMSs extend the perspective of employees as knowledge workers by providing them with the means to create knowledge and to actively contribute to a shared and dynamic body of knowledge. A KMS provides support for many information functions, including:

- Acquiring and indexing, capturing, and archiving.
- Finding and accessing.
- Creating and annotating.
- Combining, collating, and modifying.
- Tracking. (See Edmonds and Pusch, 2002.)

These KMS functions allow multiple individuals to organize meaningful activities around shared and reusable artifacts to achieve specific goals. In short, a KMS addresses the distributed nature of work and expertise (Salomon, 1993).

Within business and industry, KM technology is being used to support organizational learning (Morecroft and Sterman, 1994; Senge, 1990). The dynamics of the global economy place a premium on organizational responsiveness and flexibility. Partly as a response to the demands of a highly competitive global economy, KMS technology has emerged as a new generation of information management systems. In contrast with previous information management systems, a KMS is designed for multiple users with different and changing requirements.

British Telecommunications and Futuremedia iLearning developed Solstra 2000,[2] which is the new model of the jointly developed net-based learning and knowledge management system. It is the result of significant product development based on increasingly sophisticated and growing customer demand. Solstra 2000 is designed for hosting, delivering, and managing online learning and job support information. Additional enhancements to the new version include refined administration, management and reporting capabilities, and several new flexible options that increase the availability of learning to groups and individuals at their PCs. Solstra 2000 also claims to provide the necessary technology to allow any organization to set up a virtual "Corporate University."

Highlights include the development of Solstra 2000 to map onto an organization's structure. This reportedly makes it intuitive and straightforward for HR, training, and line managers to set up a familiar framework to administrate learning across all departments and levels of the organization, providing the natural platform for a Corporate University. Also, all staff are given the ability to "raise their hand" electronically, alerting colleagues to their expertise, interests, and areas they are looking to improve, with their own Solstra 2000 personal homepage. Searchable throughout the organization, this information provides the foundation for a knowledge management system. Solstra 2000 has increased scalability, allowing it to be used by an unlimited number of participants. Terms and text can be customized and translated into different languages, making it suitable for use by the largest global organizations.

New participants joining a group or department using Solstra 2000 are automatically able to access the learning content previously assigned to fellow group members, bringing them instantly up to speed. HR managers and trainers can tailor FAQs to specific users within Solstra 2000 and they can use a "news service" to alert participants when relevant learning content becomes available. HR and training managers can create tailored "Frequently Asked Questions" within Solstra 2000, as well as a "news service" alerting participants directly when new relevant learning content becomes available.

Key enabling technologies include object orientation, broadband communications, and adaptive systems. Object orientation provides for the creation of knowledge objects that can be easily found, modified, and reused. Broadband communication allows users separated in time or space to work on large data objects effectively as a team. Adaptive systems recognize that different users may have different requirements and preferred working styles.

A KMS can be viewed as an activity system that involves people making use of objects (tools and technologies) to create artifacts and products that represent knowledge in order to achieve a shared goal. Previous information management systems focused on a small portion of such a system, such as a narrow set of objects in the form of a collection of records or simple communication between team members. A KMS embraces the entire activity system but maintains a focus on the human-use aspects (people with shared goals) as opposed to the underlying or enabling technology aspects. KMSs have already met with significant success in the business sector and are spreading to other sectors, including education (Marshall and Rossett, 2000) and instructional design (Ganesan, Edmonds, and Spector, 2001). Table 6-5 provides some examples of KM systems.

The organizational knowledge management architecture will be comprised of at least three levels: the *data layer*, which is the unifying abstraction across different types of data, with potentially different storage mechanisms (e.g., database, text documents, video, audio); the *process layer*, which describes the logic that links the data with its use and its users (other people or other systems who use that data); and the *user interface*, which provides access to the information assets of the company via the logic incorporated in the process layer. The KM organizational architecture is shown in Figure 6-10.

KM cannot be supported, however, by the simple amalgamation of masses of data. KM requires the structuring and navigation of this content supported by metadata, the formal description of the content, and its interrelationships with other content or other knowledge objects. Metadata encompasses infor-

TABLE 6-5

EXAMPLES OF KNOWLEDGE APPLICATION SUPPORT TECHNOLOGIES

Name	Description	Website
Mindjet's Mindman	High-level visualization and mapping tool	http://www.mindjet.com
Groove	Collaboration software	http://www.groove.net
Visio	High-end flowcharting tool	http://www.microsoft.com/office/visio/
Themescape	Topographical knowledge maps	http://www.micropat.com/0/pdf/themescape.pdf
OpenText's Clarity	Automatic taxonomy creation	http://www.opentext.com/
ClearForest's ClearTags	Automatic taxonomy creation	http://www.clearforest.com/
LotusNotes Websphere	Knowledge repository	http://www.lotus.com/home.nsf/welcome/kstation
Teximus Technologies	Content management software	http://www.teximus.com
Vignette	Content management software	http://www.vignette.com/
EPSS Central	Electronic performance support systems	http://www.pcd-innovations.com/

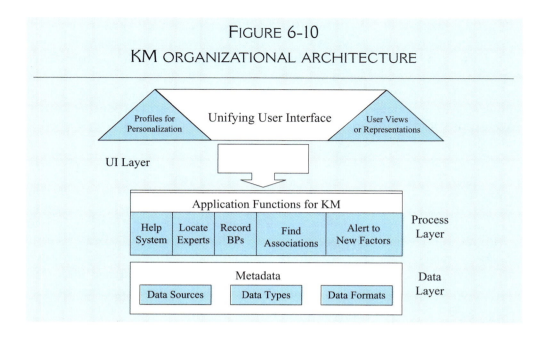

FIGURE 6-10

KM ORGANIZATIONAL ARCHITECTURE

mation about physical structures, data types, access methods, and actual content. A variety of tools and techniques are available for the knowledge application phase of the KM cycle. Dissemination and publication tools typically involve some type of knowledge repository design. They will have features such as the routing and delivery of information to those who have a need or who have subscribed (push vs. pull approach). E-mail and workflow are examples of push technologies that notify users of any changes such as newly posted or expired content. Pattern matching can be done against user profiles in order to better target where pushed content should go.

Other tools help structure and navigate through the content. They provide a classification scheme for the organization's knowledge assets. We saw examples of these knowledge taxonomies in the previous chapter. The user interface layer is where such navigation guides are to be found. Once the content has been properly indexed and organized, multiple views can be made available for the same underlying content in order to accommodate user and task needs. Electronic linkages can be used to cross-reference this content, and thesauri can encapsulate these cross-linkages. Similarly, expertise location systems should be available from the user interface layer of the KM architecture. In this way, links are made from the user interface topics to the relevant KM content, people, and processes.

Knowledge Reuse

Reusing knowledge involves recall and recognition, as well as actually applying the knowledge, if we use Bloom's taxonomy. Reusing knowledge typically begins with the formulation of a search question. It is here that expert–novice differences quickly become apparent, as experts know the right questions to ask. Next, experts are searched for and located, using expertise location systems or yellow pages as we saw in Chapter 5. The appropriate expert and/or advice is then chosen, and the knowledge nugget is applied. Knowledge application may involve taking a general guide and making it specific to the situation at hand, which is sometimes referred to as recontextualization of knowledge (where decontextualization to some degree occurred during knowledge capture and codification). An example of knowledge reuse is described in the accompanying vignette.

J.P. MORGAN CHASE

Reuse knowledge management initiatives have been established at Lab-Morgan, the Internet strategy and incubation unit of J.P. Morgan Chase & Co. The lab uses Intraspect Software technology to help employees filter the hundreds of business plan referrals received for investment or incubation possibilities each month. The platform lets users access all previous expertise and feedback on similar propositions the company has received, so they can measure new proposals against them and know what questions to ask to further probe a new plan's merits. Since the deployment, the lab says it has been able to avoid duplicate screenings of similar proposals and has generated significant gains.

But the lab thought about how it works as an organization before jumping into the technology. "The collaborative tool pushed thinking about our processes and how we work together," says J. Feldhusen, Managing Director, LabMorgan. "The core has to be a mind-set of sharing and accomplishing a common goal. We designed the software to support the processes we use." But she acknowledges that deploying knowledge management initiatives might be more challenging in dealing with very established processes. "How do you motivate people to move to new ways? [Our advantage is that] we're in an area that's highly innovative."

Source: Pflaging, 2001.

There are three major roles required for knowledge reuse: the *knowledge producer*, the person who produced or documented the knowledge object; the *knowledge intermediary*, who prepares knowledge for reuse by indexing, sanitizing, packaging, and even marketing the knowledge object; and the *knowledge reuser*, who retrieves, understands, and applies it. Of course, these roles are neither permanent nor dedicated—individuals will perform all three at some time during their knowledge work. Knowledge repackaging is an important value-added step that may involve people, information technology, or, as is often the case, a mixture of the two. For example, automatic classification systems can index content, but a human is almost always needed in the loop to validate and to add context, caveats, and other useful indicators for the most effective use of that knowledge object.

Markus (2001) suggests there are four distinct types of knowledge reuse situations according to the individual who is doing the reusing and the purpose of knowledge reuse, which is quite compatible with the user and task-adapted approach outlined in this chapter. The four reuse situations are:

1. Shared work producers, who produce knowledge they later reuse.
2. Shared work practitioners, who reuse each others' knowledge contributions.
3. Expertise-seeking novices.
4. Secondary knowledge miners.

Shared work producers usually consist of teams or workgroups that have collaborated together. A common example is an MD who consults a patient's chart to see what medications had been prescribed recently by other physicians, or special education teachers and therapists who share student files to see what sorts of interventions worked and which ones did not have any effect. This is the easiest form of knowledge reuse, for everyone is quite familiar with the knowledge content—they share the same context that makes knowledge application rapid and effective.

Shared work practitioners are members of the same community of practice. They are peers who share a profession. This form of knowledge reuse will require a higher degree of filtering and personalization, typically done by CoP knowledge librarians. Reusers would need more reassurance about the source's credibility; they would need to be able to trust that the content is valid and should be applied. Their contexts are less likely to completely overlap, so knowledge reuse would likely require contact with others knowledgeable about the knowledge object.

Expertise-seeking novices are often in a learning scenario. Unlike the previous two types of reusers, novices are the most distant or different from the knowledge object authors and those experienced with its use. Knowledge intermediaries have a much greater role to play here in making sure novices begin by accessing more general information (e.g., FAQs, introductory texts, glossaries) before they attempt to apply the knowledge object or to directly contact those who are more expert in using it. EPSS and other performance support aids such as e-learning modules would also be of great use to such reusers.

Secondary knowledge miners are analysts who attempt to extract interesting and hopefully meaningful patterns by studying knowledge repository use. They are analogous to the usage analysts who perform similar roles for a CoP library as discussed in Chapter 5. They are also analogous to librarians who periodically assess the collective holdings of a library, whether physical or digital, to see which items are no longer being actively accessed and should perhaps be archived, which have been superseded by newer and better best practices and so forth.

Different types of reusers will thus interface differently with knowledge repositories, and they will differ in their support needs. Repositories therefore need to be able to personalize—either at the extreme of treating each individual differently or, at the very least, personalizing at the level of a community of practice. Since CoPs revolve around organizational and professional themes, it makes sense to partition the global knowledge repository along similar lines. Careful attention must also be paid to the roles of intermediaries needed to develop and maintain the organization's corporate memory. Content authors are as vital to successful knowledge application and reuse as are container maintainers.

Knowledge Repositories

Knowledge repositories are usually intranets or portals of some kind that serve to preserve, manage, and leverage organizational memory. Many different types of knowledge repositories are in use today, and they can be categorized in a number of different ways. In general, a knowledge repository will contain more than documents (document management system), data (database), or records (record management system). A knowledge repository will contain valuable content that is a mix of tacit and explicit knowledge, based on the unique experiences of the individuals who are or were a part of that company as well as the know-how that has been tried, tested, and found to work in work situations.

Davenport, De Long, and Beers (1998) make a distinction between repositories that store external knowledge such as that gathered from competitive intelligence, demographic, or statistical data from data resellers and other public sources, and internal knowledge repositories that store informal information such as transcripts of group discussions, e-mails, or other forms of internal communications. Internal knowledge repositories will have a less constraining or less formal structure in order to be able to better accommodate its fluid, subjective knowledge content.

Zack (1999) classifies repositories based on the type of content they contain such as general knowledge (e.g., published scientific literature) and specific knowledge (which includes knowledge of the local context of the organization). This distinction is most useful, for knowledge reusers need to know whether the credibility of the knowledge comes from general or common knowledge or whether it was discovered by their colleagues.

STRATEGIC IMPLICATIONS OF KNOWLEDGE APPLICATION

Knowledge application implies that employees in an organization can quickly find answers to the following types of questions:

- What have we already written or published on this topic?
- Who are the experts in this area, and how can I contact them?
- Have any of our partners, contacts, and clients addressed these issues?
- What sources did we use to prepare the publications on this topic?
- What are the best websites or internal databases to find more information?
- How can I add my own experience in applying this particular piece of knowledge?

A knowledge repository should be a one-stop shop for knowledge application. Employees should be able to find out what they need in order to access, understand, and apply the cumulative experience and expertise of the organization. In this way, knowledge workers can concentrate on doing their actual work and not lose precious time trying to find all the bits and pieces of knowledge and know-how that have already been captured, coded, vetted, and made available to them. Reuse of proven knowledge not only can serve to increase efficiency and effectiveness but can free up knowledge workers to devote their efforts to innovative and creative knowledge to be added to corporate memory, as opposed to reinventing what has already been developed or solved.

In many cases, reusing knowledge is nontrivial. This counterintuitive result is generally due to two particular problems. In an organization of more than moderate complexity, it is difficult to locate the knowledge to be reused. Workers may be unaware that the knowledge they need is available. The knowledge may be held in the organization and correctly identified, but may simply be in the wrong form for the task; the essential information may be only implicit in the repository. The knowledge may have to be reconfigured in some way to meet the requirements of the task at hand. In addition, the knowledge may require some partial modification (e.g., updating). Here, understanding the knowledge requirements of both the users and their tasks is the key to understanding, identifying, and using the correct knowledge from the various sources. This in turn would enable more leverage to be gained from the knowledge already at hand, thereby increasing the returns on the investment in those knowledge assets.

PRACTICAL IMPLICATIONS OF KNOWLEDGE APPLICATION

At a minimum,

- Create an organizational knowledge base to house the intellectual assets.
- Create a corporate yellow pages so that knowledge workers can find out who is knowledgeable in which areas of expertise.
- Capture best practices and lessons learned and make them available to all others in the organization via the knowledge base.
- Empower a Chief Knowledge Officer to develop and implement a KM strategy for the organization.
- Ensure that the organizational culture will help facilitate the key phases required for the KM cycle (to capture, create, share, disseminate, acquire, and apply valuable knowledge).

Make sure that it is fairly easy to continually update and feed the corporate memory. Users should be able to contribute best practices, lessons learned, comments and questions about content, tips and tools they would recommend, working examples, and case studies. Openly encouraging and applying new ideas fosters the cooperation and innovation that is critical to a learning organization.

Knowledge application is far more likely to succeed if the type of content that is being made available can "hit the ground running." In other words, it is not just a repository of "stuff" but chunks of executable knowledge. The knowledge nuggets should always include tacit and contextual knowledge of when this should be used, where it can and cannot be applied, why and why not, and the ground truth or knowledge of how things really work and what is required for successful performance.

KEY POINTS

- There are a number of ways of ensuring that individuals apply knowledge, such as deriving user and task models in order to better match knowledge content to individual knowledge workers' preferences and requirements.
- EPSS, the Bloom taxonomies of cognitive, affective, and psychomotor skills, and content chunking are all good means of providing learning and task support to knowledge workers who apply knowledge and of optimizing the match between user needs and the content that is to be applied.
- A KM organizational architecture needs to be designed, developed, and implemented in order to facilitate knowledge application at the organizational level.
- Knowledge reuse is a good measure of how well valuable content has been preserved and managed in organizational memory management systems.
- Knowledge Support Systems can assist in organizational knowledge use and reuse, typically through some form of knowledge repository or intranet application.

DISCUSSION POINTS

1. Discuss personalization and profiling approaches to model knowledge workers. How would you make use of more information about users in order to better target valuable knowledge content to them? How would you increase the likelihood of their applying the content?
2. When would you make use of which Bloom taxonomy? Provide examples of some knowledge applications where each of the three taxonomies could provide useful information.
3. What are some of the tools used in organizational memory management?
4. What are the key components that should be addressed by an organizational KM architecture? Why are these components critical for organizational knowledge application?
5. What is reuse, and why is it an important measure of the success of KM within an organization?
6. Why is knowledge application the most important step in the KM cycle?

7. How does knowledge application relate to the internalization phase of the Nonaka and Takeuchi knowledge spiral model that was presented in Chapter 3?

8. Discuss why counting the number of "hits" to a knowledge repository (much like website statistics) would not be the best measure of knowledge application within an organization.

9. What is chunking? Why is this a good content management strategy? How would you take advantage of chunking for individual and organizational knowledge application situations?

10. Provide an example of a task analysis for a task familiar to you. What are the major challenges in designing an EPSS based on such a task analysis? How would you address these challenges?

NOTES

[1] B. Monasco, Sun's knowledge network enhances its selling skills, *Knowledge Inc.*, 1997.

[2] Solstra 2000, *International Knowledge Management News*, October 20, 1999.

REFERENCES

Barron, T. (2000, August). A smarter Frankenstein: the merging of e-learning and knowledge management. *LearningCircuits*. Available at http://www.learning circuits.org.

Bloom, B. (Ed.). (1956). *Taxonomy of educational objectives: book 1, cognitive domain*. New York: Longman.

Bloom, B., Mesia, B., and Krathwohl, R. (1964). *Taxonomy of educational objectives*. Volumes 1 and 2. New York: David McKay.

Cohen, W. M., and Levinthal, D. (1990). Absorptive capacity: a new perspective on learning and innovation. *Administrative Science Quarterly*, 35: 128–152.

Davenport, T., De Long, D., and Beers, M. (1998). Successful knowledge management projects. *Sloan Management Review*, 39(2): 43–57.

Dickleman, G. (2003). *EPSS revisited: a lifecycle for developing performance-centered systems*. Silver Spring, MD: International Society for Performance Improvement.

Dixon, N. (2000). *Common knowledge: how companies thrive by sharing what they know*. Boston: Harvard Business School Press.

Edmonds, G., and Pusch, R. (2002). Creating shared knowledge: instructional knowledge management systems. *Educational Technology & Society*, 5(1) [Online serial]. Available at http://ifets.ieee.org/periodical/vol_1_2002/.

Ford, N., Wilson, T. D., Foster, A., Ellis, D., and Spink, A. (2002). Information seeking and mediated searching. Part 4. Cognitive styles in information seeking. *Journal of the American Society for Information Science and Technology*, 53(9): 728–735.

Ganesan, R., Edmonds, G. S., and Spector, J. M. (2001). The changing nature of instructional design for networked learning. In C. Jones and C. Steeples (Eds.), *Networked learning in higher education* (pp. 93–109). Berlin: Springer-Verlag.

Gery, G. (1991). *Electronic performance support systems.* Cambridge, MA: Ziff Institute.

Greif, I. (Ed.). (1988*). Computer-supported cooperative work: a book of readings.* San Mateo, CA: Morgan Kaufmann, 1988.

Hatami, A., Galliers, R., and Huang, J. (2003). Exploring the impacts of knowledge (re)use and organizational memory on the effectiveness of strategic decisions: a longitudinal case study. In *Proceedings, 36th Hawaii International Conference on System Sciences (HICSS'03).*

Hicks, D., and Tochtermann, K. (2001). Personal digital libraries and knowledge management. *Journal of Universal Computer Systems*, 7(7): 550–565.

Kling, R. (1991). Cooperation, coordination and control in computer-supported work. *Communications of the ACM*, 34(12): 83–88.

Kuhlthau, C. (1993). *Seeking meaning: a process approach to library and information services.* Norwood, NJ: Ablex Publishing.

Malcolm, S. (1998, March). Where EPSS will go from here. *Training*, 64–69.

Markus, M. (2001). Toward a theory of knowledge reuse: types of knowledge reuse situations and factors in reuse success. *Journal of Management Information Systems*, 18(1): 57–94.

Marshall, J. M., and Rossett, A. (2000). Knowledge management for school-based educators. In J. M. Spector and T. M. Anderson (Eds.), *Integrated and holistic perspectives on learning, instruction and technology: understanding complexity* (pp. 19–34). Dordrecht, Netherlands: Kluwer Academic.

Morecroft, D. W., and Sterman, J. D. (Eds.). (1994). *Modeling for learning organizations.* Portland, OR: Productivity Press.

Myers, I., McCaulley, M., Quenk, N., and Hammer, A. (1998). *Myers-Briggs Type Indicator manual* (3rd ed.). Palo Alto, CA: Consulting Psychologists Press.

Pflaging, J. (2001). Enterprise collaboration: the big payoff. *KM World.* Special Supplement, pp. 56–57.

Preece, J., Rogers, Y., Sharp, H., Benyon, D., Holland, S., and Carey, T. (1994). *Human-computer interaction.* Reading, MA: Addison-Wesley.

Salomon, G. (Ed.). (1993). *Distributed cognitions: psychological and educational considerations.* New York: Cambridge University Press.

Senge, P. M. (1990). *The fifth discipline: the art and practice of the learning organization.* New York: Doubleday.

Solstra (2000). *International Management News*, Oct. 20, 1999.

Spector, J. M., and Anderson, T. M. (Eds.). (2000). *Integrated and holistic perspectives on learning, instruction and technology: understanding complex domains.* Dordrecht, Netherlands: Kluwer Academic.

Spink, A., Wilson, T., Ford, N., Froster, A., and Ellis, D. (2002). Information seeking and mediated searching. Part 1. Theoretical framework and research design. *Journal of the American Society for Information Science and Technology*, 53(9): 695–703.

Webb, S. P. (1998). *Knowledge management: linchpin of change.* London: Aslib.

Zack, M. (1999). Managing codified knowledge. *Sloan Management Review*, 40(4): 45–58.

THE ROLE OF ORGANIZATIONAL CULTURE

As the soil, however rich it may be, cannot be productive without cultivation, so the mind without culture can never produce good fruit.

Seneca (Roman Senator, c. 60 B.C.–c. A.D. 37)

This chapter examines the role played by organizational culture in more detail. Different types of organizational cultures are described with a view to better understanding the key dimensions of the different microcultures that thrive in organizations. Cultural enablers and obstacles to knowledge sharing are presented, together with a discussion on how to institute desired organizational changes to better accommodate knowledge management. Finally, the long-term nature of organizational culture dimensions is addressed by presenting major organizational and KM maturity models.

LEARNING OBJECTIVES

1. Define organizational culture.
2. Understand the relation between organizational culture and the business context. How does culture contribute to organizational innovation and success?
3. Appreciate the contribution of organizational culture to the management of change; understand the analytic elements of organizational culture, such as different types of cultures and organizational maturity models.
4. Describe how organizational culture intersects with knowledge management.
5. Discuss the key organizational culture enablers and the chief obstacles to effective knowledge sharing and KM.

6. List the major phases involved in initiating organizational change and review how the organizational culture would have to evolve so that KM goals can be attained.
7. Discuss to what extent organizational culture can be managed.

INTRODUCTION

A number of common myths persist in the field of KM, including the "build it and they will come" myth. Unfortunately, people rarely take the time to learn new tools; technology does not always give them what they want or need, and they often are not in a position to even know what they need. A second myth is that "technology will replace face-to-face." However, valuable tacit knowledge sharing and the important role of informal networks and peer-to-peer learning cannot and should not be ignored. The third common KM myth is that "the first thing to do is change the organizational culture to one of learning." Although a number of successful KM initiatives grew in organizations that already had a solid learning culture, in others it is very difficult, and it takes a very long time to launch (and subsequently maintain) cultural change. If you begin with this challenge, you will end up waiting a long time for KM to succeed. Most organizations can be envisaged to sit on a KM readiness gradient: some are already "there," whereas others have to move up to a cultural state that will more readily accommodate or enable KM to succeed. Regardless of position, one thing is certain: the organization's cultural environment will play a crucial role in determining what happens to knowledge management within that organization (see Figure 7-1).

What is organizational culture? The literature on organizational culture borrows heavily from anthropology and sociology. Originally an anthropological term, *culture* refers to the underlying values, beliefs, and codes of practice that make a community what it is. The customs of society, the self-image of its members, the things that make it different from other societies, are its culture. Culture is powerfully subjective and reflects the meanings and understandings that we typically attribute to situations, and the solutions that we apply to common problems. The idea of a common culture suggests possible problems about whether organizations have cultures. Organizations are only one constituent element of society. People enter them from the surrounding community and bring their culture with them. It is still possible for organizations to have cultures of their own, for they possess the paradoxical quality of being both part of and apart from society. They are embedded in the wider societal context, but they are also communities of their own with distinct rules and values.

Culture has long been on the agenda of management theorists. Culture change must mean changing the corporate ethos, and the images and values that inform action. This new way of understanding organizational life must be brought into the management process. Culture possesses a number of central aspects: one such aspect is an evaluative element that involves social expectations and standards—the values and beliefs that people hold central and that

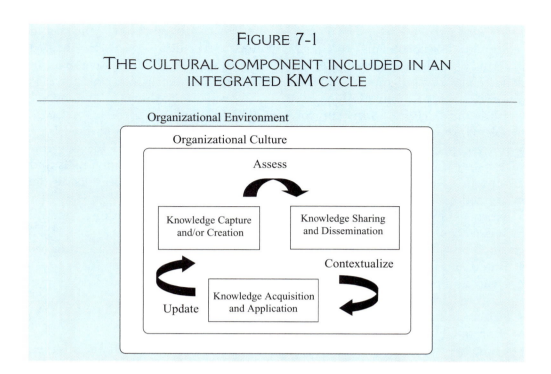

FIGURE 7-1
THE CULTURAL COMPONENT INCLUDED IN AN INTEGRATED KM CYCLE

Organizational Environment

Organizational Culture

Assess

Knowledge Capture and/or Creation

Knowledge Sharing and Dissemination

Contextualize

Update

Knowledge Acquisition and Application

bind organizational groups. Culture is also a set of more material elements or artifacts. These are not only the signs and symbols by which the organization is recognized but also the events, behaviors, and people that embody culture. The medium of culture is social interaction, the web of communications that constitute a community. Here a shared language is particularly important in expressing and signifying a distinctive organizational culture. It is especially apparent in communities of practice where members tend to have their own "jargon" or "brand."

Not surprisingly, many definitions of culture have been proposed in the literature. One of the earliest definitions was provided by Morgan (1977) who more recently (1997) describes culture as "an active living phenomenon through which people jointly create and recreate the worlds in which they live" (p. 141). For Morgan, the three basic questions cultural analysts must answer are:

- What are the shared frames of reference that make organization possible?
- Where do they come from?
- How are they created, communicated, and sustained?

Schein (1999), who is generally considered the father of organizational culture, provides the following definition: "organizational culture is a pattern of basic assumptions—invented, discovered, or developed by a given group as it learns to cope with its problems of external adaptation and internal integration—that has worked well enough to be considered valid and, therefore, to be taught to new members as the correct way to perceive, think and feel in relation to those problems" (p. 385). Organizational culture can also be defined in terms of both its causes and effects. Using an outcomes perspective, we can define culture as a manifest pattern of behavior, consistent behavioral patterns observed across a group of individuals, or "the way we do things around here." Culture thus defines consistent ways in which people perform tasks, solve problems, resolve conflicts, treat customers and employees, and so on. Using a process perspective, culture can also be defined as a set of mechanisms such as informal values, norms, and beliefs that control how individuals and groups in an organization interact with each other and people outside the organization.

Morgan (1977) found that some key elements of organizational culture include:

- Stated and unstated values.
- Overt and implicit expectations for member behavior.
- Customs and rituals.
- Stories and myths about the history of the group.
- Shop talk—typical language used in and about the group.
- Climate—the feelings evoked by the way members interact with one another, with outsiders, and with their environment, including the physical space they occupy.
- Metaphors and symbols—may be unconscious or embodied in other cultural elements.

Other authors define corporate culture as the set of understandings (often unstated) that members of a community share in common. Shared understandings consist of norms, values, attitudes, beliefs, and paradigms (Sathe, 1985). The *Webster's New Collegiate Dictionary* defines culture as the "integrated pattern of human behavior that includes thought, speech, action, and artifacts and depends on man's capacity for learning and transmitting knowledge to succeeding generations." Organizational culture can be taught to new members of the organization as the "correct" or accepted way to think, perceive, and feel with respect to organizational work, problems, and so forth.

Although every organization has its own culture, strong or weak, most organizations do not create their culture consciously. Culture is created and ingrained into people's lives unconsciously. Unless special effort is taken, people will not recognize that the attitudes, beliefs, and visions they have always taken for granted are actually standardized assumptions that they may pass on to future generations. The difficulty of making sense of culture lies in the fact that even though the artifacts of culture can be easily sensed, the core of the culture values, which are defined as "broad, nonspecific feelings of good and evil, beautiful and ugly, normal and abnormal, rational and irrational are often unconscious and rarely discussable" (Hofstede et al., 1990 p. 291). Cultural artifacts are both conceptual (such as language) and material. They mediate interaction with the world, coordinating people's activities with the physical world and with each other.

A reciprocal relationship exists between organizational culture and communication (Pepper, 1995). On the one hand, communication is the tool that helps to transmit organizational culture to each other and to the newcomers of the organization, and it also enables the culture to be maintained and developed in its certain way. In a sense, culture comes into being through constant communication among the members of the organization, and communication changes the cultural assumptions over time. Culture deeply shapes and alters the communication within this specific culture. "The culture encourages certain topics for communication and discounts others. The culture often determines who talks with whom, on what occasions, and covering what matters" (Neher, p. 127, 1997). Organizational culture, therefore, may be thought of as the manner in which an organization solves problems to achieve its specific goals and to maintain itself over time. Moreover, it is holistic, historically determined, socially constructed, and difficult to change (Hofstede et al., 1990).

DIFFERENT TYPES OF CULTURES

Of course, people do not always behave as expected, and the cultural profiles above are very generic. A good analogy can be made between organizational culture and the climate control of a large building: although the thermostat may be set at one temperature throughout the company, there are in fact a series of different microclimates depending on which part of the building one is in, how the office furniture is arranged, the number of people in a room, the number of plants, and so forth. A similar situation exists with regard to organizational culture: although an organization as a whole may be characterized as having a particular type of culture, many different types of microcultures will be in evidence throughout the company. Some of these may be picked up in examining the communities of practice that exist, the different types of professionals or skill sets that make up the company's human capital, and so forth.

One way of exploring cultures is to classify them into types. Organizational culture may be differentiated in many ways. Goffee and Johns (2000), for example, identified four types of organizational culture, which they created by using two dimensions. The first dimension, *sociability*, is a measure for friendliness. A high sociable culture indicates that people within the culture tend to be friendly to each other without expecting something in return. Sociability is consistent with a high people orientation, high team orientation, and focus on process rather than outcomes. *Solidarity*, the second dimension, measures the task orientation. High solidarity means that people can work well together toward common goals, even when they have personal disputes or conflicts.

This classification scheme produces four types of organizational cultures: communal, networked, mercenary, and fragmented (see Table 7-1).

1. A *communal culture* can give its members a sense of belonging, though it also is task-driven. Leaders of this culture are usually very

TABLE 7-1
FOUR TYPES OF ORGANIZATIONAL CULTURES

	High Solidarity	Low Solidarity
High Sociability	1. Communal Culture	2. Networked Culture
Low Sociability	3. Mercenary Culture	4. Fragmented Culture

inspirational and charismatic. The major negative is that they often exert too much influence and other members are rarely vocal.

2. In a *networked culture*, members are treated as friends and family. People have close contact with each other and love each other. They are willing to help each other and share information. The disadvantage of this culture is that people are so kind to each other that they are reluctant to point out and criticize the poor performance.

3. A *mercenary culture* focuses on strict goals. Members are expected to meet the goals and to get the job done quickly. Since everyone focuses on goals and objectivity, there is little room for political cliques. The negative is that those with poor performance may be treated inhumanely.

4. In a *fragmented culture*, the sense of belonging to and identification with the organization is usually very weak. The individualists constitute the organizations, and their commitment is given first to individual members and task work. The downside is that there is a lack of cooperation.

Culture may be characterized in a number of ways, and organizational cultural analysis must be one of the first steps to be taken in any KM initiative. One of the fundamental prerequisites of a culture that fosters rather than hinders knowledge management is the notion of trust. When organizational members feel that they are respected, that they can expect to be treated in a professional manner, and that they can trust the other members of their group, then knowledge sharing is greatly enhanced. Trust removes any potential barriers owing to lack of confidence that the person on the receiving end will not attribute the authors of knowledge or that they will make inappropriate use of the knowledge shared.

ORGANIZATIONAL CULTURE ANALYSIS

Culture surrounds us, and we need to understand how it is created, embedded, developed, manipulated, managed, and changed. To understand the culture is to understand your organization. Schein (1992) outlines three levels of culture, as shown in Table 7-2. The third level is ultimately the basis for all values and actions.

TABLE 7-2
LEVELS OF CULTURE

Cultural Level	Description
1. Artifacts	The visible organizational structures and processes.
2. Values	The stated strategies, goals, philosophies, and justifications.
3. Assumptions	The basic underlying assumptions, unconscious, taken for granted beliefs, perceptions, thought, and feelings.

Source: Adapted from Schein, 1992.

Artifacts, the first layer, are easy to detect (e.g., a dress code), but they may be difficult to understand. They represent "the tip of the iceberg," and it remains a challenge to discern or decipher what lies underneath them (i.e., what is the reason for this type of dress code or other visible structures and processes?). Basic assumptions in organizational culture are usually represented by general and abstract statements that express certain ideas and truths about human beings. They are the expression of a philosophy, of a general concept concerning individuals and society. Given the diversity of such concepts and their contradictory characteristics, these assumptions often have an eclectic, heterogeneous, fragmentary, and unilateral aspect.

The *values* shared by the members of an organization represent the second layer in culture analysis. From an organizational perspective, values express essential meanings of basic assumptions. Therefore, values define a set of its members' organizational expectations. Values are expressed and often imposed by the managerial elite and become, in some ways, a reference system for activity assessment. They are included in attitudes and behaviors, in the organizational habitat. The two levels, *assumptions* and *values*, represent the content of what we call an organization expressive area or expressive culture. Its origins can be found in both the organization and personal history of its members.

Norms form the instrumental and visible area of organizational culture. They represent the most evident layer for someone who comes in contact with the organization for the first time. They derive from cultural values and basic assumptions. Norms are expressed in a set of rules and expectations and serve to orient people's behavior within the organization. This is why, even for the organization personnel, norms constitute their contact with culture and are the conveyor of values and basic assumptions. The two basic categories of norms are *formal, institutional norms*, produced by managers or experts, hired for this purpose alone, and made mandatory, and *informal norms*, produced by the personnel or by certain groups and disseminated through legends, stories, and myths, or reflected in ceremonies or rituals. They are the expression of informal culture, based on certain values spread in an informal space. An expressive culture is one that reflects the emotions, feelings, and aspirations of the organization's personnel. An illustration follows.

Norms are directly involved in the change process because they allow for interventions in a field that is very accessible to individuals. Those who want to understand organizational culture refer to its philosophical and value layers. Those who want to change culture and use it as a maintenance or development tool refer mainly to its normative layer or see it as a normative culture. A normative culture is based on a set of formal rules, norms, prescriptions, positions, and hierarchies and emphasizes compliance with the rules.

On the other hand, norms represent one of the premises for cultural unity, the reference system for managers in personnel assessment. Such assessments sustain norms strengthening and are often accompanied by bonuses. Norms are thus a reference system for the personnel as well, whose attitude toward them represents the framework that produces organizational ethos.

Schein (1999) argues that the pattern of basic underlying assumptions can function as a cognitive defense mechanism for individuals and the group. As a result, culture change is difficult, time-consuming, and anxiety provoking. Cultures are deep seated, pervasive, and complex, and it can be extremely difficult to bring the assumptions to the surface. He uses the classic three-step approach to discuss change: unfreezing, cognitive restructuring, and refreezing. The key issue for leaders is that they must become sufficiently marginal in their own culture to recognize its maladaptive assumptions and to learn some new ways of thinking themselves as a prelude to unfreezing and changing their organization.

A number of instruments can help diagnose organizational culture (e.g., Harrison and Stokes, 1992). These are typically surveys or questionnaires that help to identify the critical aspects of an existing culture and will provide a profile of your organization's culture, typically in the form of an orientation.

The most important dimensions of an organizational culture are that culture promotes an ideal that mobilizes learning institutions in achieving it and that culture can bring uniformity and unity as well as diversity. Culture is customs and rights and the organization's "own way"—its norms, values, behavior patterns, rituals, traditions. Culture implies structural stability, patterning, and integration. It arises from shared history, and adaptation and change are not possible without making changes that affect the culture. More often than not it is not rational. For large organizations there are issues involving the development of subcultures and the integration of newcomers. Organizational learning, development, and planned change cannot be understood without considering culture as the primary source of resistance to change (Schein, 1999). It is at this junction—the resistance to any change in the organizational culture—that we first encounter the intersection between organizational culture and knowledge management.

CULTURE AT THE FOUNDATION OF KM

Implementations of knowledge management almost always require a cultural change—if not a complete transformation, at least a tweaking of the existing culture(s) in order to promote a culture of knowledge sharing and collaboration. KM will almost always trigger a change that will in turn trigger a maturing or an evolutionary process. However, the instigator of change rarely meets with a receptive audience. People do not necessarily always oppose change for the sake of opposing, but they will do so if they perceive the proposed change as an imposition rather than an improvement in their personal work lives. They are also often left out of the loop and feel neither ownership nor vested interest in whether or not the change succeeds. A knowledge-sharing culture is built upon the foundation of trust, and as such it is imperative to inform, involve, and inspire organizational participants during the organizational changes that are needed.

Corporate culture is a key component of ensuring that critical knowledge and information flow within an organization. The strength and commitment of a corporate culture will almost always be more important than the communication technologies that are implemented to promote knowledge sharing. Traditionally, knowledge flows were vertical, from supervisor to supervisee, following the lines of the organizational chart. Organizations today need to change their culture to one that rewards the flow of knowledge horizontally as well.

Communication systems can be regarded as the disseminators of culture (Bloom, 2000). In more ancient times, this role was fulfilled by physical transportation routes. For example, the Egyptians used the Nile to unite towns across 4000 miles. The Phoenicians sailed to shuttle goods and ideas 2400 miles away. Saint Paul used the Roman highway systems to send his Epistles on 170-mile journeys. The Chinese used land and river routes to pull together a 3 million square mile empire. In all of these systems, ideas flowed, were shared, exchanged, or integrated. The Romans did not just build highways—they spread a common language. The Chinese disseminated a common alphabet—the Incas a uniform system of accounting based on knots. Knowledge dissemination therefore needs some type of *lingua franca*, something in common like a language, standards, norms, or protocols.

The types of ideas that need to be disseminated for KM to be successfully implemented include a change from perceiving knowledge and knowledge creation as being a proprietary and solo undertaking to a perception of participation and collaboration. This links back to earlier discussions on the social construction of knowledge, and an understanding of the individual differences and organizational contexts that can influence such perceptions.

A knowledge-sharing culture is one where knowledge sharing is the norm, not the exception, where people are encouraged to work together, to collaborate and share, and where they are rewarded for doing so. A paradigm shift has to occur from "knowledge is power" to "sharing knowledge is more powerful" and culture will determine what you can and will do with the knowledge assets of the organization.

Sveiby and Simons (2002) suggest that a collaborative climate is one of the major factors influencing the effectiveness of knowledge work. They surveyed 8277 respondents from a diverse group of public and private organizations. The degree to which an organizational culture is collaborative can be assessed, and this in turn will provide a good indicator of how successful KM will be. It is not a surprise that the study found that distance was bad for collaboration—that is, the more dispersed a company, the less the climate is collaborative.

Gruber and Duxbury (2001) conducted an in-depth study of the research and development department of a high-technology company. They looked at the linkages between organizational culture and knowledge sharing and used the variables of trust, openness, top management support, and the reward structure of the organization to try to explain any correlations. They interviewed 30 employees, and their initial questions addressed the sharing of explicit knowledge. It was found that this was mostly through databases, intranets, and shared drives, but 28% was still through face-to-face contact (see Table 7-3). The face-to-face sharing typically involved questions such as "Where is it? How do I get it? Who should I go see?"

The study also elicited some information on what made it hard to share explicit knowledge and gave suggestions as to how it could be made easier. The major difficulties mentioned were that it was hard to find, there were different systems and no standards, the information was not where it should be, the tools were difficult to use, and the database was not easily accessible. Some of the suggestions made were to conduct training on knowledge retrieval, to define a knowledge strategy that would categorize in a standard way, to standardize the information technologies, and to create project websites.

Next, the authors looked at how tacit knowledge was shared. The most popular means (90%) was face-to-face followed by informal networks (25%).

TABLE 7-3
EXPLICIT KNOWLEDGE SHARING

Knowledge-sharing medium	Percentage of respondents who selected this
Database (LotusNotes)	55%
Intranet	40%
Face-to-face	28%
Shared drive	25%

Source: Gruber and Duxbury, 2001.

Some of the factors that made it difficult to share tacit knowledge included attitudes that knowledge was power, not knowing who the expert was, not knowing if the knowledge exists, and loss of knowledge when people left the company. Some suggestions that were made to improve tacit knowledge sharing included recognizing the value of tacit knowledge, improving relationships within the organization, and increasing opportunities for people within different parts of the organization to interact.

The ideal knowledge-sharing culture was thus one where communication and coordination between groups were emphasized, where experts would not jealously guard their knowledge, and where knowledge sharing would be actively and visibly encouraged at all levels of the hierarchy through recognizing and rewarding knowledge sharing and through embedding such statements in corporate and individual performance objectives. A culture that promotes knowledge sharing would be one where tools and taxonomies are standardized to make access and exchange easy, where there are a significant number of semi-social events such as workshops for sharing with experts and other groups, where organizational goals explicitly include knowledge sharing, where trust is prevalent in all interactions, and where the communication channels flow across geographical, temporal, and thematic boundaries.

Gruber and Duxbury (2001) concluded that an environment that truly supports the sharing of knowledge has the following characteristics:

1. Reward structure—recognition for knowledge sharing with peers.
2. Openness/transparency—no hidden agendas.
3. Sharing supported—communication and coordination between groups.
4. Trust—shared objectives.
5. Top management support—upward and downward communication.

The Effects of Culture on Individuals

How does organizational culture control the behavior of organizational members? If consistent behavioral patterns are the outcomes or products of a culture, what is it that causes many people to act in a similar manner? There are three basic ways in which a culture, or, more accurately, members of a reference group representing a culture, creates high levels of cross-individual behavioral consistency: social norms, shared values, and shared mental models.

Social norms are the most basic and most obvious of cultural control mechanisms. In its basic form, a social norm is simply a behavioral expectation that people will act in a certain way in certain situations. Norms (as opposed to rules) are enforced by other members of a reference group through use of social sanctions. Kilmann, Saxton, and Serpa (1986) characterize norms by level:

1. Peripheral norms are general expectations that make interactions easier and more pleasant. Because adherence to these norms is not essential to the functioning of the group, violation of these norms generally results in mild social sanctions.
2. Relevant norms encompass behaviors that are important to group functioning. Violation of these norms often results in noninclusion in important group functions and activities.
3. Pivotal norms represent behaviors that are essential to effective group functioning. Individuals violating these norms are often subject to expulsion from the group.

Why do individuals comply with social norms? What explains the variance among individuals with a group in the degree of compliance with norms; that is, why do some members comply with all norms, while others seem to ignore them? Individuals motivated primarily by means of acceptance, worth and status, and other forms of external validation would be most likely to comply with social norms. Since social sanctions involve the withholding of acceptance, these individuals are most likely to comply. Similarly, those characterized by weak self-concepts would be more likely to comply with social norms than those with strong self-concepts. Those with strong self-concepts are less likely to need the acceptance and other forms of affirmation contingent upon compliance with norms.

Individuals who identify with the group, that is, defining their social identity in terms of the group, are more likely to comply with the group's norms. One of the most powerful bases of compliance or conformity is internalization—that is, believing that the behavior dictated by the norm is truly the right and proper way to behave. Over time, many group members begin to internalize pivotal and relevant norms. High-status members of a group are often exempt from peripheral norms, as are those with high amounts of what is called idiosyncratic credit. Idiosyncratic credit is generally awarded to group members who have contributed a lot to the group and have earned the freedom to violate the norms free from sanctions.

As a cultural control mechanism, the key word in *shared values* is shared. The issue is not whether or not a particular individual's behavior can best be explained and/or predicted by his or her values, but rather how widely that value is shared among organizational members, and more importantly, how responsible the organization/culture was in developing that value within the individual. Value is any phenomenon that has some degree of worth to the members of given groups. Values are the conscious, affective desires or wants of people who guide their behavior.

Values influence individual behavior in many ways. For example, individuals who internalize the value of honesty feel guilty when they are cheating or stealing. This negative affect state stops them from acting in a way that is inconsistent with their internalized value. Public values arise when we believe that everyone around us holds a certain value (social value); we often act in ways consistent with that value, even though we don't personally hold that value. This is done to gain acceptance and support from the group.

A *mental model* or theory defines a causal relationship between two variables. The idea that people rely on mental models can be traced back to Kenneth Craik's suggestion in 1943 that the mind constructs "small-scale models" of reality that it uses to anticipate events. Mental models can be constructed from perception, imagination, or the comprehension of discourse. They underlie visual images, but they can also be abstract, representing situations that cannot be visualized. Each mental model represents a possibility. This phenomenon has been studied by a number of cognitive scientists for the past few decades (e.g., Johnson-Laird, 1983; Rogers, Rutherford, and Bibby, 1992; Oakhill and Garnham, 1996). The belief structure of managers can be represented as a complex set of mental models, which they use to diagnose problems and make decisions. In organizations with strong cultures, members of the organization began to share common mental models about employees, competition, customers, unions, and other important aspects of managerial decision making. Mental models are often called basic underlying assumptions. Mental models impact the behavior of individuals to a very large extent. Decisions are often based on one or more of our mental models. For example, if a manager believes that increasing satisfaction will enhance employees' performance, he or she is likely to do things that eliminate dissatisfaction among employees and work hard to increase their levels of satisfaction. When all managers of the organization share the same mental models or theories, they are likely to make similar decisions when solving problems. This leads to a consistent way of doing things and solving problems in an organization.

Cognitive schema are mental representations of knowledge. Cognitive scripts are types of schema involving action or the way to do something. Schema are generally enacted subconsciously; that is, we enact a script without much thought or deliberation. We can therefore say that cognitive scripts are like programs (like macros), which we store and call upon when certain stimuli are present. We develop scripts over time by performing a certain task many times (like driving home from work). The first time we perform a task we tend to think about every step and deliberate about the many alternative ways we can perform it. Over time, as we learn the best way to perform the task, we "lock in" the script, or program, and do not think about each step again (unless we experience a significant problem). This is called *direct schema development*. In some cases, we do not go through this deliberate step-by-step learning process; instead, we simply copy (or are told) how to perform a certain task from members of the reference group (culture). This is called *indirect schema development*. In either case, when schema become widely shared, they are called *consensual schema*, and they account for a large amount of cross-individual behavioral consistency.

In summary, organizational culture

- Establishes a set of roles (social identities).
- Establishes a set of role expectations (traits, competencies, and values) associated with each identity.
- Establishes the status or value/worth to the reference group of each social identity.
- Provides values, cognitive schema, and mental models to influence how individuals behave with respect to the various groups or communities they find themselves a member of (microculture), as well as with respect to the organizational culture as a whole.

Organizational culture is not so much a discrete "thing" that can be pointed to as the medium in which the organization resides. This medium not only is complex but is also a moving target—organizational culture as a whole is dynamic and is always in the process of changing.

CULTURAL TRANSFORMATION TO A KNOWLEDGE-SHARING CULTURE

How is culture developed, reinforced, and changed? It is often said in organizations that "we need to change the culture around here." What is usually meant is that someone desires a behavioral change, such as employees paying more attention to customers, or that they want managers to come to meetings on time, or some other set of behaviors. Although these patterns of behavior can be changed by changing the organization's structure (rules, regulations, rewards systems), altering these behaviors through culture involves changing the underlying mechanisms that drive these behavioral patterns: namely, norms, social values, or mental models. Since these underlying culture control mechanisms are often taken for granted and are subconscious, they are difficult to change.

Changing structure by changing a rule and its enforcement mechanism is rather simple when compared to changing a social value. Culture is resistant to change because many of the cultural control mechanisms become internalized in the minds of organizational members; that is what makes culture such a strong control mechanism. Changing culture often means that members have to change their entire social identity. Sometimes the statuses of various roles or identities change, causing even more resistance among high-status role holders.

While changing behavior by changing structure may have more appeal because it appears easier, this type of change is often not successful because managers have not changed the underlying culture and so they find that the culture and structure are in conflict. Although organizational change is difficult and often lengthy to undertake, it is a critical requirement for most, if not all, KM implementations. The key often lies in symbolic action, that is, dealing with important symbols of values, norms, and assumptions. Kilmann, Saxton, and Serpa (1986) provide some good general guidelines:

1. People look to leaders for cues about what is important in an organization. The leader's most important quality is to act in a manner consistent with the desired social value. When it comes to instilling cultural values, "do as I say, not as I do" does not work very well. When organizational members observe a leader making a personal sacrifice for a value, it sends a strong message that this value is important. For example, if senior managers are seen to be "practicing what they preach" by actively sharing knowledge and rewarding collaborative efforts, then the organizational members can see that this kind of behavior is in fact highly valued and practiced at all levels of the organization.

2. Culture is often transmitted through stories and myths that extol certain virtues held to be important to the organization. These stories are told in informal settings as well as published in company newsletters. For example, when new employees join an organization, they are not only handed manuals and directed at databases containing forms to be filled out but they are regaled with stories of key events in the organization's history, some of them relating spectacular successes and others disappointing failures. These stories contain a strong message that relays "how things are done around here" to the new employees.

3. In reacting to crises, leaders can telegraph the organization's values and assumptions. When a leader supports new values in the face of crisis, when emotions often run high, he or she communicates that this value is very important. For example, if the organization has repeatedly supported a strong notion of professional ethics and ends up losing a bid to a competitor who did not bother about such niceties, it is even more powerful if the organization's leaders reinforce this message in the face of and in spite of the crisis situation they are experiencing. In this way, everyone can see that values are not being treated as "fair-weather friends"—that is, values are to be adhered to not just when it is convenient to do so but are to be adhered to at all times.

4. In addition to motivating behavior directly, a reward system can send powerful messages regarding what is important. For example, if a university declines to promote a professor who has won the university-wide Outstanding Teaching award, this says loud and clear that only research productivity and not teaching is really valued at this particular institution.

5. Important and public decisions also communicate the importance of certain values. If the first item cut in budget crunches is training, then the strong message is that training is not valued. The criteria for resource allocation often become what is valued in an organization. For example, budgets that are determined by steady past performance rather than past innovation and risk taking send different messages.

6. Leaders communicate the importance of values by what they praise and what they criticize. It is important to pay attention to what leaders say. Social values are often changed through the selection process. As new members are hired, an effort is made to hire new members who hold the new value. Different organizations will elect to implement this reward (praise) and censure (criticize) cycle differently. For example, at Buckman Labs, employees who have been voted the "top 100 knowledge sharers" are invited to take a trip to the head office where the president himself bestows a gift of a fully loaded laptop to them in recognition of their excellent KM work.

BUCKMAN LABS

Buckman Labs is a specialty chemical company that serves the pulp and paper, water treatment, leather, coatings, agricultural, and wood treatment industries. Its core competency is its ability to create and manufacture innovative solutions to control the growth of microorganisms. Buckman's expertise also spans specialty chemicals such as microbicides, scale inhibitors, corrosion inhibitors, polymers, dispersants, and defoamers. When evaluated by Goldman Sachs in 1990, Buckman had a market value $175 million higher than its asset value. The difference owes a lot to the company's focus on knowledge management and knowledge transfer as effective tools to improve and sustain its competitive advantage. It saw the need for a system that would facilitate the growth in the value of knowledge that existed within the company. The best brains in the company on a particular topic were not necessarily found in the U.S. company but were spread out around Buckman's 80 worldwide offices. Hence, a system was needed to facilitate communication between sister companies so that the collective knowledge and understanding of the entire organization could be brought to bear on any problem. The resulting acceleration of knowledge would lead to a strategic advantage based on the leverage of internal as opposed to external knowledge. This thinking culminated in the Knowledge Transfer Department whose goals are to accelerate the accumulation and dissemination of knowledge by all Buckman Labs' associates worldwide, to provide easy and rapid access to Buckman Labs' global knowledge bases, and to eliminate time and space constraints in communication. The department was given a budget of about $8 million.

The primary tool employed by Buckman to enable employees to share knowledge is called K'Netix, the Buckman Laboratory Knowledge Network. KNetix is an interconnected system of knowledge that Buckman associates use worldwide to share knowledge electronically and to collaborate closely with each other, unfettered by time and distance. The principal component of KNetix is Tech Forum, a private bulletin board on CompuServe that only Buckman associates are allowed to access. An employee in Malaysia who needs information about a water treatment process can post a query to the bulletin board in the evening and the next morning find answers from a researcher in microbiology based in the U.S. office or from a field engineer in South Africa. This method of knowledge sharing recognizes that no single person can possibly know everything about a topic, and that knowledge is generally decentralized in the heads of many people, not just in a single subject matter expert's head.

Employees are encouraged to both solve their own problems and to provide solutions to others' questions on Tech Forum. The top 150 people from around the world who were rated as top-level performers in the Tech Forum with respect to answering questions are brought to the company's headquarters each year and presented with a state-of-the-art, fully loaded IBM Thinkpad by the CEO. Such incentives help boost employees' desire to participate in knowledge sharing. Besides the Tech Forum, other media like virtual conference rooms, libraries, and e-mail help employees to access knowledge rapidly. Itinerant employees are provided with laptops so that they stay connected at all times.

Tools are only one side of the equation, however—Buckman believes that tools can only act as facilitators: the company culture has to provide a conducive environment in which to use these tools. The most important cultural factor in KM is that of trust. Each employee must trust the other before providing information to each other. A distinctive feature at Buckman is that the focus is on direct communication between individual employees in order to minimize distortion and misunderstanding of the knowledge content.

Finally, Buckman freely shares its experience and expertise in KM with other organizations. Companies such as AT&T and 3M have visited Buckman to benchmark their internal KM processes.

Source: From Lipnack and Stawps, 1997.

In most cases, individuals making decisions and solving problems do not question their basic assumptions (underlying mental models). They simply use them, without thinking, and arrive at a decision or solution to their problem. If the solution does not work, they most likely question the inputs to their decision and attempt to make a better decision next time. Argyris and Schon (1978) refer to this type of learning as single-loop learning. In some cases, the individual or group begins to question the basic assumptions and models underlying the decision, which is called double-loop learning. It is through double-loop learning that changes in shared mental models take place. When attempting to change the shared mental models of a group, it is important to take time out from the day-to-day problem-solving process to outline, challenge, and agree on changes to the shared mental model.

Most change programs within companies do not work because they address content (the knowledge, structure, and data in a company) or process (the activities and behaviors), but they never address the context in which both of those elements reside. The source of people's action is not what they know but how they perceive the world around them. Context can be an individual's mind-set or the organizational culture. It includes all of the assumptions and norms that are brought to the table. Context is perception, as opposed to facts or data. People do not go off and design their context—they just inherit it. Culture is also socially constructed and reflects meanings that are constituted in interaction and that form commonly accepted definitions of the situation.

Culture is symbolic, which is why it is best described by telling stories about how we feel about the organization. A symbol stands for something more than itself and can be many things, but the point is that we invest a symbol with meaning and the symbol expresses forms of understanding derived from our past collective experiences. The sociological view is that organizations exist in the minds of their members. Stories about culture show how it acts as a sense-making device. Also, culture is unifying and refers to the processes that bind the organization together. Culture is thus consensual and not conflictual. The idea of corporate culture reinforces the unifying strengths of central goals and creates a sense of common responsibility. Culture is also holistic and refers to the essence—the reality of the organization, reflecting what it is like to work there, how people deal with each other, and what behaviors are expected. The example of Nokia describes one such holistic approach to culture.

NOKIA[1]

Nokia views KM as a combination of people, processes, technologies, and culture. It is through learning that organizations are able to improve what they do. Appropriate knowledge sharing facilitates effective learning. Various management approaches can be used in combination to produce a learning organization, which can in turn provide improved service; these include competence management and performance management. Organizational values must be reflected in the day-to-day running of an organization in order to impact on its knowledge strategy. The Nokia Way promotes a culture of learning that is premised on four pillars: customer satisfaction, respect for the individual, achievement, and continuous learning. The Nokia Way is facilitated through a series of mechanisms, mainly interactions between managers, colleagues, and employees placing power in the hands of the individual to develop in the organization. A jazz band analogy best captures Nokia's approach to KM: the company shares a common vision and creates the space for an ensemble to perform in unison without controlling the music or constraining the performance.

Change and people management are commonly believed to make up 80% of KM, whereas IT comprises only 20% of it. In Nokia no one person owns the KM process—everyone owns it. Human Resources has a crucial role to play in implementing KM, as do IT, quality, and corporate planning departments. Organizational learning overlaps performance management (individual focus), competency management (organizational focus), and knowledge management (thematic or team focus). Nokia integrates these three approaches in order to identify best practices and lessons learned.

The Nokia Saga, a novel about Nokia's history, contains about 100 stories that many employees read in order to better understand the company's values. The storytelling provides examples of what managers do and how they apply Nokia values. Nokia's annual report is called "No Limits," and it gives progress reports on how the company culture is moving toward a knowledge-sharing culture—with no limits on learning, participating, and building better futures.

Nokia does not have a Chief Knowledge Officer (CKO). It has a steering group of about 10 persons from different functional areas coordinating KM activities. The head of the steering committee is also the head of the quality department.

Many organizations have a concern that sharing all their knowledge means giving all their power away. Nokia was able to change its culture to one of knowledge sharing by designing a flat, networked, global, and multicultural organization. Speed, flexibility, opportunity, and openness are the key features. Nokia's management evaluates how well employees do with respect to supporting KM in terms of creating, sharing, and reusing knowledge. They do not have incentive systems, as they believe knowledge sharing should be part of the company culture and not something that is rewarded with money. The intention is to try to capture as much organizational knowledge as possible. As in a good jazz band, the players share a common vision, and are interested in producing good products through innovation and improvisation. The end result is not always clearly seen, but because a common vision guides their performance, these professionals allow their services to be shaped by the feelings and interactions of the various players who are part of the company.

Culture is rooted deep in unconscious sources but is represented in superficial practices and behavior codes and embodied in cultural artifacts. Some initial steps to creating a knowledge-sharing culture could include:

- Having knowledge journalists begin interviewing key people to document projects, best practices, lessons learned, and good stories.
- Instituting KM get-togethers, which could be breakfasts, lunch and learn sessions, or any type of informal gathering to help people get to know one another, sometimes with thematic talks and showing managerial support.
- Producing newsletters to publicize KM initiatives and celebrate good role models.
- Launching KM pilot projects, such as expertise location systems and intranets with space devoted to different communities of practice.

- Changing performance evaluation criteria to reflect and assess knowledge-sharing competencies and accomplishments.
- Censuring knowledge hoarders and rewarding effective knowledge sharers.
- Redesigning workplaces to allow for gathering places (e.g., Cotter, 2000; Chiem, 2001; Gladwell, 2000).

The redesign of workplaces extends beyond simple physical office layout designs to a process of facilitating more effective knowledge sharing. Owen (1997) developed the notion of Open Space Technology (OST) as a large-group facilitation process. In practice, Open Space Technology meetings take on many forms and variations, but they follow the same general guidelines. OST meetings begin with all the participants sitting in a circle and no items on the agenda. The meeting opens with an agenda-setting exercise, following which the group self-organizes into smaller discussion groups. Discussion group conveners are responsible for providing a report of the discussions, which is immediately added to a book of proceedings. At the conclusion of the meeting, or very shortly thereafter, participants receive a copy of the proceedings including all of the discussion groups' reports and any action plans that were developed.

Open Space Technology meetings operate on four principles and one law. The principles are:

- Whoever comes is the right person.
- Whatever happens is the only thing that could have happened.
- When it starts is the right time.
- When it's over it's over.

The law is known as the Law of Two Feet (sometimes referred to as the Law of Mobility). It states that "If you find yourself in a situation where you are not learning or contributing, go somewhere where you can."

Gladwell (2000) discusses how the setup and character of offices can influence innovation and knowledge sharing. He notes the importance of frequent interaction among colleagues and how far basic office layout goes in shaping the human relationships within the workplace. Gladwell states that innovation is at the heart of the knowledge economy and that it is a fundamentally social phenomenon. Companies will therefore need to design for public and semi-public spaces to promote employee interaction. Many companies provide comfortable seating and access to the knowledge repository via a few workstations to promote both tacit and explicit knowledge sharing.

The cultural approach to Open Space Technology creates an environment for innovation, teamwork, and rapid change. Open space offers a chance to gather the members of the organization in an open setting and have the work done efficiently and creatively. Open space involves much brainstorming, but it is not just brainstorming. It is the process through which people have the urge to raise the topic they are passionate about, and they are willing to share their own knowledge, especially tacit knowledge.

Whether the open space can be successful depends on the extent to which the participants are willing to share the knowledge, which is influenced by their organizational culture. For example, in an organizational culture with high sociability, people know each other and respect their companions. Therefore, they will be more likely to take an active part in the open space and to offer their knowledge to other members. However, in a low-sociability culture, where people focus more on individualism and their own work, members may well feel uneasy about talking with people whom they do not know, not to mention sharing something that is of deep concern to them.

Yet other characteristics of an organizational culture can either encourage or discourage the recognition of belonging to the organization; consequently, they will influence the member's performance in the open space. Some characteristics that are more connected with open space include individual initiative, integration, reward system, and ethical climate. The facilitators should not ignore the impact of organizational culture on the group of people who will attend the open space, and should prepare for the possible outcome that is expected from them. Then the facilitators can work out some methods to encourage the participants to understand and execute the essence of the open space.

Other good practices that encourage a knowledge-friendly culture include the following: do not impose top-down, allow cultural change to evolve over a period of time, provide positive role models wherever possible, create opportunities for people to get to know one another, and focus on connecting people rather than capturing content. Some illustrations are provided in the accompanying vignette.

GENERAL ELECTRIC

Sharing best practices is a way life at General Electric (GE)—employees live and breathe it every day.[2] A culture of what the company calls "boundarylessness" ensures that at GE whatever one person knows, everyone knows.

GE demonstrates how this process works. Beyond competence, community, and commitment, trust needs communication, both positive and negative, both best practices and lessons learned. GE is riddled with communities of practice—manufacturing councils, finance councils, technology councils—literally hundreds of interdisciplinary and interbusiness groups. Here GE's young bring their ideas to share at meetings, where other members test them, improve upon them, and take them home to be implemented in their own businesses. Individual performance reviews stress the skills that contribute to the culture. Executive evaluations cover two major areas: performance and personal values. Performance is a quantitative measure, but when the qualitative measure of an executive's personal values is considered, the only category that supersedes boundarylessness is integrity. At GE you are at least as well regarded for borrowing a best practice across business lines as you are for inventing it.

Continued

Face time is only one way GE shares best practices and other intellectual assets. MS exchange is standard on 50,000 desktops. In addition, GE has an intranet whose goal is to make the right information available at the right place and at the right time. The intranet is an important vehicle for dynamic publishing and for sharing best practices. In all divisions, executives put even their undeveloped ideas online. Others then modify those ideas using collaborative tools. For example, executives from all 12 GE divisions discuss benchmarking for computer usage via GE's intranet. Another discussion site is devoted to enterprise resource planning. GE's Technological Leadership Program is an online multimedia just-in-time training program, which is also available live on the intranet.

Then CEO Jack Welch committed GE to a 6 Sigma Program whose goal is to allow fewer than 3.4 customer-perceived defects per 1 million opportunities to err. The linchpin to the knowledge sharing necessary to achieve that goal is an intranet-accessible data warehouse dedicated to shared knowledge about quality. How important is knowledge sharing at GE? If you are a CEO at GE and you mention that you have developed a great new business procedure, the first question the chairman will ask is, "Whom have you shared this with?" People who hoard an idea for personal glory simply do not do well at GE.

VIANT

Viant[3] is a consulting company in Boston that went public in June 1999 and is often touted as a leader in knowledge sharing. New employees start off with an initiation course—three weeks in Boston. At the end of their three weeks, they know someone in each of Viant's offices, with a laptop fully loaded with off-the-shelf and proprietary software. They learn team skills and consulting strategies, including a mock consulting engagement. They bond and hear company folklore. In terms of workplace layouts, Viant has a "leaky knowledge environment"—balancing openness and privacy. People tend to underestimate how much private offices are used for meetings.

At any given time, Viant's leadership team consists of a score of official members and about an equal number of rotating "fellows" nominated by their peers in the field. Conventional reporting relationships do not work with consultants who rotate in and out of assignments, so consultants have no fixed boss. Instead senior people act as "advocates" for a number of "advocatees." Performance reviews are 360 degrees, of course, emphasizing the growth in employee skill levels, while stock options are used to recognize excellent knowledge sharers. As part of their everyday work, consultants complete a "quick sheet" that describes the knowledge they need, what can be leveraged from previous projects, and what they will need to create, along with the lessons they hope to learn from each assignment. A longer report, a sunset review, is produced at a team meeting to learn what did and did not work well. Almost every document ends up hot-linked to Viant's intranet site. Sunset reviews are always done with a facilitator who was not part of the team, which keeps everyone honest. Every six weeks, the KM group prepares, posts, and pushes a summary of what has been learned.

Viant is also unusual in that it picks "project catalysts" from top consultants in the company. They are pulled off client work for several months and assigned to other projects where they do not supervise. They are not, however, passive. Rather, they are there to help: What are you doing? How can I help? Looks like you need an example of a business plan to adapt for your client, let me get one, and so on. This is in-your-face KM—the project consultants are referred to as agitators. Knowledge sharing is natural, instinctive, and painless in all aspects of our lives, except our corporate ones. Companies that succeed in sharing knowledge somehow "force the issue." At Viant, that's the job of the agitators.

ICL

ICL Ltd.[4] developed a "conversation for change" program whereby all employees are asked to provide input in setting directions. The CEO invites all employees to participate in the program. In addition, all executives use online chat sessions with staff to discuss issues in an open and nonjudgmental environment. This open style generates a feeling of "wanting," which can be very powerful in generating commitment and loyalty. The staff feels their views and opinions are welcome and that whatever they say will influence the future vision. Every view is considered valid and important. The CEO also set up a Web space whereby any questions asked of him are posted with replies for all to see. ICL is an example of many companies where leaders are changing the way they lead. These leaders are not simply providing lip service; they genuinely believe that knowledge is a key asset, and that asset largely consists of the people in the organization.

Virtual organizations face additional challenges such as:

- No formalization, with each organization following its own norms, styles, and ideas.
- No shared values, beliefs, ideas, or norms.
- No frameworks or policies that guide individuals working in the organization.

The communication between the members of virtual organizations is so limited and is conducted through channels so impersonal (the computer) that the scope for developing a shared sense of belonging or a climate in the organization is almost nonexistent.

SIGMA

Sigma is a team-oriented, completely virtual German organization. It has grown from 20 founding members to 200 employees with home offices throughout the country. It introduced a bulletin board service, and local groups met biweekly or bimonthly. All employees meet face-to-face once a year. Each area, each branch, ended up with its own local culture. There was a great deal of resistance to any top-down implementation of a KM system as well as to any attempts to change the company's culture. In the early years, Sigma was a small group of individuals who had no trouble networking. Rapid growth and increasing virtualization changed the company's early culture. Technology could not replace its tradition of personal network-based collaboration and oral sharing of knowledge. What did succeed, however, was a highly flexible approach. Transparency about activities resulted in the creation of a culture of trust.

KM is thus an evolutionary process that needs to be embedded into the organizational culture. By allowing organizational members to participate in the development of content, rules, and goals, greater cohesion will result, and this will help move the organization to a higher level of organizational and KM maturity.

Source: From Lemken, Kahler, and Rittenbruch, 2000.

Virtual organizations are here to stay, and what they need to do today is to build a culture that will give an existence to the organization in the minds of its members and a sense of identification and belonging that will bring them together in spite of limited interactions. Within this culture it is necessary for each individual to take his or her own developmental path, which is actually the core of the functioning of virtual organizations.

A number of lessons are learned from cultural change initiatives, including:

- They provide information about the skills and experience of employees to overcome problems arising from the absence or difficulty of establishing personal relationships (e.g., virtual organizations).
- They provide support mechanisms such as feedback for effective knowledge sharing to take place.
- Active knowledge transfer requires a bidirectional communication channel.
- Common goals and mutual trust need to be developed.
- KM is an evolutionary process that must be embedded into the organizational culture.
- The introduction of new communication/information technologies that are capable of enhancing knowledge sharing can be used to catalyze cultural

changes by externalizing tacit knowledge, by building up a permanent organizational memory and by including all members in a participatory development of content, rules, goals, and systems.

Another example of cultural change is provided in the Xerox vignette.

XEROX

Xerox Corporation's global service technicians exchange most of what they know through informal networks. Technicians recount war stories face to face, but this approach is not effective across all the service teams. The Eureka system was designed to capture this tacit knowledge and make it more widely available. Technicians generally take a great deal of pride in their ability to innovate. At Xerox recognition, not financial reward, turned out to be a major motivator in the sharing of their stories. The author's name is thus displayed prominently next to each tip in the system in order to reinforce this incentive. Each tip is peer-reviewed. In its first month, over 5000 tips were entered into Eureka.

Source: From Roberts-Witt, 2002.

As Gruber and Duxbury (2002) discovered: "We have to move to a transparent organization. This means all kinds of information and knowledge is shared across the whole organization. Everyone can find out what everyone else is doing. Any kind of information that influences me and my project have to be made available to everyone else" (p. 25). The notion of organizational transparency has been recently addressed by Tapscott and Ticoll (2003), who discuss the importance of having good values of honesty and openness and being successful as an organization. The transparent organization can be viewed as an ideal form or as a target for any type of organization. Maturity models are useful frameworks that can be used to situate the current cultural state of an organization and to identify the types of cultural transformations that need to take place in order to move the organization to higher levels of organizational maturity, KM readiness, and desired transparency.

ORGANIZATIONAL MATURITY MODELS

Culture is not a static object stored somewhere in the organization. Rather, it is a fluid, dynamic medium that encompasses the organization. In fact, a series of "microcultures" are often typical of different workgroups within a given organization. Culture is a complex entity that represents a moving target of sorts. One way in which culture changes within an organization is through a maturing process. As organizations mature, so does the culture of that organization. The notion of an optimal point or a threshold point that should be reached before effective knowledge management can be implemented is inherent in a number of organizational, KM, and community maturity models.

Maturity models have their roots in software engineering. The Carnegie Mellon Software Engineering Institute (CMMI Project Team, 2002) defines a maturity model as "a descriptive model of the stages through which organizations progress as they define, implement, evolve, and improve their processes. This model serves as a guide for selecting process improvement strategies by facilitating the determination of the current process capabilities and the identification of issues most critical to quality and process improvement within a particular domain, such as software engineering or systems engineering" (p. 13). There are a number of organizational and KM maturity models, most of which are derived from the Capability Maturity Model (CMM) (Paulk et al. 1995). The CMM was developed in order to better describe the phases of software development processes, and the model was subsequently updated to the Capability Maturity Model Integration in 2000 (CMMI Project Team, 2002).

The Capability Maturity Model is an organizational model that describes five evolutionary stages (levels) in which an organization manages its processes. An organization should be able to absorb and carry its software applications. The model also provides specific steps and activities to get from one level to the next. The five stages of the CMM are:

1. *Initial*: Processes are ad hoc, chaotic, or rarely defined.
2. *Repeatable*: Basic processes are established, and there is a level of discipline to stick to these processes.
3. *Defined*: All processes are defined, documented, standardized, and integrated into each other.
4. *Managed*: Processes are measured by collecting detailed data on the processes and their quality.
5. *Optimizing*: Continuous process improvement is adopted and in place by quantitative feedback and from piloting new ideas and technologies.

CMM is useful not only for developing software, but also for describing evolutionary levels of organizations in general. The CMM and the CMMI can be extended to cover knowledge management processes, which can in turn serve to assess the organization's current level of readiness for knowledge management. For example, the maturity model shown in Figure 7-2 presents the major phases that an organization has to complete in order to integrate a new way of doing things, a new technology, or a new process. This is very relevant for KM initiatives as new processes and technologies will be introduced into the organization. These phases can keep better track of how well KM has been accepted as a way of doing business within the organization.

Table 7-4 shows a maturity model based on CMM but adapted in particular to organizational change and organizational cultural dimensions. This model serves as a good organizational culture diagnostic in that it is a fairly straightforward task to establish the status quo of a given organization. For example, if the organization exhibits multiple local cultures that do not, as yet, have much in common, then it would be advisable to select one or more of

FIGURE 7-2
STAGES OF ORGANIZATIONAL MATURITY

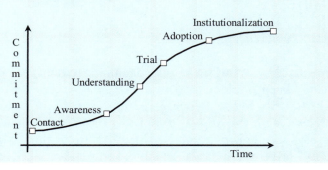

Source: Adapted from Paulk et al., 1995.

TABLE 7-4
STAGES OF ORGANIZATIONAL MATURITY

Maturity Phase	Description
1. Chaotic	▪ Noncohesive culture ▪ Decision making in-flight ▪ Leadership structure vague ▪ Operation model undefined ▪ Employees evaporating
2. Ad hoc	▪ Multiple local cultures, leadership structures, and operation models ▪ Local decision making ▪ Employee turnover high except in preferred classes of employees
3. Organized	▪ Similar local cultures ▪ Local decision making based on corporate strategy ▪ Local leadership linked to corporate leadership team ▪ Corporate operation model pushed down to local level ▪ Stable employee base
4. Managed	▪ Cohesive corporate culture and operation model ▪ Corporate strategy drives operational tactics ▪ Corporate leadership team coaches and empowers local leaders ▪ Employees recruited and retained based on strategic direction
5. Agile	▪ Culture adapts strategically ▪ Operation model changes dynamically based on environmental changes ▪ Professionals compete to work for corporation

Source: Adapted from Fujitsu Consulting.

these microcultures as pilot sites for KM interventions. If, on the other hand, the organizational maturity stage is closer to a managed phase where there is a more pervasive and cohesive culture, then it would be advisable to focus on tightly aligning the KM strategy to the overall business strategy and objectives of the organization.

KM Maturity Models

There are currently about six knowledge management maturity models. One model that has been implemented in a variety of organizations to date is the Infosys KM Maturity Model (Kochikar, 2000), shown in Table 7-5. The Infosys is also consistent with the others in that it is based on the CMM approach. In fact, the Infosys model is denoted KMM in honor of the CMM on which it is based. The five levels are default, reactive, aware, convinced, and sharing. The model associates a number of key results for each of the five levels.

The Infosys model is much more closely linked to specific KM behaviors that can be detected at the organizational, group, and individual levels. It is possible to make much more fine-grained or specific types of organizational diagnoses in order to establish the current status quo of an organization. For example, if it is possible to detect that the majority of the KM effort appears to be devoted to capturing content, then KM initiatives aimed at promoting knowledge sharing can be considered to be premature at this stage. Instead, the KM objective targets reuse when the organization is at the reactive level of organizational capability. In time, however, as KM awareness is increased and knowledge flows appear between disparate groups, then the organization can be diagnosed as being at the sharing level of organizational capability. At the sharing level, KM initiatives such as corporate yellow pages or expertise location systems are more appropriate priorities.

Paulzen and Perc (2002) have proposed a Knowledge Process Quality Model (KPQM) based on the major tenets of quality management and process engineering. The underlying premise is that knowledge processes can be improved by enhancing the corresponding management structures. The maturity model makes it possible to implement a systematic or incremental KM application. The authors assume that since software development is a knowledge-based activity, it is valid to adapt these models for KM. The Paulzen and Perc (2002) model is essentially a modification of the Capability Maturity Model (CMMI Project Team, 2002) that addresses the specific characteristics of knowledge processes and KM systems. The maturity model consists of five phases: (1) initial, (2) aware, (3) established, (4) quantitatively managed, and (5) optimizing, as shown in Table 7-6.

Note that there is a good fit with the organizational maturity models presented earlier. The major advantage of these models is that they enable organizations to progress in an orderly manner, without skipping any important stages, in order to achieve the desired end results of effective knowledge transfer, sharing, storing and distributing of experiences, learning from past experiences, and so forth.

Table 7-7 shows the Forrester Group KM Maturity Model, which describes the different stages of maturity in terms of how people are supported

TABLE 7-5
The Infosys KM Maturity Model

Level	Organizational Capability	Characteristics/Key Result Areas
1. Default	Complete dependence on individual skills and abilities.	Unstructured on-the-job learning, accidental knowledge reuse, informal knowledge sharing, teamwork virtually nonexistent.
2. Reactive	Ability to perform tasks constituting the basic business of the organization repeatably.	People are aware of knowledge as an asset through formal training and mentoring, some pockets of knowledge sharing, sporadic knowledge reuse, and some teamwork. Process focus is on basic content capture. Technology is information management.
3. Aware	Restricted ability for data-driven decision making. Restricted ability to leverage internal expertise. Ability to manage virtual teams well.	People are educated on KM, some environmental scanning, and knowledge dissemination. Process of content structure management, taxonomy of knowledge. Knowledge technology infrastructure (e.g., portal). Dedicated KM group.
4. Convinced	Quantititative decision making for strategic and operational applications widespread. High ability to leverage internal and external sources of expertise. Organization realizes measurable productivity benefits through knowledge sharing. Ability to sense and respond proactively to changes in technology and business environment.	Customized enabling. Value-added content. Quantitative KM processes (e.g., KM metrics such as percentage of content used, quality ratings). Knowledge infrastructure management for sustainable KM.
5. Sharing	Ability to manage organizational competence quantitatively. Strong ROI-driven decision making. Streamlined process for leveraging new ideas for business advantage. Ability to shape change in technology and business environment.	Expertise integration (content and expertise available organization-wide). Knowledge leverage through frictionless knowledge flows. Innovation management and cohesive teamwork.

TABLE 7-6
THE KPQM MATURITY MODEL

Maturity Phase	Description
1. Initial	Knowledge process quality is not planned; it changes randomly (chaotic).
2. Aware	Need for quality has been recognized, and initial structures have been put into place.
3. Established	A systematic structure and definition of knowledge processes are implemented and the processes are specifically tailored to identified needs.
4. Quantitatively managed	Performance measures are used to plan and track knowledge processes.
5. Optimizing	Structures are implemented to ensure continuous improvement and self-optimization of knowledge processes.

TABLE 7-7
FORRESTER GROUP KM MATURITY MODEL

KM Maturity Model Phase	Description	Typical KM Initiatives
1. Assisted	▪ Culture adapts strategically. ▪ Operation model changes dynamically based on environmental changes. ▪ Professionals compete to work for corporation. ▪ Employees find information with the help of librarians.	▪ KSO ▪ Yellow pages ▪ Communities of practice
2. Self-service	▪ Employees codify on their own without help. ▪ Employees find information using search engines.	▪ Push technologies ▪ Customized KM
3. Organic	▪ KM happens in the background; it is embedded in business. ▪ Information is provided when needed (JIT, JET).	▪ Personalized KM

Source: Shevlin et al., 1997.

throughout the knowledge management cycle. In the first phase, *assisted*, other people are needed in order for knowledge workers to find valuable content and to connect with subject matter experts. In the second phase, *self-service*, employees are able to make use of KM systems such as knowledge repositories, in order to find content and link to experts by themselves. In the final phase, *organic*, knowledge management has ceased to be an "extra" burden but has instead become part and parcel of how the knowledge work gets done every day.

The Forrester KM Maturity Model is quite useful in determining the level of knowledge support that will be needed for effective KM to be established within a given organization. For example, an organization that is at the assisted phase stands to benefit greatly from an expertise location system and a Knowledge Support Office (KSO), which is essentially a 24/7/365 (24 hours a day, 7 days a week, 365 days a year) help desk for knowledge content. Employees typically have a toll-free telephone number as well as an e-mail address through which they can contact the KSO in order to obtain help in locating, accessing, and making use of valuable knowledge content.

CoP Maturity Models

Maturity models have also been applied to the community of practice life cycle. A community of practice maturity model can serve as a good road map to show what steps need to be taken to move communities to the next stage. The Wenger CoP life-cycle model (Wenger, McDermott, and Snyder, 2002) provides a good diagnostic to assess whether informal networks exist within an organization and whether they are recognized and supported by the organization. The life-cycle model (see Figure 7-3) shows that a community needs to have attained the maturation and stewardship of knowledge levels in order to begin creating value for its members and for the organization as a whole. The life-cycle model is particularly useful for aligning any new KM roles and responsibilities that will be needed in order to optimize KM efforts throughout the life cycle—for example, a knowledge journalist to help build, identify, and extract valuable content from community members; a knowledge taxonomist to help organize content once it is being produced at a steady rate; and a knowledge archivist to help distinguish between content that should be stored or content that is no longer considered active.

Organizational and KM maturity models help to assess the current level of knowledge sharing and knowledge activities within an organization. In situat-

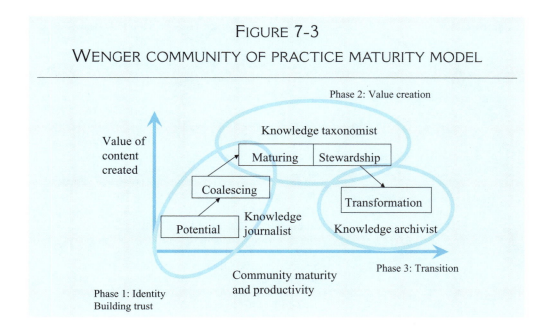

FIGURE 7-3
WENGER COMMUNITY OF PRACTICE MATURITY MODEL

ing a given company on a given maturity model, organizational change is greatly facilitated as it becomes easier to visualize what is needed in order to step up to the next level. It is important to note that there is a minimum level of maturity or readiness before KM stands a good chance of succeeding.

The major features of the six maturity models presented are summarized in Table 7-8. Each can serve as a good framework for understanding how change is introduced and eventually adopted within knowledge-based organizations. The current state of an organization can be diagnosed in order to better anticipate how both the organization as a whole and individual knowledge workers within that organization will react to KM initiatives. A better understanding of the level or phase of maturity of the organization will greatly help in identifying the potential enablers and obstacles to the organizational cultural change(s) required for KM to succeed.

TABLE 7-8
THE SIX MATURITY MODELS

Maturity Model	Key Features
1. Paulk organizational maturity	Represents the adoption of a new technology or process within an organization, which is a very good match for the introduction of new KM functions.
2. Fujitsu organizational maturity	Provides a fast and easy way of assessing how cohesive or pervasive a culture is within a given organization, which can provide valuable guidance either in selecting pilot KM sites, if the organization is in the earlier stages, or in focusing on closely aligning KM with the overall business strategy.
3. Infosys KM	A model that is much more specific and allows diagnosis of specific KM behaviors, such as content capture, knowledge sharing, and KM metrics. Greater specificity allows for more refined targeting of priority KM initiatives.
4. Paulzen and Perc KPQM	The KPQM is quite similar to the Infosys KM model and also allows for incremental introduction of KM initiatives into an organization based on the phase of KM maturity.
5. Forrester Group KM maturity model	A model that focuses on how employees acquire relevant content, which is particularly well suited for an incremental introduction of knowledge support services within an organization.
6. Wenger CoP life-cycle model	The CoP life-cycle model can also provide a good indicator of the cultural evolution of an organization, particularly as it pertains to the coalescing of informal networks of peers who regularly share valuable knowledge with one another. The CoP life-cycle model can also help identify key KM roles and responsibilities that should be introduced at each phase.

STRATEGIC IMPLICATIONS OF ORGANIZATIONAL CULTURE

Kanter (1989) refers to the paradox implicit in linking culture with change. On the surface, culture possesses essentially traditional and stable qualities, so how can you have a "culture of change" (Fullam, 2001)? Yet this is exactly what the innovative organization needs. If real change rather than cosmetic or short-lived change is to occur in organizations, it has to happen at the cultural level. Corporate culture has many powerful attractions as a lever for change. The problem is how to get a hand on the lever. First, cultures can be explicitly created: you have to be aware of what it takes to change an existing culture.

The company's ability to be culturally innovative is related to leadership, and top management must be responsible for building strong cultures. Leaders construct the social reality of the organization, shape values, and help both to create and attain the vision of the organization.

The knowledge culture change adoption process will necessarily be a long one. You should not expect results overnight. In fact, the more dispersed the organization and the longer it has been in existence, the less stable its environment and workforce, among other factors, and the longer the cultural change period that will be needed. For some organizations, this may be as long as 10 years. However, this does not mean that small, meaningful steps cannot be taken to progress toward the overall cultural change goal. The following are some recommendations for bringing about the cultural change needed for KM to succeed:

1. Clearly define desired cultural outcomes.
2. Assess the current cultural state.
3. Diagnose the existing culture with respect to desired knowledge-sharing behaviors.
4. Assess tolerance to change.
5. Identify change enablers and barriers.
6. Assess the maturity level of KM within the organization.
7. Identify KM enablers and barriers.
8. Conduct a gap analysis to yield a map on how to get from where the organization is currently to where it would like to be culturally.

PRACTICAL IMPLICATIONS OF ORGANIZATIONAL CULTURE

At a minimum, certain solutions to potential cultural barriers should be put into place in order to catalyze and successfully implement desired organizational cultural changes. For a list of these solutions, see Table 7-9.

Cultural change is often thwarted by lack of attention to some of the more basic requirements such as providing employees with a place to meet and

TABLE 7-9
COMMON BARRIERS TO CULTURAL CHANGE AND POSSIBLE SOLUTIONS

Cultural Barrier	Possible Solution
Lack of time and meeting places	Hold seminars and e-meetings; redesign physical workspaces.
Status and rewards to knowledge owners	Establish incentives and include them in performance evaluations, develop role models.
Lack of absorptive capacity	Hire for openness, educate current workforce.
Not-invented-here syndrome	Use nonhierarchical approach based on quality of ideas and not status of source.
Intolerance of mistakes and need for help, lack of trust	Accept and reward creativity and collaboration and ensure there is no loss of status for not knowing everything.
Lack of common language (not just English vs. Spanish but engineer-speak vs. manager-speak)	Establish a knowledge taxonomy and knowledge dictionary for knowledge content, standard formats, translators, metadata, knowledge support staff.

spending legitimate time in such meetings. For example, one organization set up a series of expensive employee lounges filled with computers that were linked to the organizational knowledge base. However, on any given day, these lounges were empty. The reason was that employees who spent time there were subject to comments such as "wow—you must not have much work to do if you have time to spare." When senior management took visitors around for a site visit of the office, an e-mail memo was sent out ahead of time to warn employees to be hard at work at their workstations and not "chatting in the lounges" lest the visitors leave with the wrong perception of the company. The message is very clear: management may build the physical knowledge-sharing places, but it does not provide employees with the clear message that time spent sharing knowledge is time that is productively spent. Similar examples are often found in organizations where employees are told to conduct KM activities outside of their normal working hours. In other words, KM is done in your spare time, which conveys the view that KM activities are peripheral, secondary, or even hobby-type activities when compared to "real work."

The rewarding of knowledge hoarding is another common barrier to the cultural change needed for effective KM implementations. An example is any science-based organization where recognition, performance appraisals, and promotion criteria are all linked to what has been accomplished by being the first and by being the only one who thought of a great new idea, product, or process. As long as your career prospects are enhanced if you do not share knowledge, the cultural change will not occur. It becomes imperative to integrate knowledge-sharing behaviors in performance evaluation criteria. Management can also help by publicly rewarding examples of collaboration, good teamwork, and knowledge reuse wherever possible. An example of a KM incentive strategy is that of Hill and Knowlton.

Hill and Knowlton[5] International Public Relations-Public Affairs has established a knowledge commerce methodology for its 1700 employees worldwide. The goal is to conduct consultations in such a way that the absorbed experience of that project is captured in a knowledge base and is reusable for a new client.

A product launch with a client in the United States, for instance, could be replicated worldwide without the same level of man-hours. Replication does not imply exact duplication but rather the abstraction of the key points of what makes it an effective launch. Captured knowledge could include a checklist of product launch activities, a critical path outlining execution priorities, and competitive intelligence. Hill and Knowlton had a three-pronged approach to KM implementation: decide on a technology platform; get people motivated to use the knowledge management resources; and integrate knowledge management practices with people's daily work. IT integrated the platform with in-house e-mail and also organized editors into roles as coaches and knowledge arrangers and categorizers. Senior management rejected the idea that compensation for knowledge contributions was best conducted through infrequent performance reviews.

Performance reviews are too far down the road and do not give employees this immediate market-based gratification. One day someone from the New York City headquarters suggested beenz, a sort of digital S&H Green Stamp alternative payment scheme that some e-commerce merchants use for sales incentive programs. In exchange for buying, reading an ad, or engaging in some other activity at the website, merchants will reward the visitor with beenz, which can then be redeemed at other participating merchant sites. Why not port this commerce model in-house? While collaboration software enabled knowledge contributions at H&K, beenz actually drove it because they made sense, they were fun, and they were easy to manage.

H&K buys beenz from beenz.com. They are then awarded to employees for various knowledge contributions, who can manage the beenz awards from their desktops. The company uses the ASP-like backend at the beenz.com host to track such things as beenz in circulation and total beenz redeemed. So far, employees have redeemed beenz for items like magazine subscriptions and CDs.

One of the biggest benefits of a knowledge economy is the cross-pollination of ideas and abstract thinking across the company. H&K's work is organized around practice area—crisis management or investor relations—and is industry vertical—healthcare or technology. H&K is trying to break down service silos quite a bit. If someone develops an account plan in crisis management that can be applied to other groups, H&K tries to open up people's minds and identify information applicable to those other areas, such as investor or government relations.

Continued

The relative value of a beenz reward is more important than the absolute number awarded for a contribution. Also, many employees seem reluctant to redeem their beenz. People tend to hold onto them; this suggests that the beenz possess intrinsic value as a rough proxy for an employee's perception of worth to the company. Or perhaps they are saving for a Caribbean villa. A villa is available to H&K employees for 105,000 beenz.

Absorptive capacity refers to the individual and/or organizational openness to change and innovation and the capability or preparedness for being able to integrate it. The term originally referred to the related knowledge that a firm already possessed (see Cohen and Levinthal, 1990). If an organization's existing absorptive capacity is low, it will be very difficult to carry out significant cultural changes. The organization could augment its existing employee base by recruiting and hiring individuals who have been selected for their openness to new ideas, eagerness to learn, and innovativeness in approach. The existing employees can be provided with awareness seminars, creativity-building workshops (e.g., thinking out of the box approaches), and other training opportunities to give them a chance to reframe their perceptions of themselves and of the planned cultural changes.

Change is greatly hindered if mistakes and any requests for help or collaboration are perceived as undesirable behaviors and/or manifestations of weakness or incompetence. For example, if an organization expects you to have all of the answers and if asking someone for assistance implies that you are not qualified to be in your job, this will greatly reduce the number of requests for help. If, on the other hand, the organization's role models and reward systems actively promote, support, and value such interactions, then cultural change will be greatly facilitated. Steps must be taken to ensure that employees do not lose face or status if they admit to not knowing everything and, concurrently, that employees who provide knowledge and assistance are rewarded.

Finally, another important cultural barrier lies in the lack of a common language among knowledge workers. Natural language barriers exist, particularly in multinational companies, and translation costs can be prohibitively high. However, other types of languages, such as jargon or shared technical or professional languages, can cause a great deal of confusion. For example, some may understand the word "network" to mean contacts for sales and marketing people, whereas telecommunication engineer may interpret the same word to mean a system of towers. A knowledge dictionary of commonly used terms within the organization, together with a good, up-to-date thesaurus that cross-references all known synonyms, would greatly help overcome this type of cultural change barrier.

KEY POINTS

- Culture penetrates to the essence of an organization. It is almost analogous to the concept of personality in relation to the individual. This acute sense of what an organization is—its mission, core values—seems to have become a necessary asset of the modern company.
- There is the challenging question of whether or not organizational culture can be changed and/or managed.
- Organizational culture consists of the set of norms, routines, and unspoken rules of how things are done in that organization.
- An organization's culture may be in differing states of maturity, and these can be assessed using a variety of organizational and KM maturity models.

DISCUSSION POINTS

1. What is the culture of an organization? Why is it important to understand?
2. What contribution does organizational culture make to the intellectual capital of the organization?
3. What do we mean when we talk about changing the culture of an organization? What would be some examples?
4. How would we go about assessing the cultural readiness of an organization with respect to planned KM interventions? How would we modify our KM implementation strategy based on the results of such an assessment?
5. What are some of the maturity models that can be used to situate a company with respect to its KM culture? Discuss the strengths and weaknesses of each of these maturity models.
6. What are some of the key enablers and major obstacles to effective knowledge sharing that can be attributed to the overall organizational culture? to the diverse microcultures?
7. Describe how you would initiate an organizational change. Provide an estimate of how long you believe each stage would last.
8. What are some of the ways of assessing whether or not the culture is changing, or maturing, toward an intended end state? Provide examples.
9. What are some of the ways you would go about learning what an organization's values are? How would you collect and analyze stories, myths, and the typical language used by a particular community of practice?
10. How would you forge a bridge between the largely tacit cultural knowledge of an organization and the largely explicit organizational memory system that should serve to preserve this knowledge?

NOTES

[1] KM and the Learning Organization: A European Perspective. APQC Report (http://www.apqc.org)

[2] T. Stewart, "Whom Can You Trust? It's Not So Easy to Tell," *Fortune*, June 12, 2000.

[3] T. Stewart, "The House That Knowledge Built," *Fortune*, October 2, 2000.

[4] Dilip Bhatt, "EFQM: Excellence Model and Knowledge Management Implications," ICL/Fujitsu.

[5] Berkman, E. (2000). Don't lose your mind share. CIO Magazine, Oct. 21, 2000. Available at: http://www.cio.com

REFERENCES

Argyris, C., and Schon, D. (1978). *Organizational learning: a theory of action perspective*. Reading, MA: Addison-Wesley.

Bloom, H. (2000). *The global brain*. New York: John Wiley and Sons.

Chiem, T. (2001, October). Form follows strategy: open and interactive office design supports cultural changes at the new BP. *Knowledge Management Magazine*. Available at http://www.destinationkm.com/articles/default.asp?ArticleID=369.

CMMI Project Team (2002). Capability Maturity Model Integration (CMMI). Version 1.1. *Report CMU/SEI-2002-TR-011*. Software Engineering Institute, Pittsburgh.

Cohen, W., and Levinthal, D. (1990). Absorptive capacity: a new perspective on learning and innovation. *Administrative Science Quarterly, 35*: 128–152.

Cotter, M. (2000, January). Workplace design: the anti-office of the future. *Knowledge Management Magazine*. Available from http://www.destinationkm.com/articles/default.asp?ArticleID=80.

Craik, K. (1943). *The nature of explanation*. Cambridge: Cambridge University Press.

Fullam, Michael. (2001). *Leading in a culture of change*. San Francisco: Jossey-Bass.

Gladwell, M. (2000, December 11). Designs for working. *The New Yorker*.

Goffee, R., and Jones, G. (2000). *The character of a corporation: how your company's culture can make or break your business*. New York: HarperBusiness, HarperCollins Publishers.

Gruber, H., and Duxbury, L. (2001, January 11). Does organizational culture affect the sharing of knowledge? Presentation Health Canada. Available from http://www.hc-sc.gc.ca/iacb-dgiac/km-gs/english/duxbury_en.pdf.

Harrison, R., and Stokes, H. (1992). *Diagnosing organizational culture*. San Francisco: Jossey-Bass.

Hofstede, G., Neuijen, B., Daval Ohayv, D., and Sanders, G. (1990). Measuring organization cultures: a qualitative and quantitative study across twenty cases. *Administrative Science Quarterly, 35*: 286–316.

Johnson-Laird, P. N. (1983). *Mental models: towards a cognitive science of language, inference, and consciousness*. Cambridge: Cambridge University Press.

Kanter, R. (1989). *When giants learn to dance: mastering the challenge of strategy, management and careers in the 1990s*. New York: Simon and Schuster.

Kilmann, R. H., Saxton, M. J., and Serpa, R. (1986). Issues in understanding and changing culture. *California Management Review, 28*: 87–94.

Kochikar, V. (2000, September). The knowledge management maturity model —a staged framework for leveraging knowledge. In *Proceedings, KM World 2000.* Available at http://www.infy.com/knowledge_capital/knowledge/KMWorld00_B304.pdf.

Kotter, J. (1996). *Leading Change.* Boston: Harvard Business School Press.

Lipnack, J., and Stawps, J. (Eds) (1997). Virtual teams: Reaching out across space, time, and organization with technology. Chapter 2. New York, NY: John Wiley.

Lemken, B., Kahler, H., and Rittenbruch, M. (2000). Sustained knowledge management by organizational culture. In *Proceedings, 33rd Hawaii International Conference on Systems Sciences.*

Morgan, G. (1977). Bureaucratic organizations. In C. Brown, P. Guillet de Mouthoux, and A. McCullough (Eds.), *Research Access*, pp. 138–150. Sweden: THS Co.

Morgan, G. (1997). *Images of organization.* Thousand Oaks, CA: Sage Publications.

Neher, W. (1997). *Organizational communication.* Needham Heights, MA: Allyn & Bacon.

Oakhill, J., and Garnham, A. (Eds.) (1996). *Mental models in cognitive science.* Mahwah, NJ: Lawrence Erlbaum Associates.

Owen, H. (1997). *Open space technology: a user's guide.* San Francisco, CA: Berrett-Koehler.

Paulk, M. C., Weber, C., Curtis, B., and Chrissis, M. (1995). *The capability maturity model: guidelines for improving the software process.* Reading, MA: Addison-Wesley.

Paulzen, O., and Perc, P. (2002). A maturity model for quality improvement in knowledge management. In A. Wenn, M. McGrath, and F. Burstein (Eds.), *Enabling organizations and society through information systems*, pp. 243–253. Proceedings of the 13th Australasian Conference on Information Systems (ACIS 2002), Melbourne, Australia.

Pepper, G. (1995). *Communicating in organizations: a cultural approach.* New York: McGraw-Hill.

Roberts-Witt, S. (2002, March 26). A "Eureka" moment at Xerox. *PC Magazine.* Available at http://www.pcmag.com/article2/0,4149,28792,00.asp.

Rogers, Y., Rutherford, A., and Bibby, P. A. (Eds.). (1992). *Models in the mind: theory, perspective and application.* London: Academic Press.

Sathe, V. (1985). *Culture and related corporate realities.* 1st ed. Homewood, IL: Richard D. Irwin.

Schein, E. (1992). *Organizational culture and leadership.* 2nd ed. San Francisco: Jossey-Bass.

Schein, E. (1999). *The corporate culture survival guide: sense and nonsense about cultural change.* San Francisco: Jossey-Bass.

Shevlin, R., Maney, R., Sawyer, J., and Edwards, B. (1997, November–December). The stages of knowledge management. *The Forrester Report—Leadership Strategies, 3*(2). Forrester Group.

Sveiby, K., and Simons, R. (2002). Collaborative climate and effectiveness of knowledge work—an empirical study. *Journal of Knowledge Management, 6*(5): 420–433.

Tapscott, D., and Ticoll, D. (2003). *The naked corporation. How the age of transparency will revolutionize business.* Toronto, Ontario: Viking Canada Press.

Wenger, E., McDermott, R., and Snyder, W. (2002). *Cultivating communities of practice.* Boston: Harvard Business School Press.

KNOWLEDGE MANAGEMENT TOOLS

Any sufficiently advanced technology is indistinguishable from magic.

Arthur C. Clarke (1917)

This chapter provides an overview of KM tools, which are all too often treated as black boxes (i.e., data goes in and knowledge magically comes out the other end). Knowledge management implementations require a wide range of quite diverse tools that come into play throughout the KM cycle. Technology is used to facilitate primarily communication, collaboration, and content management for better knowledge capture, sharing, dissemination, and application. Major categories of KM tools are presented, as new ones are being developed at a rapid pace.

LEARNING OBJECTIVES

1. Describe the key communication technologies that can be used to support knowledge sharing within an organization.
2. Illustrate the major advantages and major drawbacks of synchronous versus asynchronous KM technologies.
3. Define data mining and list some cases where it would be used.
4. Compare and contrast the different types of intelligent agents and show how they can be used to personalize KM technologies.
5. Define the difference between push and pull KM technologies.
6. Characterize the major groupware tools and explain how they would be implemented within an organization.
7. Sketch out the major components of a knowledge repository and explain how organizations and organizational users would make optimal use of one.

INTRODUCTION

Many dimensions are involved in describing knowledge management tools. Ruggles (1997) provides a classification of KM technologies as tools that

1. Enhance and enable knowledge generation, codification, and transfer.
2. Generate knowledge (e.g., data mining that discovers new patterns in data).
3. Code knowledge to make knowledge available for others.
4. Transfer knowledge to decrease problems with time and space when communicating in an organization.

Rollet (2003) classifies KM technologies according to the following scheme:

1. Communication
2. Collaboration
3. Content creation
4. Content management
5. Adaptation
6. E-learning
7. Personal tools
8. Artificial intelligence
9. Networking

Rollet's (2003) categories can also be grouped according to the particular phase of the KM cycle in which they are used (see Figure 8-1).

The initial knowledge capture and creation phase does not make extensive use of technologies. Methods of converting tacit knowledge into explicit knowledge were discussed in Chapter 4. A wide range of diverse KM technologies may be used to support knowledge sharing and dissemination as well as knowledge acquisition and application. Table 8-1 lists the major KM tools, techniques, and technologies currently in use. The underlying theme is that of a toolkit. Many tools and techniques are borrowed from other disciplines, and others are specific to KM. All of them need to be mixed and matched in the appropriate manner in order to address all the needs of the KM discipline, and the choice of tools to be included in the KM toolkit must be consistent with the organization's overall business strategy.

KNOWLEDGE CAPTURE AND CREATION TOOLS

Content Creation Tools

Robertson (2003) predicts that content management systems (CMS) will become a "commodity" in the future. Many content management system projects fail owing to a lack of good implementation standards and a lack of an understanding of usability issues. Technology-only approaches will continue to

FIGURE 8-1

THE TECHNOLOGY COMPONENT IN AN INTEGRATED
KM CYCLE

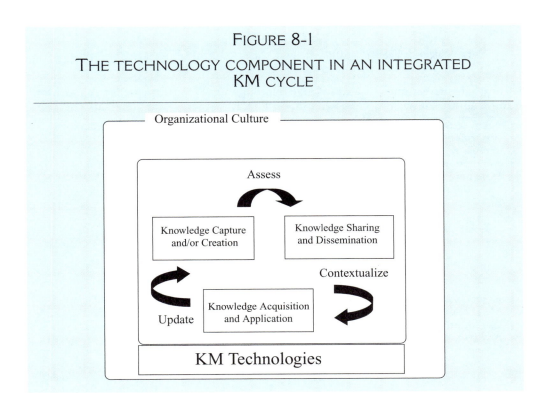

generate unsuccessful projects. CMS should be handled in a strategic way. These failures provide a valuable source of learning. The move toward open standards would greatly assist the evolution of CMS, which is likely to proceed with the use of XML-based protocols for communicating with and between content management systems. Additional standards are needed for storing, structuring, and managing content. Eventually, content, document, records, and knowledge management will converge, which will be of greatest benefit to organizations. As yet, there is no merged platform to accommodate such a convergence.

Authoring tools, the most commonly used content creation tools, range from the general (e.g., word processing) to the more specialized (e.g., web page design software). Annotation technologies enable short comments to be attached to specific sections of a text document, often by a number of different authors (e.g., by making used of the track changes feature in Word). This allows a "running commentary" to be built up and preserved. Annotations may be public (visible to all who access and read the document) or private (visible to the author only).

Data Mining and Knowledge Discovery

The data mining and knowledge discovery processes automatically extract predictive information from large databases based on statistical analysis (typically, cluster analysis). Using a combination of machine learning, statistical analysis, modeling techniques, and database technology, data mining detects

TABLE 8-1
MAJOR KM TECHNIQUES, TOOLS, AND TECHNOLOGIES

Knowledge Creation and Capture Phase	Knowledge Sharing and Dissemination Phase	Knowledge Acquisition and Application Phase
Content creation ■ Authoring tools ■ Templates ■ Annotations ■ Data mining ■ Expertise profiling ■ Blogs	Communication and collaboration technologies ■ Telephone ■ Fax ■ Videoconferencing ■ Chat rooms ■ Instant messaging ■ Internet telephony ■ E-mail ■ Discussion forums ■ Groupware ■ Wikis ■ Workflow management	E-learning technologies ■ CBT ■ WBT ■ EPSS
Content management ■ Metadata tagging ■ Classification ■ Archiving ■ Personal KM	Networking technologies ■ Intranets ■ Extranets ■ Web servers, browsers ■ Knowledge repository ■ Portal	Artificial intelligence technologies ■ Expert systems ■ DSS ■ Customization–personalization ■ Push/pull technologies ■ Recommender systems ■ Visualization ■ Knowledge maps ■ Intelligent Agents ■ Automated taxonomy systems ■ Text analysis—summarization

hidden patterns and subtle relationships in data and infers rules that allow the prediction of future results. Raw data is analyzed in order to offer a model that attempts to explain the observed patterns. This model can then be used to predict future occurrences and to forecast expected outcomes (see Figure 8-2).

A large number of inputs are required, usually over a significant period of time, and the types of models produced range from "easy" to "almost impossible" to understand. Examples of easy-to-understand models are decision trees. Regression analyses are moderately easy to understand, and neural networks remain black boxes. The major drawback of the black box models is that it becomes very difficult to hypothesize about causal relationships (see Figure 8-3).

Variables may be correlated, but this relationship may not have any meaning or usefulness. For example, a major bank found a correlation between the state an applicant lived in and a higher percentage of defaults on loans given out. This finding should not be the basis for a policy that would automatically reject any applicants from that state! Reality checks are always needed with statis-

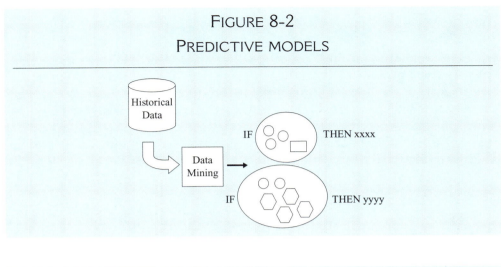

FIGURE 8-2
PREDICTIVE MODELS

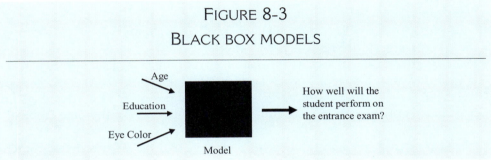

FIGURE 8-3
BLACK BOX MODELS

tics before any conclusions can be drawn; as Disraeli put it so wittily, "there are three kinds of lies: lies, damned lies and statistics."

Typical applications of data mining and knowledge discovery systems include market segmentation, customer profiling, fraud detection, evaluation of retail promotions, credit risk analysis, and market basket analysis (as described in the following vignette). However, there are usually a few gems to be mined with data mining applications. These are often unexpected correlations that upon further study yield some useful (and often actionable) insights into what is occurring. The famous example is that of the relationship between purchases of beer and purchases of diapers.

BEER WITH YOUR DIAPERS?

A chain of convenience stores conducted a market basket analysis as an aid in product placement. Market basket analysis is a statistical analysis of items that consumers tend to buy together (and are found in the same "basket" at checkout). One of the store managers' hypotheses was to place all items related to infant care together, and they ran a simple correlation

Continued

check to validate that mothers of newborns did in fact tend to buy items such as baby powder or cream when they came in to purchase diapers. To their surprise, the highest correlation for an item that tended to be bought at the same time as diapers (in the newborn size and format) was a case of beer. This was later explained by the observation that it was the fathers of newborns who were more likely to be sent to the store to buy more diapers, and while they were there, they tended to pick up other items they considered equally essential.

Data mining tools that are currently in use include:

- Statistical analysis tools (e.g., SAS).
- Data mining suites (e.g., EnterpriseMiner).
- Consulting/outsourcing tools such as EDS, IBM, and Epsilon. (Note that these tools are models, not just software.)
- Data visualization software that coherently presents a large amount of information in a small space. They make use of human information processing capabilities—your eyes—to detect patterns, for example, in a virtual reality or simulation environment where you can "walk around the data points."

It is also possible to apply this technique and use these tools to mine content other than data—namely, text mining and thematic analysis and webmining—to look at what content, how often, for how long (e.g., number of hits), which is very helpful in content management. Similarly, skill mining or expertise profiling can be used to detect patterns in online curriculum vitae of organizational members. Expertise location systems can be automatically created based on the content that has been mined. Commercial software systems can also be used to mine e-mail data in order to determine who is answering what types of queries or themes. Organizational experts and expertise can be detected by looking at the patterns of questions and answers contained within the e-mails. The same caveat applies to all of these data mining applications: a human being is always needed in the loop in order to carry out "reality checks" (i.e., to verify and validate that the patterns do indeed exist and that they have been interpreted in a useful and valuable manner).

Blogs

A *blog* is a slang term for a web log. For the uninitiated, a web log is a popular and fairly personal content form on the Internet. A person's web log is much like an open diary. It chronicles what a person wants to share with the world on an almost daily basis (Blood, 2002; see also http://www.rebeccablood.net/). A blog is a frequently updated, publicly accessible journal. Although the "blogosphere" started off as a medium for mostly personal musings, it has evolved into a tool that offers some of the most insightful information on the web. Furthermore, blogs are becoming much more common, as businesses, politicians, policy makers, and even libraries and library associations have begun to blog as a way of communicating with their patrons and constituents.

Several librarians publish blogs that offer a wealth of information about social software and its uses. SNTReport.com focuses on the social software industry and how social software tools are being used to help people collaborate. Blogs not only offer a new way to communicate with customers, but they have internal uses as well. For example, large organizations can use a well-formed blog to exchange ideas and information about web development projects, training initiatives, or research issues. These questions and answers can be cross-indexed and archived, which helps build a knowledge network among the participating members. Most importantly, the price of setting up a well-formed, secure blog and leveraging it into a knowledge and content management tool is a pittance when compared to the cost of other, proprietary solutions.

At present, the majority of blogs are published exclusively in text. The next generation of blogs, however, will implement audio and video elements, bringing a sophisticated multimedia blend to the medium (Dames, 2004).

Pikas (2004) adds the notion of searching to blogs. Blogs are collections of articles or stories arranged in reverse chronology and are generally updated more frequently than regular web pages. Just like any other information on the net, there is no guarantee of authority, accuracy, or lack of bias. In fact, personal blogs are frequently biased and can be good sources of opinion and information from the "man on the street." Because blogs can be updated on the fly, they frequently have access to unfiltered information faster from war zones and sites of natural disasters than the mainstream media outlets. Blogs are also good sources of unfiltered information on either faulty or very useful products.

In the beginning, blogs appeared in search results alongside regular web pages. Since blogs are not technologically any different from other web pages (that is, they are HTML, XML, javascript, etc.—it is their format, not their coding that is different). Spiders and bots (or webcrawlers, knowledge robots) automatically search for information online and collect posts (i.e., messages that are submitted to a computerized messaging system) the same way as they collect other online information. Search engines that place greater value on sites that are recently and frequently updated and are highly linked tend to rank blog posts very highly. Because the barrier to publication is so low in blogs, arguably much lower than that for standard web pages, these high rankings were introducing a lot of noise into online searches. The odds are that if you have searched on a controversial topic in the past year you have run across several archived blog posts. Recently, most major search engines have altered their algorithms to push blogs down in the search results. Engines that only return two results from any one site use this feature to limit the impact of blogs on the search results.

Blog searching breaks down into at least two categories: (1) information from within blogs/across blogs or (2) addresses of feeds from blogs so that you may subscribe in your aggregator (i.e., a piece of software or a remotely hosted service that periodically reads a set of news sources, such as blogs, identifies what is new, and displays them on single page). Feeds and blogs are two different concepts, but they are closely linked because most blogs have feeds and many feeds are generated by blogs. Just as in other web search tools, there are search engines and directories. At this time, blog search engines are where general search engines were before the Google Age: there are many competing smaller products, but no product dominates the scene.

Content Management Tools

Content management refers to the management of valuable content throughout the useful lifespan of the content. Content lifespan will typically begin with content creation, handle multiple changes and updates, merging, summarization, and other repackaging, and will typically end with archiving. Metadata (information about the content) is used to better manage content throughout its useful lifespan. Metadata includes such information as source/author, key words to describe content, date created, date changed, quality, best purposes, annotations by those who have made use of it, and an expiry or "best before" date where applicable. It is also useful to include attributes such as storage medium, location, and whether or not it exists in a number of alternative forms (e.g., different languages). XML is increasingly being used to tag knowledge content, and taxonomies serve to better organize and classify content for easier future retrieval and use.

XML (eXtensible Markup Language) gives you the ability to structure and add relevance to chunks of information (that is why many CM solutions use XML), and in theory to exchange data more easily between applications (e.g., with your suppliers, customers, and partners). However, you may all use the same words (tags), but if each of you defines and applies them differently, then we remain in the land of Babel. Common agreed schemas are essential. Keep tabs with developments on the schemas and metadata standards in your field. Useful sources are XML.org (http://www.xml.org) in the W3C XML schemas section (http://www.w3.org/XML/Schema).

Taxonomies are hierarchical information trees for classifying information, analogous to the library subject catalog. They can help overcome differences of language usage in different parts of an organization and even clarify the use of different languages. Traditionally, taxonomy development is manually intensive in that it is created and maintained by people. The growing problem of information overload means that taxonomies are receiving significant attention. But how do you cope with the evolution of terms whose meanings seem to change from one year to the next? Automatic (or semiautomatic) classification of information objects uses software such as natural language analyzers, text summarizers, and other technology to understand some of the meaning —the concepts—behind blocks of text, and to tag and index it appropriately to aid subsequent retrieval. Automated classifiers find patterns in textual content, produce categories, and classify the content using these categories.

Personal capital is a term coined to explain a divergence from the traditional notion of capital, which is an asset "owned" by an organization (Cope, 2000). In fact, the future of KM will blur the boundaries between the individual, the group or community, and the organization. KM will become a pervasive part of how we conduct our everyday business lives. Personalized KM (PKM) will gain increasing importance given the ever-increasing momentum of information overload with which we must deal. In other words, some of the key principles, best practices, and business processes of KM that have to date been focused at the organizational level will filter down to be used by individuals managing their own personal capital.

PKM and traditional knowledge management differ depending on whether an organizational or personal perspective is adopted. Tools for personal information management are impressive and, if you think about e-mail and portals, are already widely used. Newer tools such as blogs, news aggregators and instant messaging, represent a new toolset for PKM.

Personal portals—which were once known as "enterprise" portals—are now focused on the needs of the individual—all a person's information and application needs harmoniously brought together into a preferred arrangement on the desktop. This is mass customization in front of your eyes! Again, the aims are laudable, but reality and theory are often miles apart. PKM brings many of the key principles of KM to bear on the personal productivity and specific work requirements of a given knowledge worker. Definitions of PKM revolve around a set of core issues: managing and supporting personal knowledge and information so that it is accessible, meaningful, and valuable to the individual; maintaining networks, contacts, and communities; making life easier and more enjoyable; and exploiting personal capital (Higgison, 2004). On an information management level, PKM involves filtering and making sense of information and organizing paper and digital archives, e-mails, and bookmark collections.

KNOWLEDGE SHARING AND DISSEMINATION TOOLS

Although Rollet (2003) made a distinction between communication technologies (such as telephone and e-mail) and collaboration technologies (such as workflow management), it is very difficult to draw a line between the two. Communication and collaboration are invariably intertwined, and it is quite difficult to establish where one ends and the other begins. Both types of tools have been grouped under the category of groupware or collaboration tools. Although all organizational members will make use of communication and collaboration, including project teams and work units, communities of practice will be particularly active in making use of many, if not all, of the communication and collaboration technologies described in this section.

Groupware and Collaboration Tools

Groupware represents a class of software that helps groups of colleagues *(workgroups)* attached to a communication network (e.g., Local Area Networks [LANs]) to organize their activities. Typically, groupware supports the following operations:

- Scheduling meetings and allocating resources
- E-mail
- Password protection for documents
- Telephone utilities
- Electronic newsletters
- File distribution

The most commonly used communication technologies include the telephone, fax, videoconferencing, teleconferencing, chat rooms, instant messaging, phone text messaging (SMS), Internet telephone (voice over IP or VOIP), e-mail, and discussion forums. Communication is said to be dyadic when it occurs between two individuals (e.g., a telephone call). Teleconferencing, on the other hand, may have more than two participants interacting with one another in real time. Videoconferencing introduces a multimedia component to the communication channel as participants can not only hear (audio) but also see the other participants (audiovisual). Desktop videoconferencing is similar but does not require a dedicated videoconference facility. Simple and inexpensive digital video cameras can be used to transmit images. The visual component is especially useful when demonstrations are presented to all participants.

Chat rooms are text-based but synchronous. Participants communicate with one another in real time via a web server that provides the interaction facility. Instant messaging is also real-time communication, but in this case participants sign on to the instant messaging system and they can immediately see who else is online or "live" at that same time. Messages are exchanged through text boxes. The SMS (Short Messaging System) allows text messages to be sent via a cellular phone rather than through the Internet.

E-mail continues to be one of the most frequently used communication channels in organizations. Although e-mail messaging is dyadic, it can also be used in a more broadcast mode (e.g., group mailings) as well as in an asynchronous group discussion mode (by forwarding previous discussion threads).

Communication technologies are almost always integrated with some form of collaboration, whether it be planning for collaboration or organizing collaborative work. Collaboration technologies are often referred to as groupware or as workgroup productivity software. It is technology designed to facilitate the work of groups. This technology may be used to communicate, cooperate, coordinate, solve problems, compete, or negotiate. Although traditional technologies like the telephone qualify as groupware, the term is ordinarily used to refer to a specific class of technologies relying on modern computer networks, such as e-mail, newsgroups, videophones, or chat.

Groupware technologies are typically categorized along two primary dimensions (see Table 8-2):

1. Whether users of the groupware are working together at the same time ("real-time" or "synchronous" groupware) or different times ("asynchronous" groupware).
2. Whether users are working together in the same place ("colocated" or "face-to-face") or in different places ("non-colocated" or "distance").

TABLE 8-2
CLASSIFICATION OF GROUPWARE TECHNOLOGIES

	Same Time—Synchronous	Different Time—Asynchronous
Same place—co-located	Voting Presentation support	Shared computers
Different place—distant	Videophones Chat	E-mail Workflow

Coleman (1997) developed a taxonomy of groupware that lists 12 different categories:

1. Electronic mail and messaging
2. Group calendaring and scheduling
3. Electronic meeting systems
4. Desktop video, real-time synchronous conferencing
5. Non-real-time asynchronous conferencing
6. Group document handling
7. Workflow
8. Workgroup utilities and development tools
9. Groupware services
10. Groupware and KM frameworks
11. Groupware applications
12. Collaborative Internet-based applications and products

E-mail is by far the most common groupware application (besides, of course, the traditional telephone). Although the basic technology is designed to pass simple messages between two people, even relatively basic e-mail systems today typically include interesting features for forwarding messages, filing messages, creating mailing groups, and attaching files with a message. Other features that have been explored include automatic sorting and processing of messages, automatic routing, and structured communication (messages requiring certain information).

Newsgroups and mailing lists are similar in spirit to e-mail systems except that they are intended for messages among large groups of people instead of one-to-one communication. In practice, the main difference between newsgroups and mailing lists is that newsgroups show messages to a user only when they are explicitly requested (an "on-demand" service), while mailing lists deliver messages as they become available (an "interrupt-driven" interface).

Workflow systems allow documents to be routed through organizations by means of a relatively fixed process. A simple example of a workflow application is an expense report in an organization: an employee enters an expense report and submits it, a copy is archived and then routed to the employee's manager for approval, the manager receives the document, electronically approves it, and sends it on, and the expense is registered to the group's account and forwarded to the accounting department for payment. Workflow systems may provide features such as routing, development of forms, and support for differing roles and privileges.

Hypertext is a system for linking text documents to each other, with the web being an obvious example. Whenever multiple people author and link documents, the system becomes group work, constantly evolving and responding to others' work. Some hypertext systems include capabilities for seeing who else has visited a certain page or link, or at least seeing how often a link has been followed, thus giving users a basic awareness of what other people are doing in the system. Page counters on the web are a crude approximation of this function. Another common multiuser feature in hypertext (that is not found on the web) is allowing any user to create links from any page, so that others can be informed when there are relevant links not known to the original author.

Group calendars allow scheduling, project management, and coordination among many people and may provide support for scheduling equipment as well. Typical features detect when schedules conflict or find meeting times that will work for everyone. Group calendars also help to locate people. Typical concerns are privacy (users may feel that certain activities are not public matters) and completeness and accuracy (users may feel that the benefits of the calendar do not justify the time it takes to enter schedule information).

Collaborative writing systems may provide both real-time and non-real-time support. Word processors may provide asynchronous support by showing authorship and by allowing users to track changes and make annotations to documents. Authors collaborating on a document may also be given tools to help plan and coordinate the authoring process, such as methods for locking parts of the document or linking separately authored documents. Synchronous support allows authors to see each other's changes as they make them, and usually needs to provide an additional communication channel to the authors as they work (via videophones or chat systems).

Synchronous or real-time groupware is exemplified by shared workspaces, tele- or videoconferencing, and chat systems. For example, shared whiteboards allow two or more people to view and draw on a shared drawing surface even from different locations. This system can be used, for instance, during a phone call, where each person can jot down notes (e.g., a name, phone number, or map), or people can work collaboratively on a visual problem. Most shared whiteboards are designed for informal conversation, but they may also serve structured communications or more sophisticated drawing tasks, such as collaborative graphic design, publishing, or engineering applications. Shared whiteboards can indicate where each person is drawing or pointing by showing telepointers, which are color-coded or labeled to identify each person.

Video communications systems allow two-way or multiway calling with live video, providing essentially a telephone system with an additional visual component. Cost and compatibility issues limited the early use of video systems to scheduled videoconference meeting rooms. Video is advantageous when visual information is being discussed, but may not provide substantial benefit in most cases where conventional audio telephones are adequate. In addition to supporting conversations, video may also be used in less direct collaborative situations, such as by providing a view of activities at a remote location.

Chat systems permit many people to write messages in real time in a public space. As each person submits a message, it appears at the bottom of a scrolling screen. Chat groups are usually formed by listing chat rooms by name, location, number of people, topic of discussion, and so on.

Many systems allow for rooms with controlled access or with moderators to lead the discussions, but most of the topics of interest to researchers involve issues related to unmoderated real-time communication, including anonymity, following the stream of conversation, scalability with number of users, and abusive users.

Although chat-like systems are possible using nontext media, the text version of chat has the rather interesting aspect of having a direct transcript of the conversation, which not only has long-term value, but allows for backward reference during conversation, making it easier for people to drop into a conversation and still pick up on the ongoing discussion.

Groupware applications from Teamware, the U.S. Army, Chevron, and BP are the topics of the following vignettes.

TEAMWARE

Teamware Group, a Fujitsu subsidiary, has implemented an interactive web community solution for the city of Kerava in Finland. The solution enhances communication between and within the city managers, city board, city council, and other elected officials, and offers them facilities to interact and distribute information regardless of time or location. The objective of the system is to facilitate the daily work of the city administrators by providing them with a new virtual means of interaction in addition to the traditional meetings and sessions. "It has become more and more difficult for the city administrators to take care of their duties within the normal working hours and premises. Therefore, it is essential to provide them with facilities to communicate and obtain information without the boundaries of time or location," says IT manager Ari Sainio from the city of Kerava.

The new system was built on the Teamware Pl@za® platform and integrated with the existing Teamware Office™ groupware solution, which means that now e-mail, city archives, electronic calendars, and bulletin boards will be available for the city administrators through the standard web browser. To enhance interaction between the city officials, the system is augmented with discussion facilities where individuals can exchange opinions and discuss different issues. Various archives and files are created for content management purposes. Different user groups are provided with their own virtual workspaces that can be accessed only by authorized members. Through Teamware Pl@za's decentralized and easy-to-use updating functionality the city officials can update the pages themselves. The new web service was launched in October 2001.

Source: http://www.teamware.com.

The Army's After Action Review (AAR) is an excellent example of a process that ensures lessons are learned after an event. British Petroleum (BP) and Chevron have introduced similar systems whereby they learn before, during, and after the undertaking of a large project. Major cost savings have been realized by introducing these learning processes. For example, Chevron introduced a lessons learned tool for its drilling processes. Every time drilling takes place in a particular area, lessons are recorded. The next time drilling takes place in a similar area, lessons learned during the last drilling operations are available. This results in fewer errors and less "reinventing of the wheel." Chevron has also recorded waste savings in its drilling operations.

The United States Air Force (USAF) is utilizing Open Text's Livelink to manage its Business Solutions Exchange (BSX), which involves integrating the people, process, and policies of the USAF's service contracting into a single system, paving the way for the group to meet the Pentagon's goal of a completely paper-free acquisition process by January 1, 2000. Prior to installing Livelink, the USAF employed a variety of client-server-based systems that had difficulty managing this process across different geographic locations. With the new collaborative KM approach, the USAF has shortened the time spent from identifying point of need to completing a performance requirement document (PRD) from seven months to eight weeks; this represents a 70% reduction in processing time.

The USAF's KM initiative is part of the Pentagon's requirement to simplify and modernize the U.S. Defense Department's acquisition process in the area of contract writing, administration, finance, and auditing. Since July 1998, the USAF has been using Livelink on a variety of outsourcing projects. The first and largest project can be found at Maxwell Air Force Base in Alabama. The goal of the Business Solutions Exchange process is to continually improve USAF business practices. BSX goes to work as soon as a requirement is identified and a Business Strategy Team is formed. The collaborative software is used throughout the life cycle of the project—from requirements definition to contract close-out, connecting a cross-functional team dispersed across a given base and the command.

This implementation of Livelink runs on Windows NT Server, Microsoft SQL Server, Microsoft Office, and Microsoft Exchange and is accessed through Microsoft Internet Explorer. A team, often composed of people from six different locations within the United States, is formed to create a performance requirement document (PRD). It uses the collaborative software as its central knowledge library to gather market research, establish an acquisition plan, record baseline costs, eliminate regulatory constraints, draft requirements, and gather feedback from customers and industry on the contract requirements. The BSX team works together throughout the planning, execution, and supplier management phases. Teams use the public folders (found at http://www.bsx.org) to gather feedback from industry on ways to improve existing requirements documents. In addition, the public sites include process-oriented libraries of best practices that are available to other agencies, whether or not they use the collaborative capabilities of Livelink.

Wikis

Wikis are web-based software that supports concepts such as open editing, which allows multiple users to create and edit content on a website (for more information, see http://en.wikipedia.org/wiki/Wiki). A wiki site grows and changes at the will of the participants. People can add and edit pages at will, using a Word-like screen, without knowing any programming or HTML commands. More specifically, a wiki is composed of web pages where people input information and then create hyperlinks to another page or new pages for more details about a particular topic. Anyone can edit any page and add, delete, or correct information. A search field at the bottom of the page lets you enter a key word for the information you want to find. Today, two types of wikis exist: public wikis and corporate wikis. Public wikis were developed first and are freewheeling forums with few controls. In the last year or two, corporations have been harnessing the power of wikis to provide interactive forums for tracking projects and communicating with employees over their in-house intranets.

An example of a wiki is *Wikipedia*, a free encyclopedia written, literally, by thousands of people around the world. Wikis exist for thousands of topics (see WorldWideWiki: SwitchWiki), and if one does not exist for your favorite subject, you can start one on it and add it to the list.

Wikis support new types of communications by combining Internet applications and websites with human voices. That means people can collaborate online more easily, whether they are working together on a brief or working with a realtor online to tour office space in another city. Outside the law office, it means customer service representatives can interact with customers more readily, which should advance e-commerce (Leuf and Cunningham, 2001).

The first wiki was started in 1995 by Ward Cunningham, a programmer who decided to build the most minimal working database possible. The idea was to provide a simple website where programmers could quickly and easily exchange information without waiting for a webmaster to update the site. He named the site "wiki," after the quick little wiki-wiki shuttle buses in Hawaii.

A public wiki survives thanks to the initiative, honesty, and integrity of its users. Sites can be vandalized, derogatory remarks—called "flames"—can be posted, and misinformation can be published. However, a vandalized site can be restored, a flame can be erased, and information can be corrected by anyone who knows better. The community polices itself. Corporate wikis differ from public wikis in that they are more secure and have many more navigation, usage, and help features. Corporate wikis are used for project management and company communications as well as discussion sites and knowledge databases. For example, a wiki can be established for a particular project, with the project team given access to update the status of tasks and add related documents and spreadsheets. Its central location makes it easy to keep everyone informed and up to date regardless of their home office, location, or time zone. A wiki is more reliable than continually e-mailing updates back and forth to the team members, it is faster than e-mail since updates are available instantly, and it is more efficient than e-mail since each team member does not have to maintain his or her own copies. Managers like wikis because they allow them to see what progress the team is making or what issues it is facing without getting involved or raising concern (e.g., a new way of project management reporting).

For security reasons, corporations usually buy wiki software rather than lease space on the Internet, and they set up the wiki behind the company's firewall as part of an intranet or as an extranet if customers or vendors are allowed access. Also, corporations look for wiki software that has authorization and password safeguards, "rollback" versions so that information can be restored to its former state, and easy upload capabilities for documents and images. Some wikis notify users when new information is added; this is an especially nice feature for corporate projects where fast responses are required.

Networking Technologies

Networking technologies consist of intranets (intraorganizational network), extranets (interorganizational network), knowledge repositories, knowledge portals, and web-based shared workspaces. Liebowitz and Beckman (1998) define knowledge repositories as an online computer-based storehouse of expertise, knowledge, experiences, and documentation about a particular domain of expertise. In creating a knowledge repository, knowledge is collected, summarized, and integrated across sources. Such repositories are sometimes referred to as *experience bases* or *corporate memories*. The repository can either be filled with knowledge through what van Heijst, van Der Spek, and Kruizinga (1997) call *passive collection*—where workers themselves recognize what knowledge has sufficient value to be stored in the repository—or *active collection*—where some people in the organization are scanning communication processes to detect knowledge.

Davenport and Prusak (1998) describe three types of knowledge repositories:

1. External knowledge repositories (such as competitive intelligence).
2. Structured internal knowledge repositories (such as research reports and product-oriented market material).
3. Informal internal knowledge repositories (such as "lessons learned").

A knowledge repository differs from a data warehouse and an information repository primarily in the nature of the content that is stored. Knowledge content will typically consist of contextual, subjective, and fairly pragmatic content. Content in knowledge repositories tends to be unstructured (e.g., works in progress, draft reports, presentations). Knowledge repositories also tend to be more dynamic than other types of architectures because the knowledge content is continually updated and splintered into varying perspectives to serve a wide variety of different users and user contexts. To this end, repositories typically end up being a series of linked mini-portals distributed across an organization.

Most repositories contain the following elements (adapted from Tiwana, 2000):

1. Declarative knowledge (e.g., concepts, categories, definitions, assumptions—knowledge of *what*).
2. Procedural knowledge (e.g., processes, events, activities, actions, manuals—knowledge of *how* or *know-how*).
3. Causal knowledge (e.g., rationale for decisions, for rejected decisions—knowledge of *why*).
4. Context (e.g., circumstances of decisions, informal knowledge, what is and what is not done, accepted, etc.—knowledge of *care-why*).

The knowledge repository is the one-stop-shop for all organizational users providing access to all historical, current, and projected valuable knowledge content. All users should be able to connect to and annotate content, connect to others who have come into contact with the content, as well as contribute content of their own. The interface to the repository or repositories should be user-friendly, seamless, and transparent.

Personalization in the form of personalized news services through push technologies, in the form of mini-portals for each community of practice, and so forth will help maintain the repository in a manageable state. To this end, use of a term such as a *knowledge warehouse* should be strongly discouraged. The knowledge repository should instead be visualized as a lens that is placed on top of the organization's data and information stores. The access and application of the content of a repository should be as directly linked to professional practice and concrete actions as possible.

The knowledge repository typically involves content management software tools such as a Lotus Notes platform and will be run as an intranet within the organization, with appropriate privacy and security measures in place. An example is described in the accompanying vignette.

PRICEWATERHOUSECOOPERS (PWC)

PriceWaterhouseCoopers[2] focused on sharing knowledge across what had been boundaries following the merger of Price Waterhouse and Coopers & Lybrand. The Chief Knowledge Officer, Elen Knapp, supported this effort by putting into place the KnowledgeCurve, where employees can find a

Continued

repository of best practices, consulting methodologies, tax and audit rules, news services, online training, directories of experts, and more, plus links to specialized sites for various industries or skills. The site gets 18 million hits a month, mostly from workers downloading forms or checking news, but also from employees looking things up. Yet there is a feeling that it is under-used—when looking for expertise, most people still go down the hall.

In parallel, a British-based PWC consultant and his colleagues set up a network where they could be "more innovative." Over five months they set up a Lotus Notes e-mail list with no rules, no moderator, and no agenda other than what is set by the messages people sent. Any employee was able to join. Kraken, as it came to be known, now has 500 members, and although it still has no official status, it has become the premier forum for sharing. As an analogy, Kraken is to KnoweldgeCurve what Carlos was to Eureka.[2] On a busy day, members may get 50 Kraken messages, but they are welcomed because they are relevant and useful.

What are some of the reasons for this grassroots CoP success over corporate top-down KM systems? It is demand-driven ("does anyone know. . . ."); it gets at tacit knowledge; it allows fuzzy questions rather than structured database queries; it is part of your everyday routine; it is full of opinions—points of views rather than dry facts. KnowledgeCurve preserves explicit knowledge, whereas Kraken enables the sharing of tacit knowledge. Kraken is about learning, whereas KnowledgeCurve is about teaching. You cannot have one without the other.

Knowledge portals provide access to diverse enterprise content, communities, expertise, and internal and external services and information (Collins, 2003; Firestone, 2003). Portals are a means of storing and disseminating organizational knowledge such as business processes, policies, procedures, documents, and other codified knowledge. They typically feature searching capabilities through content as well as through a taxonomy (categorized content). The option to receive personalized content through push technologies as well as through pull technologies (intelligent agents) may exist. Communities can be accessed via the portal for communication and collaboration purposes. There may be a number of services that users can subscribe to as well as web-based learning modules on selected topics and professional practices. The critical content will consist of the best practices and lessons learned that have been accumulated over the years and to which many organizational members have added value.

The purpose of a portal is to aggregate content from a variety of sources into a one-stop shop for relevant content. Portals enable the organization to access internal and external knowledge that can be consolidated, analyzed, and used as inputs to decision making. Ideally, portals will take into account the different needs of users and the different sorts of knowledge work they carry out in order to provide the best fit with both the content and the format in which the content is presented (the portal interface). Knowledge portals link people, processes, and valuable knowledge content and provide the organizational glue or common thread that serves to support knowledge workers. First-generation portals were essentially a means of broadcasting information to all organizational members. Today, they have evolved into sophisticated shared workspaces where knowledge workers can not only contribute content and share content but also acquire and apply valuable organizational knowledge. Knowledge portals support knowledge creation, sharing, and use by allowing a high level of bidirectional interaction with users.

Portals serve to promote knowledge creation by providing a common virtual space where knowledge workers can contribute their knowledge to organizational memory. Portals promote knowledge sharing by providing links to other organizational members through expertise location systems. Communities of practice will typically have a dedicated space for their members on the organizational portal and their own membership location system included in the virtual workspace. The portal organizes valuable knowledge content using taxonomies or classification schemes to store both structured (e.g., documents) and unstructured content (e.g., stories, lessons learned, and best practices). Finally, portals support knowledge acquisition and application by providing access to the accumulated knowledge, know-how, experience, and expertise of all those who have worked within that organization. An application is described in the accompanying vignette.

KPMG

KPMG International[3] has implemented KWORLD, an advanced global knowledge management system. KWORLD, an online messaging, collaboration, and knowledge-sharing platform, is reportedly the first system of its kind built entirely from standard Microsoft components—Microsoft Windows NT Server, including Microsoft Exchange, Site Server, and Microsoft Office, Outlook, and Internet Explorer. KWORLD is KPMG's digital nervous system based on the Microsoft concept.

KPMG invested over one year and $100 million in developing this "universally" accessible knowledge-sharing environment, which allows its nearly 100,000 professional workers to conduct active conferences and public exchanges, locate customized and filtered external and internal news, and access global- and country-specific firm information. As acknowledged by Microsoft, KPMG is one of only five organizations to embark on its fast-track program to exploit fully the power of the web browser, integrate Microsoft-based messaging, collaboration, and knowledge-sharing applications, and push current web technology to the "limit." Knowledge is content in context, and KPMG's global communities of practice—who marry knowledge about complex services to specific industries—determine KWORLD's contextual frames. KWORLD brings qualified internal content and filtered external content to each community with a click. KPMG foresees developing KWORLD extranets to make KPMG a virtual extension of its clients.

KNOWLEDGE ACQUISITION AND APPLICATION TOOLS

A number of technologies play an important role in how successful knowledge workers are in acquiring (i.e., understanding) and applying (i.e., making use of) knowledge content that is made available to them by the organization. E-learning systems provide support for learning, comprehension, and better understanding of the new knowledge to be acquired. Tools such as electronic performance support systems (EPSS), expert systems, and decision support systems (DSS) help knowledge workers to better apply the knowledge on the job. Adaptive technologies can be used to personalize knowledge content push or pull. Recommender systems can detect similarities or affinities between different types of users and make recommendations of additional content that others like them have found to be useful to acquire and apply. Knowledge maps and other visualization tools can help to better acquire and apply valuable knowledge, and a number of tools derived from artificial intelligence can at least partially automate processes such as text summarization, content classification, and content selection.

E-learning applications started out as computer-based learning (CBT) and web-based training (WBT) applications. The common feature is the online learning environment provided for learners. Courses can now be delivered via the web or the company intranet. The particular knowledge and know-how to be acquired can be scoped and delivered in a timely fashion in order to support knowledge acquisition. E-learning technologies also greatly increase the range of knowledge dissemination because knowledge that has been captured and coded or packaged as e-learning can be easily made available to all organizational members, regardless of any time or distance constraints.

Decision support systems are designed to facilitate groups in decision making. They provide tools for brainstorming, critiquing ideas, putting weights and probabilities on events and alternatives, and voting. Such systems enable presumably more rational and even-handed decisions. Primarily designed to facilitate meetings, they encourage equal participation by, for instance, providing anonymity or enforcing turn-taking.

Visualization technologies and knowledge mapping are good ways of synthesizing large amounts of complex content in order to make it easier for knowledge workers to acquire and apply knowledge.

Artificial intelligence (AI) research addressed the challenges of capturing, representing, and applying knowledge long before the term *knowledge management* entered popular usage. AI developed automated reasoning systems that could make use of explicit knowledge representations in order to provide expert-level advice, troubleshooting, and other forms of support to knowledge workers. Expert systems are decision support systems that do not execute an a priori program but instead deduce or infer a conclusion based on the inputs provided. Natural language processing also grew out of AI research. Linguistic technologies resulted in automating the parsing (breaking into subsections) and analysis of text. Common applications today are voice interfaces or natural language queries that can be typed in to search databases. Similar AI technologies can also be applied to analyze and summarize text or to automatically classify content (e.g., automated taxonomy tools). Many of the automated reasoning capabilities studied in AI research are encapsulated in autonomous pieces of software code, called intelligent agents or software robots ("softbots"). These agents act as proxies for knowledge workers and can be tasked with information searching, retrieving, and filtering functions.

Intelligent Filtering Tools

Intelligent Agents can generally be defined as software programs that assist their user and act on his or her behalf: a computer program that helps you in newsgathering, acts autonomously and on its own initiative, has intelligence and can learn, improving its performance in executing its tasks (Woolridge and Jennings, 1995). These agents are autonomous computer programs, where their environment dynamically affects their behavior and strategy for problem solving. They help users deal with information. Most agents are Internet based—that is, software programs inhabiting the Net and performing their functions there.

The following features define a true Intelligent Agent (Khoo, Tor, and Lee, 1998):

1. *Autonomy*: the ability to do most of their tasks without any direct assistance from an outside source, which includes human and other agents, while controlling their own actions and states.
2. *Social Ability*: the ability to interact with, when they deem appropriate, other software agents and humans.
3. *Responsiveness*: the ability to respond in a timely fashion to perceived changes in the environment, including changes in the physical world, other agents, or the Internet.
4. *Personalizability*: the ability to adapt to its user's needs, by learning from how the user reacts to the agent's performance.
5. *Proactivity*: the ability of an agent to take initiatives by itself, autonomously (out of a specific instruction by its user) and spontaneously, often on a periodical basis, which makes the agent a very helpful and time-saving tool.
6. *Adaptivity*: the capacity to change and improve according to the experiences accumulated. This has to do with memory and learning: an agent learns from its user and progressively improves in performing its tasks. The most experimental *bots* even develop their "own" personalities and make decisions based on past experiences.
7. *Cooperation*: the interactivity between agent and user, which is fundamentally different from the one-way working of ordinary software.

Many knowledge management applications make use of intelligent agents (e.g., see Elst, Dignum, and Abecker, 2003). This range includes personalized information management (such as filtering e-mail), electronic commerce (such as locating information for purchasing and buying), and management of complex commercial and industrial processes (such as scheduling appointments and air traffic control). These tasks/applications can generally be grouped into five categories (Khoo, Tor, and Lee, 1998):

1. *Watcher Agents*: look for specific information.
2. *Learning Agents*: tailor to an individual's preferences by learning from the user's past behavior.
3. *Shopping Agents*: compare "the best price for an item."
4. *Information Retrieval Agents*: help the user to "search for information in an intelligent fashion."
5. *Helper Agents*: perform tasks autonomously without human interaction.

In the age of computers, information, whether useful or useless, is readily available on the Internet. So much data is available that we often claim to be "overloaded with information." Having too much data can cause as much trouble as having no data, as we must sift through so much information to get what we need. We can categorize this information overload problem into two divisions:

1. *Information filtering*: We must go through an enormous amount of information to find the small portion that is relevant to us.
2. *Information gathering*: There is not enough information available to us, and we have to search long and hard to find what we need.

Information filtering is a particularly important function in KM because users need a way of filtering this data into a more manageable situation. Knowledge workers (such as managers, technical professionals, and marketing personnel) need information in a timely manner as it can greatly affect their success. Tasks that are redundant or routine need to be minimized by some individuals who can otherwise spend their time more productively (Roesler and Hawkins, 1994).

Some companies receive so much e-mail that they have to employ clerical workers to sift through the flood of e-mail, answering basic queries and forwarding others to specialized workers. Others use intelligent filtering software such GrapeVine for Lotus, which reads a preestablished "knowledge chart" to determine who should receive what mail. Intelligent Agent services can supplement but not replace the value of edited information. As information becomes more available, it becomes more and more crucial to have strong editors filter that information (Webb, 1995). There is so much content out there that the tools that filter content are going to be as important as the content itself (Wingfield, 1995). As stated by Rutherford Rogers,[3] "we are drowning in information but starved for knowledge."

An end user, required to constantly direct the management process, contributes to information overload. But having agents to perform tasks such as searching and filtering can ultimately reduce the information overload to a degree. Maes (1994) describes an electronic mail-filtering agent called Maxims, which is a type of learning agent. The program "learns to prioritize, delete, forward, sort, and archive mail messages on behalf of a user." The program monitors the user's actions and treats these actions as a lesson on what to do.

Depending upon threshold limits that are constantly updated, Maxims will guess what the user will do. Upon surpassing a degree of certainty, it will start to suggest action for the user to take.

Maes (1994) also presents an example of an Internet news-filtering program called NewT. This program takes as input a stream of Usenet news articles and gives as output a subset of these articles that is recommended for the user to read. The user gives NewT examples of articles that would and would not be read, and NewT then retrieves articles. Next the user gives feedback about the articles, and thus NewT is trained further on which articles to retrieve and which articles not to retrieve. NewT retrieves words of interest from an article by performing a full-text analysis using the vector space model for documents. Some additional examples of information-filtering agents are shown in Table 8-3.

News Agents are designed to create custom newspapers from a huge number of web newspapers throughout the world. The trend in this field is toward autonomous, personalized, adaptive, and very smart agents that surf the Net, newsgroups, databases, and so on and deliver selected information to their users. "Push" technology is strictly connected to news bots developments, consisting basically in the delivery of information on the web that appears to be initiated by the information server rather than by the client. Some examples are shown in Table 8-4.

TABLE 8-3
SAMPLE INFORMATION-FILTERING AGENTS

Name	Description	Reference
Search Pad	An advanced bot that finds and categorizes relevant information based on the user's preferences, also learning from them.	http://www.searchpad.com
Copernic	An agent that carries out Net searches by simultaneously consulting the most important search engines on the web.	http://copernic.com
KOS (Knowledge Object Suite)	A new class of intelligent information retrieval tool built by modeling how we learn. Cognitive science, collaborative knowledge sharing, and knowledge modeling that continues where search drops you by "reading" the knowledge in search results.	http://www.cirilab.com
NetAttachePro v1.0	A "second-generation web agent" that features a powerful information-filtering Intelligent Agent. It allows and organizes offline browsing.	http://www.tympani.com/

Table 8-4
Examples of Personalized News Services

Name	Description	Reference
myCNN	Personalized news service	http://my.cnn.com
Excit News Tracker	Pulls information from a collection of databases	http://nt.excite.com
Infoseek Personal News	Personalized news service	http://www.infoseek.com/news?pg=personalize.html
Dogpile	Fast, efficient news service that draws upon a large database for its searches	http://www.dogpile.com

Information overload is a worldwide problem today, but Intelligent Agents help reduce this problem. Using them to filter the oncoming "traffic" of the "information highway" can help reduce cost, effort, and time. Yet the development of Intelligent Agents is still in its infancy. As it gains in popularity and use, we can expect to see more sophisticated and better developed Intelligent Agents.

Information studies research has examined information-seeking behavior for over five decades now and can serve as an excellent theoretical basis for the study of the Internet as an information source and Intelligent Agents as mediators in this digital environment (e.g., Kulthau, 1991, 1993; Rasmussen, Pejtersen, and Goodstein, 1994; Spink, 1997; Wilson, 1981). Detlor (2003), using a case study to explore how knowledge workers made use of Internet-based information systems, found that information studies theory provides an appropriate framework for examining Internet-based information-seeking behaviors. Detlor, Sproule, and Gupta (2003) made use of a similar conceptual framework to explore goal-directed behavior in online shopping environments. Choo, Detlor, and Turnbull (2000) investigated how knowledge workers use the web to find information external to their organizations as part of their daily work life. A typology of different complementary modes of using the web as an information source was identified and described (e.g., formal search, informal search).

Detlor (2004) adopts an information vantage point and views enterprise knowledge portals as more than tools to merely deliver content. Instead, he sees them as shared workspaces that can facilitate communication and collaboration among knowledge workers. Intelligent Agents can play a significant role in improving the interaction between knowledge workers and knowledge portals for the successful completion of everyday work tasks. Empirical research studies on information seeking help define a web use model based on information-seeking motives and modes. The advantage of using a theoretical framework as a starting point is that online behavior and preferences can be better understood, explained, and predicted. These online behavioral preferences can then be used to better design both online environments and mediators such as Intelligent Agents.

Adaptive Technologies

Adaptive technologies are used to better target content to a specific knowledge worker or to a specific group of knowledge workers who share common work needs.

Customization refers to the knowledge workers "manually" changing their knowledge environment—for example, selecting user preferences to change the desktop interface, specifying certain requirements in content to be provided to them (language, format), or subscribing to certain news or listserv services.

Personalization, on the other hand, refers to the automatic changing of content and interfaces based on the observed and analyzed behaviors of the intended end user. For example, many MS Office applications offer the option of dynamically reordering pop-down menu items based on frequency of usage (the ones used most often will be displayed on top). One way of automatically personalizing knowledge acquisition makes use of recommender systems. Recommendations regarding content that is likely to be considered useful and relevant by a given knowledge worker may be based on a user profile of that knowledge worker (e.g., with themes checked off), or the recommendation may be based on affinity groups. Affinity groups make use of similarity analysis of users in order to develop groups of individuals who appear to share the same interests. Amazon, for example, uses affinity groups when, after ordering a book online, visitors to the site are provided with information on related books that others who have bought the same book have also purchased.

Communities of practice are affinity groups to some extent, and personalization technologies are often used to target or push certain types of content that are of interest to a given community. Community profiles can be established just as individual profiles and can be used in the same manner in order to better adapt content and interfaces to the community members.

STRATEGIC IMPLICATIONS OF KM TOOLS AND TECHNIQUES

Historically, the IT horse has always been placed before the KM carriage, and it is crucial to think of KM tools in strategic terms. It is often said that if we hold a hammer in our hand, then all the problems we see look very much like nails. It is important to avoid this bias in knowledge management. Tools and techniques are a means and not an end in themselves. First, the business objectives must be clearly identified, and then a consensus must be reached on priority application areas to be addressed. For example, an initial KM application will typically be some form of content management system on an internally managed intranet site. This is a good building block for subsequent applications such as yellow pages or expertise finders and groupware tools to enable newly connected knowledge workers to continue to work together. An illustration is provided in the accompanying vignette.

MERCEDES-BENZ

The Mercedes-Benz[5] Customer Assistance Center in Maastricht, The Netherlands, serves as a central customer contact point for the whole of Europe, handling all customer needs in 17 European countries, in 12 languages, 24 hours a day, 365 days a year. In order to share knowledge of product information, technical information, business procedures, as well as sample letters, FAQs, and best practices, CMG, a leading European IT services business, developed a web-based knowledge management solution for Mercedes-Benz. Called BRAiN (Backbone Repository for Archiving Information), this KM-based IT solution enables Mercedes-Benz Customer Assistance Center employees to share and retrieve knowledge through the company's corporate intranet. Full-text searching and dynamic knowledge maps allow users to navigate intuitively to the information needed. Direct search facilities enable quick retrieval of all information related to a specific vehicle, country, or market, and have been fine-tuned to support business needs. Web technology facilitated a quick roll-out within the organization and helps to minimize maintenance. Attention has been paid to all business aspects throughout the project phases. A staged business approach, supported with incremental system development (RAD—Rapid Application Development), has been applied. Both technical and organizational goals have been identified at each stage. Procedures have been defined for sharing knowledge, and these are directly supported by the knowledge management system. BRAiN offers the possibility to identify knowledge users, publishers, advanced publishers, and knowledge administrators, each with their own rights and authorities.

A number of the techniques presented here address the phenomenon of emergence that can help discover existing valuable knowledge, experts, communities of practice, and other valuable intellectual assets that exist within an organization. Once this is done, the intellectual assets can be better accessed, leveraged, and employed. The KM tools and techniques have an important enabling role in ensuring the success of KM applications.

PRACTICAL IMPLICATIONS OF KM TOOLS AND TECHNIQUES

A number of techniques and tools, though never having been specifically developed for or targeted to KM applications, have proven to be quite useful. A pragmatic toolkit approach is needed for KM, for there is no single end-to-end solution that can be simply bought "off the shelf" in order to address all the critical dimensions of a knowledge management initiative. It is therefore important to understand what is out there already and what some of the new emerging tools are in order to adapt them and make use of them for KM purposes.

KEY POINTS

- Content creation and management tools are used to structure and organize knowledge content for each retrieval and maintenance.
- Groupware and other collaboration tools are essential enablers of knowledge flow and knowledge-sharing activities among personnel.
- Data mining and knowledge discovery techniques can be used to "discover" or identify emergent patterns that could not have otherwise been detected. Some of these techniques may provide valuable insights.
- Intelligent filtering agents are a KM technology that can help address the challenges of information overload by selecting relevant content and delivering this in a just-in-time and just-enough format.
- A knowledge repository will often be the most frequently used and most visible aspect of a KM technology. What is important is not so much the container but the content and how this content will be managed.
- Knowledge management technologies help support emergent phenomena involved in the creation, sharing, and application of valuable knowledge assets.

DISCUSSION POINTS

1. Discuss the pros and cons of the major technologies used in:
   a. The knowledge creation and capture phase.
   b. The knowledge-sharing and dissemination phase.
   c. The knowledge acquisition and application phase.
2. Data mining technologies can be used on a number of different types of knowledge content. What are the major categories, and what sorts of patterns would this technology detect?
3. Describe an application of blog technology within an organization. What potential benefits would accrue to the individual, the community of practice, and the organization as a whole if blogs were implemented?
4. Describe some of the ways in which unstructured content may be managed. Do standards exist? What are some best practices in the management of the useful life cycle of knowledge content?
5. How would you categorize the different forms of groupware or collaboration technologies? What sort of criteria would you make use of in order to determine when and where each type would be the best means of sharing and disseminating knowledge? How would you adopt a cost-benefit approach to such a technology selection decision?

6. What role can a wiki play in promoting group collaboration? What advantages does a wiki offer when compared to a discussion forum?
7. Describe the push and pull technologies that can be used in conjunction with knowledge repositories. What types of profiling or personalization are required? What are the benefits? Can this be done at the community level as well as the individual level? Why or why not?
8. What are some of the artificial intelligence technologies that can play a role in knowledge management? What benefits are offered by adaptive technologies?
9. What role do e-learning tools play in knowledge management?
10. How can intelligent agents help knowledge workers find relevant knowledge content?

NOTES

[1] Dilip Bhatt, *EFQM: Excellence Model and Knowledge Management Implications*, ILS/Fujitsu, 2000.

[2] Velker L. (1999). A combined knowledge leader. KM World, 8(4). Available at http://www.kmworld.com.

[3] Manohar, H. (2005). KPMG: Leveraging KM tools for practice areas and clients. Ch. 16 in M. Rao (Ed.) KM Tools and Techniques. Elsevier.

[4] Attributed to Rutherford Rogers, Yale librarian, *New York Times*, p. A-10, February 25, 1985.

[5] Sturz, W., and Schniertshauer, A. (2001). KM02: KM is critical for us. TC-Forum, March 2001. Available at http://www.tc-forum.org.

REFERENCES

Blood, R. (2002). *The weblog handbook: practical advice on creating and maintaining your blog.* Cambridge, MA: Perseus Publishing.

Choo, C. W., Detlor, B., and Turnbull, D. (2000). Information seeking on the web: an integrated model of browsing and searching. *First Monday*, 5(2). Available from http://www.firstmonday.org/issues/issue5_2/choo/index.html.

Coleman, D. (1997). *Groupware: collaborative strategies for corporate LANS and intranets.* San Francisco: Prentice Hall.

Collins, H. (2003). *Enterprise knowledge portals.* New York: American Management Association.

Cope, M. (2000). *Know your value. Value what you know.* London: Pearson Education Ltd.

Dames, M. (2004, July 26). Social software in the library. *LLRX online.* Available at http://www.llrx.com/features/socialsoftware.htm.

Davenport, T., and Prusak, L. (1998). *Working knowledge: how organizations manage what they know.* Boston: Harvard Business School Press.

Detlor, B. (2003). Internet-based information systems use in organizations: an information studies perspective. *Information Systems Journal*, 13(2): 113–132.

Detlor, B. (2004). *Towards knowledge portals: from human issues to intelligent agents.* Dordrecht, Netherlands: Kluwer Academic Publishers.

Detlor, B., Sproule, S., and Gupta, C. (2003). Pre-purchase online information seeking: search versus browse. *Journal of Electronic Commerce Research, 4*(2): 72–84.

Elst, L., Dignum, V., and Abecker, A. (Eds.). (2003). Agent mediated knowledge management. International Symposium AMKM 2003, Stanford, CA. March 24–26, 2004. Lecture.

Firestone, J. (2003). *Enterprise information portals and knowledge management.* Boston: Butterworth-Heinemann.

Higgison, S. (2004). Your say: personal knowledge management. *KM Magazine, 7*(7). Available at http://www.kmmagazine.com.

Khoo, L-P, Tor, S., and Lee, S. (1998). The potential of intelligent software agents in the World Wide Web in automating part procurement. *International Journal of Purchasing and Materials Management, 34*(1): 46–47.

Kulthau, C. C. (1991). Inside the search process: information seeking from the user's perspective. *Journal of the American Society for Information Science, 42*(5): 361–371.

Kulthau, C. C. (1993). A principle of uncertainty for information seeking. *Journal of Documentation, 49*(4): 339–455.

Leuf, B., and Cunningham, W. (2001). *The wiki way: collaboration and sharing on the Internet.* Boston: Addison-Wesley.

Liebowitz, J., and Beckman, T. (1998). *Knowledge organizations: what every manager should know.* Boca Raton, FL: CRC Press.

Maes, P. (1994). Agents that reduce work and information overload. MIT Media Laboratory, Cambridge, MA. Available at http://pattie.www.media.mit.edu/people/pattie/CACM-94/CACM-94.p1.html.

Pikas, C. (2004). Trends in blog searching. *Bulletin of the Information Technology Division of SLA, 21, (2/D).*

Rasmussen, J., Pejtersen, A., and Goodstein, L. (1994). *Cognitive systems engineering.* London: John Wiley and Sons.

Robertson, J. (2003). Looking towards the future of content management. *IT Toolbox.* Available at http://knowledgemanagement.ittoolbox.com/documents/document.asp?i = 2094.

Roesler, M., and Hawkins, D. (1994). Intelligent agents: software servants for an electronic information world (and more!). *Online, 18*(4): 18–29.

Rollet, H. (2003). *Knowledge management processes and technologies.* Norwell, MA: Kluwer Academic Publishers.

Ruggles, R. (1997). *Knowledge tools: using technology to manage knowledge better.* Boston: Butterworth-Heinemann.

Spink, A. (1997). Study of interactive feedback during mediated information retrieval. *Journal of the American Society for Information Science, 48*(5): 382–394.

Tiwana, A. (2000). *The knowledge management toolkit: orchestrating IT, strategy and knowledge management platforms.* Upper Saddle River, NJ: Prentice Hall.

van Heijst, G., van Der Spek, R., and Kruizinga, E. (1997). Corporate memories as a tool for knowledge management. *Expert Systems with Applications, 1*(13): 4–54.

Webb, W. (1995). Intelligent agents on the Internet. *Editor and Publisher, 128*(12): 50–52.

Wilson, T. (1981). On user studies and information needs. *Journal of the American Society for Information Science, 37*(1): 3–15.

Wingfield, N. (1995). Internet apps to get intelligent search agents. *InfoWorld, 17*(20): 16–17.

Woolridge, M., and Jennings, N. (1995). Intelligent agents: theory and practice. *Knowledge Engineering Review, 10*(2): 115–152.

KM STRATEGY AND METRICS

Price is what you pay. Value is what you get.

Warren Buffet (1930–)

This chapter addresses the common building blocks that are developed in order to be able to apply and gain benefits from KM applications. The major steps involved in developing a knowledge management strategy are presented. Innovation and reuse will be discussed in terms of how best to balance creativity with organizational structure. Finally, the area of KM metrics is assessed, with a discussion of three commonly used techniques: benchmarking, the balanced scorecard method, and the house of quality metric.

LEARNING OBJECTIVES

1. Provide examples of major KM objectives and how specific KM initiatives can be implemented to address them.
2. Outline the major barriers to good organizational memory management.
3. Define corporate amnesia and cite the reasons it may occur.
4. Illustrate the major elements of a KM strategy and discuss the processes involved in each step.
5. Outline the key steps in the evolution of an innovative new idea and the institutionalization of a best practice that forms the object of reuse.
6. Discuss and evaluate the different approaches that may be undertaken in order to achieve an optimal balance between creativity and organizational structure.
7. List the different types of knowledge assets that result from KM initiatives.
8. Understand the major advantages and shortcomings of the three KM metrics.

9. Apply the benchmarking, house of quality, and balanced scorecard method metrics to knowledge management performance measurement systems.

INTRODUCTION

This chapter discusses two more additions to the integrated KM cycle: a sound KM strategy that is linked to the overall business objectives of the organization and a good metrics framework to monitor progress toward those organizational goals (see Figure 9-1).

The two most commonly encountered objectives of knowledge management are innovation and reuse. Innovation is closely linked to the generation of new knowledge or new linkages between existing knowledge. It is a popular misconception, however, to think that innovation occurs in isolation. Actually, innovation rests firmly on a large body of accumulated experiences, both positive and negative, based on what has and has not worked in the past. Creativity often involves lateral thinking such as seeing an analogy in a completely different context. Similarly, reuse is often mistakenly equated with dull, routine, and unproductive work. In fact, reuse forms the basis for organizational learning and should be viewed more as a dissemination of innovation.

An evolutionary framework begins to emerge in which new knowledge in the form of innovations eventually ends up becoming incorporated into orga-

FIGURE 9-1

KM STRATEGY AND KM METRICS IN AN INTEGRATED KM CYCLE

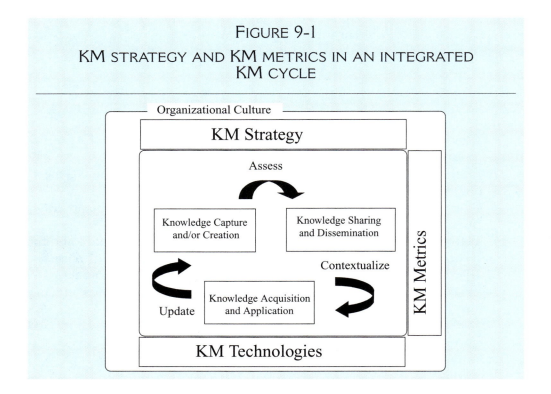

nizational memory to form the object of reuse so that the benefits of this new knowledge, know-how, can be spread throughout the organization. The KM strategy provides the basic building blocks used to achieve this organizational learning and continuous improvement so as to not waste time repeating mistakes and so that everyone is aware of new and better ways of thinking and doing. In addition, a number of important knowledge by-products should be recognized and inventoried as knowledge assets of the organization. These typically include familiar, tangible items such as patents as well as "softer" or more intangible assets such as core competencies. Leibowitz (1999) developed a comprehensive framework for KM strategies in the industrial sector, such as telecommunications companies.

Sveiby (2001) developed a three-part framework for categorizing the different types of KM initiatives.

1. *External structure initiatives* (e.g., gain knowledge from customers, offer customers additional knowledge).
2. *Internal structure initiatives* (e.g., build a knowledge-sharing culture, create new revenues from existing knowledge, capture the individual's tacit knowledge, store it, spread it, and reuse it, and measure knowledge-creating processes and intangible assets produced).
3. *Competence initiatives* (e.g., create careers based on KM, create microenvironments for knowledge transfer, and learn from simulations and pilot projects).

Lev (2001) uses different labels for the three main "nexuses" or sources of intangibles: (1) discovery (innovation), (2) organizational practices, and (3) human resources.

The sources of innovation and knowledge reuse consist of either internal or external discoveries, or they may stem from business practices or from knowledge workers' competencies. More often, improvements will result from some combination of these types of sources, as is illustrated in the vignette on Monsanto.

MONSANTO

Monsanto Company[1] develops products for the agricultural, pharmaceutical, food ingredients, and chemical industries. The products it manufactures include Roundup herbicide, Wear-Dated carpet, arthritis treatments Daypro and Artrotec, Ortho lawn and garden products, and the NutraSweet brand artificial sweetener. Management realizes that more can be accomplished in the way of serving customers better at lower costs, developing new products and new businesses around the world, and addressing the global challenge of sustainable development. Knowledge management is seen as a way of ensuring that the right combination of autonomy and

Continued

interaction is achieved, thus producing a faster, more focused, and more effective workforce.

The KM process at Monsanto is known as Knowledge Management Architecture (KMA) and was developed due to the flattening of the organization. The primary purpose of the architecture was to create enterprisewide capabilities that would allow Monsanto to leverage its collective intellect, thereby creating value. Decentralization actions included changing the company's organization from four large business units into a dozen strategic business units. This caused a further diffusion of knowledge among the 28,500 employees, creating duplication of effort and lost opportunities. Monsanto wanted these units to be small and connected. Increased global competition highlighted the need for a shorter decision cycle. Furthermore, management wanted inputs (shared knowledge) from the business units to produce tangible outputs for customers (goods and services) and shareowners (income and equity). Through the capture, codification, and use of the company's knowledge, employees in these strategic CoPs were able to make more educated decisions.

Monsanto's KMA adds value to the raw material of information; it creates insight/knowledge that then becomes intellectual capital. Once knowledge is created, Monsanto perpetuates its value by continuing to update it and refresh it through a learning process. The system focuses on futuristic or market information as well as historical information. Structured information is provided by data warehousing technology and is useful in developing and carrying out business processes. Unstructured information is derived from Notes, the WWW, e-mail, and the Internet in general. This information is used to generate insight and appropriate leveraging of both structured and unstructured information. The enterprisewide KM capabilities focus primarily on connecting people with people and encapsulating knowledge so that it can be shared. The barriers to Monsanto's internal KM process have not been technical. The technical architecture is flexible and capable of accommodating Monsanto's business strategy. The criteria of speed, reliability, capacity, and geographic availability are more than well met by the technology. The challenge lay in orienting Monsanto toward learning and sharing corporate culture with initiatives that focused on empowering people and in helping the company find new ways to bring information and learning to its everyday work efforts. The positive outcomes of Monsanto's KMA were captured in anecdotal form and were shared widely throughout the company via an electronic newsletter. The ultimate benefit has been that Monsanto is now able to bring innovations to market more quickly, its operational efficiency has been improved, and it can serve its customers better. This has not only increased profits for Monsanto but has also provided benefits to its customers by providing better value and more new product offerings.

A knowledge management strategy should target one or more of these objectives, but the strategy needs to go further than high-level goals. Robertson (2004) points out that a good KM strategy should identify the key needs and issues within the organization and provide a framework for addressing these issues. A number of different types of business requirements may trigger the need for KM. The most commonly encountered business drivers include:

1. Imminent retirement of key personnel.
2. Need for innovation to compete in a dynamic, challenging business environment.
3. Need for internal efficiencies in order to reduce costs and effort (e.g., time to market a new product).

The resources and skills required to develop a KM strategy depend on the size and complexity of the organizational unit and on the depth of information gathering and analysis. The ideal mix of skills on the KM strategy team would be a KM expert, access to people who are knowledgeable about the organization, and a KM advocate who will "sell" the strategy to the senior member of management who mandated the strategy development.

KNOWLEDGE MANAGEMENT STRATEGY

A KM strategy is a general, issue-based approach to defining operational strategy and objectives with specialized KM principles and approaches (Srikantajah and Koenig, 2000). The result is a way of identifying how the organization can best leverage its knowledge resources. Once this fundamental KM strategy is defined, baselining and technology options may be explored. A KM strategy helps address the following questions:

1. Which KM approach, or set of KM approaches, will bring the most value to the organization?
2. How can the organization prioritize alternatives when any one or several of the alternatives are appealing and resources are limited?

Once the KM strategy is defined, the organization will have a road map that can be used to identify and prioritize KM initiatives, tools, and approaches in such a way as to support long-term business objectives. The strategy is used to define a plan of action by undertaking a gap analysis. The gap analysis involves establishing the current and desired states of knowledge resources and KM levers. Specific projects are then defined in order to address specific gaps that were identified and agreed upon as being high-priority areas.

A good KM strategy possesses the following components:

1. An articulated business strategy and objectives
   a. Products or services.
   b. Target customers.
   c. Preferred distribution or delivery channels.
   d. Characterization of regulatory environment.
   e. Mission or vision statement.
2. A description of knowledge-based business issues
   a. Need for collaboration.
   b. Need to level performance variance.
   c. Need for innovation.
   d. Need to address information overload.
3. An inventory of available knowledge resources
   a. Knowledge capital: tacit and explicit knowledge, know-how, expertise, experience in the minds of individuals and in communities or embedded in work routines, processes, procedures, roles, artifacts such as documents or reports.
   b. Social capital: culture, trust, context, the informal networks, and reciprocity (e.g., willingness to experiment and take risks, or able to fail without fear of repercussions).
   c. Infrastructure capital: physical knowledge resources; e.g., LAN/WAN, file servers, intranets, PCs, applications, physical workspaces and offices, and the organizational structure.
4. An analysis of recommended knowledge leverage points that describes what can be done with the above-identified knowledge and knowledge artifacts and that lists KM projects that can be undertaken with the intent to maximize ROI and business value; for example:
   a. Collect artifacts and exploit them (e.g., best practices database, lessons learned database).
   b. Store for future use (e.g., data warehouses, intelligence gathering for specific issue/problem, data mining, text mining).
   c. Focus on connecting—connect knowers to each other and to a problem through communities of practice or expertise location systems. Hypothesize to carry out scenario planning, informal cross-pollination to produce new insights and breakthrough thinking.

The major steps involved in developing a KM strategy are to first understand the organization in terms of its current state ("as is") and its desired business objectives ("to be"). The analysis of the difference between the two states is often referred to as a gap analysis, and the means of getting from the "as is" to the "to be" state is often represented in the form of a KM strategic road map. The road map typically represents a three- to five-year strategy with clear milestones or targets to be achieved throughout that time.

The current or baseline state of the organization is assessed using information gathering from a variety of sources such as key documents (e.g., annual report) and interviewing key stakeholders (e.g., senior managers, human resources, information technology, and major business unit managers). It is at this point that existing KM initiatives will also be identified in the form of a knowledge audit or inventory.

Knowledge Audit

A knowledge audit service identifies the core information and knowledge needs and uses in an organization. It also identifies gaps, duplications, and flows and how they contribute to business goals. A knowledge inventory (sometimes called an information audit or a knowledge map) is a practical way of coming to grips with "knowing what you know." This inventory is usually performed by applying the principles of information resources management (IRM). A knowledge audit identifies owners, users, uses, and key attributes of core knowledge assets. Willard (1993) discusses five key activities of IRM:

1. *Identification*: What information is there? How is it identified and coded?
2. *Ownership*: Who is responsible for different information entities and coordination?
3. *Cost and Value*: What is a basic model for making judgments on purchase and use?
4. *Development*: How can we increase the value of information or stimulate demand?
5. *Exploitation*: What is the best way to proactively maximize the value for money?

A knowledge audit is often carried out in conjunction with a knowledge management assessment, which provides a baseline on which one can develop a knowledge management strategy (Skyrme, 2001). This typically involves taking stock of current KM capabilities and is often carried out as part of a KM strategy formulation exercise.

A knowledge audit can produce the following types of results:

- Identification of core knowledge assets and flows—who creates, who uses.
- Identification of gaps in information and knowledge needed to manage the business effectively.
- Areas of information policy and ownership that need improving.
- Opportunities to reduce information-handling costs.
- Opportunities to improve coordination and access to commonly needed information.
- A clearer understanding of the contribution of knowledge to business results.

An example from Northrop-Grumman is provided in the accompanying vignette.

Northrop-Grumman[2] faced consolidation and downsizing during the late 1990s. The Air Combat Systems (ACS) group in particular was in danger of losing the expertise it needed to support and maintain a complex machine that would be flying—carrying precious lives and cargo—for years to come. So ACS instituted KM procedures designed to capture the so-called tacit knowledge, or know-how and experience, with the B-2, locked in its employees' heads. But before designing a program, ACS wanted to find out what barriers, if any, prevented employees from sharing knowledge with their peers. With a good picture of knowledge culture attitudes, ACS would then have a better road map for designing a unitwide KM program. It conducted a knowledge audit, surveying employees about their knowledge-sharing habits, polling nearly 5000 employees with a 97-question survey (KM2) to determine their knowledge needs, sharing practices, and prejudices. The survey asked questions such as, "From your perspective, to what extent is the knowledge that you and your team generate reused by other teams?" This not only highlighted ACS's readiness for a formal KM effort but also pointed out areas where sharing was not happening. The Delphi Group was hired to conduct the audit and derive a baseline pulse of the unit's knowledge-sharing culture. Participation was voluntary—employees were given a free lunch for giving 30 minutes of their time. The survey response rate was better than 70% (typically, mail-in surveys return a 10–30% response). Delphi consultants analyzed the preliminary results and targeted 125 employees for face-to-face follow-up interviews.

ACS had established a 10-person KM team to identify subject matter experts and capture the content of their expertise. After creating about 100 knowledge cells and identifying 200 subject matter experts within those cells, the KM council turned its attention to knowledge capture. The team created websites for each knowledge cell and logged information about the knowledge experts into an expert locator system called Xref, short for cross-reference. Using Xref, employees can search for information in any number of ways, including by employee name, program affiliation, or skill area. If, for example, the B-2 landing gear is locking up, one can find the landing gear expert through Xref. The knowledge audit helped ensure that this centralized database not only would be useful but would actually be used.

The results of the knowledge audit confirmed that employees were eager to share their knowledge in an automated, centralized system but that challenges, such as integrating the systems across lines of business, remained. The willingness of employees to participate in systems intended to minimize the impact of their own eventual layoff is, of course, highly dubious. Other key findings showed that employees recognized the value of their fellow employees' expertise; they spent at least eight frustrating hours each week looking for information they needed to do their job (costing $150 million annually); only 6% of their knowledge was reused by others; and 31%

believed that ideas generated by junior staffers were not valued and were likely to get smothered by ACS's bureaucracy.

ACS's knowledge strategy based on these results made use of three dimensions. (1) On the human side, the KM team set out to identify experts and communities of practice to facilitate sharing among employees (e.g., the CoP of project managers on different ACS programs). CoPs exist informally—it is important to identify the ones that are strategically important, raise their visibility, and provide funding and support systems for them. (2) On the process side, the KM team focused on finding out how people captured, organized, and reused existing knowledge. A central repository was created to amalgamate knowledge previously found in personal employee files in order to share lessons learned. The F/A-18 fighter jet program, for example, now has a web-based system that capitalizes on years of technical expertise by tracking structural problems with the aircraft. When an issue arises—a cracked part, for example—the first thing an engineer does is search the tracking system's 900 previously encountered experiences. If it is a new problem, he inputs the relevant information using a PowerPoint template that can include pictures, drawings, and notes on the appropriate sections. Each week engineers meet to discuss unresolved issues. Once the problem is resolved, it is automatically entered as a lesson learned. (3) The technology piece of the strategy serves as the glue holding the KM initiative together—the homegrown Xref system, collaboration applications, and document management systems. The five technology areas are portals, expert locator, knowledge capture, media management, and collaboration. These address the key barriers found in the knowledge audit: paper-based filing systems, disparate locations, and inability to locate internal expertise. Other initiatives, including portals that push personalized information, are in the pilot phase. The KM team plans to conduct follow-up audits every 18 months or so to keep tabs on the evolution of KM initiatives and the knowledge-sharing culture.

A knowledge management program or system should never be implemented without a knowledge audit having been conducted. Most importantly, the precursor to "big spending" on knowledge management technology is a proper knowledge audit to determine exactly what tools and solutions are most appropriate to enable better knowledge management by the knowledge people in the organization. It is people who will be required to use the newly procured technology and adapt to the new KM system. It is therefore prudent that every attempt be made to consult with all or most knowledge people in the organization before any KM system is purchased and implemented. This is where the knowledge audit plays a pivotal role in a new knowledge management initiative. The company's "knowledge people" form the core of its knowledge audit, and hence no knowledge person should be marginalized during the knowledge audit initiative/process.

It is of vital importance that an organization's knowledge management initiators or practitioners always seek to assess the company's current knowledge management health, before proceeding to implement knowledge management. The knowledge audit provides evidence-based information and knowledge of the audited units' current knowledge status or "knowledge health." This evidence-based knowledge is the launching pad into a new knowledge management program. The knowledge audit is also extremely useful as a regular review and assessment of existing knowledge management practices in the company. Management and exploitation of corporate knowledge is intrinsically intertwined in the corporate knowledge culture, which is in turn determined and maintained by the corporate knowledge people. This is why a knowledge audit must be focused on people.

Stakeholder interviews can help identify key knowledge needs to yield a knowledge map (Robertson, 2004). Typical sample questions include:

- What are your job role and your major responsibilities?
- How long have you been working for the organization?
- With whom do you communicate most frequently on work matters?
- Do you have policies or guidelines for your work? If so, how do you access them?
- What information do you rely upon during a normal working day? What is the source of this information?
- If you have a question, where do you go to find the answer?
- Who asks you what types of questions?
- What sort of orientation and refresher training have you received?
- How do you find out what is happening in the organization?
- What kind of news do you read regularly?
- What type of knowledge do you need to do your work?
- How do you add value to the organization? Where do your knowledge artifacts reside?
- How do you think knowledge flow could be improved?
- What would make your work easier?

Knowledge mapping is an ongoing endeavor—not a one-time activity. The knowledge map is a navigation aid to explicit/codified information and tacit/uncodified knowledge (Grey, 1999). The map should provide an inventory and evaluation of the organization's intellectual or knowledge assets.

Once the "as is" portrait of the organization has been completed through information gathering and the knowledge audit, a gap analysis can be performed.

Gap Analysis

The difference between the organization's existing and desired KM state is analyzed in terms of enablers and barriers to successful KM implementation. A good gap analysis should address the following points (Zack, 1999; Skyrme, 2001):

1. What are the major differences between the current and desired KM states of the organization?
2. List barriers to KM implementation (e.g., culture where "knowledge is power" or where individual possession of knowledge is consistently rewarded).
3. List KM leverage points or enablers (e.g., existing initiatives that could be built upon).
4. Identify opportunities to collaborate with other business initiatives (e.g., combine knowledge continuity goals with succession planning initiatives in Human Resources).
5. Conduct a risk analysis (e.g., knowledge that will soon "walk out the door" due to imminent retirements or knowledge that is at risk because only a few individuals are competent in this area and very little of their expertise exists in coded or tangible knowledge assets).
6. Are there redundancies within the organization (e.g., the case of the right hand not knowing what the left hand is doing)?
7. Are there knowledge silos (e.g., groups, departments, or individuals that hoard knowledge or block fluid knowledge flows to other groups, departments, or colleagues)?
8. How does the organization rank with respect to others within the industry? (e.g., are they early adopters of KM, KM leaders who are emulated by others, or are they just becoming aware of KM needs within their organization?)

This analysis can then be used to list and prioritize KM objectives to be addressed by the organization. The results of the gap analysis should be validated by returning to the stakeholders who were initially involved in the information-gathering and needs analysis phases. The priorities should be determined by a consensus of the organization's key stakeholders. The result will be a KM strategy document that can be used as road map to implement KM within the organization.

The KM Strategy Road Map

The final recommended strategy will typically cover a three- to five-year period, outlining the key priorities for each year. The road map addresses questions such as:

1. How will the organization manage its knowledge better for the benefit of the business?
2. How will the organization manage explicit knowledge (content) as well as tacit knowledge (community) priorities?
3. How will the processes, people, products, services, organizational memory, relationships, and knowledge assets be identified as high-priority knowledge levers to focus on?

4. What is the clear or direct link between KM levers and business objectives?
5. What are some quick wins (i.e., early relatively inexpensive KM successes)?
6. How will KM capability be sustained over the long term (e.g., defined KM roles)?

The last point is a crucial one that should not be overlooked in a KM strategy. One key component of a sustainable KM program is the efficient and effective management of organizational memory. Other key components include clearly defined KM roles and responsibilities (discussed in Chapter 10) and a framework that can be used to evaluate how well KM initiatives succeed (discussed in the KM metrics section of this chapter). An illustration of the critical importance of closely aligning KM strategy to the overall organizational business goals is described in the accompanying vignette.

FORD[1]

Ford and Firestone suffered the "death of 1000 cuts," in part because of the two companies' catastrophic failure to share knowledge. Information that might have alerted them to the calamitous mismatch of Ford Explorers and Firestone tires was scattered in different places in both companies, each item innocuous in isolation. Yet Ford's knowledge-sharing scheme is one of the best in the world. The company's Best Practices Replication Process has produced a billion-dollar benefit for the automaker. Why didn't it help in this case?

The Ford process began in 1995 when a VP of manufacturing on a trip to Europe saw that the plant there had ideas Americans could use and vice versa. Back home he assembled his operations people and asked them to figure out a way to share best practices. At the same time, another Ford group was addressing reengineering issues through the Rapid Actions for Process Improvement Deployment (RAPID). These were workshops aimed to eradicate small inefficiencies. They soon turned to the challenge of replicating the solutions so that they need not be reinvented again. The two merged to become Ford's Best Practices Replication Process. In 4.5 years, more than 2800 proven superior practices have been shared across Ford's manufacturing operations. The documented value of this shared knowledge so far is $850 million. Another $400 million stands to be won from work in progress, bringing the grand total to $1.25 billion. Royal Dutch/Shell and Nabisco have licensed the process, and portions have been patented.

Ford made three key decisions. First, the process would be managed with distinct roles and responsibilities. Second, no practice would get into the system unless proven. Third, every improvement would be described in the

---

language of the workgroup involved: time, head count, gallons, and quality. These workgroups are communities of practice. Each CoP has a company-wide administrator, picked by the director of manufacturing. The role takes half a day a week. At the plant level, each community chooses someone as the focal point, and that role takes one to two hours a week. No one is paid extra. The best practices process has 42 steps. The focal point looks for a neat new process (or its inventors go to him). He makes up a web page that prompts him to quantify benefits such as time or material saved. He then e-mails it to the community administrator, who compares it with other plants, and if it passes muster, designates it as a gem. Next it is immediately posted on the intranet and e-mailed to every focal point in the community. One way or another, each focal point must report a decision: to adopt or adapt it, and say when; to investigate it; or to reject it and explain why. The web maintains and displays a scorecard to all users—by community and by plant. It may show, for example, that of 61 gems in painting, the St. Louis plant has done or agreed to 42, was investigating 2, had rejected 7 as inapplicable and 9 as economically not feasible, and had originated and contributed 2.

So if Ford is so good at knowledge sharing, why did no one know about the tire problem? There are two reasons: first, knowledge is best shared within communities—people with something in common talk more than strangers do. Neither Ford's nor Firestone's social networks were rich enough to support the kind of extramural communication that might have uncovered the problem. Second, the more widely dispersed the knowledge is, the more powerful the force required to share it. Every year, Ford head-quarters hands down a "task" to managers: they are required to come up with a 5 to 7% gain in, say, costs, throughput, or energy use. The best prac-tices database is the first place they turn to—like a magnet, the task draws knowledge from its hiding places. This is an important lesson for KM: if KM is not tightly linked to your business model, it will never amount to much.

It is particularly important to pay attention to the optimal management of organizational memory, for this is often forgotten or weakly addressed by KM strategies. In the absence of a strong bridge between the individual, commu-nity, and organizational levels, a KM strategy will not live up to the expecta-tions created. A second area of concern should be to attain the optimal balance between openness, transparency, and creativity to increase innovativeness on the one hand and institutionalization to improve efficiency on the other hand. KM strategies must take a long-term view of the organization, one that envis-ages how the organization will mature, how KM readiness will increase, and above all, how the KM strategic objectives will be sustained.

THE MANAGEMENT OF
ORGANIZATIONAL MEMORY

There are significant technical and cultural barriers to capturing informal knowledge and making it explicit. As outlined in Chapter 8, groupware tools such as e-mail and Lotus Notes tend to make informal knowledge explicit, but they generally fail to create an accessible organizational memory. On the other hand, attempts to build organizational memory systems have generally failed because they required additional documentation effort with no clear short-term benefit, or, like groupware, they did not provide an effective index or structure to the mass of information collected in the system. Organizational memory extends and amplifies this asset by capturing, organizing, disseminating, and reusing the knowledge created by its employees. There are good reasons to pursue creating organizational memory. Organizations routinely forget what they have done in the past and why they have done it. These organizations have an impaired capacity to learn, owing to an inability to represent critical aspects of what they know. Sutton (2005) refers to this as organizational stupidity, and others use the term *corporate amnesia* (Kransdorff, 1998).

CORPORATE AMNESIA

A large mining company was examining its predictive maintenance procedures. This form of maintenance relies upon scheduled parts changes and "tune-ups" that take place according to expected useful lifespans of the various types of equipment used, as opposed to waiting until something fails and brings the whole operation to a costly stop. In the case of one particular type of valve used in the refinery, technological advances had resulted in the use of a new type of polymer that was just now available. The question was: could this new polymer be used to cap the valves? Could it withstand the high temperatures that the valve would be subjected to during operations? At first, this seemed to be an easy, almost trivial question. Engineers began looking for the equipment specification documents, but these documents proved more elusive than expected. When, after about six weeks, they were found, they were located not within the company but within the archives of a design firm that had been subcontracted to design that particular piece of equipment—roughly 25 years ago. Unfortunately, nothing in the specifications helped answer the question.

The use of a polymer would represent a significant cost savings, but the team was reluctant to go ahead—"a slow dime is worth more than a fast penny" was the conventional wisdom. In other words, we may save a few pennies now, but if the polymer melts under the high temperatures, the whole refinery will have to be shut down, costing many, many more dollars to the company. Finally, after about six months of searching, the HR department of the design company tracked down the original design engineer who had worked on the equipment. He was happily retired and playing golf in Florida but was still receiving a pension, which is how they found an address for him. Luckily for the mining company, this engineer was a bit of a pack rat and/or nostalgic: he had kept his original hand-drawn specifications with his own annotations. It was by checking these annotations that he was able to confidently answer "No, the polymer would not be a safe alternative; metal should continue to be used." The next question posed by the mining team was: now, where can we write down this valuable information? Where is the company "book" to look this up when the next five-year cycle comes up?

Organization memory contributes to the overall governance and compliance with regulatory guidelines. An organizational memory can also help increase the transparency of the organization as well as how knowledge workers perceive this transparency. Given the nature of organizations and the competitive environment within which they exist, organizational learning and the accumulation of knowledge will be a source of immediate health as well as long-term survival (McMaster, 1995, p. 113). The management of organizational memory must play a paramount role in any KM strategy, as illustrated in the following vignette.

LESSONS LEARNED AND BEST PRACTICES IN TEACHING

A specialized school for students with severe behavioral problems undertook to build a repository of lessons learned and best practices. The primary motivation was driven by the fact that there was a high turnover among teachers employed by the school. The average stay was about two years, and most left owing to burnout as the responsibilities are quite demanding. A number of best practices and lessons learned were gathered and preserved. Templates were developed and used in order to facilitate this knowledge capture process, and access was provided through each student's profile. This is an example of a nontraditional KM application—one that is not situated in a for-profit commercial organization. The same principles and methods apply and can be successfully used to create a corporate memory. The greatest benefit is that it will no longer be necessary to reinvent the wheel each time a new teacher works with the same student. The new teacher will have access to all of the accumulated successes and failures of the various techniques that have been tried out by each previous teacher working with the same student.

Frequently, the usual approach to organizational memory, preserving documents, fails to preserve the context that gives the documents meaning, the very thing that allows them to be useful in the future, when the context has changed. Because current notions of organizational memory assume a repository of artifacts, they focus on preserving, organizing, indexing, and retrieving only the formal knowledge as it is stored in documents and databases. For some tasks, formal knowledge alone is sufficient; for example, when it is time to write the new annual report, you might start with last year's annual report as a template. However, most knowledge work addresses problems for which there is no clear and agreed-upon definition of the problem, and, indeed, in which the problem itself is apt to change over time. An organizational memory that consists only of formal knowledge is bare and lifeless. Conklin (1993) likens this to describing a ball game by giving the statistics or the mystery novel by simply relating the plot outline. Such formal, structured content also lacks the history and context behind the formal documents, and as a result, the organizational memory is essentially an immense heap of disconnected items, a giant "organizational attic." Documents that contain formal knowledge that the organization has paid dearly to create live somewhere on the corporate network with enlightening names like .H:\org\finan\arc\drg\693plan.doc.8. If, however, an organization embraces its informal knowledge, then the rationale behind decisions and documents becomes the glue that holds the formal knowledge documents together and preserves their meaning (Conklin, 1993).

In this context, formal documents are not rich enough to support knowledge work. For example, a team may come together for many meetings in the course of resolving a problem, but the practice of creating and circulating meeting minutes is a relatively laborious instrument for creating continuity and coherence among these meetings. Meeting minutes are summaries that often represent only one person's point of view, and they usually capture only a small part of the conversations that took place. Projects can often stretch into months and years, which necessitates some form of project memory. An explicit project memory provides more continuity among these sessions, allowing the group to pick up where it left off, with a minimum of repetition and loss of important issues. As team membership changes over time, or the project is handed off to a completely new team, the project memory can in principle reduce the likelihood of false starts and duplication of previous work.

A system that includes informal knowledge tends to lose its relevance, and thus its value, over time. Informal knowledge, being more contextual, is even more dynamic in this way. An organizational memory system, like human memory, should therefore have the capacity to recall whatever is relevant and salient to the moment. Closely related to this problem is that of the sheer size of organizational memory. There will be ever-increasing volumes of corporate knowledge accessible online, which will make it even more difficult to pinpoint those particular items relevant to users.

To summarize, a knowledge management strategy should address the cultural and technical factors that influence effective organizational memory management. Potential *cultural barriers* include:

1. A cultural emphasis on artifacts and results to the exclusion of process.
2. Resistance to knowledge capture because of the effort required, the fear of litigation, and the fear of loss of job security.
3. Resistance to knowledge reuse because of the effort required, and the low likelihood of finding relevant knowledge.

Potential *technical barriers* include:

1. How to make the knowledge capture process easy or even transparent.
2. How to make retrieval and reuse easy or even transparent.
3. How to ensure the relevance and intelligibility (i.e., through sufficient context) of retrieved knowledge.

Current implementations of organizational memory fail for a variety of reasons, including a KM strategy that adopts a broad cultural focus on work products over process and a lack of tools that make capture and reuse of knowledge transparent. The challenge is to design an organizational memory system that offers sufficient short-term payoffs to knowledge workers who will use the system, both to capture knowledge as they are creating it and to look for and reuse existing knowledge, as well as a system that is compatible with the long-term, sustainable KM strategic objectives of the organization.

BALANCING INNOVATION AND ORGANIZATIONAL STRUCTURE

A balance between innovation and organizational structure should be the desired outcome of a good KM strategy. In the past, innovation and reuse (efficiency garnered through institutionalization of KM processes) have often been presented as mutually exclusive objectives. Organizational KM strategies were characterized as *either* aimed toward promoting innovation *or* increasing efficiency through organizational structure. Klein (1999) discusses the importance of maintaining a balance between fluidity and institutionalization as the dynamic equilibrium that should ideally exist between innovation and organizational structure. The fluid intellectual domain consists of individuals with ideas originating and growing from a given person (intuition), personal networks that form outside formal organizational charts (CoPs), chance encounters that occur between people, and improvisation that ignores standard procedures to discover better ways of doing things. In contrast, the organization strives to structure work and to control processes and measure outcomes. Explicit knowledge is defined in procedures, reports, memos, and databases. This knowledge is usually selectively shared through official chains of command or organizational hierarchies. How then does one strike the right balance?

If the organization is too fluid, there will be no solid connection of knowledge work to business goals, and it will be difficult to have clear accountability. If the balance shifts too much in favor of institutionalization, however, the organization risks becoming too formal, which can stifle innovation and the open communication necessary for creative work to take place (see Figure 9-2).

Some companies, including Buckman Labs, 3M, KAO in Japan, and AES, have managed to strike the right balance (Klein, 1999). Some of their critical success factors were:

- Consistency between core values, business strategy, and actual work environment.
- Stress on personal freedom, cooperation, and community.
- Top leaders as good role models—"they walk the talk."

AES set up a task force that conducted a historical study of the company's 10 biggest mistakes. It also provided physical meeting space and time for people from different parts of the company to meet and share what they were doing and to get advice on problems.

3M incorporated stories into its corporate training. It adopted the slogan "conservatism with creativity," and the company realized that 30% of revenues come from products that are less than four years old. Technology was used to connect knowledge workers to a database so that they could share their expertise systematically. The company used the 15% rule: 15% of the employees' time should be set aside to pursue personal research interests. 3M also instituted a storytelling culture with such legends as "remember the time they tried to kill the Thinsulate idea . . .").

KAO is a company that focuses on organizational learning and bases its approach on values derived from Buddhist principles. It encourages continuous cross-functional interactions, and every company meeting is open to all. The Value-Added Network (VAN) is KAO's digital memory. ECHO is a system

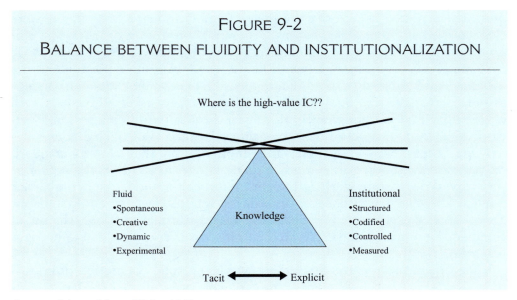

FIGURE 9-2

BALANCE BETWEEN FLUIDITY AND INSTITUTIONALIZATION

Source: Adapted from Klein, 1999.

that adds customer call information to VAN, and the company can receive about 250 calls a day. In this way, corporate experiences are preserved and made available for future customer interactions.

Buckman Labs developed K'Netix as its knowledge network. This knowledge repository is available in the 90 countries where Buckman has its offices. The users are both the sales and technical workforce. K'Netix connects the Buckman communities of practice. The KM application consists of e-mail and forums residing in the knowledge repositories. Each forum has a message bulletin board, library, and virtual conference room. In configuring for a balanced knowledge framework, successful companies such as these need to identify strategic business drivers: what is the business all about? This is the logical starting point for deciding how to organize and manage intellectual assets. They need to identify products' services, cost, value, quality, and differentiating factors and to characterize the environment in terms of competitive forces, regulations, and socioeconomic trends. The organization can thus establish the knowledge core and interrelationships: what knowledge assets are needed to maximize value for customers, shareholders, employees, and other stakeholders? Both tangible and intangible assets (e.g., values, culture, people, technology, and business capabilities) need to be clearly identified, together with where this critical knowledge exists and where it goes (knowledge flow analysis). The knowledge flow can then be further analyzed to assess how fluid or how institutionalized the knowledge has become and whether any gaps in key competencies exist.

In summary, there is a need to continually monitor and rebalance, to reconfigure, or expand an organization's knowledge assets as triggered by mistakes, and changes in environment, in competencies, and/or in performance. It is important to remember that an organization is a complex adaptive system operating in a complex dynamic environment, and the ultimate goal is that of a dynamic equilibrium between fluidity and institutionalization pressures. Just-in-time discipline can be applied, together with a focus on culture. The speed and accuracy with which knowledge is transmitted must be optimal. The best example of nonoptimal conditions is a reenactment of the telephone game—when the message that is transmitted to the first individual becomes progressively more garbled with each repetition. Other useful questions to ask are:

1. How changeable is the knowledge?
2. What is the useful half-life of the knowledge?
3. What type of information technology is being used for knowledge sharing?
4. What about innovation support systems?

A comprehensive KM strategy should target an equilibrium between innovation and structure as a key objective rather than forcing a choice between the two types of successful KM outcomes.

The next section addresses methods of assessing whether or not desired KM outcomes have been achieved. KM metrics are a series of techniques that are currently used to measure how successful the KM strategy was and how well the recommended KM initiatives were implemented.

Many present-day business managers are intrigued by the potential hidden value that the intellectual capital perspective suggests lies untapped within their businesses. None, however, seems to know what kinds of value they can obtain from their company's intangible assets or how they might go about it. They just know that there is hidden value in their companies and that it is somehow wrapped up in the thoughts, skills, innovations, and abilities of their employees. They want to learn more about this value: how to harness it, direct it, and extract value from it (Sullivan, 2000).

Intellectual assets are intellectual materials that have been formalized, captured, and leveraged to produce higher value for the firm. As organizations gain a fuller recognition of the role these assets play in marketplace success, efforts to more accurately identify and value them become a top priority. Although most managers readily recognize that their most important organizational investments are in talents, capabilities, skills, and ideas, often they must rely on surrogate, tangible-resource measures such as people, capital, inventory, and money for performance decisions.

Being intangible, intellectual assets have historically been difficult to measure and manage. The accounting concept of "goodwill," which is simply the amount left after deducting measurable costs from the selling price, has and continues to be used by many organizations as a type of "miscellaneous" category in which intellectual assets can be placed. A more organizationally appealing approach was introduced by Stewart (1997) where intellectual assets are classified as:

1. A semipermanent body of tacit and explicit knowledge about a task, person, or organization.
2. The capital resources (human, structural, and relational) that augment this body of knowledge.

This classification scheme, if applied properly, produces intellectual asset measures that can be targeted for KM value assessment.

Bolita (2001) states that with more than half the value of U.S. corporations now considered intellectual assets, organizations are increasingly looking for ways to identify, quantify, and capitalize on those intangibles. Over the last seven years, the value of intellectual assets has increased by 700%. An organization's intellectual assets are computed in a number of ways (none of them precise). The difference between a company's book value and the value of all its fixed assets is one measure. The Coca-Cola Company (www.thecoca-colacompany.com) is often cited as a reference model for evaluating intellectual assets. Discounting the extensive value of the sugar, water, bottling facilities, and distribution system, the bulk of the company's value lies in the formula to make Coke and in the brand awareness the company has established.

For example, Microsoft (www.microsoft.com) paid $425 million for WebTV (www.webtv.com), a company with few fixed assets and only modest revenue. However, WebTV held 35 patents for delivering the Internet over television.

For that intellectual property and the expectation of revenue it could generate, Microsoft was willing to pay dearly. Intellectual capital may be represented by documents, recordings, or images—all different structured data types. Those data types embody the knowledge and a substantial portion of a company's value. Quantifying an organization's intellectual property should therefore begin by making it as tangible as possible. By converting ideas, processes, concepts, and business intelligence into archived documents, computer-assisted design (CAD) drawings, database entries, procedure manuals, or even patents, organizations are much better able to count intellectual assets in their bottom line.

Edvisson and Malone (1997) proposed that knowledge assets can be placed in one of three categories:

1. *Human capital*, or all the brainpower that "leaves at 5:00 P.M." Human capital represents the knowledge inherent in employees and contractors, and it is difficult to calculate. The best way to assess it is to calculate the potential inherent in human knowledge—the value that has not yet manifested itself.
2. *Structural capital*, or all the brainpower that "stays after 5:00 P.M." Structural capital includes policies and procedures, customized software applications, training courses, patents, and the like. The financial community can more easily calculate the value of structural capital because it has physical properties.
3. *Customer capital* (also called relationship capital), or all the corporate relationships with customers and prospects. The value of customer relationships can be calculated in terms of the business they have provided and the trend in those relationships. (The value of future relationships or lapsed contracts is difficult to calculate.)

Organizations can take an inventory of these assets and, in some cases, can sell them to others. (For example, organizations can sell training courses and license patents.) Identifying and extracting intellectual assets is the process of determining the obvious and nonobvious assets that a company owns. Often as a company goes through a systematic process of inventorying its known assets, it finds many surprises. For example, a company might start an inventory by listing its patents and patentable discoveries. It then becomes clear that some of the company's most valuable intellectual assets are in the form of processes or know-how that are not patentable.

Examples that should be included in an inventory of intellectual assets are product formulas, manufacturing processes, new product plans, packaging specifications, product compositions, research direction, test methods, alliance relationships, business plans, strategic direction, vendor terms, competitive analysis, customer lists, marketing plans, sales projections, budgets, financial projections, pricing analysis, and employee lists.

Intellectual assets also come from widening the aperture of the lens used to see intellectual assets. For example, by looking to contractors and consultants who develop intellectual assets for the company, the company is likely to discover assets it owns that had not been considered. In the process that links identifying intellectual assets to extracting them for profit, a company will often see opportunities to create new intellectual assets. A company can cultivate creativity to create assets that can be identified and extracted for profit to the organization.

Lev (2001) views intangible assets as nonscarce. Deployment of an intangible asset is possible at the same time in multiple uses. The value of intangibles increases when used. This is also referred to as scalability: the value of intangibles increases when the scale in which they are used increases. Intangibles are not subject to diminishing returns as are tangible assets, but they have increasing returns. Intangibles also have strong network effects. Though not exclusively applicable to intangibles, network effects are characteristic for intangibles in the sense that intangibles often form the core of important networks. Intangibles create future value. All intangibles are future-oriented, and as a result they are ignored by traditional accounting systems based on conservatism and materialism.

Intangibles are difficult to manage and to exclusively control. Taking full advantage of the tacit knowledge that resides in employees is more difficult than exploiting the value of a building or a machine to its maximum. Copying or reengineering intellectual assets is often relatively easy, and we have limited ability to protect by property rights. Cost accounting systems are not well geared toward intangible assets and are even wholly inaccurate for managing intangible assets–intensive corporations. Intangibles cannot be owned (except legal property rights). Intangible investments are therefore typically more risky because intangibles play the most dominant role in the early stages of the innovation process. Proper management can deal with this situation—that is, R&D alliances and diversified innovation project portfolios.

Intangible assets are nonphysical and therefore inherently difficult to trade. Legal protection is weak, and there are large sunk costs as well as low marginal costs. Open exchanges for intangibles are in their infancy. In addition, intangibles cannot be measured directly, and so valuing intangibles is difficult. Unlike tangibles, intangibles are not evidenced by financial transactions.

KM METRICS

Many businesses are finding that in order to gain buy-in from senior management, they need to prepare and present a solid KM business case, usually presented in the form of a KM strategy. Ideally, the KM strategy should include the assessment framework that will be used to monitor progress toward and successful attainment of the targeted KM objectives and initiatives. Unfortunately, traditional accounting standards do not provide the guidance necessary to value all intangible assets (Lev, 1997). The International Accounting Standard Number 38 named "Intangible Assets" only discusses patents, copyrights, goodwill, and research and development costs (ISAC, 1998). It makes no mention of employee knowledge, best practices, or investments in training. Despite the difficulty in valuing such intellectual capital, it remains one of the more important KM techniques to learn and to apply in practice (Brown and

Woodland, 1999). Traditional financial statements would not show the loss of intellectual capital, and the subsequent impact to the company, if 1000 employees were to suddenly leave (Roos & Roos, 1998). However, KPMG's research indicates that, after losing key employees, 43% of organizations experienced damage to a main customer relationship, 50% had lost knowledge of best practices information, and 10% had lost significant income (Warren, 1999).

Most current approaches place a value on intellectual capital in the following way: for publicly traded companies, the value of intellectual capital (IC) is the difference between the market capitalization and the book value (summation of assets less depreciation) of the company (Roos & Roos, 1998; Skandia, 1998; Saint-Onge, 1999). For example, Intel's market capitalization in 1997 was $110 billion, and its financial book value was $17 billion. This hidden value of $93 billion is stated as the value of Intel's intellectual capital (Sveiby, 1997). Roos and Roos (1998) made a similar comparison with Microsoft. A recent study by the Brookings Institute in Washington shows that this "missing value" grew from 38% of a company's market capitalization in 1982 to 62% in 1995 (Dzinkowski, 1999).

Skandia, a Swedish insurance company, has made strides to quantify its intellectual capital through further exploration. Using work that won the 1992 Nobel Prize in Economics, Skandia has divided IC into several subsets: customer capital, human capital, and organizational capital (Roos and Roos, 1998; Skandia, 1998). Skandia's annual *Intellectual Capital Prototype Report* (1998) defines these terms with supporting details regarding how calculations of value are made. Skandia's advancements, as well as efforts by KPMG (KPMG, 2000), Buckman Laboratories, and McKinsey & Company (Davenport, 1996), are providing tools by which management can determine the company's present intellectual capital (IC) value and foresee future IC growth (or shrinkage). Deutsche Bank is using these tools to give loans with only IC as collateral (Henry and King, 1999).

The Skandia Intellectual Capital model is called the Skandia Navigator (Wall, Kirk, and Martin, 2004). Four key dimensions of business form the core of this model:

1. *Financial focus*, represented in monetary terms.
2. *Customer focus*, a financial and nonfinancial measure of the value of customer capital.
3. *Process focus*, which addresses the effective use of technology within the organization.
4. *Renewal and development focus*, which attempts to capture the innovative capabilities of the organization.

All four dimensions are in turn related to a *human focus*, which is a measure of the organization's human capital. This model is quite similar to the balanced scorecard method (BSC) discussed later in this chapter. The Navigator can be thought of as a combination of Sveiby's (1988) Intangible Assets Monitor and the BSC.

The valuation of IC is receiving much attention in today's literature. However, the cost of implementing KM techniques is not as clear. McKinsey

& Company has an objective of spending 10% of revenues on developing and managing knowledge (Davenport, 1996). Keeping with the earlier Intel example, these estimates would place the cost of managing knowledge within Intel between $595 million and $1.7 billion in 1997. By not clearly understanding the "intellectual liabilities," or cost of KM, it remains difficult for companies to calculate any balance sheet effects. Buckman Labs estimates that companies spend 3.5% of their revenues on KM (Davenport, 1996). The founder of Buckman Labs, Robert Buckman, estimates that the first benefits from KM were seen as an improved speed of new product development (Angus, 2003), which increased to 30–35% from 13–18% a year. Some additional examples are provided in the accompanying vignettes.

ACCENTURE

Accenture (formerly known as Arthur Andersen) and the ICM Group[4] formed an alliance to help organizations identify and measure the value of their intangible assets, and use those assets to generate new revenue. Services provided to firms were to include evaluating a company's intangible assets—patents, licenses, trademarks, copyrights, and all the knowledge or "know-how" of its employees—and then recommending and implementing systems and processes to manage those assets. Clients could expect to pay in the region of $25,000 for an analysis of their intellectual property portfolios.

In 1995, the ICM Group co-founded the ICM Gathering, which includes more than 30 global companies dedicated to improving the way they manage their intellectual assets and maximizing their financial return. ICM defines intellectual assets as ideas that can be converted into profit. Organizations are sitting on untapped wealth in the form of hundreds of ideas that were never developed. Arthur Andersen and the ICM Group enable organizations to find these hidden gems and translate them into increased revenue and higher market value. The alliance also will emphasize the link between research and development and business strategy, as organizations need to look at where new value is being created and focus the dollars spent on R&D. Organizations need to understand how intellectual assets are created and managed in order to get the most benefit from those assets. R&D can help organizations identify future market direction and the competitive landscape.

CHEVRON

For Chevron[5] the guiding concept of KM has not been a buzzword but a culture, dubbed "The Chevron Way." This concept, which provides an integrated framework for the company's objectives and principles, actively encourages the internal transfer of information to make every employee's life easier. For Chevron, as for other oil companies, the sharing of knowledge is a necessity. According to Chevron's chairman and chief executive Kenneth Derr, the long-term forecast for the energy business is still "one of growth and opportunity." By using best practice sharing, Chevron can cut costs, reduce production cycle times, and still grow in targeted areas.

That extends to ensuring that the projects the company is undertaking are the most important ones and offering the best rate of return. Knowledge is applied to all business, and sharing knowledge is no longer merely a performance issue; it is a reputation issue as well. It directly affects every major company's ability to win new business and to keep top employees. One of the drivers for Chevron's focus on sharing best practices throughout the organization was a series of benchmarking studies that showed Chevron's management that the company was spending more than its competitors on large projects.

The oil industry is very capital-intensive, and any way of cutting investment costs will improve the company's bottom line. On the basis of the survey results, a tool was created and deployed throughout the company called the Chevron Project Development and Execution Process. Better known throughout Chevron as "Chip-Dip," this process is estimated to have resulted in a 15% improvement in capital efficiency since 1991. Chip-Dip is, in effect, a best practice sharing work process system involving networks of Chevron staff to help improve capital project selection and execution. At the same time, achieving best practice sharing can also have a marked effect on safety and environmental performance. In a world where disasters are headline news—as Exxon found to its cost with the Alaskan oil disaster in 1989—Chevron believes its employee safety performance has improved by 50% through facilitating the transfer of knowledge throughout the company. Overall, although there are hundreds of individual areas within the company that contribute to best practice sharing, key labels under which they could be categorized include exploration, production, refining operations, energy management, marketing, and transportation.

Chevron's goal has been one of steady, "continuous improvement," based more on cultural than on technology "buy-in." The key factor for Chevron was not that everyone within the company had IT tools, but that the tools were "standardized, compatible, and connected." Chevron's technology configuration involves a base of Windows NT running on Hewlett-Packard machines, with Microsoft Office and other Microsoft tools. But for the swapping of knowledge, the company uses Lotus Notes, with Fulcrum as its main search vehicle. Web usage within the company is also growing rapidly, doubling every 100 days. Training to encourage the growth of the knowledge-sharing culture across the company, especially for new employees, is also important.

Continued

Chevron's best practice culture extends to the evaluation of employees for salary purposes. An individual's evaluation is based on individual growth and team performance. Those who practice the sharing of knowledge are more likely to be the ones rising up the organizational ladder. Staff who are not ingrained with the culture probably will either not know who to share information with, or not share their information because they do not feel it is of value to anyone. It is establishing that culture—and most important, doing it for business needs—that is the difference between those who practice knowledge management and those who just talk about it. Best practice sharing has helped Chevron cut annual operating costs by $1.8 billion, reduce cost structure by $400 million, reduce debt by $2.3 billion in two years, cut capital cost of projects by 15% since 1991, and improve employee safety performance by 50%.

The shift toward knowledge-driven business models has created a strong need for knowledge management metrics. The literature has only recently begun to explore the cost of KM, with little empirical data showing true organizational costs (Harvey and Lusch, 1999). Three popular approaches—benchmarking, the balanced scorecard method, and the house of quality—are presented next.

The Benchmarking Method

Benchmarking is the search for industrywide best practices that lead to superior performance. It usually consists of a study of similar companies to determine how things are done best in order to adapt these methods for their own use. This technique is best summed up by the Hindu proverb: "know the best to become the best."

Benchmarking as a tactical planning tool originated with Xerox Business Systems in the late 1970s. At that time, Japanese affiliates were selling better-quality copiers for less than the manufacturing costs of similar products in the United States; Xerox wanted to know why as well as whether or not they could emulate them. Similarly, one of the first experiments in benchmarking was in the production logistics area (warehousing, picking, packing, and shipping) when Xerox Business Services benchmarked with L. L. Bean, a clothing manufacturer, which had one of the best logistics operations in the world.

Benchmarking is a fairly straightforward KM metric that often represents a good starting point. There are two general types of benchmarking: *internal benchmarking*, which involves comparisons against other units within the same organization or a comparison of a single unit over different time periods; and *external benchmarking*, which involves a comparison with other companies.

In addition, Spendolini (1992) describes three different types of benchmarking:

1. *Industry Group Measurements*: the measurement of various facets of your operation and comparing these to similar measurements. Often the measures have little to do with productivity, customer satisfaction, or "best practice." Many industry groups publish comparative data either privately (for members of the group or service only) or publicly, or both. The Institute of Internal Auditors' GAIN (Global Audit Information Network) provides this kind of data privately to subscribers. The Institute also publishes biannual salary surveys and occasionally special studies of external audit fees and research on effective audit departments ("best practices").

2. *Best Practice Studies*: studies and lists of what works best. These are useful to benchmarking research, but they are not useful as metrics. What works best for an entity in its specific environment may not work the same way in another environment. These studies can be useful simulators, but they are not benchmarks per se. There are books, consultants, and public accounting firms that report internal audit "best practices" gathered from research and consulting practice. The IIA published a book for audit committees that was a study of best practices.

3. *Cooperative Benchmarking*: the measurement of key production functions of inputs, outputs, and outcomes with the aim of improving them. In internal audit, we would study, for example, comparisons of costs per audit hour, time elapsed to distribute final report, and percentage of recommendations accepted. Cooperative benchmarking is performed with the assistance of the entity being studied (the benchmark "partner"). Often the entity selected as a benchmark is one that has "best practices" in the area of interest or has won a major national or international quality award. Internal audit departments are increasingly interested in this method. A version of cooperative benchmarking is collaborative benchmarking. In the collaborative method, both entities study each other and work together to improve. Some audit departments are now doing this.

4. *Competitive Benchmarking*: the study and measurement of a competitor without its cooperation for the purposes of process or product quality improvement. The latter is called reverse engineering. A version of competitive benchmarking is the commisioning of a third party to study a group of competitors and share the results with all. The third-party consultant is the only one who knows what data belong to which entity. (You obviously know your own, but not necessarily anyone else's.)

In the long term, this approach lacks sufficient value and flexibility, which leads to other measurement tools and techniques eventually being brought in to measure the effectiveness of KM. Benchmarking is essentially a comparison that is undertaken with key leaders in the industry in order to identify any best practices that the company can emulate in order to improve its own organizational effectiveness. This technique was pioneered by Carla O'Dell at the American Productivity and Quality Center (APQC, http://www.apqc.org).

Benchmarking is a good way of avoiding reinventing the wheel by looking at what has worked and what has not worked for other companies operating in comparable environments or industrial sectors.

The benefits of benchmarking are not limited to improvements in process or the promotion of reuse. Tiwana (2000) lists the following potential benefits:

1. Overall productivity of knowledge investments.
2. Service quality.
3. Customer satisfaction and the operational level of customer service.
4. Time to market in relation to other competitors.
5. Costs, profits, and margins.
6. Distribution.
7. Relationships and relationship management.

Benchmarking can help an organization evolve to higher maturity levels, whereby it becomes a learning organization by identifying where it stands with respect to KM in relation to the competition.

Accenture (formerly Arthur Andersen) developed a Knowledge Management Assessment Tool (KMAT) that is essentially a benchmarking questionnaire where responses by a given company can be easily compared against industry standards in order to come up with a relative standing or ranking for the company on specific indicators. The KMAT was developed by the American Productivity and Quality Center and Arthur Andersen in 1995 to help organizations self-assess where their strengths and opportunities lie in managing knowledge. The tool is divided into five sections: the KM process; leadership; culture; technology; and measurement. A subset of the items and information in the KMAT, with a simplified scoring system, is available at (http://www. kwork.org/White%20Papers/KMAT_BOK_DOC.pdf).

The first step in benchmarking is to compile the short list of companies that you will be comparing. Recent trends toward globalization indicate that international companies should not be automatically excluded from your short list. In the end, it is a fairly subjective decision as to which companies and which criteria you will be benchmarking against. Some typical targets include innovation metrics (how fast are new products being developed? How much is invested in R&D?), customer loyalty, KM integration, leveraging of IT, and quality management.

Tiwana (2000) adapted Spendolini's (1992) key benchmarking steps in order to arrive at a better fit with KM. These key steps can be summarized as:

1. Determine what to benchmark: which knowledge processes, products, services? Why? With what scope?
2. Form a benchmarking team.
3. Select a benchmarking short list—which companies will you be benchmarking against?
4. Collect and analyze data.
5. Determine what changes should be made as a result of the metrics obtained.

6. Repeat when an appropriate amount of time has lapsed to measure progress.

Benchmarking is of greatest value when a company has clearly identified its strategic objectives and they have thought long and hard about which best practices might or might not be transferable and effective within their own particular context, with its own KM drivers and constraints.

The Balanced Scorecard Method

The balanced scorecard method (BSC) is a measurement and management system that enables organizations to clarify their vision and strategy and to translate them into action. It provides feedback on both the internal business processes and external outcomes in order to continuously improve strategic performance and results. The BSC is a conceptual framework for translating an organization's vision into a set of performance indicators distributed among four dimensions: Financial, Customer, Internal Business Processes, and Learning and Growth. Indicators are maintained to measure an organization's progress toward achieving its vision; other indicators are maintained to measure the long-term drivers of success. Through the BSC, an organization monitors both its current performance (finances, customer satisfaction, and business process results) and its efforts to improve processes, motivate and educate employees, and enhance information systems—its ability to learn and improve. A high-level balanced scorecard is shown in Figure 9-3.

Variations in the basic design are common. Typical changes include changes in the categorization of perspectives (Innovation and Learning, or Employees, in place of Learning and Growth, for example) and the number of perspectives

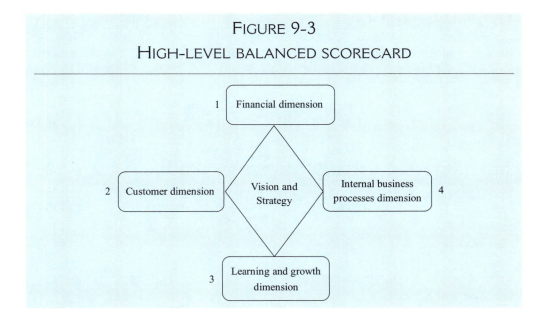

FIGURE 9-3
HIGH-LEVEL BALANCED SCORECARD

(adding Stakeholders as a separate, fifth perspective, for example). Balance is achieved through the four perspectives, through the decomposition of an organization's vision into business strategy and then into operations, and through the translation of strategy into the contribution each member of the organization must make to successfully meet its goals. The BSC translates the organization's strategy into four dimensions with a balance between:

1. Internal and external measures.
2. Objective and subjective measures.
3. Performance results and drivers of future results.

The financial dimension typically includes measures such as operating income, return on capital employed, and economic value added. The customer dimension deals with such measures as customer satisfaction, retention, and market share in targeted segments. The internal business process dimension includes measures such as cost, throughput, and quality. The learning and growth dimension addresses measures such as employee satisfaction, retention, and skill sets.

Each dimension of the BSC can be further expanded to include objectives, metrics, targets, and initiatives, as shown in Table 9-1. Objectives are the major goals to be achieved (e.g., profitable growth). Metrics are the parameters that will be monitored in order to measure progress toward these stated goals (e.g., growth in net margin). Targets are the specific thresholds to be met for each metric (e.g., 2% or greater growth in net margin). Finally, initiatives describe the actions, projects, programs, and so on to be put into place in order to be able to meet the stated goals.

The balanced scorecard method was intended to be a performance improvement metric, but it quickly became apparent that it also serves as an effective strategic management system. It is applicable to both profit and nonprofit organizations as well as to both private- and public-sector companies. The BSC offers a number of significant advantages, including the translation of abstract goals into action items that can be continuously monitored. It provides objec-

TABLE 9-1
SAMPLE BSC IMPLEMENTATION

	Objectives	Metrics	Targets	Initiatives
Financial				
Customer				
Internal Processes				
Learning and Growth				

tive measures of the current situation, and it also helps initiate the changes required to move from the current to the desired future state of the company. This is a much more difficult technique to use than benchmarking. Each BSC must be developed "from scratch" because it is customized to individual organizations. Some templates and automated tools are now becoming available to help implement a BSC from, for example, Six Sigma (available at http://www.sixsigma.com/me/balanced_scorecard/) and QPR (available at http://www.qpr.com/balancedscorecard/).

The House of Quality Method

The house of quality method was developed to show the connections between true quality, quality characteristics, and process characteristics. This was done using the Fishbone Diagram, with true quality in the heads and quality and process characteristics in the bones. In 1988, Hauser and Clausing developed an evaluation matrix metric that measures how customer needs are linked to the business processes and internal decisions of an organization. A simplified matrix is shown in Figure 9-4.

This technique is also referred to as Quality Function Deployment (QFD) by Mazur (1993) because it links the customer's needs with marketing, design, development, engineering, manufacturing, and service functions (see also the Quality Function Deployment Institute, http://www.qfdi.org). It can be used for service and software products as well. QFD is the only comprehensive quality system aimed specifically at satisfying the customer. It concentrates on maximizing customer satisfaction (positive quality), measured by metrics, such

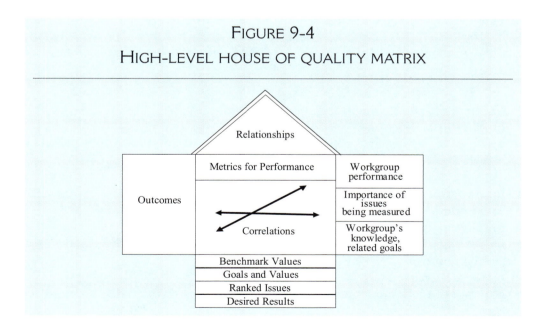

FIGURE 9-4

HIGH-LEVEL HOUSE OF QUALITY MATRIX

as repeat business and market share. QFD focuses on delivering value by seeking out both spoken and unspoken needs, translating these into design targets, and communicating the targets throughout the organization. Furthermore, it allows customers to prioritize their requirements, tells us how we are doing compared to our competitors, and then directs us to optimize those features that will bring the greatest competitive advantage.

The goals and objectives are placed to the left of the house. Ideally, these desired outcomes should be short- to mid-term and observable. Some examples would be:

- Increase the number of communities of practice by 3.
- Decrease the number of customer complaints by 50%.
- Decrease the number of unsolved problems by 60%.
- Decrease the time to market for newly developed products and services by 40%.

Priorities are next assigned to each of these goals by placing weights to the right of the house. Useful metrics can then be listed on top of the house (the ceiling). At the center of the matrix, we will see the level of correlation between the metrics and the performance outcomes; these can be numerical correlations or low-moderate-high type values. By analyzing these correlations, we can zoom in on those aspects of KM that are more likely to have an impact on overall company performance and thus will contribute more significantly to progress made toward the stated goals.

A blank house of quality template is also available at http://www.gsm.mq. edu.au/cmit/hoq/Example%20HOQ%20Matrix.doc. Advice on interpreting, analyzing, and reiterating the house of quality design is provided in the form of a checklist by Mazur (1993) and is available at http://www.mazur.net/works/9checks.pdf.

Tiwana (2000) recommends using indicators and other useful parameters from the Skandia Intellectual Capital annual report instrument as house of quality outcomes in order to analyze KM effectiveness. These indicators include:

- Competence development expenses ($ per employee).
- Employee satisfaction.
- Time spent on systematic packaging of know-how for future reuse when a project has been completed.
- Training expenses per employee.
- Information-gathering expenses per existing customer.
- Total number of patents held.
- Employee attrition rate.
- Dollar figure value of loss per employee who leaves (and who leaves for a competing firm).
- Expense of reinventing solutions per year.
- Number of ideas implemented compared to those suggested (e.g., suggestion box).

KEY POINTS

- Knowledge management auditing is often the first step in any KM initiative because it serves to inventory what knowledge-intensive resources exist within a company. This provides a snapshot of the "as is" or current state of the organization with respect to KM and helps in measuring progress toward organizational culture change and other KM goals.
- The two most commonly encountered KM application goals are reuse and innovation.
- It is crucial that a balance be maintained between fluidity and institutionalization in a given organization.
- Lessons learned and best practices are flip sides of the same coin—they represent the accumulated results and learning from trial-and-error experiences that the organization has accumulated.
- Organizational memory systems serve to identify and preserve valuable lessons learned and best practices.
- Corporate amnesia is a risk when no systematic approach has been applied in creating organizational memory systems.
- Intellectual assets are generally categorized as human capital (the know-how of knowledge workers that is "rented" by an organization), structural capital (the policies, procedures, and applications that the organization "owns"), and customer or relationship capital (the value of customer relationships and loyalty that has been built up over the years).
- A number of fairly sophisticated KM measurement techniques are available now that can help assess how well an organization is progressing. These include benchmarking, the balanced scorecard method, and the house of quality matrix.

DISCUSSION POINTS

1. Compare and contrast KM applications that are driven by an objective of reuse versus those driven by an objective of innovation.
2. What are the major steps involved in developing a KM strategy? What sorts of information are needed in order to recommend a KM strategy to an organization? List the major categories of stakeholders who should be involved in the strategy formulation process.
3. What are some of the key challenges in developing and managing an organizational memory system? Outline some of the key obstacles that may be encountered and how you would address each one.
4. What does the term *corporate amnesia* mean? How would you characterize the costs involved in corporate amnesia? Provide some examples to illustrate your points.
5. Why is it important to maintain a balance between fluidity and institutionalization? What are some of the mechanisms that can be used to achieve this balance? How can KM applications upset this balance?

6. List and provide examples for some different types of knowledge assets. What are some typologies that can be used to categorize them?
7. What is the relationship between human, structural, and relationship capital?
8. Why are intellectual assets difficult to manage?
9. KM metrics remain an issue because it is often only too easy to measure the costs of implementing KM whereas the benefits prove too elusive to measure. Discuss this KM issue: what are some of the methods and measures that can be used to make KM benefits less elusive?
10. Explain how you would approach intellectual assets in developing KM applications. What are some of the key challenges? Why can't we use traditional approaches such as traditional accounting methods when dealing with intellectual assets?
11. Compare and contrast the three KM metrics of benchmarking, BSC, and house of quality. What are their major advantages and major drawbacks in monitoring progress toward strategic KM and business goals?

NOTES

[1] Karlenzig, W. (1998). Monsanto picks up KM pieces after merger plan collapses. KM Magazine, December 1998. Available at http://www.destination.com.
[2] Santosus, M. (2001). Thanks for the memories. CIO Magazine, Sept, 21, 2001. Available at: http://www.cio.com.
[3] Kwiecien (2005).
[4] Falk, S. (2005). KM at Accenture. Ch. 2 in M. Rao (Ed.). KM Tools and Techniques. Amsterdam: Elsevier.
[5] "Managing Knowledge The Chevron Way" Speech by K. T. Derr, Chairman of The Board and CEO, Chevron Corporation, to the Knowledge Management World Summit, San Francisco, CA, January 11, 1999. Available at http://www.chevrontexaco.com/news/archive/chevron_speech/1999/99-01-11.asp.

REFERENCES

Angus, R. (2003, March 14). KM's father figure: Robert Buckman. *InfoWorld* interview. Available online at http://www.infoworld.com.
Bolita, D. (2001). Intellectual assets—corporate value moves from top minds to bottom lines—a price on (what's in) your head. *KM World*, 8(2). Available at http://www.kmworld.com/publications/.
Brown, R., and Woodland, M. (1999, December). Managing knowledge wisely: a case study in organizational behaviour. *Journal of Applied Management Studies*, 8(2): 175–198.
Conklin, E. (1993). Capturing organizational memory. In D. Coleman (Ed.), *Proceedings of GroupWare*, pp. 133–137. San Mateo, CA: Morgan Kaufmann.
Davenport, T. (1996, 1st Quarter). Some principles of knowledge management. *Strategy and Business*, 10(5):105–116.

Dzinkowski, R. (1999, October). Managing the brain trust. *CMA Management, 7(8)*: 14–18.

Edvisson, L., and Malone, M. (1997). *Intellectual capital: realizing your company's true value by finding its hidden brainpower.* New York: Harper-Business.

Grey, D. (1999). Knowledge mapping: a practical overview. Available at http://www.smithweaversmith.com.

Harvey, M. G., and Lusch, R. F. (1999, February). Balancing the intellectual capital books: intangible liabilities. *European Management Journal, 17(1)*: 85–92.

Hauser, J., and Clausing, L. (1988). The house of quality. *Harvard Business Review, 3*: 63–73.

Henry, J. M., and King, A. M. (1999, November). Valuing intangible assets through appraisals. *Strategic Finance, 81*: 32–37.

IASC. (1998). International Accounting Standard IAS 38: Intangible Assets. Available at: http://www.iasplus.com/standard/ias38.htm.

Klein, D. (1999). *The strategic management of intellectual capital.* Boston: Butterworth-Heinemann.

KPMG. (2000). The KPMG Value Explorer. Available at http://www.kpmg.interact.nl/value-expl/index.shtml.

Kransdorff, A. (1998). Corporate Amnesia. Keeping know-how in the company. Oxford: Butterworth-Heineman.

Kwiecien, S. (2005). KM processes and tools at Ford Motor Company. In M. Rao (Ed.), *KM tools and techniques*, pp. 155–165. Amsterdam: Elsevier.

Lev, B. (1997, April 7). The old rules no longer apply: intellectual capital measurement. *Forbes Magazine, 72(13)*: 34–38.

Lev, B. (2001). *Intangibles—management, measurement, and reporting.* Washington, DC: Brookings Institute Press.

Liebowitz, J. (1999). *Building organizational intelligence: a knowledge management primer.* Boca Raton, FL: CRC Press.

Mazur, G. (1993, June). QFD for service industries: from voice of customer to task deployment. *Transactions from the Fifth Symposium on Quality Function Deployment*, Novi, MI.

McMaster, M. (1995). *The intelligence advantage: organizing for complexity.* Douglas, Isle of Man, UK: Knowledge Based Development Co. Ltd.

Robertson, J. (2004). Developing a knowledge management strategy. *KM Column. August 2, 2004.* Available at http://www.steptwo.com.au/papers/kmc_kmstrategy/.

Roos, G., and Roos, J. (1998). *Intellectual capital.* New York: New York University Press.

Saint-Onge, H. (1999). *Knowledge management: according to Saint-Onge.* Available at http://www.knowinc.com/saint-onge/primer/hso1.htm.

Skandia. (1998). *Intellectual capital prototype report.* Available at http://www.skandia.com/capital/concept.htm.

Skyrme, D. (2001). *Capitalizing on knowledge: from e-business to k-business.* Boston: Butterworth-Heinemann.

Spendolini, M. (1992). *The benchmarking book.* New York: AMACOM.

Srikantajah, T., and Koenig, M. (2000). *Knowledge management for the information professional.* Medford, NJ: Information Today.

Stewart, Thomas A. (1997). *Intellectual capital: the new wealth of organizations.* New York: Currency/Doubleday.

Sullivan, P. (2000). *Value driven intellectual capital: how to convert intangible corporate assets into market value.* New York: John Wiley and Sons.

Sutton (2005). Ignorance and Stupidity Management—an Irreverent Look at Knowledge Management "a bit off-kilter" Presentation to the Columbus Technology Council, Columbus, Ohio, 4 Feb, 2005.

Sveiby, K. E. (1997). *The new organizational wealth: managing and measuring knowledge-based assets*, San Francisco: Berrett-Koehler.

Sveiby, K. (2001). What is knowledge management? Available at http://www.sveiby.com/articles/KnowledgeManagement.html.

Tiwana, A. (2000). *The knowledge management toolkit*. Upper Saddle River, NJ: Prentice Hall.

Wall, A., Kirk, R., and Martin, G. (2004*). Intellectual capital. Measuring the immeasurable?* Burlington, MA: CIMA Publishing (Elsevier).

Warren, L. (1999, December). Knowledge management: just another office in the executive suite? *Accountancy Ireland*, 31(6): 20–22.

Zack, M. (1999). Developing a knowledge strategy. *California Management Review*, 41(3): 125–145.

THE KM TEAM

He is wise who knows the sources of knowledge—where it is written and where it is to be found.

A. A. Hodge (1823–1886)

This chapter provides an overview of the professionals who form part of the KM team. The key skill sets required to carry out KM responsibilities are described using a variety of frameworks. The new role of CKO (Chief Knowledge Officer) and CLO (Chief Learning Officer) are introduced, and their evolution from the more traditional CIO (Chief Information Officer) is discussed. The different types of KM jobs that exist and the potential KM employers are outlined, and the chapter concludes with a discussion of the emerging KM profession and some of the ethical issues involved in its practice.

LEARNING OBJECTIVES

1. List the key KM skills required to carry out KM professional work and justify the need for each one.
2. Describe the different roles that are required for a KM team and list the key responsibilities of each.
3. Understand how a CIO role can evolve into a CKO role or even a CLO position.
4. Identify the different types of potential KM employers.
5. Relate the critical cognitive and attitudinal attributes that an ideal KM professional should possess.
6. Critically evaluate ethical issues in KM situations in order to make recommendations on how to successfully prevent and correct any morally challenging hurdles to KM implementations. Outline the key

tenets that should be included in a KM code of ethics and justify your recommendations.

INTRODUCTION

This chapter introduces the final component to complete the integrated KM cycle: the KM team (see Figure 10-1).

The brief historical overview of KM in Chapter 1 discussed how the KM field has been transformed from one led primarily by consultants and other KM practitioners to a bona fide discipline, with a distinct body of knowledge. This change has been paralleled by the growing number of academic programs that offer KM as compared to the predominately private-sector training that had been the only way to learn about KM up until now (e.g., Al-Hawamdeh, 2003).

One approach to forming an effective KM team is to define the different types of KM professionals and the types of skills, attributes, and background they should ideally possess. The ultimate goal is to develop a list of cognitive, affective, and psychomotor skills together with the required competency levels for each skill.

TFPL (www.tfpl.com) is a specialist recruitment, advisory, training, and research services company with offices in London focusing on knowledge management, library and information management, records management, and web and content management. Since 1987, TFPL has worked with organizations in both public and private sectors to help them develop and implement

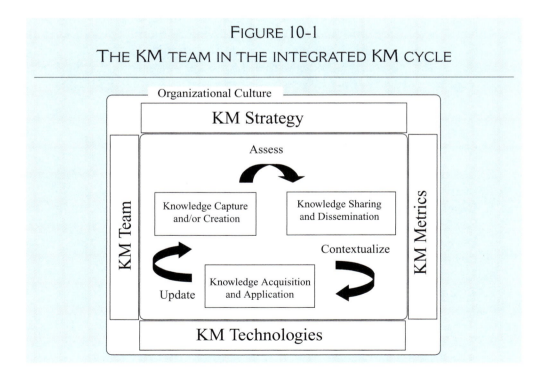

FIGURE 10-1

THE KM TEAM IN THE INTEGRATED KM CYCLE

knowledge and information strategies and to recruit and train information and knowledge leaders and their teams. TFPL has drafted a KM skills and competencies guide to provide a clear and practical overview of KM skills and competencies that draws on the practical experience of organizations in a wide range of sectors and with varying approaches to KM.

In general, these KM skills include:

- Time management to use their time and energy effectively for acquiring knowledge (spending all day surfing the net is probably counterproductive).
- Use of different learning techniques to absorb key knowledge and learning quickly.
- Effective skills of advocacy and inquiry to present knowledge to, and gather knowledge from, others.
- Informal networking skills to build your influence to gain access to people with knowledge.
- Resource investigation skills.
- Effective IT skills for recording and disseminating information.
- Skills of cooperative problem solving.
- Open dialogue skills.
- Flexibility and willingness to try new things and take educated risks.
- Active review of learning from mistakes, risks, opportunities, and successes.

The TFPL knowledge management skills map (available at http://www.tfpl.com/resources/skills_map.cfm) is based on extensive international research. The project team contacted over 500 organizations involved in implementing KM and identified the roles that they had created, the skills needed in those roles, and the additional skills required across the organization. These key skills included (1) an understanding of the KM concept—the philosophy and theory, (2) an awareness of the experience of other organizations in developing KM solutions and approaches, (3) an understanding of, and the ability to identify, the business value of KM activities to the organization, and (4) an appreciation of the range of activities, initiatives, and labels employed to create an environment in which knowledge is effectively created, shared, and used to increase competitive advantage and customer satisfaction (see Table 10-1).

The KM team's skill requirements can be built up from the set of critical skills or core competencies, such as an ability to learn, autonomous, wait to be told, collaborative team player, sees the big picture, makes connections, learns from mistakes, ability to think and do, with a focus on outcome, and an appreciation of information management techniques.

A KM dream team would collectively possess the skills of communication, leadership, expertise in KM methodology/processes/tools, and negotiation and strategic planning, together with the following attributes: know the organization, remain connected to the top, adopt a systems view, and be an intuitive risk taker.

TFPL has developed a competency framework that allows managers to define knowledge and information management roles and their competencies in consultation with the staff who will hold the posts. The KM Skills Toolkit (available at http://www.tfpl.com/skills_development/skills_toolkit.cfm) is a

TABLE 10-1
EXCERPT FROM THE TPFL KM SKILLS MAP

Business Awareness/Experience	Management Skills	Intellectual and Learning Skills
Business planning	Change management	Ability to deal with ambiguity
Entrepreneurial	Coordination	Analytical
Forward thinking	Cost control	Bigger picture view
Globalization issues	Financial management	Conceptual thinking
Industry/sector knowledge	Leadership	Emotional intelligence
Leadership	Measurement performance impact, value	Self-awareness, self-motivation, persistence, read emotion in others
Organizational design	People management	Innovation
Organizational skills	Project management	Lateral thinking
Risk management	Quality assurance	Organizational skills
Strategic thinking	Team building	Original thinking
Strategic planning	Time management	Perspective
Understanding value chain	Training and development	Problem solving
Visioning	Needs analysis	Positive thinking

diagnostic tool that can help organizations to assess recruitment needs and develop job descriptions and personnel specifications for knowledge and information roles.

Moving up one level, Goade (2000) groups key KM skills within the following seven categories:

1. Retrieving information.
2. Evaluating/assessing information.
3. Organizing information.
4. Analyzing information.
5. Presenting information.
6. Securing information.
7. Collaborating around information.

The skill of retrieving information involves everything from the low-tech skills of asking questions and listening and following up to the more complex skills of searching for information using Internet search engines, electronic library databases, and relational databases. Concepts of widening and narrowing one's search, Boolean logic, and iterative search practices are an important part of the effective exercise of this skill.

Evaluating information entails not only being able to judge the quality of information, but also to determine its relevance to some question or problem at hand. Although this has no necessary computer mechanism for implementation (though Internet search engines have crude relevant raters), the greater availability of information in the current information-rich environments gives this skill much greater importance.

Organizing information involves using various tools to draw connections between items of information. In the manual environment, we use file folders, drawers, and other mechanisms to organize information; in more high-tech environments, we use electronic folders, relational databases, and web pages. Effective organizational principles must underlie effective implementation of information organization regardless of the environment.

Analyzing information entails the challenge of "tweaking" meaning out of data. Integral to analyzing information is the development and application of models, often quantitative, to "educe" relationships out of the data. Tools such as electronic spreadsheets and statistical software provide the means to analyze information, but the human element is central in framing the models embodied in that software.

The key aspect of presenting information is the centrality of the audience. Presenting information—whether through PowerPoint presentation, website, or text—builds on principles of chunking information to enable audiences to understand, remember, and connect. Web styles and monographs on designing website usability provide concrete content for this KM skill.

Although securing information employs a KM skill different from that of the other six, it is no less important. Securing information entails developing and implementing practices that assure the confidentiality, quality, and actual existence of information. Practices of password management, backup, archiving, and use of encryption are important elements of this effectively practiced KM skill.

Increasingly, information technology tools called groupware are being provided to support collaborative work. To use that technology effectively requires not just understanding how to use those tools, but understanding the underlying principles of effective collaborative work. The principles of e-mail etiquette illustrate important knowledge underlying the effective exercise of this KM skill.

Most organizations are still defining their KM roles, and some are repurposing or extending existing roles in order to better accommodate knowledge work. While KM in every organization is unique and necessarily tailor-made, a number of "generic" KM roles can be identified.

MAJOR CATEGORIES OF KM ROLES

KM roles are quite diverse. They may include categories such as:

- Senior and middle management roles—Chief Knowledge Officer, Knowledge Manager.
- Knowledge leaders, also referred to as KM champions, who are responsible for promoting KM within the organization.
- Knowledge managers, responsible for the acquisition and management of internal and external knowledge.
- Knowledge navigators, responsible for knowing where knowledge can be located, also called knowledge brokers.

- Knowledge synthesizers, responsible for facilitating the recording of significant knowledge to organizational memory, also called knowledge stewards.
- Content editors, responsible for codifying and structuring content, also called content managers; roles involving capturing and documenting knowledge—researchers, writers, editors.
- Web developers, electronic publishers, intranet managers, content managers.
- Learning-oriented roles such as trainers, facilitators, mentors, and coaches—including those with responsibility for developing information and knowledge skills.
- Human resources roles with specific responsibility for developing programs and processes that encourage knowledge-oriented cultures and behaviors.
- Knowledge publishers, responsible for internal publishing functions, usually on an intranet, also called Webmasters, knowledge architects, and knowledge editors.
- Coaches and mentors, responsible for assisting individuals throughout the business unit or practice to develop and learn KM activities and disciplines.
- Help desk activities, including the delivery of KM and information related to training, also called KSO (Knowledge Support Office).

In seeking to recruit relevant professionals for knowledge management roles, a key challenge lies in defining the objectives and deliverables of those roles, and in specifying the skills and experience of the people needed to fill them. Some of these roles may be newly created, whereas others may involve redefining or extending existing roles.

Different organizations will necessarily have different approaches describing knowledge management roles. A sample KM job description may look something like this:

SAMPLE JOB DESCRIPTION: KNOWLEDGE AND INFORMATION MANAGER[1]

Responsibilities will include:

- Systematically recording and storing health-related information and expertise.
- "Packaging" organizational expertise, health information, knowledge, and learning for use by a variety of clients.
- Maximizing the usability and usefulness of health resources/information products for different user groups.
- Promoting the meaning and purpose of information and knowledge resources/products to clients within and outside of the organization.
- Ensuring that information/knowledge resources can be readily accessed and easily retrieved.

The Knowledge and Information Manager:

- Will provide leadership in the area of knowledge management as a technique for managing the intellectual assets of the organization.

- Will assist with the development of knowledge and information as a core business function for all business units.
- Will provide the "hands-on" expertise required to manage organizational expertise in the form of both knowledge and information resources/products.

Selection criteria:

- Tertiary qualifications preferably in a relevant field, for example, Information Science, KM.
- In-depth appreciation of the capabilities and limitations of information technology.
- The ability to manage knowledge and information via online databases, collaborative technologies, and web-based services.
- Understanding of knowledge processes such as organizational learning and development.
- Understanding of the principles of knowledge management as a management technique to enable organizational development in the knowledge economy.
- Excellent computer skills preferably with experience with database and website management.
- Experience in systems development and implementation.
- Experience managing small teams and budgets.
- Leadership and planning skills.
- Superior communication and relationship-building skills.
- Strong project management skills.

Role responsibilities:

- Develop, implement, and achieve a knowledge management plan for the organization.
- Establish a Health Information Center for the knowledge and information resources/products of the organization.
- Develop and maintain a Health Internet and intranet site.
- Train and develop staff in information literacy and knowledge awareness, that is, in systematically identifying, collecting, reviewing, sharing, and retaining high-value knowledge.
- Ensure compliance with relevant legislation (e.g., copyright and intellectual property).
- Oversee development and achievement of business and project plans for the unit.
- Monitor and report on relevant activity levels in operational and business plans.
- Establish and maintain links with relevant internal and external stakeholders.

KM professionals require a multidisciplinary skill set that consists of such competencies as finding, appraising, and using knowledge, reformulating questions, navigating through content, evaluating the relevance of content, filtering out what is not needed, and synthesizing from diverse sources in order to apply the knowledge (e.g., to make a decision). Last but not least, they must contribute to the recording of such valuable experiences to organizational memory systems.

Senior Management Roles

Most people are familiar with the role of a Chief Executive Officer (CEO), Chief Operating Officer (COO), and Chief Financial Officer (CFO). There are also Chief Technology Officers (CTOs) and Chief Information Officers (CIOs), positions typically reserved for heads of information technology. An analogous role exists for a knowledge management executive, sometimes referred to as the Chief Knowledge Officer (CKO) or Chief Learning Officer (CLO). The CKO or CLO position heads the KM team and is primarily responsible for:

- Formulating knowledge management strategy.
- Handling knowledge management operations.
- Influencing change in the organization.
- Managing knowledge management staff (Rusonow, 2003).

The KM executive must decide how information is evaluated, created, processed, inventoried, retrieved, and archived, so that KM activities are aligned with the business goals of the organization. There are huge ramifications when an organization creates records, installs a new online catalog or a firewall, designs a website, creates virtual workplaces, copyrights information, and creates policies and procedures on how one department communicates information to another (or too many times, it does not). The head of KM must be present in all these events. This executive KM role often incorporates change management as well.

Thurow (2003, 2004) maintains that in our increasingly knowledge-based economy, every company will eventually have a senior manager responsible for KM, and those who get there first will have a competitive edge. Just what this person will do is still being invented and will differ from industry to industry. The KM executive's duties may be as varied as recommending whether a company should buy, sell, or make its technologies, or determining where technology is going and where new competitors may arise. KM executives identify critical knowledge needs within a company as well as any knowledge gaps that need to be addressed. KM executives need to be good relationship builders as the fundamental issues revolve around people, culture, roles, behaviors, and the business processes in the organization.

Skyrme (1997) defines a CKO as a senior executive who is responsible for ensuring that an organization maximizes the value it achieves through one of its most important assets—knowledge. Although only a few companies have people with this explicit title, those with similar responsibilities include Director of Intellectual Capital and Director of Innovation. CKOs will typically contribute to the following KM goals:

1. Maximize the returns on KM investment in knowledge—people, processes, and intellectual capital.
2. Exploit intangible assets (e.g., know-how, patents, customer relationships).
3. Repeat successes and share best practices.
4. Improve innovation and the commercialization of ideas.
5. Avoid knowledge loss and leakage after organizational restructuring.

The responsibilities associated with the job function of KM executive revolve around converting the KM strategy into specific KM initiatives that help achieve organizational business goals. KM initiatives fall into four general categories:

1. Promoting the importance of knowledge sharing.
2. Creating a technical infrastructure to ease that sharing.
3. Promoting a cultural climate that rewards knowledge-sharing behaviors.
4. Measuring the value of knowledge and KM practices to the organization.

Potentially the most important job function is promoting a corporate culture that encourages knowledge sharing. A long-term proposition, the CKO works as a change agent to build a cultural climate that rewards sharing behavior (Earl and Scott, 1999). Because of the power associated with expertise, employees may be reluctant to share their knowledge and skill. "A person who has unique or special knowledge, skills and experience may use this expertise as a source of influence and a way of building personal power" (Gordon, 2002).

The CKO argues against perceived reasons for hoarding knowledge (Stewart, 1998), persuades workers that knowledge-sharing initiatives are to their benefit (Earl and Scott, 1999), and uses motivational techniques to reward a sharing climate. The CKO also creates an environment that makes it easier to build communication networks between employees who do not normally work together, but would generate value from exchanging information (Earl and Scott, 1999). The CKO works with formal and informal communication networks and supports "communities of practice" or groups of experts who could learn from knowledge exchange (Stewart, 1998).

Davenport and Prusak (1997) argue that these organizational changes will necessarily require changes to the information technology structure, since IT is the key enabler in leveraging intellectual capital. Having fostered a sharing culture, the CKO uses IT as a way of creating a structured means of knowledge exchange and of generating opportunities to connect workers together across organizational units and geographies. The CKO designs ways for workers to present and receive knowledge and is responsible for developing and maintaining an information infrastructure to harness the collective knowledge of the organization.

While working to foster a cooperative culture and creating mechanisms to exchange knowledge, the CKO keeps a sharp eye on the rewards of these endeavors. The results of KM activities must translate into real business value. In business ventures, the bottom line is the measure of success to an organization. The CKO evaluates the return on investment before making cultural and design decisions and proceeding with KM initiatives. A final function for many CKOs is that of manager to a team of knowledge professionals. Although not all CKOs have a team, Earl and Scott (1999) found that most have a small staff of 3 to 12 specialists working under their supervision. In addition to leading the management of intellectual capital in an organization, CKOs must therefore also supervise the work and careers of their employees.

Some KM executives have the title of Chief Learning Officer (CLO). There is a journal dedicated to this new role, called Chief Learning Officer, available at http://www.clomedia.com/. Like CKOs, most Chief Learning Officers are first-generation incumbents. They typically started their jobs less than three years ago and did so without clearly defined roles, responsibilities, and daily activities. Chief Knowledge Officer positions are typically created to leverage knowledge into tangible business benefits. Similarly, CLO positions are designed to leverage learning through the culture of an organization, the type of knowledge and learning it wants to emphasize, and how technologically focused it is.

Unlike CKOs, the roots for most Chief Learning Officer positions, on the other hand, are in human resources, organization development, or sales and marketing (Bonner, 2000). Most incumbent CLOs have strong backgrounds in learning strategies and a strong orientation toward setting and reaching business goals. They have been selected from such positions as director of training or vice president of sales and marketing. CLOs are committed to the strategic integration of organizational and individual learning at all levels and across all functional silos. Their primary objectives are often to change their organizations' mind-sets from training (usually defined as a classroom-based delivery system) to continuous learning and human performance improvement, and to use a wider variety of delivery methods such as virtual learning options, corporate universities, and self-directed learning.

Chief Learning Officers are not glorified training directors. Baard (2002) points out that initially the CLO was concerned primarily with organizational learning and initiatives such as e-learning, but the role has expanded to help transform the organization into a learning organization. The CLO's primary success factor is being a businessperson first and then understanding how to drive through a strategic initiative. CLOs must be able to communicate in business-tangible results, think strategically, and talk the language of other executives. CLOs are strategic leaders who help senior management translate learning into strategic business capabilities.

Gale (2003) describes Dell's CLO role, filled by John Coné who retired as Dell's Chief Learning Officer in August 2001, but the company never replaced him—not because the CLO position is a passing concept but because Coné believed that his work as the CLO was done. He had been with Dell since 1995 and was given the official title of CLO in 1999, although he says that actually he always worked in that capacity. His job was to define the policies and infrastructure that would make Dell a distributed learning organization where employees have access to training whenever and wherever they need it. Ultimately, that meant making learning such an inherent part of how they did their jobs that it became an unremarkable event in employees' lives, he says. He achieved that goal in part by making training a necessary piece of every new product release. "We wanted training to be a natural part of the development process," he says. Today, new products at Dell do not move forward unless the necessary training for the product release is in place and deployed. Since Dell comes out with thousands of new products every year, training quickly became a constant in employees' lives.

During his six years at the company, Coné also oversaw the organization's vast e-learning program. His team transformed more than 90% of the company's learning content to technology-based formats, putting employees in control of their own learning, 24 hours a day, seven days a week. Admittedly, Coné is not sure if he was successful in making learning a permanent part of the culture at Dell. The traditional measures for training success, including the number of hours people are in training, executive involvement, and the percentage of payroll dedicated to learning, show that his efforts are still going strong, but it has been only two years. "I don't know if the ideas are deep enough in the fabric of the culture to survive long-term."

Willis and May (2000) describe the CLO as:

- A strategic, lead player in today's business organization.
- One whose core responsibility is to make sure learning across an entire system is leveraged, not sacrificed.
- Accountable to the whole system and given broad discretionary power.
- One who operates by using knowledge about how adults learn, how learning affects work, and how value systems operate, and how social and technical systems in an enterprise or in their environment may either support or counteract each other.

CLOs work with the "know-how" of knowledge—the tacit knowledge that is hard to codify. They integrate thinking and acting, and their work involves lots of errors and mistakes. CLOs need to create an environment that fosters knowledge sharing informally so that they can interact with a team in a work context. The CLO's work begins and ends with the customers. His or her work is applicable at each point in the continuous cycle that becomes spirals of need and need satisfaction. Customers validate and confirm the mission of the organization, which in turn drives the business strategy. Strategy involves inventing and choosing options, determines the culture needed to accomplish the strategy, and leads to modification of the systems in use to create competitive advantage. If there is advantage to the customers, they are satisfied and the mission of the company is once again ratified.

Some typical CLO initiatives would include:

1. *Cultural Transformation*—assisting with the development and communication of a new vision and strategy for the organization and tending to the cultural transformation to support the new corporate direction. Watkins and Marsick (1993) noted that training programs can help deliver skills needed for organizations to change, but do not address the deep-seated mental models and attitudes or the organizational structures and norms that perpetuate them.
2. *Culture Maintenance*—designed to support the marketplace strategy and to address deficiencies in skills essential to maintain the new culture developed.
3. *Contemporary Initiatives*—related to business development, like developing a new marketing plan, account manager development, or promotional process redesign. These require the CLO's in-depth experience in the industry, comfort/ease in working across all functions of the organization, and a whole systems viewpoint/thinking.

Because of the nature of work, CLOs have a limited number of quantitative performance indicators, most of which are budget related. The CLO's job focuses on management of projects, preparation of plan documents for projects including problem or opportunity synopsis, proposed solutions, action steps and timetable, deliverables, and projected costs. A CLO's performance is evaluated in terms of meeting objectives on target, on time, and on budget. The CLO serves as an unprecedented catalyst in organizations, combining technical and social work factors through communication and paving the way for employees to contribute their very best to the collective enterprise.

KM executives, whether they have a CKO or CLO title, are primarily responsible for ensuring that KM goals are in line with organizational strategies and objectives.

KM ROLES AND RESPONSIBILITIES WITHIN ORGANIZATIONS

The main types of KM roles observed in a wide range of private- and public-sector organizations can be summarized as follows:

1. Designing information systems (designing, evaluating, or choosing information content, database structures, indexing and knowledge representation, interfaces, networking, and technology.

2. Managing information systems (maintaining the integrity, quality, currency of the data, updating, modifying, improving the system, and operating the system).

3. Managing information resources (managing organizational information resources to support organizational missions and for competitive advantage).

4. Training (coaching, mentoring, community of practice start-up and life-cycle training support, and feeding back lessons learned, best practices into training content).

5. Serving as information agencies (acting as information consultants or guides for clients: advising, training, guiding on information, information sources, information use; acting as agents on behalf of clients: gathering, evaluating, analyzing, synthesizing, and summarizing information for clients).

6. Providing competitive intelligence.

7. Maintaining customer relations for information systems/technology (acting as intermediaries between clients and information system designers, translating client needs into functional specifications and sales).

8. Designing and producing information services and products publications, databases, information systems, multimedia products, and stories from storytelling workshops).

9. Serving as knowledge journalists.

10. Acting as organizational information and KM policy analysts (designing corporate, organizational information and KM policies access, quality control, maintaining proprietary information and KM, and mapping corporate intellectual assets).

11. Functioning as government KM policy analysts (formulating government policies at all levels regarding such issues as the KM infrastructure, access to and use of government information, intellectual property, privacy and public/private roles in knowledge creation, dissemination, and use, government acquisition of information and information technology).

KM roles can be found typically in those organizations concerned primarily with information content, such as publishers, database creators and providers, the press/mass media, new media companies (e.g., multimedia developers), information collectors (e.g., Reuters), data service companies (e.g., Mead), value-added providers (e.g., Standard and Poor's), and disciplinary societies (e.g., American Chemical Society). Also, organizations concerned primarily with information delivery offer a number of major KM roles. These would include companies such as telecommunications and cable companies, database vendors (e.g., DIALOG and networks), and service providers (e.g., BARNET, ANS).

Organizations concerned primarily with information technology have long had a number of key KM positions. These include the software industry, computer hardware companies, and systems integrators, especially to develop criteria for hardware and software and to optimize systems for customers and instructional technology development companies. Similarly, KM can be found in organizations concerned with information organization, access and preservation such as libraries (e.g., college/university libraries, public libraries, corporate libraries, school libraries, research libraries, and other special-purpose libraries such as hospital libraries), museums, archives, data centers, and hospitals and other medical organizations.

KM can be found in almost every type of organization today: law firms, medical practices, pharmaceutical companies, utilities, engineering firms, healthcare, government departments, banks and insurance companies, and the military sector. KM roles include the application of information technology—evaluation, selection, applications design; research and information gathering, synthesis, and evaluation—in libraries, competitive intelligence units, and records management. The government has been a KM leader in many areas. KM jobs are often found at governmental agencies engaged in information production and distribution (e.g., Bureau of Labor Statistics, Department of Commerce, National Center for Education Statistics, National Technical Information Service (NTIS), Education Resource Information Center (ERIC), U.S. Geological Survey, National Institutes of Health, Bureau of the Census, Patent and Trademark Office, United Nations, World Bank, and foreign governments); governmental agencies involved in information regulation; governmental agencies engaged in information technology assessment, development, and policy; information resources management to help agencies accomplish their missions; the intelligence community (e.g., CIA); and agencies involved in policy formulation/decision making as consumers of information (e.g., the Food and Drug Administration [FDA]).

A number of important KM functions are also found in other academic and research institutions such as large scientific enterprises (e.g., Human Genome Project, Mission to Planet Earth) and in the design and management of discipline-specific information systems. Ph.D.s in KM also follow an academic career path at universities or find employment in information industry firms for R&D and government agencies.

THE KM PROFESSION

Al-Hawamdeh (2003) refers to KM as an emerging profession. The field of KM has slowly evolved from a consulting service to an internal business function and has become an academic discipline that is being taught in universities worldwide. At the same time, many organizations are still in the process of defining their KM roles. There are a wide range of differing job titles and an even wider diversity in the backgrounds of KM practitioners. These factors are all contributing to the emergence of the KM profession. The KM field is fairly young when compared to older more established professions such as law, medicine, or engineering. As the KM skill set continues to grow and shows valuable contributions to the overall organizational goals, the profession will also continue to mature and coalesce as a distinct field of professional activity. A number of certification initiatives now under way will help solidify KM's position as a bona fide field of professional practice (e.g., the KMCI Certificate in

Knowledge and Information Management, www.kmci.org). At the same time, university programs in KM are proliferating, and a new class of KM graduates will soon be entering the KM job market. At the same time that KM has emerged and coalesced as both an academic discipline and a professional field of practice, there has been a growing awareness of the need to incorporate ethics into the job description of each KM team member.

The Ethics of KM

Ethics establishes a framework for making decisions based on values and for determining what is right and wrong. Laws create public policy built on government's presumption of what is best for its citizens. Legal aspects frequently attempt to codify ethical responsibilities but can differ from an individual's or organization's moral standards. An ethical code for a profession is a system of standards to which those in the field agree to conform (Rogus, 1997). Professionals in formal leadership roles have a responsibility to model the highest possible standards for those whom they manage. Perhaps our most important aspiration is that we understand how the larger culture supports a set of values centering on personal success, power, and popularity, and tends not to care about the means by which they are achieved.

The field of ethics, also called moral philosophy, involves systematizing, defending, and recommending concepts of right and wrong behavior (the Internet Encyclopedia of Philosophy, available at http://www.iep.utm.edu/e/ethics.htm). Philosophers today usually divide ethical theories into three general subject areas:

1. *Metaethics* investigates where our ethical principles come from and what they mean. Are they merely social inventions? Do they involve more than expressions of our individual emotions? Metaethical answers to these questions focus on the issues of universal truths, the will of God, the role of reason in ethical judgments, and the meaning of ethical terms themselves.
2. *Normative* ethics takes on a more practical task, which is to arrive at moral standards that regulate right and wrong conduct. This may involve articulating the good habits that we should acquire, the duties that we should follow, or the consequences of our behavior for others.
3. *Applied ethics* involves examining specific controversial issues, such as environmental concerns and how whistleblowers will be treated. By using the conceptual tools of metaethics and normative ethics, discussions in applied ethics try to resolve these controversial issues.

McElroy (2002) discusses recent accounting scandals that highlight the dangers of allowing dysfunctional knowledge processing in a corporate context. He points out that knowledge management can help generate a greater sense of openness in managerial decision making. KM can promote ethics by enhancing transparency in management where transparency is defined as openness with respect to knowledge and knowledge processes. In this way, it becomes possible to identify dysfunctional knowledge processes and bad practices or ideas. KM deals explicitly with the manner in which organizational knowledge is produced and integrated into practice. Openness should contribute not only to more ethical business practices but to innovation as well.

KM is the one management discipline that concerns itself with managing the quality and complexity of knowledge processing. No other body of management practice deals explicitly with the manner in which organizational knowledge is produced and integrated into practice. The transparency problem in business is fundamentally a knowledge management problem because bad practice is nothing more than bad knowledge in use, and bad knowledge in use is the product of dysfunctional knowledge processing. Separately, we can see that a move toward more openness or transparency in organizations not only has an impact on illicit behaviors, but also serves to enhance innovation through greater inclusiveness in knowledge processing. By involving higher proportions of stakeholders in knowledge production and integration, organizations can avail themselves of both more quality control over knowledge in use and more stakeholder participation in the process, thereby adding to the depth and breadth of organizational creativity. Openness is, at once, a prescription for enhancing both corporate responsibility and business innovation.

It is also clear that knowledge management is uniquely well equipped to assist organizations in making the transition from relative states of "closedness" to greater openness in knowledge processing, primarily because KM is a management discipline that seeks to enhance knowledge processing. The targets of its interventions are always knowledge processing behaviors, not just their outcomes. This is often referred to as the "transparency" of an organization (Tapscott and Ticoll, 2003).

In terms of knowledge processing behaviors, ethics in KM consists of valuing human beings. Ethics is often considered to be a simple matter, but that is a fallacy. Much of ethics can be distilled down to boundaries—boundaries that can help employees of an organization stay on the correct side of organizational policy and help clarify ethical issues (Groff and Jones, 2003). Some examples of boundaries are landmarks, fences, and DMZs (demilitarized zones). A *landmark* is a high-level ethical guideline often built upon the company's culture (e.g., value the demonstration of social responsibility among their employees, promote recycling, donate to local charities, pay employees to work on community events), and these landmarks often can be conveyed through good stories. *Fences* are explicit boundaries that show exactly where an important ethical line lies (e.g., official company policies on ethics). They should be ubiquitous as policies define the fence and the procedures define operating within the limits of the ethical fence. *DMZs* are concerned with active compliance monitoring (e.g., monitoring of software licenses). They define exactly where the ethical line is, and they prevent employees from crossing the ethical line in order to monitor and report any violations.

Managing ethical liabilities involves four major processes:

1. *Prevention*, using codes of conduct and standard operating practices and providing landmarks, fences, and DMZs.

2. *Detection*, using automated systems to enforce and monitor ethical compliance and to verify appropriate use of company assets.
3. *Reporting*, where employees are able to report unethical behaviors ("whistleblowers") without suffering any retaliation.
4. *Investigation*, which often requires outside assistance in order to be thorough, fair, and neutral.

The challenge is, once again, a question of establishing and maintaining a dynamic balance: too much monitoring and regulation can lead to lack of innovation. Organizations must be able to continue rewarding and motivating innovative and creative behaviors, but this cannot be at the expense of cutting corners so drastically that ethical values become compromised.

What is needed is a KM code of ethics to help govern the professional practice of knowledge management work. A number of good examples exist that can serve as a basis or starting point, and a great deal of work is being done on this issue by the KMCI (Knowledge Management Certification Institute, http://www.kmci.org/). A good illustration is the code of ethics developed for health science librarians (available at http://www.mlanet.org/about/ethics.html) shown in Table 10-2.

Another good example exists in the U.S. federal government, particularly in the forestry sector. A list of key questions is used to assess and monitor the

TABLE 10-2
SAMPLE CODE OF ETHICS FROM MEDICAL LIBRARIES
ASSOCIATION (MLA)

Goals and principles for ethical conduct	The health sciences librarian believes that knowledge is the sine qua non of informed decisions in healthcare, education, and research, and the health sciences librarian serves society, clients, and the institution by working to ensure that informed decisions can be made.
Society	The health sciences librarian promotes access to health information for all and creates and maintains conditions of freedom of inquiry, thought, and expression that facilitate informed health care decisions.
Clients	The health sciences librarian works without prejudice to meet the client's information needs, respects the privacy of clients, protects the confidentiality of the client relationship, and ensures that the best available information is provided to the client.
Institution	The health sciences librarian provides leadership and expertise in the design, development, and ethical management of knowledge-based information systems that meet the information needs and obligations of the institution.
Profession	The health sciences librarian advances and upholds the philosophy and ideals of the profession, advocates and advances the knowledge and standards of the profession, conducts all professional relationships with courtesy and respect, and maintains high standards of professional integrity.

ethical "health" of the particular federal organization, such as: do senior leaders generate high levels of motivation and commitment in the workforce and promote ethical behavior through modeling, communication, training, accountability systems, and disclosure mechanisms? Some performance indicators that are used include the promotion of teamwork, continual feedback, and whistleblower rights and employee protection if they report wrongdoings.

Morris (1997) emphasizes that the business world does not exist in isolation. Indeed, the way people think and act in clearly business contexts filters into all other social contexts as well. How can we overcome short-term, bottom-line thinking in order to do the right thing? Ethical decision making emerges when we abandon our self-centeredness. Why are ethical rules of conduct not enough? Because we can never have enough rules; moreover, rules have exceptions, they can conflict, and they require interpretation. Here one should observe the Golden or Universal Rule: Treat others the way you would want to be treated in their place.

KEY POINTS

- A number of studies have been undertaken to better describe the knowledge, skills, capabilities, and attitudes that good KM professionals require.
- KM skills span the range from business awareness and experience to management skills, learning abilities, communication and interpersonal skills, as well as information management and information technology expertise.
- In general, KM professionals should be proficient in retrieving information, evaluating/assessing information, organizing and analyzing content, presenting content, ensuring the security of content, and collaborating around valuable content.
- Major types of KM roles include knowledge manager, knowledge journalist, KM champion, KM navigator, knowledge synthesizer, content editor, knowledge publisher, coach or mentor, and help desk activities. More senior roles are Chief Learning Officer and Chief Knowledge Officer.
- CKOs ensure that KM goals are in line with organizational strategies and objectives.
- CLOs ensure that the organization acts like a learning organization, improving over time with the help of accumulated best practices and lessons learned.
- A wide range of organizations employ KM professionals, including private, academic, and public-sector companies.
- The KM profession is an emerging one and is in the process of examining the ethics that KM professionals should be espousing in their work. As with all professions, KM must be practiced in an ethical fashion. A KM Code of Ethics should be formulated and shared with key stakeholders for all KM projects.

DISCUSSION POINTS

1. What are some of the major types of KM roles or jobs that exist in organizations today? Describe the types of tasks each would be expected to carry out.
2. How would you devise a training program or a course curriculum to train KM professionals in the critical job skills they will need in the workplace?
3. What types of competencies should be present in a good KM team? What is the contribution of each skill set?
4. List some of the major types of organizations that offer KM positions and discuss why they need these KM skills.
5. Compare and contrast professional KM training courses with academic degree programs that integrate KM within their curricula.
6. What core skills will KM professionals need in the next five years? Why do you feel these will be important in the future?
7. In your opinion, what are the three critical ethical issues facing KM? Why have you selected these as being critical?
8. Draft a sample code of ethics for KM professionals. Explain/justify each element in your proposed code. What would be the best way of publicizing this code? How would you make sure that KM professionals practice KM in an ethical fashion?

NOTE

[1] Posted on www.brint.com.

REFERENCES

Abell, A., and Oxbrow, N. (2001). *Competing with knowledge.* London: Library Association.

Al-Hawamdeh, S. (2003). *Knowledge management: cultivating knowledge professionals.* Rollinsford, NH: Chandos Publishing.

Baard, M. (2002). Chief learning officer role taking on new importance. *Search-CIO.com.* Available at http://searchcio.techtarget.com/originalContent/0,289142, sid19_gci858958,00.html.

Davenport, T. H., and Prusak, L. (1997). *Information ecology: mastering the information and knowledge environment.* New York: Oxford University Press.

Davenport, T. H., and Prusak, L. (1998). *Working knowledge: how organizations manage what they know.* Boston: Harvard Business School Press.

Earl, M. J., and Scott, I. A. (1999). Opinion: What is a chief knowledge officer? *Sloan Management Review, 40*(2): 29–38.

Gale, S. (2003). For some chief learning officers, one of the goals is job insecurity. *Workforce Management, 11*: 79–81. Available online at http://www.workforce.com/section/11/feature/23/53/77/.

Goade, J. (2000). Problem solving skills for the information age: from concept to practice. JMS Project, Millikin University. Available at http://www.millikin.edu/pkm/pkm_ascue.html.

Gordon, J. R. (2002). *Organizational behavior: a diagnostic approach*. Englewood Cliffs, NJ: Prentice Hall.

Groff, T., and Jones, T. (2003). *Introduction to knowledge management*. Boston: Butterworth-Heinemann.

McElroy, M. (2002). Ethics, innovation and the open enterprise. *Knowledge Management*, 6(1). Available at http://www.kmmagazine.com/xq/asp/sid.0/articleid.20C04C34-11CE-45AE-8815-CAAB07EE516D/qx/display.htm.

Morris, T. (1997). *If Aristotle ran General Motors: the new soul of business*. New York: Henry Holt and Company.

Rogus, J. (1997). Being ethical: maintaining a perspective of vigilance. *School Business Affairs*, 63(2): 58–59.

Rusonow, G. (2003). *Knowledge management and the smarter lawyer*. New York: ALM Publishing.

Skyrme, D. (1997). Do you need a chief knowledge officer. Available at http://www.skyrme.com/insights/27cko.htm.

Stewart, T. A. (1998). Is this job really necessary? *Fortune*, 137(1): 154–155.

Tapscott, D., and Ticoll, D. (2003). *The naked corporation. How the age of transparency will revolutionize business*. Toronto, ON: Viking Canada Press.

Thurow, L. (2003). *Fortune favors the bold: what we must do to build a new and lasting global prosperity*. New York: HarperBusiness.

Thurow, L. (2004). Help wanted: a chief knowledge officer. *Fast Company*, 78. Available online at http://www.fastcompany.com/magazine/78/helpwanted.html.

Watkins, K., and Marsick, V. (1993). Sculpting the learning organization. Lessons in the art and science of systematic change. San Francisco: Jossey-Bass.

Willis, V., and May, G. (2000). Strategy and the chief learning officer. In J. Phillips and D. Bonner (Eds.), *In action: leading knowledge management and learning*, pp. 55–70. Alexandria, VA: American Society for Training and Development.

FUTURE CHALLENGES FOR KM

The gem cannot be polished without friction.

—Chinese proverb

Knowledge management objectives are ambitious and almost always involve change at the individual, group and organization levels. As a result, the objectives are almost never easily achieved or straightforward. A number of critical challenges must be successfully addressed in order to obtain the maximum value for KM investments—in terms of both budget and time and human resources. This chapter explores some issues facing knowledge management, such as political issues regarding Internet search engines, the shift to knowledge-based assets, and how to provide incentives for knowledge sharing to successfully incorporate KM into organizations.

LEARNING OBJECTIVES

1. Discuss the politics of information seeking and what this implies for successful knowledge management applications. Be able to outline how this would impact the design of an organizational memory management system.
2. Describe the five major types of information politics models and how knowledge-sharing activities would take place in each of them. Be able to evaluate each model with respect to "goodness of fit" with KM requirements.
3. Define the paradox of value and explain how it impacts the design of KM solutions. Describe ways in which this impact can be minimized.

303

4. Compare and contrast the different ways incentives can be provided for knowledge sharing.
5. Understand and critically debate where KM stands today, particularly with respect to how well initial expectations of KM have been met.
6. Outline the major reasons why KM may be perceived as a success or a failure and discuss how you would improve upon ROI measures for KM.
7. Describe the key areas of research in the field of KM today and make educated guesses about how these new developments will impact KM.
8. List the key challenges KM faces today and in the near future and provide some recommended approaches to best address them.
9. Summarize the history of KM to date and predict some directions that the field may take with respect to the profession, the education of KM professionals, and the types of KM implementations that will be undertaken in organizations.

INTRODUCTION

The major challenges facing KM include focusing on people or cultural issues, overemphasizing technology, conducting KM in isolation from business goals, ignoring the dynamic aspects of content, and opting for quantity of content over quality. Although this is not an exhaustive list, there does appear to be a fairly good consensus on the most important challenges that are facing KM. These can be found as recurring themes in KM discussion groups, conferences, and publications (e.g., Firestone and McElroy, 2003; Tannenbaum and Alliger, 2000).

The major problems that occur in KM usually result because companies ignore the people and cultural issues. In an environment where an individual's knowledge is valued and rewarded, establishing a culture that recognizes tacit knowledge and encourages employees to share it is critical. The need to sell the KM concept to employees should not be underestimated; after all, in many cases employees are being asked to surrender their knowledge and experience— the very traits that make them valuable as individuals. One way companies motivate employees to participate in KM is by creating an incentive program. However, there is the danger that employees will participate solely to earn incentives, without regard to the quality or relevance of the information they contribute. The best KM efforts are as transparent to employees' workflow as possible. Ideally, participation in KM should be its own reward. If KM does not make life easier for employees, it will fail. This is why the role of organizational culture is so important, together with any cultural change that needs to take place in order to better accommodate any KM initiatives.

KM is not a technology-based concept. All-inclusive KM solutions, despite any vendor claims to the contrary, simply do not exist. Companies that implement a centralized database system, electronic message board, web portal, or any other collaborative tool in the hope that they have established a KM program are wasting both their time and money. Although technology can support KM, it is not the starting point of a KM program. KM decisions should be based on who (people), what (knowledge), and why (business objectives), and you should save the how (technology) for last. In other words, successful KM begins with a sound KM strategy combined with a fostering organizational culture that enables and rewards the sharing of valuable knowledge.

A KM program should never be divorced from a business goal. For example, whereas sharing best practices is a commendable idea, there must be an underlying business reason to do so. Without a solid business case, KM is a futile exercise. Knowledge is also not static. Since knowledge can get stale fast, the content in a KM program should be constantly updated, amended, and deleted. What is more, the relevance of knowledge at any given time changes, as do the skills of employees. Therefore, a KM program has no end point. Like product development, marketing, and R&D, KM is a constantly evolving business practice. Finally, companies need to be vigilant for information overload. Quantity rarely equals quality, and KM is no exception. Indeed, the point of a KM program is to identify and disseminate knowledge gems from a sea of information.

Three key critical issues are discussed in this chapter:

1. *Access issues*: What political issues govern Internet information seeking? What are some of the factors hindering employees from accessing critical knowledge within their organizations?
2. *Organizational issues*: What is the political context of the organization, and how does this context affect KM? How can a KM-friendly culture be encouraged? How can one provide incentives for knowledge sharing?
3. *Valuing issues*: What is the impact of a shift from resource-based assets to knowledge-based assets (i.e., from tangible, measurable assets to intangible ones)? How can knowledge assets be valued?

These three major categories of KM issues are presented in greater detail in the following sections.

POLITICAL ISSUES REGARDING ACCESS

The term *Googlewhacking*, which has entered our language recently, refers to the "challenging pursuit of searching the popular Google search engine with a two-word or more search argument that will produce exactly (no less and no more than) one result. That is, only one web page in the world (at least as indexed by Google) will happen to have the combination of words you've entered in the search box" (see http://www.googlewhack.com/). Some examples of past "Googlewhacks" that have been successful include word pairs such as comparative unicyclist, maladroit wheezer, blithering clops, and demurrable insufficiencies. Both the term and the occupation of Googlewhacking are the inventions of Gary Stock (see http://www.googlewhack.com/ and http://www.unblinking.com), Chief Innovation Officer, Nexcerpt, Inc.

The raison d'etre of this phenomenon lies with the information overload issue: the number of hits that are returned for a given search term is incredible and yet not particularly useful. For example, what results from typing "knowledge management?" It is interesting to compare the results to the concept analysis technique that was presented in Chapter 1. For example, Weinberger (1998) used the key words *human, user, change management, knowledge worker,* and *person* and kept a tally of the number of hits returned using those key terms. This can then be compared to the hits obtained when technology-related key terms are used such as *processor, RAID, mouse, Internet,* and *repository.* The number of hits obtained with KM technology terms far exceeds the number of hits obtained with nontechnology terms. This finding is partially attributable to the fact that there are possibly more technology publications, but it illustrates that the "human" is often the last thing considered as organizations change their technology. This is a key reason many technology initiatives result in failure: neglecting the human element.

To make matters worse, there is a common misconception that the commercial search engines perform an objective and exhaustive search of all things digital and that the hits are ranked—that is, the first hit is the most relevant to what you were looking for. Nothing, of course, could be further from the truth. Introna and Nissenbaum (2000) argue that search engines raise not merely technical issues but also political ones. Their study of search engines suggests that they systematically exclude (in some cases by design and in other cases accidentally) certain sites and certain types of sites in favor of others, systematically giving prominence to some at the expense of others. Such biases would lead to a narrowing of the web's functioning in society and run counter to the basic architecture of the web as well as to the values and ideals that have fueled widespread support for its growth and development. It is doubtful that the market mechanism could serve as an acceptable corrective.

Users are largely ignorant of what goes on "under the hood," and this ignorance is compounded by their unusually high degree of trust in "what the computer says." A study conducted by Lawrence and Giles (1999) found that *none* of the search engines individually indexed more than 16% of the total indexable content of the Web. Taken together, they indexed about 42% of the accessible content. Search engines are only partially effective at finding things, and a great deal of the web remains "hidden." This is not, however, simply due to technological constraints (Kautz, Selman, and Shah, 1997) as is popularly believed. The politics of information seeking must be taken into account with organizational knowledge management systems in order to ensure that the best possible (i.e., the most relevant, valid, and up-to-date) content is found, retrieved, and made available to the organization's knowledge workers.

The politics of information seeking on the Internet are mirrored by problems experienced by employees who seek knowledge from their organizational sources. Organizations typically approach their intranets or knowledge repositories as knowledge warehouses. Given the relatively low cost of storing digital content, many companies simply decide to "keep everything," believing that the content will someday be required by someone. This is true of course—

except that "the someone" needing to access that content someday will likely not be able to find it!

Access remains a critical KM issue, and the situation can only worsen with time. Business drivers such as increasing globalization, mobilization, doing more faster, and the expectation to be "on" 24/7/365 due to connection technologies such as cell phones and the Internet only serve to increase the expectations of being able to find the best possible information almost instantaneously. Tolerance for delays (a two-week turnaround time by surface mail!) has evaporated, and today's work environment is increasingly knowledge-intensive and scarce in resources such as time. Organizations need to tackle the thorny issue of content organization, management, and optimization if they are to survive the deluge of information and knowledge that is being created, shared, stored, and accessed.

THE POLITICS OF ORGANIZATIONAL CONTEXT AND CULTURE

KM must address not only the information itself but also the business practices and processes that generate the information. Hence, the politics of organizational context and culture must also be taken into consideration. For example, at Dow Chemical, managers believe there should be a common set of financial processes around the world to create common measures of financial performance, whereas IBM relies on more traditional measures such as customer satisfaction, time to market, and cost evaluation. The organizational context will thus affect KM implementation and the evaluation of how successful this implementation was.

Five models of information politics can be used to characterize the politics of the organizational context and culture (Klein, 1999; Davenport, Eccles, and Prusak, 1992). They are: (1) technocratic utopianism, (2) anarchy, (3) feudalism, (4) monarchy, and (5) federalism.

In *technocratic utopianism*, a heavily technical approach is taken to information and knowledge management stressing categorization and the modeling of an organization's full information assets (often in the form of an exhaustive inventory). There is heavy reliance on emerging technologies, and content tends to be driven by the information system. The focus is on detailed corporate data rather than knowledge. The underlying assumption is that technology will resolve all problems, with the consequence that little attention is paid to content and its use. Data is perceived as a corporate asset.

In the *anarchy* model, there is an absence of overall information management policy. Individuals are left to their own devices to obtain and manage their own information, which is made possible by the introduction of the personal computer. Anarchy models are often seen in early stages of start-ups. They stand at the opposite end of the spectrum from the technocratic model with little if any classification of corporate information possible (e.g., of revenues, costs, and customer order levels). This model rarely represents a conscious choice but instead, with time, tends to evolve into some sort of order.

The *feudalism* model is based on the management of information by individual business units or functions, which define their own information needs and report only limited information to the overall corporation. This is the most commonly encountered model, with its emphasis on "the control of information" and "knowledge is power." The "king" decides on content, language, format, distribution list, and the analysis. Key organizational and environmental information is often ignored, and it is quite difficult to make informed decisions.

In the *monarchy* model, the firm's leaders define information categories and reporting structures and may or may not share the information willingly after having collected it. The CEO, or someone empowered by the CEO, dictates the rules for how information will be managed. This model represents an extreme top-down model that is commonly found in entrepreneurial profiles and among small business owners and micromanagers. This model is appropriate when consensus cannot be reached.

A constitutional monarchy can evolve directly from feudalism or monarchies. There is a document (a "Magna Carta")—an information management charter—that states the monarch's limitations. This document identifies what information will be collected, rules, processes, platforms, common vocabulary, and so on.

Finally, the *federalism* model emphasizes an approach to information management based on consensus and negotiation on the organization's key information elements and reporting structures. This is the preferred model for most intellectual capital management applications because it makes extensive use of negotiation to bring potentially competing and noncompeting parties together. People with different interests work out among themselves a collective purpose and a means of achieving it. Federalism requires strong (but not too strong) central leadership and a culture of trust, cooperation, and learning. It is important to understand the value of information itself as well as that of the technology that stores, manipulates, and distributes it. Federalism encourages the use of cooperative information resources to create a shared information vision for genuine leveraging of a firm's knowledge assets in the form of data marts, not exhaustive data warehouses. As a result, this model is also a very good fit with communities of practice.

It is important to critically assess an organization and to identify the type of political model that is in place so that potential KM barriers can be better anticipated. Organizational diagnostics such as an assessment of the prevailing culture, attitudes toward knowledge (sharing vs. hoarding), and the reward and censure systems that are in place can help understand the level of KM readiness that exists within a given organization. This baseline measure will help devise strategies to move the organization one level up, to transform the culture of the organization, and to move it toward a "KM-enabled" cultural context that will promote successful KM implementations. A key ingredient of the KM-enabled culture lies with incentives to promote knowledge sharing. Culture remains one of the critical KM issues to be addressed, and change management increasingly goes hand in hand with any KM objective.

How to Provide Incentives for Knowledge Sharing

KM practitioners often neglect the crucial management issues of organizational learning, motivation, and culture when formulating a knowledge management strategy. Knowledge workers need to have a climate in which knowledge sharing is encouraged, and they need a reason for sharing the knowledge. Incentives remain one of the more important challenges facing KM today. An incentive is a reward or some form of positive feedback given when a desired behavior is exhibited. Since human beings are purposeful creatures who would tend to continue to exhibit behaviors associated with positive rewards and to avoid those behaviors that lead to negative consequences, it seems reasonable to expect that incentives for knowledge sharing should lead to more sharing of knowledge. This being said, the situation is, as always, not so clear cut.

Incentives can be quite tricky to get right because what is perceived as a reward by some may be seen as an insult by others. An example is the system of recognition. In one company, the public posting of a "knowledge sharer of the month" serves to motivate employees to share more knowledge. In another context, employees feel that as highly educated professionals, they should not be reduced to something that reminds them of a plaque used by fast-food companies to motivate their staff. *De gustibus non disputatum*—of tastes there is no disagreeing. In other words, the reward should fit the person being rewarded. At a minimum, employees should be allowed to choose their reward from a list of possibilities. At Buckman Labs, as noted earlier, this problem was resolved by polling the employees, and the top choice turned out to be a fully equipped laptop computer to be conferred on the top KM citizens flown in to headquarters for a public remittance of the prize by the president himself.

It may be helpful to look at how incentives can be classified according to the different ways in which they motivate agents to take a particular course of action. One common and useful taxonomy developed by Callahan (2004) divides incentives into three broad classes:

1. *Remunerative incentives* (or *financial incentives*) are said to exist where an agent can expect some form of material reward—especially money—in exchange for acting in a particular way.
2. *Moral incentives* are said to exist where a particular choice is widely regarded as the right thing to do, or as particularly admirable, or where the failure to act in a certain way is condemned as indecent. A person acting on a moral incentive can expect a sense of self-esteem and approval or even admiration from her community; a person acting against a moral incentive can expect a sense of guilt and condemnation, or even ostracism, from the community.
3. *Coercive incentives* are said to exist where a person can expect that the failure to act in a particular way will result in physical force being used against him or her (or her loved ones) by others in the community—for example, by punishment, imprisonment, firing, or confiscating or destroying their possessions.

These categories are not an exhaustive list of all types of incentives. For example, personal incentives are related to preferences, personal objectives that may motivate actions of individual people. The reason for setting these sorts of incentives to one side is not that they are less important to understanding human action. Personal incentives are essential to understanding why a specific person acts the way he or she does, but social analysis has to take into account the situation faced by any individual in a given position within a given society, which means mainly examining the practices, rules, and norms established at a social, rather than a personal, level.

Quite intuitively, if there is no economic, social, or personal incentive for any individual to do work, it will not get done. Therefore, a society must provide incentives for the work necessary for its own maintenance. Similarly, a company or organization that provides incentives for its members to improve said institution will usually have better results. One that provides no or little incentive will suffer from weak morale.

Incentive is very much a double-edged sword. For example, corporate policies—especially of the "extreme incentive" variant popular during the 1990s—with the goal of encouraging productivity may not have the intended effect. For example, stock options, intended to boost CEO productivity by tying CEO compensation to company performance, were blamed for many of the falsified earnings reports and public statements in the late 1990s and early 2000s. Throughout the 1990s and 2000s, many corporations have sought to increase individual incentives by increasing the sizes of bonuses (to the point where they exceed salaries, sometimes by a factor as high as 10) for star performers while also laying off large proportions of their workforce, hoping to cultivate fear-factor-related gains. The most extreme version of this is "forced ranking," a scheme by which workers are annually ranked and a set proportion (usually between 10 and 15%) is automatically fired. The results of these programs are mixed but in extreme cases usually negative.

Whereas competition among firms often has beneficial results, lowering prices and encouraging innovation, competition within firms has almost uniformly negative results. Designed to encourage production, extreme incentive schemes actually create a cutthroat working environment where office politics dominate and actually overshadow the productive goals of the company. An example is the now-defunct Enron Corporation. According to Callahan (2004), the environment at that company was so cutthroat (as a result of extreme incentive management) that employees feared leaving their computer terminals, worried that co-workers might steal information for their own purposes.

Obviously, some issues exist with KM as it is applied in many organizations, and care needs to be taken that the application of this effective approach is accepted and supported. It is *not* the information collection but the processes and systems that must be acceptable to those involved. Business issues as well as people issues are involved, and a simple framework might be helpful in understanding and rolling forward. Remember, nobody ever washes a rental car, so address issues of ownership and involvement as you progress.

Denning (2000) points out that since knowledge sharing usually entails a change in the way the business of an organization is conducted—often, it entails a shift from vertical "look up and yell down" modes of behavior to horizontal knowledge-sharing behaviors—relevant behaviors should be reflected in whatever incentive systems are in place in the organization. The value of knowledge sharing should be reflected in the ongoing personnel evaluation, periodic merit review, or pay bonuses of the organization, so that managers and staff can see that knowledge sharing is one of the principal behaviors that the organization encourages and rewards.

Knowledge sharing should be designated as one of a small number of core behaviors that are rewarded in the performance review system. It is not easy to get agreement across a large organization to focus on knowledge sharing as one of a small number of core behaviors, and even when it is accomplished, there is no instant effect. In the short run, there is often cynicism and posturing, but the experience of organizations, particularly the large consulting firms, is that over time such a change sends an unmistakable signal throughout the organization, which accelerates the intended behavioral change.

In practice, informal incentives, in the form of recognition by management, and visibility within the organization can often be more powerful incentives than the formal incentive system. Although the establishment of formal incentives is important for the long-run sustainability of a knowledge management program, it is easy to overestimate the value of incentives. The absence of formal incentives in the early days of knowledge sharing can become a pretext for not implementing the program. The establishment of rewards for individual knowledge-sharing activities can signal the importance of knowledge sharing, but can also run the risk of creating expectations of rewards for behavior that should be part of the normal way of conducting the business of the organization.

In the long term, however, the establishment of incentives through the organization's regular personnel and reward system can establish a clear value framework that confirms that knowledge sharing, rather than being a mere management fad, is part of the permanent fabric of the organization.

Stevens (2000) discusses how organizations use a variety of incentives to show that they are serious about sharing knowledge. For example, some organizations have rewards and recognition programs for knowledge sharers; these range from kudos in the company newsletter to substantial pay bonuses. Other companies evaluate employees for raises, advancement, and even extra vacation time on the basis partly of how much they participate in knowledge-sharing activities. Government departments are beginning to focus on social or group incentives over individual incentives by rewarding team projects or exemplary success in mentoring or otherwise sharing valuable knowledge. Buckman Labs invites top knowledge sharers to visit the headquarters to personally receive a state-of-the-art laptop as recognition. This incentive was chosen by surveying employees to ascertain what they felt a good reward for being a good knowledge sharer should be. Given that the "value is in the eye of the beholder," asking employees to suggest rewards they would like to receive is probably the best way to proceed. What is thought of as a reward may not necessarily be perceived in the same light as it was intended. In a science and technology group, for example, being named "Top Knowledge Sharer" was perceived as being slightly insulting (someone explained it was too much like "Employee of the Month" at a fast-food restaurant). In a multinational consulting company, a $50 bonus was offered for each contribution made to the organization's knowledge base. Again, the members of the organization perceived this as slightly embarrassing, yet this type of reward was quite welcome in a similar, albeit smaller, consulting company located in the same European country. Instead of trying to guess and risking sabotage of the incentive scheme, a representative needs assessment survey of the target group is by far the preferred option.

Traditional incentives, such as pay bonuses, are not always enough to change behavior. Stevens (2000) surveyed seven organizations about their efforts to encourage knowledge sharing. The following list is adapted from the best practices identified in the survey:

1. Hire people who are willing to encourage knowledge sharing from the beginning and to catalyze the necessary cultural change. This can be done by having current employees participate in the hiring process.
2. Develop trust. At Buckman Labs, a code of ethics is formally posted and deals with how to treat fellow employees properly, with respect, and to recognize and reward all contributions.
3. Vary motivations by providing different types of incentives at different levels within the organization in order to better reward executives, department heads, and individuals.
4. Show public recognition via plaques and newsletters as well as adding mentions to employees' permanent files.
5. Reorganize for sharing to leverage the fact that people naturally share knowledge with others in their own team and/or community of practice. Formalize natural inclinations to group around certain projects, themes, or professional skills.
6. Encourage, support, and sustain communities to promote the sharing of expertise, skills, technical knowledge, or even just professional interest in a particular subject matter. Enlarge the network of contacts that each employee has, and thus enlarge the scope of knowledge sharing that is possible.
7. Develop leaders and role models, for even a small group of KM enthusiasts within a company can be a powerful catalyst for knowledge sharing.

SIEMENS MEDICAL SOLUTIONS

Gale (2002) describes the case of Siemens Medical Solutions and how it decided to change its "knowledge is power" culture into one in which "knowledge sharing" was the norm. The company wanted employees to have easy access to information and expertise across business units so that they could do their jobs better and faster without reinventing the wheel. The problem was that many employees associated sharing knowledge with losing power. Taking the time to share information or to coach someone in a new skill was also perceived as a burden by busy employees. Employees saw no value in this activity.

In order to change that attitude, employees had to perceive an immediate and personal advantage to sharing information. To support the new environment, the company built three web-based knowledge-sharing tools through which employees could collect and disseminate useful information to the rest of the company. The first, "People of Med," is an online database of employee profiles that includes each member's contact information, experience, areas of expertise, and photograph. The second, "Communities of Practice," is an online meeting place where employees volunteer to host forums on specific topics, such as ISO 9001 certification challenges. Any employee interested in that topic can register and participate in conversations, and share materials that may be of value to the group. The third knowledge-sharing tool is the "Knowledge Square," an online database filled with presentations, websites, technical papers, specs, and any other materials of value to the company. Employees can search the database to quickly find information related to their area of interest. To encourage employees to take advantage of the knowledge-sharing opportunities, they receive bonus points every time they use one of the three tools. These bonus points can be used to purchase items from a gift catalog that includes everything from T-shirts to vacations. Whether they store their profiles in People of Med, participate in a community, or download information from the Knowledge Square, they get rewarded. Community leaders are also encouraged to throw parties for their members where they can share stories of successful knowledge-tool users in company newsletters, marketing materials, and broadcast e-mails.

SHIFT TO KNOWLEDGE-BASED ASSETS

The paradox of value (Boisot, 1998) lies in the fact that the easier it is to extract the knowledge, the less value it actually embodies. That is to say, the greater the tacitness of knowledge, the greater its value (see Figure 11-1).

Knowledge assets are a source of competitive advantage for firms that possess them. Yet the way the possession of knowledge translates into a competitive advantage is not well understood. Of course, obtaining this advantage does not happen automatically—a firm has to know how to *extract* value from knowledge assets. There are also definite costs incurred in managing knowledge assets (Boisot, 1998), notably:

- In moving knowledge, data processing and data transmission costs.
- Codification costs due to searching, selections made under uncertainty.
- Abstraction costs arising from generalizing knowledge over wider problem spaces.

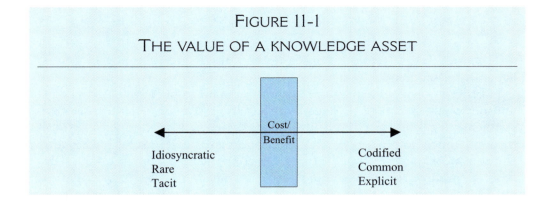

FIGURE 11-1

THE VALUE OF A KNOWLEDGE ASSET

Cost/Benefit

Idiosyncratic
Rare
Tacit

Codified
Common
Explicit

- Diffusion costs when communicating with potentially large audiences in ways that can be understood and can lead to effective responses.
- Absorption costs when getting potential recipients of new knowledge to internalize it and familiarize themselves with it.
- Costs of applying internalized knowledge in a variety of concrete situations.

Classical theories of value focus on resource-based, largely renewable, nature's bounty with little concern about the role of information or knowledge. Labor power put into the equation is largely unadulterated by knowledge, skills, or expertise. Technical advances are made on behalf of all individuals and not for any single individual. Land, labor, and physical factors of production constitute the basis of this traditional approach.

We need to consider the value of information goods more closely, however. In the second half of the nineteenth century, value ceased to be regarded as an intrinsic property of the energy inputs required for production. Instead, value became relational and contingent. The focus was still primarily on physical goods but knowledge played a supporting role. An information good cannot be inspected prior to purchase. The value of a knowledge asset is derived from the utility of services it renders over time and the fact that it offers a competitive advantage over those who do not possess it. This lies at the core of the definition of an intellectual asset as discussed in Chapter 9.

This leads to another paradox associated with a knowledge asset: knowledge transfer does not require physical contiguity. It does require codification and abstraction, however. Since cost is involved with this approach, one should only select information with potential value and utility that will justify the time and effort required. Yet the more "transferable" we make knowledge, the less scarce it becomes. We therefore need reliable ways of measuring intangibles when valuing intellectual capital. An excellent overview of the major measures and techniques used to assess intellectual capital can be found in Sveiby (2001). In general, most approaches agree that three different types of intellectual capital need to be considered:

1. *Human capital*, the ability of individuals and teams to apply solutions to customer needs, competencies, mind-sets.

2. *Organizational capital*, the codified knowledge, culture, values, norms.
3. *Customer capital*, the strength of customer relationship, superior customer-perceived value, and customized solutions.

The intellectual capital model is thus the relationship between human, customer, and organizational capital that maximizes the organization's potential to create value (see Figure 11-2).

Measurement success stories in a number of companies such as Dow Chemical, Skandia, Buckman Labs, the World Bank, and CIBC are outlined in the Knowledge Management of Internal Best Practices Report, available at http://www.bestpracticedatabase.com.

In 1993, before the words "Intellectual Capital" and "Knowledge Management" became industry buzzwords, Dow Chemical began to realize that its database of over 29,000 patents represented a gold mine in underutilized intellectual capital. Over time, the company's database had become little more than a dusty, neglected filing cabinet. To combat this neglect, Gordon Petrash was hired to direct Dow's intellectual asset management. Once in office, Petrash took immediate action to identify and index all of Dow's patents. His initial review revealed that fewer than one-half of Dow's patents were being utilized. Understanding the value waiting to be discovered, Petrash worked to develop patent portfolios for each of Dow's business units. All unused patents were indexed and checked for royalty opportunities, including:

- Projected costs until expiration.
- Percentage of annual intellectual asset management costs of R&D budget.

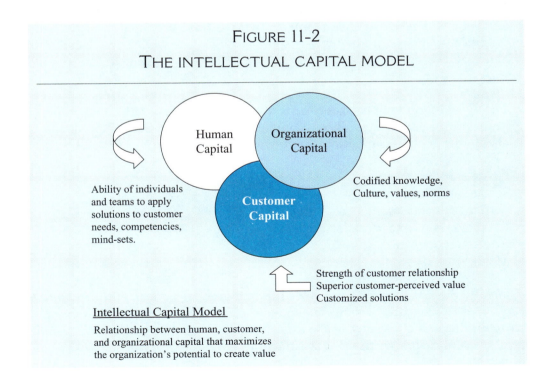

FIGURE 11-2

THE INTELLECTUAL CAPITAL MODEL

Human Capital

Organizational Capital

Customer Capital

Ability of individuals and teams to apply solutions to customer needs, competencies, mind-sets.

Codified knowledge, Culture, values, norms

Strength of customer relationship
Superior customer-perceived value
Customized solutions

Intellectual Capital Model

Relationship between human, customer, and organizational capital that maximizes the organization's potential to create value

- Percentage of competitive samples analyzed that initiate business actions by purpose.
- Percentage of business using.
- Percentage of business will use . . .

Dow credits Petrash's actions for saving more than $1 million in patent maintenance fees within the first 18 months. Petrash estimated that, in addition to an estimated $50 million in tax savings, Dow would increase its annual licensing and patent revenue to $125 million in the year 2000. In effect, Dow expected to reap a benefit of $175 million by better managing its most obvious intellectual assets.

The Skandia Navigator (Edvinsson, 1997) makes use of four types of dimensions:

1. *Financial Focus*: gross premium income, insurance result.
2. *Customer Focus*: satisfied customer index, customer loyalty, market share.
3. *Human Focus*: number of employees, average age, empowerment index.
4. *Process Focus*: operating expense ratio, premium income/salesperson; net claims ratio.

In addition, renewal and development are assessed by looking at training expense/employee and sales-oriented operations. In all, 21 indicators are used to measure IC, with 9 indicators used to measure efficiency of use of IC.

At Buckman Labs, the following metrics are used:

- Percentage of company effectively engaged with customer (target = 80%).
- Percentage of revenues invested in knowledge transfer system.
- Number of college graduates.
- Sales of new products less than five years old as a percentage of total sales.

The World Bank emphasizes the creation of knowledge, public expenditure on education relative to GNP, and public expenditure on education absolute. It also looks at the assimilation of knowledge through such metrics as:

- Gross enrollment rate.
- Secondary education.
- Tertiary education.
- Literacy—newspaper readership.
- Adult literacy rate.
- Mean years of schooling.

Finally, the CIBC takes three major dimensions into consideration: *human capital* consisting of the skills individuals need to meet customer demands, *structural capital* consisting of the information required to understand specific markets, and *customer capital* consisting of essential data about the bank's customer base.

Similarly, Sveiby's Intangible Asset Monitor (Sveiby, 1997) focuses on external structure, internal structure, and the competencies of people. External structure contains customers, suppliers, and other "external" stakeholders, and one selects those that are relevant. Most private companies will use customers, and in the public sector organizations will use other stakeholders, such as community members. Many companies have so many valuable alliances with their suppliers that they must be included too. Internal departments will have internal "customers," which will form their external structure. Tobin's q (Tobin, 1998) is a metric that looks at the ratio between the market value stock price multiplied by the outstanding shares and replacement value of physical assets. This metric serves to quantify the value of knowledge at the global level on an objective basis.

In order to complete the cycle, it is also extremely important to know when to divest knowledge assets. We need to understand why, when, where, and how to formally divest parts of the knowledge base. After having invested so much, how can we throw it away? An opportunity cost analysis should be carried out to identify which knowledge assets are no longer contributing to competitive advantage. Examples of divesting knowledge would include:

- Selling, licensing, and donating a patent.
- Spinning off or selling a business unit.
- Outsourcing a function of the operating process.
- Terminating a training program.
- Retaining, relocating, or firing individuals with obsolete or ill-fitted skills.
- Replacing or upgrading information technology systems.
- Terminating partnerships, alliances, and contracts.

Figure 11-3 summarizes the different types of intellectual assets and the relative ease with which their value can be extracted.

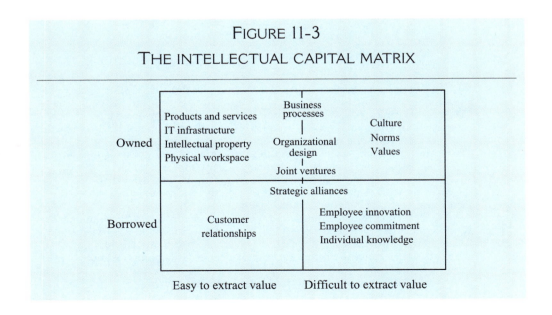

FIGURE 11-3
THE INTELLECTUAL CAPITAL MATRIX

What lies ahead for KM? One camp predicts no future for KM, citing a number of KM failures to deliver. This gloomy forecast can be mitigated somewhat: it is true that, as with all innovation, initial expectations were on the unrealistic side, partly because the people component of KM was underestimated at the same time that the role of KM technology in KM solutions was overemphasized. According to Pollard (2003), this failure was the result of the unrealistic expectation that human organizational behavior could be easily and rapidly changed. Of course, behavioral change at the individual level and cultural change at the organizational level are two very difficult and lengthy processes. The KM "quick fix" was therefore vastly misleading.

The return on KM investments should not be perceived exclusively as short-term gains but rather should be seen as long-term process, people, and organizational improvements. Unfortunately, people change their behavior only when there is an overwhelmingly compelling argument to do so (there is no "leap of faith" on which much of KM was predicated), or where there is simply no alternative. Skyrme (2002), for example, discusses some of the cornerstones of KM as summarized in Table 11-1.

Before KM, the way in which people shared knowledge was person-to-person, just-in-time, and in the context of solving a specific business problem. With the increasingly widespread adoption of KM, knowledge management processes such as knowledge creation/capture, knowledge sharing/dissemination, and knowledge acquisition/application have begun to form part and parcel of how organizations conduct their core business and how knowledge workers conduct their work activities in an efficient and effective manner.

Another way of looking at what lies ahead for KM is to inventory the types of research that are being conducted on KM issues.

TABLE 11-1
SUMMARY OF KM CORNERSTONES

1.	Steady and pervasive growth—into almost every business function and geographic location.
2.	The holistic perspective of people, processes, and technology—as many organizations still find out to their cost, you cannot simply put in KM technical solutions and leave the realization of business benefits to chance.
3.	The knowledge cycle—from creation to identifying, gathering, classifying, storing, accessing, exploiting, protecting (and many activities in between).
4.	Conducting of information audits and development of knowledge maps.
5.	The classification of intellectual capital into customer capital, structural (organizational) capital, and human capital.
6.	The need for KM to demonstrate its value to the organization's "bottom line."
7.	Communities of practice, and the importance of nurturing, and not trying to manage or control them.
8.	The Internet as an infrastructure for communication, collaboration, and information sharing.
9.	The need to root knowledge into its environment and context.

Some examples of research being conducted in the area of KM include Thomas, Kellogg, and Erickson (2001), who are exploring the role of social and cognitive factors in knowledge codification. The simple picture of knowledge management as getting the right information to the right people at the right time is wrong. Knowledge management is not just a matter of managing information. It is deeply social in nature, and it must be approached by taking human and social factors into account. As the field of knowledge management develops, and more widespread and varied experience with different approaches to KM is gained, it will become clearer how all the pieces fit together to create a rich picture of social and intellectual capital within organizations. Certainly, looking toward the future of work, as it becomes more centered in virtual relationships and spaces both within and across organizations, creating and maintaining knowledge and its social context will only become more vital.

One of the most important aspects of a knowledge management system is that it becomes what Thomas et al. (2001) termed a *knowledge community*: a place within which people discover, use, and manipulate knowledge, and can encounter and interact with others who are doing likewise. They discuss two approaches for supporting knowledge communities, namely, social computing and knowledge socialization. A fundamental characteristic of a knowledge community is that it includes conversation and other forms of narrative, for example, stories and/or unguarded discussion among people who know one another, who share professional interests, and who understand the contexts within which their remarks are being made. Thomas et al. outline a variety of specific techniques that can contribute to a realistic and effective approach to knowledge management, including supporting new forms of group interaction (e.g., Bohm Dialogue, stories), methods for enhancing creativity (e.g., the use of metaphor), and support for expressive communication. When such techniques are incorporated into knowledge communities, they result in organizational opportunities to build social capital, including trust and cooperation among colleagues.

The notion of a knowledge management environment as a "trusted place" is an interesting and challenging one for system designers and for organizations. How—technically, socially, and organizationally—can we balance the need for a safe and trusting place, within which so much knowledge creation and social capital building take place, with the organizational imperative to share information more broadly? A greater understanding of how to design socially translucent systems that permit social mechanisms to come into play will help developers of technological systems to negotiate such issues. Similarly, a better understanding of how to socialize knowledge through techniques such as storytelling and scenarios will offer organizations greater mastery and scope in creating, sharing, and reusing the knowledge that is critical to survival in the twenty-first century.

Others, such as Bouthillier and Shearer (2002), have undertaken survey research to investigate whether KM is an emerging discipline or just a new label for Information Management (IM). The authors gathered empirical evidence of how KM is practiced in several types of organizations, demonstrating the variety of organizational approaches used and the processes involved. Based on an exploratory study of KM practices, they present a typology of methodologies employed in various organizations to illustrate what may be considered as the particular nature of KM to show potential differences with IM.

The field of knowledge management is fairly new; this explains why its research base is still under development. Despite its vagueness, its potential overlaps with IM, and its weak theoretical base, KM is practiced in many organizations. Examining empirical evidence is certainly a valid approach for identifying building blocks of theories and concepts to support the development of new scientific fields. Indeed, scientific knowledge is often rooted in practice: culture and society existed before we had anthropology and sociology. The empirical evidence gathered for one study shows that KM involves human/soft and technical/hard aspects (Hlupic, Pouloudi, and Rzevski, 2002). KM seems to comprise various organizational practices requiring changes in policies, work routines, and organizational structures. More specifically, these authors found the following general principles:

1. Knowledge, in practice, is most often defined as tacit knowledge in spite of the conceptual problems mentioned above. Explicit knowledge was included only in those initiatives where the focus was on converting tacit knowledge into explicit knowledge.
2. Knowledge management, as it is practiced, really means facilitating the sharing of tacit knowledge. Despite the fact that other processes were part of the KM projects, sharing was the primary emphasis of all case studies.
3. There are slight differences in the practices between private- and public-sector knowledge management. Private-sector organizations use KM for internal knowledge sharing, targeted in specific areas of the organization, and the KM initiatives are most often concerned with managing business and administrative knowledge. Public-sector organizations use KM for both internal and external knowledge sharing throughout the organization, and the KM initiatives are most often concerned with managing product-related knowledge.
4. Finally, KM practices could benefit from the skills already held by information professionals. These skills include identification of knowledge needs and helping to distinguish between information and knowledge, and will facilitate a broader and more inclusive KM initiative.

One can claim that the ontological and epistemological aspects of knowledge are still so ill-defined and poorly understood that KM cannot be considered an emergent discipline. Indeed, although the concepts of tacit and explicit knowledge, knowledge sharing, and knowledge technologies are often used, they are not clearly defined. However, the question remains why large private and public organizations bother to use unclear terminologies. The reason likely stems not from a lack of clarity but from a lack of consensus or use of standardized terms across organizations. The IM community cannot continue to claim that it has for years addressed the same issues addressed now by KM experts. Dismissing KM as simply a management fad could be a missed opportunity to understand how knowledge is developed, gained, and used in organizations and, ultimately, in society. New labels can be misleading, but they can also force some reflections. There continues to be a need to examine why there is such an interest for KM in both academic and business communities, and in governments.

Researchers have also begun to study KM technologies. For example, Studt (2003) found that drug discovery is one of a handful of technologies that create value by transforming vast amounts of data into knowledge that is then used to create useful products—in this case drugs for human health. Unfortunately, the creation of that data in the drug area is growing at a faster rate than researchers are able to manage it. Genomics and proteomics, and the biotech industry based on them, have turned the traditional, mostly linear flow of information into a dynamic, iterative loop.

Along with new types of biotech data, information capture throughout the development process has also become more critical. Decisions to advance and prioritize targets and potential leads require the integration and capture of whole new types of information using new research technologies.

The use of knowledge management tools is becoming a critical part of reducing development times and costs and improving the overall success rate of testing new compounds. Understanding the different components of knowledge management and how they interact in a drug development environment is the first step in implementing a workable system. A knowledge management process consists of creation, collection, interpretation, storage, and interaction with data. A number of pharmaceutical and biotechnology companies have reported significantly improved R&D productivities with the implementation of knowledge management initiatives. Bristol-Myers Squibb's SMART-IDEA, for example, incorporates data repositories, data integration technologies, data visualization, and data mining tools, as well as having decision support functionalities.

Finally, a growing number of doctoral theses address KM themes. Some sample KM research topics include:

- What are the exact mechanisms by which knowledge and learning are institutionalized and embedded in the corporate memory?
- How can communities of practice support and enhance professional education?
- When do stories work best and why? Is there a best practice for creating and telling stories?
- What drives employees to share their knowledge with each other or, conversely, to hoard it? What can management do to increase knowledge sharing among employees?
- How can weblogs be used in KM research? What types of data can be collected, and how can they be analyzed?
- Is there a gap between theory and implementation of knowledge management systems and principles?

- Do top-down knowledge management initiatives meet bottom-up organizational learning?
- How do business ethics relate to the use of IT? What methods effectively assess ethical quality in business systems and processes?
- How do we evaluate and improve the facilitation of group workshops?
- How do we implement strategy (or change programs) and adapt strategy to new pressures?

As Schulz and Jobe (2001) point out, empirical research in the corporate knowledge management world is limited. Many opportunities exist for further detailed empirical research.

A POSTMODERN KM?

Weinberger (2001) introduced the term *postmodern KM* to distinguish it from traditional KM, which he views as having traditionally suffered from the belief that we can discover ultimate truths and organize the world according to rational principles using clever code. The idea was that we should capture and organize bits of "knowledge" in central databases. The people involved were relevant only as donors to the common ontology or as empty vessels into which knowledge could be poured. Postmodernism holds that our concept of reality is always warped by the lenses of individual subjectivity and group power dynamics. Therefore, postmodern KM cannot be about management at all because management implies external control of some definable resource. Its goal is simpler, yet deeper: leveraging people. Postmodern KM operates within and on the basis of existing behavior patterns, mining conversation streams and relationships automatically to incorporate structure and context into the information human users already manipulate. It fosters human intelligence and interaction rather than trying to replace them. Concretely, that means things like automatically parsing e-mail messages and other internal content to draw out useful context and associations (an approach being pursued by Lotus and a bevy of start-ups including Tacit Knowledge Systems, Abridge, ContextPortal, EcoCap, Krypteian and Neomeo); mining discussion content and user feedback on intranets (Newknow); adding workflow directly into e-mail messages (Zaplet); and building on web logs as a powerful web-native tool for knowledge sharing (Onclave and Slashdot derivatives). In other words, tools help to manage knowledge.

Miller and Morris (1999) discuss the impending transformation of R&D from its historical, product-centric past to its emerging knowledge-centric future. In addition, their focus on "discontinuous" and "fusion" innovation promises to lead the way for industry, in general, whose R&D functions typically produce less than one new product innovation per decade and whose new products, when they are produced, tend to fail in under four years. The authors' explicit embrace of knowledge management is also welcome inasmuch as the value of most companies now tends to rest more on the weight of their intellectual assets than on so-called hard assets. The focus is on distributed, enterprisewide innovation. It signals the tearing down of R&D's overly centralized and compartmentalized profile in most firms, and it offers strong support for the view that innovation should be structured as a distributed, whole-firm social process, not an administrative one.

A KM strategy enables an organization to act proactively (acting before the problem occurs) rather than reactively (acting after a crisis has arisen). This means trying to anticipate potential problems, potential areas of resistance to organizational change, the lack of incentives for knowledge sharing, and the very thorny ethical issues associated with KM applications. Some good practices and lessons learned from an organization's experiences with KM to date can help guide us in being proactive, namely:

1. Improve access to information and knowledge—covering the availability, accessibility, and affordability of information (especially of scientific information in developing countries).
2. Promote knowledge sharing through learning circles and vertical/horizontal coalitions, peer-to-peer technology, communities of practice, infomediaries, help desks, e-learning, and better interaction/mutual learning with target groups (the poor).
3. Network: international and regional cooperation—covering networking models, "digital solidarity," collaboration tools such as portals and common terminology (thesaurus), network effectiveness, strengthening existing structures, and resource centers.
4. Develop local content in local languages and dissemination channels besides the Internet, capacity building, and quality control/standards.
5. Avoid weak incentives—incentives that do not encourage maximization of an objective because they are ambiguous or satisficing. For example, payment of weekly wages is a weak incentive because by construction it does not encourage maximum production, but rather the minimal performance of showing up every workday. This can be the best kind of incentive in a contract if the buyer does not know exactly what he wants or if output is not straightforwardly measurable.

CONCLUDING THOUGHTS

As gold which he cannot spend will make no man rich,
so knowledge which he cannot apply will make no man wise.
Samuel Johnson (1709–1784)

In the short term, knowledge management will continue to contribute to the improved exploitation of the information and knowledge resources available to the company because as John Dewey states: "information is an undigested burden unless it is understood" (Demetrion, 2003). In the longer term, knowledge management will continue to build the foundation for improved business advantages and strengthen the capabilities for a sustainable future. It is a somewhat ironic twist that the success of KM is often accompanied by its disappearance—in the sense that successful KM is KM embedded in an organization.

KM processes simply become part of "how knowledge workers conduct their everyday work." As KM permeates the core business processes of the organization, there will be less and less need to refer to KM as "something completely different" or something that is done apart from and in addition to "real" work. The Gartner Group (1998) has stated that knowledge management "will be the standard way of running a business." Some authors (e.g., Davenport, 2002) have even started to use terms such as *mundane KM* to describe what KM should look like when it is actually used and useful in conducting everyday knowledge work. The evolution of KM will continue to integrate more seamlessly with core business processes, and the scope of KM will continue to expand to all types of organizations whether they be for-profit or nonprofit, regardless of the type of industry.

The introduction of KM should be viewed as a catalytic process that significantly transforms the organization—ranging from impacting individual behaviors, collaborative knowledge sharing within groups, and organizational dimensions such as culture. KM initiatives are more likely to provoke a snowball effect—gaining momentum exponentially over time. The snowball metaphor is in stark contrast to some of the gardening metaphors that have prevailed to date: for example, sowing KM seeds, harvesting knowledge, or patiently nurturing knowledge sharing. KM succeeds when it has disrupted the status quo—when it has moved beyond rhetoric into the realm of the organization's pragmatic business needs.

The value of KM will be reaped through the thoughtful application of the knowledge and know-how stemming from the organization's collective experience. KM educational programs will solidify KM as a field of study, prepare students for careers as KM professionals, and contribute to the evolution of professional KM practice. As more and more organizations transform themselves into KM-enabled enterprises, KM will no longer be a shiny new thing to point at or a lofty ideal to strive for—KM will be an essential ingredient of all successful organizations.

KEY POINTS

- Knowledge management is a complex undertaking that involves people and cultural issues, not just technology-related decisions.
- Information seeking, particularly on the World Wide Web, should not always be taken prima facie. There are political, commercial influences in addition to technical constraints, and all these will affect the type and volume of content that can be easily retrieved.
- Organizational knowledge repositories should ensure that information seeking is both objective and optimized—if not to each individual user at least to the different thematic groups or CoPs that exist within the company.
- The type of organizational culture will often prove to be a KM barrier. This profile needs to be assessed and characterized in order to allow for proactive actions to be taken.

- The paradox of the value of an intellectual or knowledge asset is one of the major issues facing KM today. Human, structural, and customer capital will need to be codified to some extent, and their sharing promoted actively throughout the organization.
- One of the most important challenges in ensuring the success of KM applications is to put into place the appropriate rewards and "punishments" to motivate knowledge workers to share knowledge. This means there has to be "something in it for me" as well as for the CoP and the organization.
- KM has enjoyed a steady and pervasive growth into many business functions, and its future lies in its becoming part of how knowledge workers carry out their professional tasks.
- There continues to be a need for KM to be able to demonstrate its value.
- KM requires a holistic perspective, one that encompasses business goals, people, processes, technologies, and organizational context.
- KM requires a comprehensive approach that addresses each step in the KM cycle.
- KM must rest on solid theoretical foundations. Current research studies will add to, complete, and complement KM theoretical models.
- Knowledge capture and codification will evolve as knowledge taxonomy development methods and tools are increasingly available.
- Knowledge sharing will be leveraged throughout the organization via communities of practice that act as a two-way bridge between individual and organizational learning.
- Knowledge application in the future will be increasingly based on organizational memory management systems that will contain valuable lessons learned and best practices.
- Organizational cultures will continue to transform and be guided to offer environments that are more conducive to effective knowledge management.
- KM continues to evolve as a profession as demonstrated by the fact that more empirical research is being undertaken, professionals can attend academic KM programs, KM skill sets are being more clearly identified, and a new wave of KM-related doctoral theses are well on their way.

DISCUSSION POINTS

1. What are some of the critical issues facing the successful implementation of KM applications? How do they play out in your organization?
2. What do we mean when we refer to the "politics of information seeking"? Why would this be a potential risk for KM?
3. What are the five major types of organizational cultures? Critically evaluate their strengths and weaknesses. How would you analyze or identify these organizational profiles? Where does your organization lie?
4. The "paradox of value" is one of the greatest challenges facing KM today. Do you agree with this statement? Why or why not? Provide illustrative examples to support your arguments.

5. KM often fails to live up to its ideal goals of knowledge sharing due to a lack of incentives. How would you set up a system of rewards and censures to motivate knowledge workers to share knowledge? What are some typical obstacles that you would expect to encounter? How would you address these obstacles? Outline an incentive strategy and describe how you would evaluate its success.

6. Many of the expected benefits of KM stem from being able to deliver the "right information to the right person at the right time in the right format." What are the implications of this statement for issues of privacy of information?

7. If after six months of effort, you found that your KM project was still not making headway, what actions would you take? What information would you seek out in order to decide the best course of action to take? How and when would you assess progress again?

8. Provide a brief history of the field of KM and describe where you feel it is today and where it is heading.

9. Which do you feel are the key priorities to be addressed in order for KM to continue to evolve and become better embedded in critical business processes?

10. Describe some research themes in the field of KM. What do you see as the Next Big Thing in KM? What breakthroughs would be needed before KM could make a quantum leap in its evolution?

REFERENCES

Boisot, M. (1998). *Knowledge assets.* Oxford: Oxford University Press.

Bouthillier, F., and Shearer, K. (2001). Understanding knowledge management and information management: an empirical perspective. *Information Research, 8*(1). Available at http://informationr.net/ir/8-1/paper141.html.

Callahan, D. (2004). *The cheating culture: why more Americans are doing wrong to get ahead.* Orlando, FL: Harcourt.

Davenport, E. (2002). Mundane knowledge management and microlevel organizational learning: an ethological approach. *Journal of the American Society for Information Science and Technology, 53*(12): 1038–1046.

Davenport, T., Eccles, R., and Prusak, L. (1992). Information politics. *Sloan Management Review, 34*(1): 53–63.

Demetrion, G. (2003). John Dewey's educational philosophy. Core concepts. Available at http://www.nald.ca.

Denning, S. (2000). *The springboard: how storytelling ignites action in knowledge-era organizations.* Boston: Butterworth-Heinemann.

Edvinsson, L., and Malone, M. (1997). *Intellectual capital: realizing your company's true value by finding its hidden brainpower.* New York: HarperBusiness.

Firestone, J., and McElroy, M. (2003). *Key issues in the new knowledge management.* Boston: Butterworth-Heinemann/KMCI Press.

Gale, S. (2002, November). Knowledge-sharing earns bonus points. *Workforce Management*, p. 85. Available at http://www.workforce.com/section/02/feature/23/35/70/233574.html.

Gartner Group. (1998). Knowledge management. *October 1997/June 1998.* Available at http://gartnergroup.com.

Hlupic, V., Pouloudi, A., and Rzevski, G. (2002). Towards an integrated approach to knowledge management: "hard," "soft," and "abstract" issues. *Knowledge and Process Management*, 9(2): 90–102.

Introna, L., and Nissenbaum, H. (2000). Shaping the web: why the politics of search engines matters. *The Information Society*, 16: 169–185.

Kautz, H., Selman, B., and Shah, M. (1997). The hidden web. *AI Magazine*, 18(2):27–36.

Klein, D. (1999). *The strategic management of intellectual capital*. Boston: Butterworth-Heinemann.

Lawrence, S., and Giles, C. (1999). Accessibility of information on the web. *Nature 400*: 107–109.

Miller, W., and Morris, L. (1999). *Fourth generation R&D: managing knowledge, technology and innovation*. New York: John Wiley and Sons.

Pollard, D. (2003). The future of knowledge management. Discussion paper. Available at http://blogs.salon.com/0002007/images/TheFutureofKnowledgeManagement.doc.

Schulz, M., and Jobe, L. A. (2001). Codification and tacitness as knowledge management strategies: an empirical exploration. *Journal of High Technology Management*, 12(1): 139–165.

Skyrme, D. (2002). What's next for knowledge management? *I³ Update Entovation International News*. Available at http://www.skyrme.com/updates/u57_f1.htm.

Stevens, L, (2000). Incentives for sharing. *Knowledge Management Magazine*. Available at http://www.kmmag.com/articles/default.asp?ArticleID=778.

Studt, T. (2003). Knowledge management is key to improving drug R & D cycles. *R & D*, 45(4): 18.

Sveiby, K. (1997). *The new organizational wealth: managing and measuring knowledge-based assets*. San Francisco: Berrett-Koehler Publishers.

Sveiby, K. (2001). Methods for measuring intangible assets. Available at http://www.sveiby.com/articles/IntangibleMethods.htm.

Tannenbaum, S., and Alliger, G. (2000). *Knowledge management: clarifying the key issues*. Burlington, MA: IHIRM.

Thomas, J., Kellogg, W., and Erickson, T. (2001). The knowledge management puzzle: human and social factors in knowledge management. *IBM Systems Journal*, 40(4): 863–884.

Tobin, Daniel R. (1998). *The knowledge-enabled organization: moving from "training" to "learning" to meet business goals*. New York: AMACON.

Weinberger, D. (1998). KM and the human element. *KMWorld*, 7(6). Available at http://www.kmworld.com/publications/magazine/index.cfm?action=readarticle&Article_ID=181&Publication_ID=6.

Weinberger, D. (2001, August 15). Postmodern KM: a one-question interview. *Journal of the Hyperlinked Organization*. Available at http://www.hyperorg.com/backissues/joho-aug15-01.html#pomo.

GLOSSARY

Absorption costs Costs incurred when recipients of knowledge content understand and internalize the knowledge in order to be able to apply it.

Absorptive capacity The individual and/or organizational openness to change and innovation and the capability or preparedness for being able to integrate it.

Abstraction costs Costs incurred when knowledge context is generalized over a wider scope.

After Action Review (AAR) An assessment that is conducted after a project or major activity to allow employees and leaders to discover what happened and why (popularized by the U.S. Army); a professional discussion of an event that enables participants to understand what worked well, what did not, and what they learned from the experience. An AAR need not be performed at the end of a project or activity; it can also be performed after each identifiable event or milestone, thus becoming a live learning process to help support a learning organization.

Aggregator A piece of software or a remotely hosted service that periodically reads a set of news sources, such as blogs, identifies what is new, and displays them on a single page.

Anarchy An organizational political model where there is an absence of any information/knowledge management policy.

Applied ethics The examination of specific controversial issues to try to resolve them, to come up with a stand or accepted way of proceeding with respect to the specific issue.

Artifact Material objects manufactured by people to facilitate culturally expressive activities; the signs and symbols by which the organization is recognized; the events, behaviors, and people that embody a culture.

Audit trail A documented history of a piece of knowledge in the knowledge base from knowledge acquisition/capture source to subsequent use and reuse.

Balanced scorecard A measurement and management system that enables organizations to clarify their vision and strategy and translate them into action. It provides feedback around both the internal business processes and external outcomes in order to continuously improve strategic performance and results.

Belief   An idea with emotional or spiritual appeal that has not been tested and/or is not considered accepted knowledge.

Benchmarking   The search for industrywide best practices that lead to superior performance. A study of similar companies to see how things are done best in order to adapt these methods for a company's own use.

Best practice   An improvement in a particular process, approach, technique, or subject matter knowledge that is good enough to replace an existing practice and general enough to merit being disseminated widely throughout an organization; a "good work practice" or innovative approach that is captured and shared to promote repeat applications.

Boundary   What separates a system and its environment. Just as there is a subjective element in defining a system, there is a subjective element in choosing a boundary. Defining a boundary is tantamount to defining the thing that is to be considered a "system" and those other things that are to be considered a system's "environment."

Brainstorming   A commonly used group problem-solving technique whose goal is to generate as many solutions to a problem as possible.

Censure   Harsh criticism or disapproval; to rebuke formally, to blame, criticize adversely, or to express disapproval. If you are censured for something you have done, someone in authority is telling you that he or she strongly disapproves of your action.

Change   An event that occurs when something passes from one state or phase to another; a relational difference between states, especially between states before and after some event.

Change management   Activities involved in (1) defining and instilling new values, attitudes, norms, and behaviors within an organization that support new ways of doing work and overcome resistance to change; (2) building consensus among customers and stakeholders on specific changes designed to better meet their needs; and (3) planning, testing, and implementing all aspects of the transition from one organizational structure or business process to another.

Chief Knowledge Officer (CKO)   Officer responsible for managing intellectual capital and custodian of KM practices in an organization.

Chief Learning Officer (CLO)   An enterprise-level position that typically reports to the Chief Executive Officer (CEO) of a corporation. The CLO's overall goal is to improve organizational effectiveness and efficiency by facilitating increased knowledge and skill proficiency in individuals, teams, and the enterprise as a whole. Ultimately, the goal is to transform an enterprise into a learning organization.

Chunking   A letter, syllable, word, phrase, or even a sentence. Chunking is defined as the organization of blocks of content that are conceptually related. The amount of information that is processed as a chunk depends on the learner's ability, maturity, motivation, and prior knowledge related to the content being processed. For example, to a poor or beginning reader a chunk may be a letter. Good readers generate chunks in the form of words. S-t-u-d-y becomes study. The effect of prior knowledge on processing speed is obvious when we try to read a complex article out of our area of expertise. Short-term memory can usually handle only about seven chunks.

Climate The prevailing psychological state; "the climate of opinion"; "the national mood had changed radically since the last election."

Closed questions Questions that set limits on the type, level, and amount of information a respondent provides; often used to validate content and can be answered by a finite number of responses such as yes/no (e.g., is it true that this project was initiated by yourself?).

Cluster analysis Generic term for a set of statistical analysis techniques that elicit or produce classifications from seemingly unordered data.

Codification costs Costs incurred in rendering tacit knowledge explicit.

Coercive incentive Some form of punishment—physical force, firing, disbarring—brought about by failure to act in the desired manner.

Cognitive maps Theoretical representations of how humans organize and process some type of knowledge.

Collaboration A coalition of diverse people with diverse values and expectations working together at the community level to solve problems; a social skill involving working together with two or more persons. Collaboration is the process of shared creation: two or more individuals with complementary skills interacting to create a shared understanding that none had previously possessed or could have come to on their own.

Combination The reassembling of existing explicit knowledge into new, systematically organized forms such as a database, a summary document, or a trend analysis.

Community of practice An affinity group or information network that provides a forum where members can exchange tips and generate ideas; a group of professionals who try to face common problems to solve and who strive to improve their profession and thereby themselves. An informal network or forum where tips are exchanged and ideas are generated. A group of professionals, informally bound to one another through exposure to a common class of problems, common pursuit of solutions, and thereby themselves embodying a store of knowledge. A group of practitioners held together by shared practices and common beliefs.

Complex adaptive systems Organizations that are composed of a large number of self-organizing components, each of which seeks to maximize its own specific goals but also operates according to the rules and context of relationships with the other components and the external world.

Concept analysis A technique used to clarify the meaning of subjective, value-laden terms such as "democracy." Derived from science education and philosophy, the technique explicitly distinguishes between related terms to pinpoint the boundaries of the concept and lists exemplars and nonexemplars of the concept in order to extract a set of "necessary and sufficient" attributes that a definition must have in order to adequately reflect the meaning of the concept.

Concept clustering A methodology for organizing and summarizing domain data by producing an abstraction of the domain based on the analysis of clusters.

Concept dictionary A conceptual analysis technique that provides a mechanism to visualize an abstraction of the primary concepts in a domain and the terminology used to label them.

Concept hierarchy   A structural taxonomy or arrangement of the associations that make up a concept.

Concept sorting   A psychological paradigm that can be used to tap into the way in which a subject matter expert has organized key concepts.

Content management   The processes and workflows involved in organizing, categorizing, and structuring information resources so that they can be stored, published, and reused in multiple ways. A content management system (CMS) is used to collect, manage, and publish content, storing the content either as components or whole documents, in such a way as to maintain the links between components. "Content" in this context generally refers to computer-based information such as the content of a website or a database. Content management is about making sure that content is relevant, up to date, accurate, easily accessible, and well organized, so that quality information is delivered to the user.

Content Steward   Person responsible for improving the management of an organization's knowledge assets, driving new processes and promoting behaviors for creating higher-quality information and sharing knowledge.

Continuous process improvement   An ongoing effort to incrementally improve how products and services are provided and internal operations are conducted.

Core competency   Set of skills that confer a competitive advantage on an organization; required to carrry out the mission-critical business of the organization.

Core or key process   Business processes that are vital to the organization's success and survival.

Corporate memory   All the information, data, and know-how that a company possesses; accumulation of historical events and experiences. The knowledge and understanding embedded in an organization's people, processes, and products or services, along with its traditions and values. Organizational memory can either assist or inhibit the organization's progress.

Corporate yellow pages   Also called expertise location systems; detection, discovery, and management of human knowledge resources, including subject matter experts. An expertise directory provides a map to subject matter experts in an organization or "virtual" organization (as in communities of practice). Expertise directories usually exist as part of a knowledge management software environment, sometimes as a fallback resource for computer-based knowledge retrieval systems.

Cultural assumptions   Beliefs about the internal workings and external environment of an organization, which, having worked well in the past, have gradually come to be taken for granted and which provide the basis for group consensus about common events and circumstances. Cultural assumptions function as the unifying themes of organizational culture.

Culture   A people's ways of being, knowing, and doing; all the knowledge and values shared by a cohesive group or organization; the attitudes and behavior characteristic of a particular social group or organization; the accumulated habits, attitudes, and beliefs of a group of people that define for them their general behavior and way of life; the total set of learned activities of a people; the beliefs, traditions, habits, and values controlling the behavior of the majority of the people in a social-ethnic group, including the people's way of dealing with their problems of survival and existence as a continuing group.

Custom A usage or practice that is common to a group of people or to a particular place; accepted or habitual practice.

Cybrarian One of many new terms being used to define a "virtual librarian." Others include electronic services librarian, digital librarian, and Internet information specialist.

Data Directly observable or directly verifiable facts; decision tree; a technique for organizing knowledge that divides sets of elements into subsets such that each node has only one "parent" based on discriminating evidence provided by attributes and their values.

Data mining An information extraction activity whose goal is to discover hidden facts contained in databases. Using a combination of machine learning, statistical analysis, modeling techniques, and database technology, data mining finds patterns and subtle relationships in data and infers rules that allow the prediction of future results. Typical applications include market segmentation, customer profiling, fraud detection, evaluation of retail promotions, and credit risk analysis.

Demilitarized zone (DMZ) Prevents employees from breaching ethical boundaries. They monitor compliance and report any violations.

Diffusion costs Costs incurred in the dissemination and distribution or publishing of knowledge.

Digital library A collection of a very large number of digital objects, comprising all types of material and media, that are stored in distributed information repositories and accessed through national computer networks. Digital libraries can include reference material or resources accessible through the World Wide Web. Digitized portions of a library's collection or original material produced for the web can also be included in a digital library.

Environment Those variables whose changes affect the system and that are in turn affected by the system's behavior; things outside a system that are important to it. Understanding the system's behavior usually requires some understanding of its context or environment.

Epistemology The scientific study of knowledge; knowledge science.

EPSS (Electronic Performance Support System) Any computer software program or component that improves employee performance by reducing the complexity or number of steps required to perform a task, providing the performance information an employee needs to perform a task, or providing a decision support system that enables an employee to identify the action appropriate for a particular set of conditions.

Ethics The "science of morality." In *philosophy*, ethical *behavior* is that which is "*good*." The philosophical study of the moral value of human conduct and of the rules and principles that ought to govern it; moral philosophy. A social, religious, or civil code of behavior considered correct, especially that of a particular group, profession, or individual. The moral fitness of a decision, course of action, and so on.

Expectation   Belief about (or mental picture of) the future. The anticipation of what is to happen next (see curiosity and suspense), what a character is like, or how he or she will develop, what the theme or meaning of the story will prove to be, and so on.

Explicit knowledge   Knowledge that has been rendered visible (usually through transcription into a document or an audio/visual recording); typically, captured and codified knowledge.

Expressive culture   Reflects emotions, feelings, and aspirations of the organization's personnel.

Externalization   The conversion of tacit knowledge into explicit knowledge— rendering previously unarticulated, undocumented, uncaptured content into a visible, tangible, and concrete form (e.g., recording a meeting, writing up minutes of a meeting).

Facilitation   A collaborative process used to help parties discuss issues, identify and achieve goals, and complete tasks in a mutually satisfactory manner. This process uses an impartial third party, the facilitator, who focuses on the processes and procedures of dispute resolution and decision making. The facilitator is impartial to the issues being discussed, rarely contributes substantive ideas, and has no decision-making authority.

Federalism   An organizational political model where information/knowledge management is approached using negotiation processes to reach a consensus.

Fence   Explicit ethical boundaries that show exactly where the important ethical lines lie, typically encapsulated in formal policy statements or laws.

Feudalism   An organizational political model where individual business units act fairly autonomously in defining their information/knowledge needs.

Googlewhacking   Searching the popular Google search engine with a two-word or more search argument that will produce exactly (no less and no more than) one result.

Googling   Use of the Google search engine (http://www.google.com) to locate content and information about people.

Groupware   Software that enables a group of users to collaborate on a project by means of network communications; software that supports collaborative work. It may include conferencing, shared files, or facilities to allow several people to work in one document. This software enables members of a network workgroup to communicate and collaborate through e-mail, scheduling, bulletin boards, conferencing, project management, file sharing, and other means.

Heuristic   A set of instructions for searching out an unknown goal by exploration, which continuously or repeatedly evaluates progress according to some known criterion. A method of achieving a goal where the exact means of doing so cannot be precisely specified: we know what it is but not where it is . . . general rules, guidelines but not prescribing a specific route to the goal (antonym: algorithm).

Ideal   Model of excellence or perfection of a kind; one having no equal. Conforming to an ultimate standard of perfection or excellence; embodying an ideal. Constituting or existing only in the form of an idea or mental image or conception.

Incentive   A reward for a specific behavior, designed to encourage that behavior; also called inducement. In economics, an incentive is anything that provides a motive for a particular course of action—that counts as a reason for preferring one choice to the alternatives.

Information   Analyzed data—facts that have been organized in order to impart meaning.

Information literacy   A set of abilities requiring individuals to recognize when information is needed and to have the ability to locate, evaluate, and use effectively the needed information.

Information Resource Management (IRM)   An emerging discipline that helps managers assess and exploit their information assets for business development. It draws on the techniques of information science (libraries) and information systems (IT related). It is an important foundation for knowledge management, in that it deals systematically with explicit knowledge. Knowledge centers often play an important part in introducing IRM into an organization.

Innovation   A new idea applied to initiating or improving a product, process, or service. All innovations involve change, but not all changes necessarily involve new ideas or lead to significant improvements. The concept of innovation encompasses new production process technologies, new structures or administrative systems, and new plans or programs pertaining to organizational members. The creation of something new or different; the conversion of knowledge and ideas into a new benefit, such as new or improved processes or services. An improvement of an existing technological product, system, or method of doing something. Organizational innovation is the process by which new products or new methods of production are introduced, including all the steps from the inventor's idea to bringing the new item to market.

Intellectual asset/capital   An organization's recorded information (and, increasingly, human talent itself), where such information is typically either inefficiently warehoused or simply lost, especially in large, physically dispersed organizations. An asset is a claim to future benefits (value, cash flows). An intangible asset can be defined as a nonphysical claim to future value or benefits. Intangibles, intangible assets, knowledge assets, and intellectual capital are more or less synonyms. All are widely used—intangibles specifically in the accounting literature, knowledge assets by economists, and intellectual capital predominantly in the management literature.

Intelligent agent   Also called an Internet agent. Most commonly found on websites, a mini-program designed to retrieve specific information automatically. Agents rely on cookies to keep track of the user's preferences, store bookmarks, and deliver news through push technology. Intelligent agents cannot perform their duties if the user's browser rejects cookies, and some web pages (especially online ordering sites) will not function properly without the agent's information.

Internalization   The conversion of explicit knowledge into tacit knowledge; understanding of new knowledge and its integration into existing mental models; accepting that this new knowledge is valuable and acting accordingly.

Invisible college   An informal communication network, typically consisting of scholars or researchers working around a common theme; jargon. A characteristic language of a particular group (as among thieves); "they don't speak our lingo." The technical language of an occupation or group. The informal or technical language used by members of the same profession or industry.

Job analysis   An analytical technique that entails structuring the major responsibilities of a job and high-level description of the key tasks encompassed by that job.

Knowledge   Subjective and valuable information that has been validated and that has been organized into a model (mental model); used to make sense of our world; typically originates from accumulated experience; incorporates perceptions, beliefs, and values.

Knowledge acquisition   The process of extracting, transforming, and transferring expertise from a knowledge source.

Knowledge audit   A more qualitative evaluation. It is essentially a sound investigation into an organization's knowledge "health." The knowledge audit provides an evidence-based assessment of where the organization needs to focus its knowledge management efforts. It can reveal the organization's knowledge management needs, strengths, weaknesses, opportunities, threats, and risks.

Knowledge base   The fundamental body of knowledge available to an organization, including the knowledge in people's heads, supported by the organization's collections of information and data. An organization may also build subject-specific knowledge bases to collate information on key topics or processes. The term is also sometimes used to describe a database of information.

Knowledge broker   A person who facilitates the creation, sharing, and use of knowledge in an organization. Many organizations have created knowledge broker roles such as Knowledge Coordinator. The term is also sometimes used to describe companies or individuals who operate commercially as knowledge traders or provide knowledge-related services.

Knowledge center (KSO, Knowledge Support Office)   A place where knowledge is gathered and stored and can be accessed and used by other people. It may be a physical place like a library, a virtual place like an interactive website or an online discussion board, or a place where people gather such as a café or an informal meeting room or discussion area created to encourage knowledge sharing. A focal point for collecting, structuring, and disseminating information. That does not mean people do it all themselves. They set the framework and structures, develop the good practice guides, and provide information management expertise. A central services group that consists of information specialists who manage content and provide services to the organization's members.

Knowledge codification   The process of producing a knowledge or intellectual artifact—anything that allows knowledge to be communicated independently of its holder (e.g., a document, a picture, a sound recording, a film, or a video).

Knowledge elicitation The process of interacting with experts using techniques to stimulate the articulation of the expertise—to convert tacit knowledge into explicit knowledge.

Knowledge management The deliberate and systematic coordination of an organization's people, technology, processes, and organizational struc-ture in order to add value through reuse and innovation. This value is achieved through the promotion of creating, sharing, and applying knowledge as well as through the feeding of valuable lessons learned and best practices into corporate memory in order to foster continued organizational learning.

Knowledge management assessment A systematic analysis of your organization's current knowledge management capabilities. It assesses your current performance against world-class practice and identifies critical areas for applying knowledge management.

Knowledge management system Centralized databases in which employees enter information about their jobs and from which other employees can seek answers. This system often relies on groupware technologies, which facilitate the exchange of organizational information, but the emphasis is on identifying knowledge sources, knowledge analysis, and managing the flow of knowledge within an organization—all the while providing access to knowledge stores. A system or tool that manages the sum of all knowledge within the organization as its "intellectual assets."

Knowledge manager A role with developmental and operational responsibility for promoting and implementing knowledge management principles and practices.

Knowledge repository A place to store and retrieve explicit knowledge. A low-tech knowledge repository could be a set of file folders. A high-tech knowledge repository might be based on a database platform.

Knowledge researcher Individual who is responsible for searching, retrieving, and delivering knowledge that is in explicit or codified form.

Knowledge Steward Individual whose responsibility is to convert tacit knowledge to explicit knowledge that can be more easily codified; person who interviews a project team and then captures and summarizes the learnings from that session.

Knowledge taxonomy A scheme that partitions a body of knowledge and defines the relationships among the pieces; used for classifying and better understanding the body of knowledge.

Knowledge worker Term coined by Peter Drucker to refer to professionals who are relatively well educated and who create, modify, and/or synthesize knowledge as a fundamental part of their jobs. Someone whose primary job focus is the accumulation, processing, or analysis of data and information, as opposed to physical goods.

Landmark A high-level ethical guideline often built upon tenets of an organization's culture and conveyed through stories.

Learning organization An organization that possesses the practices, systems, and culture that actively promotes sharing of experiences and lessons learned to encourage quality performance and continuous improvement.

Legitimate peripheral participation Formally referred to as "lurking"; refers to a quite different kind of learning theory, situated learning, which is primarily social rather than psychological. It is legitimate because all parties accept the position of "unqualified" people as potential members of the "community of practice." It is peripheral because they hang around on the edge of the important stuff, do the peripheral jobs, and gradually get entrusted with more important ones. It is participation because it is through "doing."

Lessons learned Knowledge that results from a postmortem or after-the-fact analysis of a project, a new technique, or the application of new knowledge; the "opposites" of best practices. Lessons learned are caveats, hard-earned experiences of unsuccessful endeavors that should be disseminated widely throughout an organization in order to prevent the same mistakes from being made again or to ensure that valuable innovations are not lost. A work practice or experience that is captured and shared to avoid a recurrence.

Likert Scale A scale developed by R. Likert for the purpose of measuring a person's degree of agreement or disagreement with a set of carefully constructed statements.

Maturity The state of being fully developed; attainment of a desired goal when growth and progress toward that goal have been successfully completed.

Mental model The result of internal psychological representations of peoples' interactions with the world. One purpose of these representations is that they allow us to solve problems and use artifacts such as computer systems and the like. An individual's existing understanding and interpretation of a given concept, which is formed and reformed on the basis of experiences, beliefs, values, sociocultural histories, and prior perceptions. Mental models are representations in the mind of real or imaginary situations. Scientists sometimes use the term mental model as a synonym for mental representation.

Metaethics Investigation of the origins of ethical principles and their meaning.

Metaknowledge Knowledge about knowledge; conscious knowledge about what is known. It is a process of self-assessment about knowledge levels and abilities while planning, changing strategies, and evaluating/revising throughout task completion.

Model A representation of the essential features of a system from the perspective of the observer or participant in that system. It can be as simple as a mental picture or as complex as a computer simulation or model of the world (e.g., Club of Rome).

Monarchy An organizational political model that is an extreme top-down hierarchical model, where information is controlled at the very top.

Moral incentive When a particular alternative is widely regarded as the right thing to do.

Myth A dramatic narrative of imagined events, generally used to explain the origins of transformations of something. An unquestioned belief about the practical benefits of certain behaviors; techniques not supported by demonstrated facts.

Needs assessment The process of determining or isolating needs to develop a KM initiative that meets specific objectives.

Nominal group technique A group problem-solving technique that reduces the negative effects that may be triggered by face-to-face interaction among members of a group or team.

Nonreflective skills Behaviors that initiate, guide, or transition communication (e.g., conversational ice-breakers, attentive silence).

Nonverbal communication Communication that takes place through media other than talking (e.g., gestures, observation of a demonstration).

Norm Expectation of how a person or persons will behave in a given situation based on established protocols, rules of conduct, or accepted social practices; a way of behaving or believing that is normal for a group or culture. All societies have their norms; they are simply what most people do. Deviants break norms. Some norms are enshrined in law, and society punishes those who deviate from them. Breaches of unwritten norms are unofficially punished.

Normative culture A set of formal rules, norms, prescriptions, positions, and hierarchies; a culture that emphasizes compliance with the rules.

Normative ethics The attempt to arrive at moral standards to regulate what is right and wrong, to ensure compliance.

Ontology An explicit formal specification of how to represent the objects, concepts, and other entities that are assumed to exist in some area of interest and the relationships that hold among them; a formal, explicit specification of a shared conceptualization. "Conceptualization" refers to an abstract model of phenomena in the world by having identified the relevant concepts of those phenomena. "Explicit" means that the type of concepts used, and the constraints on their use, are explicitly defined. "Formal" refers to the fact that the ontology should be machine readable. "Shared" means that ontology should capture consensual knowledge accepted by the communities.

Open questions Broad questions that impose few restrictions on the respondent and encourage free response (e.g., what do you think about this project?).

Open Space Technology (OST) A large group facilitation process that consists in setting an agenda by all members present, self-organization into smaller groups, and conveners who report each group's findings into proceedings, which are then distributed to all participants. The cultural approach to open space technology serves to create an environment for innovation, teamwork, and rapid change.

Organizational knowledge A complex network of knowledge and knowledge sets held by an organization consisting of declarative and procedural rules (validated knowledge claims).

Organizational learning A process involved in human interaction, knowledge claim formulation, and validation by which new organizational knowledge is created; the ability of an organization to learn from past behavior and information and to improve as a result; the capture and use of organizational knowledge to make organizational decision making more efficient and effective. Working and learning become increasingly collaborative activities based on the limitations of the individual human mind. Individual learning needs to be complemented by organizational learning.

Organizational memory   Extends and amplifies knowledge as the key asset of the knowledge organization by capturing, organizing, disseminating, and reusing the knowledge created by its employees. Also called a knowledge repository or corporate memory.

Participant observation   A fundamental method of research used in cultural anthropology. It involves a researcher, or researchers, living within a given culture for an extended period of time, to take part in its daily life in all its richness and diversity. The anthropologist in such an approach tries to experience a culture "from within," as a person native to that culture might do.

Personalization/profiling   Using continually adjusted user profiles to match content or services to individuals. Includes determining a user's interest based on his or her preferences or behavior, constructing business rules to select relevant content based on those preferences or behaviors, and presenting the content to the user in an integrated, cohesive format. For example, the process that occurs upon page request to a webserver and is handled by either (a) a general application server, (b) a specialized one-to-one application server, or (c) a specific personalization engine; or the capability for electronic library users to choose the information to be "pushed" or delivered directly to them through the e-library.

Portal   A grand and imposing entrance (often extended metaphorically); "the portals of the cathedral"; "the portals of heaven"; "the portals of success." A site that the owner positions as an entrance to other sites on the Internet; "a portal typically has search engines and free e-mail and chat rooms, etc."

Post   A message that is submitted to a computerized messaging system.

Process tracing   Any of a set of techniques that enables the determination of an individual's train of thought while he or she completes a task or reaches a conclusion.

Productivity paradox   The question: why were U.S. employers investing more and more heavily in computers and information technologies when standard measures of labor productivity in the United States suggested that computers, at least until 1995, were not improving productivity?

Protocol analysis   A method used to discern an individual's general problem-solving approach and the specific operations used to move from one knowledge state to another.

Protocols   Verbal reports or transcripts that are typically the result of a process-tracing or interview session to acquire/code knowledge.

Reflective listening   Listening behaviors that provide feedback that the message was communicated (e.g., paraphrasing, clarifying, summarizing).

Remunerative incentive   A financial reward, when money is exchanged for acting in a particular, desired way.

Repertory grid   A psychological technique for eliciting and analyzing a model of the expert's world so that similarities and differences among objects can be represented in a grid.

Requisite variety   According to the Law of Requisite Variety (B. Clemson, 1984. Cybernetics: A New Management Tool. Kent, UK: Abacus Press, p.

45.), the notion that regulation can be measured. The maximum possible effectiveness of a regulator will be directly measurable by a comparison between the variety (number of possible states) of the regulator and that which is being regulated. In other words, only variety can absorb variety. If a thermostat is to control temperature over a range, it must have more than two settings (on/off). Management must similarly find ways to increase variety through the use of models that present decision makers with the required information.

Retrospective verbalization   A variation on the process-tracing technique that asks the expert to verbalize his or her reasoning process after completing the task being investigated.

Reuse   Organization of meaningful activities around shared and reusable artifacts to achieve specific goals, typically within the context of distributed work and expertise. These artifacts may be any number of knowledge objects such as executable procedures, sections of text, or audiovisual "sound bites." Reuse is the use of a previously used material in the same or different process. Organizational reuse aims to make additional use of standard parts or components such as reusable code, designs, architectures, test cases, templates, references, and other valuable knowledge-based components.

Reward   An act performed to strengthen approved behavior; act to give compensation in recognition of someone's behavior or actions to reinforce good behavior. Money, or anything else of value to the recipient, is given, usually in exchange for a service.

Rite   Relatively elaborate, dramatic, planned sets of activities that consolidate various forms of cultural expressions into one event, which is carried out through social interactions, usually for the benefit of an audience.

Ritual   A standardized, detailed set of techniques and behaviors that manage anxieties but seldom produce intended consequences of practical importance.

Semantic networks   Cognitive models that illustrate associations among elements. A semantic network is a graph structure in which nodes (or vertices) represent concepts, while the arcs between these nodes represent relations among concepts. From this perspective, concepts have no meaning in isolation and only exhibit meaning when viewed relative to the other concepts to which they are connected by relational arcs. In semantic networks, then, structure is everything.

Social capital   The degree to which a community or society collaborates and cooperates (through such mechanisms as networks, shared trust, norms and values) to achieve mutual benefits. The value of social networks that people can draw on to solve common problems. The benefits of social capital flow from the trust, reciprocity, information, and cooperation associated with social networks.

Social constructivism   Emphasizes the importance of culture and context in understanding what occurs in society and constructing knowledge based on this understanding. Social constructivists believe that reality is constructed through human activity and that knowledge is also a human product that has been socially and culturally constructed. Learning is a social process in which individuals create meaning through their interactions with each other and with the environment in which they live.

Social network analysis The mapping and measuring of relationships and flows between people, groups, organizations, computers, or other information/knowledge processing entities.

Sociogram A diagram that shows interaction patterns between people; for instance, a diagram with a node to represent each individual and lines drawn between individuals to indicate that they interact frequently. These diagrams can be used to study workflows, the clustering of groups, communication needs, and inefficiencies in work processes.

Structured interview An interview that is organized, planned, and appropriate for the sessions that require specific information.

Symbol An arbitrary sign (written or printed) that has acquired a conventional significance; something visible that by association or convention represents something else that is invisible. For example, the eagle is a symbol of the United States.

System A set of interrelated elements; an entity comprised of at least two elements and a relation that holds between each of the elements and at least one other in the set. A system is also a holistic or gestalt—it cannot be understood by simple reductionist inquiry because "the whole is greater than the sum of the parts."

Tacit knowledge From the Latin *tacitare*, which refers to something that is very difficult to articulate, to put into words or images; typically highly internalized knowledge such as knowing how to do something or recognizing analogous situations.

Task analysis The process of determining or describing the nature of a task, job, or procedure by breaking it down into its primitive components; analyzes what a user is required to do in terms of actions and/or cognitive processes to achieve a task.

Task model User-centered representations of goals and actions a user needs to perform in the context of information processing. They help to characterize tasks that might be fruitfully supported by current or future systems and therefore are promising aids for a deeper understanding of user activities in certain application domains.

Taxonomy Basic classification system that enables the conceptual identification of concept hierarchies and dependencies. A hierarchical structure used for categorizing a body of information or knowledge, allowing an understanding of how that body of knowledge can be broken down into parts, and how its various parts relate to each other. Taxonomies are used to organize information in systems, therefore helping users to find it.

Technocratic utopianism An organizational political model where the emphasis is on technology and corporate data.

Thesaurus An organized language used for inputting and searching information systems, which predefines the relationships between terms and concepts used in its vocabulary.

Transparency The quality of being clear and transparent. Evolving global standard for state institutions and international organizations, requiring open processes according to general rules subject to monitoring; regarded as the basis of accountability, diminishing corruption. Sharing information and acting in an open manner. Transparent systems have clear procedures for public decision making and open channels of communication between stakeholders and officials, and make a wide range of information accessible.

Trust   Certainty based on past experience; the trait of trusting, and of believing in the honesty and reliability of others; complete confidence in a person or plan.

Unstructured interview   Interviews that have the goal of exploring an issue, used primarily in early stages of knowledge acquisition/capture.

User model   Defines the types of users of the interface and the relevant attributes of those users. Its main purpose is to influence interface generation. It is not designed to be a model of the user's mental state at a particular time during the interaction.

Value   An ideal accepted by some individual or group. The quality (positive or negative) that renders something desirable or valuable.

Variety   The total number of possible states of a system or an element of a system. It is a measure of the complexity of the system. The total number of distinguishable states—that is, dependent on the observational powers of a given observer. A useful managerial measure that conveys the amount of requisite variety that will be required to model the system (and to base decisions on).

Virtualness   "As-if-reality"—an object that has an effect and shows behavior without physically existing in reality.

Virtual organization   Structure in which organization members in different locations work together using e-mail, phone, fax, and other communication methods; a cluster of organizations united by a series of electronic linkages.

Weak incentive   An incentive that does not encourage maximization of an objective because it is ambiguous or satisficing.

Web log   Also called a blog. Basically a journal that is available on the web. The activity of updating a blog is "blogging," and someone who keeps a blog is a "blogger." Blogs are typically updated daily using software that allows people with little or no technical background to update and maintain the blog. Postings on a blog are almost always arranged in chronological order, with the most recent additions featured most prominantly. An online diary or journal, typically documenting the day-to-day life of an individual; often very personal.

Wiki   From the Hawaiian "wiki wiki" for "quick" or "super-fast"; refers to a website or other hypertext document collection that gives users the ability to add content, as on an Internet forum, but also allows this content to be edited by other users. The term can also refer to collaborative software used to create such a website.

XML   eXtensible Markup Language; a subset of SGML constituting a particular text markup language for interchange of structured data. The Unicode Standard is the reference character set for XML content. XML is a trademark of the World Wide Web Consortium. It is a flexible way to create standard information formats and share both the format and the data on the World Wide Web.

INDEX

NOTE:
Italicized *f* or *ff* following page numbers indicate a figure or figures on that page, respectively.
Italicized *t* or *tt* following page numbers indicate a table or tables on that page, respectively.